The Changing Roles of Women in the Criminal Justice System

Offenders, Victims, and Professionals

Second Edition

IMOGENE L. MOYER

WAVELAND
PRESS, INC.
Prospect Heights, Illinois

For information about this book, write or call:

Waveland Press, Inc.
P.O. Box 400
Prospect Heights, Illinois 60070
(847) 634-0081

Contents

Part II: Women Victims and the Criminal Justice System

Part III: Women Professionals and the Criminal Justice System

Contents

Dedicated to
Ruth Shonle Cavan
Friend, Colleague
Pioneer Woman in Criminology

Preface

The Second Edition of this book, *The Changing Roles of Women in the Criminal Justice System: Offenders, Victims and Professionals*, applies conflict theory throughout the book to examine the slow, but progressive, changes in the major roles of women in criminal justice agencies. Each new/revised chapter reflects changes in the discipline regarding the feminist perspective and incorporates race, ethnicity and international data wherever this information is available and/or appropriate.

The first section presents a collection of essays regarding the processing of women offenders through the various criminal justice agencies. Four of these chapters remain unchanged. A new chapter on women offenders has been added and the chapter on police and women offenders has had major revisions. These chapters are either reviews of the literature and of current issues on women offenders and the criminal justice system or present primary data from empirical research studies.

The second section concerns women as victims of rape, spouse abuse, incest, and sexual harassment. Three of these chapters are new, and the chapter on child sexual abuse is revised. With the changes in women's roles and the impact of the resurgence of the feminist movement, the victimization perspective of most traditional criminologists has been replaced with a concern for the re-victimization of women by attitudes and policies of officials in the system. The chapters in this book reflect these changes as the authors examine legal issues and criminal justice policies from the point of view of the women who are victims of these crimes.

Chapters in section three examine the changing roles of women as professionals in criminal justice agencies. While the absolute numbers of women employed in professional positions in the criminal justice agencies are small, the roles of women professionals have changed somewhat. There is a new chapter on women police officers, two of the chapters are major revisions with new authors, and our chapter remains essentially the same. The essays presented here are a mix of position papers suggesting the need for more women professionals in the various agencies as well as discussing some of the conflict situations and problems that women employed in these agencies confront today.

An important feature of the volume is that all of the chapters are original essays written especially for this book. All of the papers are pertinent to conflict theory as well as to the changing roles of women in the criminal justice system. The chapters are written by a combination of women and men who are established scholars in the field and enthusiastic young scholars who bring a challenging, new perspective and originality to the book. These scholars represent a variety of disciplines including sociology, psychology, criminology/criminal justice, political science, history, law, women's studies and education.

Thus, the book should be of interest as a supplementary text for a large number of college classes including criminology and women's studies courses. Most importantly, the works in this volume will provide academic researchers and officials in various criminal justice agencies with useful research information on women and their changing roles in the criminal justice system. The book also should make various categories of officials aware of the issues and perspectives important to women.

The people to whom this author owes the most appreciation are Ruth Shonle Cavan and Joseph W. Rogers. Both of these scholars were influential in the development of my initial, student interest in women and crime. The rare chapter on women offenders in Cavan's Criminology text was the original stimulus for my study of women offenders. Through his excellent instruction and intellectual support, Rogers challenged me to begin research in the vastly neglected area of the post-institutional adjustment of women released from prison. Both Rogers and Cavan possess a unique talent to point out weaknesses in a manuscript while, at the same time, strengthening the writer's confidence in her own ability to produce an excellent final product.

I would like to express my appreciation to several colleagues, friends, and graduate students at Indiana University of Pennsylvania who have provided encouragement and assistance in a variety of ways throughout the writing process. Nanci Koser Wilson has read and provided thoughtful comments on several of the manuscripts. Her knowledge of the feminist literature and her insights have been invaluable in the writing of my chapters. Kate Hanrahan also read and evaluated manuscripts and made many helpful suggestions during the process of revising the manuscript. Jake Gibbs kept me calm during the last week of the revisions of the book by providing reassurance and helpful interpretations of resources used in one of the chapters. Four graduate students, Marian Whitson, Nancy Koehler, Elizabeth Grossi, and Jamie Cassium assisted in a variety of ways, including bibliographic information, copy editing, Index preparation, and other helpful suggestions. I especially would like to acknowledge and offer sincere gratitude to the authors who contributed the original essays for this book. Their enthusiasm and dedicated interest in the subject matter made working with all of these people a pleasure.

Dorothy Shubra, our faithful departmental secretary, willingly used her computer skills to re-type bibliographies and tables that were not in the proper format. I owe her a very special thanks. I am also grateful to Indiana University of Pennsylvania for granting me a reduction in my teaching load for the spring semester, 1991 so that I could begin the revisions of the book. Finally, I would like to thank Carol S. Rowe and Jeni Ogilvie for providing editorial work and advice regarding the manuscript style and organization.

chapter 1

Crime, Conflict Theory, and the Patriarchal Society

Imogene L. Moyer
Indiana University of Pennsylvania

The neglect of women by criminologists has been well documented (e.g., Moyer, 1985a, 1985b, 1986; Wilson and Rigsby, 1975; and Wright, 1987a and 1987b). Moyer (1985b and 1986) notes the hierarchical structure both in society and in the discipline of criminology that places men in positions of power and diminishes the importance of women. She further highlights the failure of male criminologists to include women in textbooks, curricula, and professional journals. The "gatekeeping" activities of publishers and professional associations keep many women criminologists at the lower levels of academia. The systematic analyses of textbooks and journals by Wilson and Rigsby (1975) and Wright (1987b) provide substantial empirical evidence that little space is devoted to women and crime in mainstream criminological books and journals. Yet, a large body of literature on women and crime has emerged during the last three decades.

The historical account of the development of the research on women and crime presented in this chapter reflects the changing roles of women in a patriarchal society. The application of conflict theory to the development of this research will allow the reader to see how a criminal justice system dominated by white, middle class men fails to meet the needs of powerless groups, particularly women.

Research/Theories Prior to the 1960s

Rasche (1974:307), in discussing early views of women, indicates that works on women offenders prior to the twentieth century involved moral, ethical, and armchair theorizing. Women were seen as essentially virtuous unless they "fell" from their pedestals or were led astray by others. Females who deviated from their expected roles and transgressed the law were viewed as immoral, corrupt, hysterical, diseased, manipulative, and devious. They were considered "fallen" or "errant" (Rasche, 1974:307; Simpson, 1989:605).

Feinman (1986) traces this chivalrous conception of women through historical religious thought and expresses it as the madonna/whore duality. Implicit in this syndrome is women's subservience to men. Men assumed the roles of protectors of good women and punishers of bad women. Moyer (1985a:12) suggests that in "this tradition of chivalry, the criminal justice system has tried to shield women in order to help the whores become madonnas and to ensure that the madonnas do not fall from grace."

The positivist criminologists of the nineteenth century were concerned with what's wrong with the individual. This research involved a search for physiological and mental characteristics that cause crime. Students of criminology associate Caesare Lombroso with positivism. Lombroso had conducted extensive research on prisoners to find evidence for his theory of the "atavistic throwback," which characterized male prisoners who had not fully evolved to a higher state. In 1895, as a footnote to his larger study of males, Lombroso published his study, *The Female Offender*, in which he argued that women were innately inferior to men. He further stated that biological factors led to unusually sinister forms of crime in women:

> We have seen that the normal woman is naturally less sensitive to pain than a man. . . . We also saw that women have many traits in common with children; that they are revengeful, jealous, inclined to vengeances of a refined cruelty. . . . In ordinary cases

these defects are neutralized by piety, maternity, want of passion, sexual coldness, by weakness and an underdeveloped intelligence. But when a morbid activity of the physical centers intensifies the bad qualities of women, and induces them to seek relief in evil deeds . . . it is clear that the innocuous semi-criminal present in the normal woman must be transformed into a born criminal more terrible than any man. . . . (Lombroso, 1895:150-52).

Thus, women criminals were more evil than born male criminals. While most criminologists today discredit Lombroso's theory as biased and unscientific, his work is found in all theory books and most criminology texts.

Most criminology texts contain no reference to early women researchers (e.g., Pauline Tarnowsky, Jean Weidensall, and Eugenia Lekkerkerker) of crime. These women were first mentioned by Bowker (1978) and Rasche (1974). Pauline Tarnowsky studied Russian peasant murderesses in the late nineteenth century and found that they were biologically different from normal women. Tarnowsky also found that poison was the most frequent method used. Tarnowsky concluded that there was definitely a quantitative sex differential in the commission of crime, and this differential was due to biological and social influences.

While most traditional criminological theory books credit Goddard with research indicating that low intelligence and criminality are related, Jean Weidensall also tested intelligence of women prisoners in the 1900s, (Bowker, 1978:36-37; Rasche, 1974:310). Weidensall conducted research at Bedford Hills Reformatory for Women in New York. Her study compared reformatory inmates to working girls and school girls in a variety of tests measuring intelligence, skill, and mechanical ability. The reformatory inmates generally did worse on all tests. Weidensall believed there were different types of criminals. Some were intelligent but too lazy to go to work; some were truly criminal; and some were just so unintelligent they drifted into crime (Bowker, 1978:37). With training, however, many of the women learned to be quite efficient at a task. Weidensall concluded that "when one has recognized and satisfactorily explained this slow, yet really existent, ability to learn and then evaluated it in terms of their social requirements and facilities for training, the problem of how to understand and deal with the criminal woman will have been in large part solved" (Rasche, 1974:310).

Eugenia Lekkerkerker, a Dutch lawyer who visited the United States in the late 1920s to study female reformatories, conducted a completely different type of study (Bowker, 1978:44; Rasche,

1974:312-13). Her book, *Reformatories for Women in the United States*, published in 1931, traced the growth of separate reformatories for women and provided lengthy descriptions of those institutions she visited. She noted that women committed to reformatories or prisons in the first six months of 1923 had been convicted of "prostitution, fornication, adultery, disorderly conduct or vagrancy. . . ." (Rasche, 1974:312). She further observed that women offenders were regarded as "erring and misguided" and in need of protection and help. The purpose of the institution was to rehabilitate through shame and to instill "standards of sexual morality" and "sobriety." Also, the reformatory trained women in duties as homemakers and mothers.

In 1950, women accounted for only 10 percent of arrests reported in the Uniform Crime Reports. Otto Pollak attempted to explain this disparity between the arrests of men and women. Believing that women were actually as involved in crime as men, Pollak relied on biology to explain the low crime rate for women. He claimed that women were more deceitful and had learned to mask their real behavior during the sex act. He stated:

> Man must achieve an erection in order to perform the sex act and will not be able to hide his failure . . . and pretense of sexual response is impossible for him, if it is lacking. Woman's body, however, permits such pretense to a certain degree and lack of orgasm does not prevent her ability to participate in the sex act (Pollak, 1950:10).

It is interesting to note that in the 1930s theories of men's crimes, e.g., Merton's anomie and Sutherland's differential association theories, were refuting the biological explanations of the early positivists. Although women were largely ignored by criminological theorists, when criminologists did attempt to explain women's crime they still relied on the physiological analysis. This trend continued for women into the 1980s.

The conclusions from the research in this early positivist period have been rejected by most reputable criminologists today. Yet, their work laid the groundwork for modern scientific research and made important contributions. It is thus equally important to recognize the work of these women (i.e., Tarnowsky, Weidensall, and Lekkerkerker). The exclusion of their research from traditional accounts of this period is evidence of the gatekeeping power of those in authority to control whose works are included in scholarly publications.

Research Conducted in the 1960s

In the 1960s a few sociological studies of women offenders began to appear in the scholarly literature. In 1964, Mary Owen Cameron published her dissertation, *The Booster & the Snitch: Department Store Shoplifting*. Cameron reports a study of shoplifting using data from one large department store (1943-1950) and from the Chicago Women's Court (1948-1950).

Several early *Criminology* textbooks included chapters on women offenders, (e.g., Cavan, 1962 and Reckless, 1967). In 1962, Cavan also introduced a short chapter on "Delinquency of Girls" in her *Juvenile Delinquency* book. This chapter was expanded in Cavan's later edition of *Juvenile Delinquency*. In this way, Cavan introduced thousands of students to the issues regarding the female offender.

Sociological research studies of women's prisons emerged in the 1960s. Although Lekkerkerker and Weidensall had studied women's prisons in the 1920s and 1930s, this work was largely ignored. Prior to the 1960s most other works on women's prisons were accounts of the experiences of women who were wardens (e.g., Harris, 1942 and O'Hare, 1923).

The actual forerunners of the sociological research on women's prisons were the studies of men's maximum security prisons by Donald Clemmer, *The Prison Community* (1940) and by Gresham Sykes, *The Society of Captives* (1958). There were no comparable works on women's prisons until the mid-1960s, when Ward and Kassebaum published, *Women's Prison: Sex and the Social Structure* (1965) and Rose Giallombardo published, *Society of Women* (1966). Prior to the publication of these two studies it was assumed that women prisoners experienced prison in the same manner that men prisoners did.

Research in women's prisons was designed to test some of the findings in men's prisons. For example, Giallombardo (1966) utilized Sykes' (1958) pains of imprisonment and argot roles to examine the social world of imprisoned women. Recently, Moyer (1980) used the findings of Clemmer (1940) and Schrag (1954) regarding leadership in men's prisons to explore leadership patterns among women in the prison she had studied in 1973. Giallombardo (1966) found significant differences in the way men and women experience the pains of imprisonment and Ward and Kassebaum (1965) and Moyer (1978) found important differences in the patterns of homosexual involvement in men's and women's prisons. There were also differences found among the various women's prisons studied with reference to homosexual alliances and interaction patterns.

Research/Theories in the 1970s

The conceptualization of the woman offender, woman victim of crime, and the woman co-worker in the criminal justice system began to change somewhat in the 1970s. The 1960s had been times of controversy and struggle with the civil rights movement, the Vietnam War protests, the children's rights movement and the resurgence of the women's rights movement. The decade of the seventies saw changes in academia with students taking a more active role in matters of curriculum and policies. Women were also entering the academic professions in larger numbers and curricula were changing to integrate classes on women and minorities. Children's rights advocates were attaining changes in courtrooms and police stations, and the concept of "child abuse" emerged.

The 1970s brought academic controversies regarding issues such as spouse abuse and women offenders. Some women and crime researchers and the mass media attributed changes in women's involvement in crime to the women's movement. They also treated the women's movement as though it had originated in the 1960s. This ignores the rich history of feminism that can be traced through centuries of history.

Abigail Adams was very aware of the sexual inequities of her time when she wrote to John Adams in 1776:

> Remember the Ladies and be more generous and favourable to them than your ancestors. Do not put such unlimited power into the hands of Husbands. Remember all men would be tyrants if they could. (Spender, 1983, 113).

Although Abigail Adams' words were not heeded by her husband, other women continued the cause. For example, Mary Wollstonecraft's feminist treatise, *A Vindication of the Rights of Women* was published in 1792.

During the late eighteenth century, the Women's Movement and the Anti-Slavery Movement worked together toward common goals. The first women's rights convention in the United States was held at Seneca Falls, New York in 1848. Susan B. Anthony and Elizabeth Cady Stanton met in 1850 and joined forces to work for the Women's Suffrage Movement. Anthony was the organizer (she went to jail in 1872 for registering to vote and actually voting) and Stanton was the writer. Other women's voices were also heard.

Of particular importance was the voice of Sojourner Truth in her great speech calling for "Woman's rights and niggers!" commonly titled, "Ain't I a Woman?" (Spender, 1983:366-67). Also noteworthy was the courageous work of Harriet Tubman with the underground railroad to help free the slaves and her stand on the rights and dignity of black women (Spender, 1983:362). Feminists in the early twentieth century included women like Margaret Sanger (Spender, 1983:507), who led the fight for the rights of women to birth control and to control their own bodies.

It is not necessary to name the hundreds of women and men who were active in the women's rights movement which helped enlighten criminologists to the flaws in their interpretation of the trends in women's crime in the 1970s.

In the mid-1970s, a new stage of research on the woman offender emerged and was sensationalized by the press. In *Sisters in Crime* (1975) Freda Adler claimed that the women's movement was producing a "new breed" of female offenders. Adler argued, "In the same way that women are demanding equal opportunity in the field of legitimate endeavor, a similar number of determined women are forcing their way into the world of major crimes" (1975:13). Adler stated specifically that this "new breed" of female offender was moving into the traditionally male crimes, i.e., robbery and burglary. Unfortunately, her major support for this argument was anecdotal.

Rita Simon (1975) conducted research for the National Institute of Mental Health in which she analyzed the Uniform Crime Reports. Simon also credited the women's movement for the increase in women's crime but predicted these increases would occur in the traditional women's property crimes. Specifically, Simon (1975:41) predicted that "if present trends in these crimes persist approximately equal numbers of men and women will be arrested for fraud and embezzlement by the 1990s and for forgery and counterfeiting the proportions should be equal by the 2010s."

These predictions by Adler (1975) and Simon (1975) have been challenged by numerous researchers (e.g., Feinman, 1980; Giordano, et al., 1981; Laub and McDermott, 1985; Naffine, 1987; Steffensmeier, 1978; and Young, 1980). While Steffensmeier (1978) agreed with Simon (1975) that increases in women's crime would occur in the traditional women's crimes such as fraud, embezzlement, forgery and counterfeiting, and larceny/theft, he stated emphatically that absolute differences were still large and that female crime levels continue to lag far behind those of males (1978:577). The research by Feinman (1980:19) and Giordano, et al., (1981:73) provides evidence that most of the increases in female property crime involves petty, unsophisticated crimes, e.g., shoplifting, misuse of credit cards, passing bad checks, defrauding an innkeeper, and falsification to obtain welfare.

By the late 1970s, most researchers of women and crime were

convinced that the "new breed" of woman offender was based on speculation. Feminists also recognized that the work of Adler (1975) and Simon (1975) had made an important contribution to the development of research interest in the woman offender. Research and scholarship in the area of women and crime was now more acceptable and respected among some mainstream criminologists. In fact, the first women and crime classes were taught in the 1970s, including classes taught by Nanci Koser Wilson in 1973 and Freda Adler in 1974.

By the late 1970s and the 1980s, feminists were having an influence on criminology in areas that impacted the lives of women offenders, women victims, and women professionals in criminal justice agencies. This occurred partially as a result of the upsurge of the women's movement in the 1960s but also in response to the work of earlier scholars such as Adler (1975), Giallombardo (1966), Simon (1975), and Ward and Kassebaum (1965) who opened the door of credibility for criminologists to study women.

Research in the 1980s

Women Offenders and the Criminal Justice System

The research of scholars such as Curran (1983), Moulds (1978), Moyer (1981), Stone (1985), and Visher (1983) was conducted largely in response to claims by Pollack (1950) and Haskell and Yablonsky (1973) that women actually committed more crimes but were receiving chivalrous treatment by the police and court officials. Research studies on the police and especially on the behavior of court officials reported mixed findings with regard to paternalism and chivalry toward the female offender.

Moyer's (1982) study of police questionnaire responses in a metropolitan area in a southeastern state found little support for the chivalrous/paternalistic behavior of police based on race and/or sex. On the other hand, Visher (1983:23) in her analysis of data from field observation of police-citizen encounters in three metropolitan areas reported chivalrous behavior and preferential treatment varying somewhat with the race, age, and demeanor of the woman offender.

The mixed findings regarding the legal handling of women by the judicial system are partially the result of different methodologies and differences in the stages of the judicial decisions studied.

Moulds conducted a re-analysis of the state and federal judicial sentencing data examined by Nagel and Weitzman (1971) and reported a significant relationship between the female sex and gentle treatment in the justice system (1978:426). Curran (1983:43) suggests that Moulds' results may be spurious because she controlled for the variables of race, type of offense, and prior criminal record one at a time rather then simultaneously. In contrast, Curran (1983:45) reports finding no support for any existing theory of differential legal handling of male and female offenders. It should be noted that Moulds argues that even if women do receive preferential treatment, women pay a price for this gentler treatment. Moulds states:

> A major cost to them, however, is the continuation of a state of public consciousness which holds that women are less able than men and are thus in need of special protective treatment. This results in extensive personal psychological, social, economic, and political damage to the democratic notions of self-determination and quality. . . . To the extent that paternalistic views of women dominate the criminal justice system, programs designed for women within that system will be affected by those views (1978:430).

Rafter and Natalizia (1981) continue Moulds' argument using a Marxist Feminist perspective to examine the oppression of women by the criminal justice system. These authors argue that "the entire justice system in America has been dominated by men" (1981:83-84) and that the legal system "oppresses women . . . through its almost total failure to respond to issues of concern to women."

Research in women's prisons by feminists (e.g., Baunach, 1985; Chapman, 1981; Mahan, 1982; Moyer, 1984; and Shaw, 1982) provide strong support for Moulds' (1978) suggestion that women pay a price for preferential treatment and for Rafter and Natalizia's (1981) argument that the criminal justice system oppresses women by its failure to respond to issues of concern to women. This research suggests that women's prisons are isolated and neglected.

Baunach (1985), Chandler (1973), Chapman (1981), and Moyer (1984) have documented the low educational and vocational training skills of women offenders. These authors also indicate that most women in prison are the sole support of their children. Baunach (1985) and Moyer (1984) especially point to the economic needs of these women to support their children and the failure of the prison systems to provide meaningful vocational training and educational programs for women.

While Moyer ([Simmons], 1975) provides some evidence for the inadequate nature of the health programs for women in prison, the best documentation for the failure of the prisons to meet the medical needs of women prisoners has been provided by Shaw (1982) and Shaw, Browne, and Meyer (1981). Shaw (1982:264-65) points to the overuse of psychotropic drugs for women prisoners. This research also reports that basic health care needs, such as routine dental work, most gynecological services (including PAP smears), general checkups, prenatal and postnatal care, and specialized services such as drug and alcohol treatment, psychiatric care, and dietary assistance, will not be met in most prisons (Shaw, 1982:262). The powerlessness that most patients feel in their relationships with members of the medical profession are intensified in the prison environment where women prisoners are controlled through rules and regimentation.

Finally, Baunach (1985) and Mahan (1982) discuss the traumas of mothers in prison. Mahan (1982) conducted interviews with women in prison in New Mexico to explore the personal histories of women defined by society as "unfit mothers." Baunach's (1985) study of mothers in prison used questionnaires, standardized scales, and individual interviews to examine the experiences/attitudes of women in prison who are separated from their children. She also explored the development and operations of programs designed to retain mother-child bonds in women's prisons in a variety of states.

Women Victims of Crimes

The power of the patriarchal system to control and oppress women through men's historical authority in both the family and the criminal justice system is perhaps most evident in the crimes of domestic violence and rape. As stated by Rafter and Natalizia:

> Wife abuse, sexual harassment, incest, rape, production of unsafe methods of birth control, forced sterilization for eugenic purposes — these are critically important problems to women, whose needs the legal system has either failed to consider or has glossed over with token, ad hoc efforts. Such problems, moreover, have the greatest significance for poor and working-class women, indicating that class is at least as critical as sex in the struggle to obtain legal equality for women (1981:84).

Spouse Abuse.

Taub (1983:153-55) traces the origins of lawful wife beating to Roman law which gave authority to men over their wives and children without regard to the judgments of others. In Anglo-American legal tradition, this power became the power of moderate chastisement. In Blackstone's words:

> The husband . . . might give his wife moderate correction. For, as he is to answer for her misbehavior, the law thought it reasonable to entrust him with this power of restraining her, by domestic chastisement, in the same moderation that a man is allowed to correct his apprentices and his children (1768:445).

Common law further allowed men to discipline their spouses as long as they did not use a stick thicker than their thumb and did not disturb the neighbors. Jolin (1983:451) notes that "as recently as 1976 a Pennsylvania town ordinance sanctioned a husband's violence against his wife provided he not do so after ten o'clock in the evening and on Sundays."

The resurgence of the women's movement in the 1960s brought women together in consciousness raising groups to discuss their concerns. Physical abuse soon emerged as a problem shared by many women. While Straus (1973) and Gelles (1974) were among the early researchers of domestic violence, the work of feminists such as Klein (1981), Martin (1976), Pagelow (1981), Pizzey (1974), and Walker (1979) pointed to spouse abuse as economic exploitation, political domination, and psychological oppression. These works mobilized women to establish shelters for battered women and their children.

In addition to seeking changes in the legal statutes and establishing shelters for victims, researchers such as Berk, et al, (1980); Bowker, (1982); and LaFree, (1981) have pointed to the need for establishing new police policies to protect the victim. In the 1960s and 1970s police officers were being trained for "crisis intervention" of domestic violence. Crisis intervention involved two officers who would separate the victim and offender and talk to them to resolve the problem. If they could not calm the couple down, they would try to get the offender to leave and/or the victim to press charges. The application of crisis intervention in many cases did not end the violence in the home and eventually the police would be called back when one of the partners in the domestic violence was murdered.

Studies of police calls and murder cases indicate that domestic violence cases handled by crisis intervention are not successful. One such study was conducted in Kansas City in 1972-73. The study reported that in 85 percent of the homicide and aggravated assault cases, police had been called to the house one time before the murder/assault. In almost 50 percent of the cases, the police had responded to five or more prior domestic disturbance calls (Jolin, 1983:452).

Several researchers (Browne, 1987; Kuhl, 1985; and Totman, 1978) have examined the legal issues involved when battered women kill. Applying the psychological approach to understanding these women, Walker (1979) points to the "cycle of violence" in which battered women experience "learned helplessness." Kuhl (1985) argues that this learned helplessness involves the "battered wife syndrome" in which women perceive no alternative but to kill their abusers. She further indicates that the traditional self-defense laws are not appropriate when applied to battered women who kill.

Rape

Although the exact statutes varied from one legal jurisdiction to another, the traditional definition of rape was generally: "Carnal knowledge of a woman by a man (not her husband) by force and without her consent." Thus, traditional statutes made it impossible for a husband to rape his wife and placed the responsibility for proving the rape on the victim.

Historically, rape has been defined as a sexual act and women have been blamed for wearing seductive clothing and for enticing men to rape them by saying "no" when their eyes say "yes." In the words of Amir, "In a way, the victim is always the cause of the crime. . . . If the victim is not solely responsible for what becomes the unfortunate event, at least she is often a complementary factor" (1967:493). This perspective of rape is reflected in the way victims are dealt with in the criminal justice system. Robin (1977) refers to institutionalized sexism in the criminal justice system and outlines in detail the kind of evidence that must be presented by the victim in order for the rapist to be convicted.

Feminists, such as Brownmiller (1975) and Schwendinger and Schwendinger (1983; 1984), have analyzed how a patriarchal society has historically and cross-culturally interpreted incidents of rape so that women, who are victims, are made to share the legal responsibility for the acts with the male offenders. Brownmiller argues that women have historically been subjected to the physical/sexual conquest of men. She further states that:

> Female fear of an open season of rape, and not a natural inclination toward monogamy, motherhood, or love, was probably the single causative factor in the original subjugation of woman by man, the most important key to her historic dependence, her domestication by protective mating (Brownmiller, 1975:6).

In return for male protection, women sacrificed their autonomy and ownership of their bodies. Schwendinger and Schwendinger (1984:43) further indicate that "rape was an invasion of male property rights; therefore, when the rape laws were finally developed, their focus was on property, not persons."

Other researchers, e.g., Groth, et al., (1977), have presented evidence that rape is not a sexual act but an act of power and anger. As this perspective has become more widely accepted, feminists have lobbied legislatures to revise the statutes to define degrees of sexual assault, e.g. , indecent assault, involuntary deviant sexual intercourse etc. Not only is this a more accurate definition of the act but also assures a greater conviction rate, since many jurors and judges are reluctant to convict if the sentence is viewed as too severe (the death penalty, for example).

In changing the definitions of the offense, most states also have removed the requirement that the victim prove that she did not consent and that force was used. Thus, a woman's reputation and previous sexual activities are not allowed as evidence in court cases in many states today.

Although the legal system is changing somewhat, Stanko (1985:9) states that "To be a woman — in most societies, in most eras — is to experience physical and/or sexual terrorism at the hands of men." She further argues that the daily possibility of being threatened by male behavior creates a sense of powerlessness. This powerlessness is the result of women's inability to predict and control men's behavior or to anticipate when it might lead to violence. Stanko further argues that because violence is a normal part of life for most women, women learn early to negotiate their safety.

Women Professionals in Criminal Justice Agencies

Historically, information on women employed in criminal justice agencies has been limited to brief articles in the newspapers and popular magazines. There also were a few women officers and correctional personnel who published accounts of their professional experiences (e.g., Hamilton, 1924; Harris, 1942; and Sullivan, 1956). Women workers in criminal justice have been the last women to be included in scholarly research.

The scarcity of research in this area reflects the hierarchical power structure described in conflict theory. Women have had a difficult time gaining entrance into the traditional male occupations. Not only were men in positions of authority to determine research projects but historically too few women have been employed by the criminal justice agencies to make research feasible.

The late entrance of women professionals into criminal justice agencies reflects the dominance of men in a patriarchal society that has made women's entrance into nonclerical positions in these agencies difficult. Wilson (1982:360) points to a "close connection between gender and criminal justice occupations" as many criminal justice professions are "gender specific." She further states that "the link between masculinity and criminal justice is so tightly bound that we may say it is true not merely that only men can be crime fighters, but even that to be a crime fighter means to be a man."

Historical studies of women professionals in criminal justice have found that the few women who entered police work in the nineteenth century were social workers assigned to protect women and children. An interesting fact is that these women were better educated than the men in the system (Feinman, 1986:84-88). Feinman also notes that the number of women in most police departments was kept low by quotas, usually 1 percent (1986:88). In a historical account of the origin of women's prisons, Freedman (1981) also reports that nineteenth century white, middle class women were the reformers who rescued women prisoners from male administrators, male inmates, and male prisons. These women became the administrators and matrons who created a home environment to reform the "fallen women" in prisons.

Although a few women were employed in criminal justice agencies, the agencies generally remained "bastions of classical male chauvinism which operate in a variety of unspoken ways to effectively exclude women" (Wilson, 1982:366). One of these ways was to admit women as women but not as professionals. Thus women in police work, judicial positions, and corrections were limited to selected tasks that involved assignments to handle women and children—clerical and administrative tasks that virtually eliminated contact with offenders. In relegating women to positions as supplementary professionals, women were not given the opportunity to demonstrate skills or to develop experiences that would make them promotable.

In the 1960s and 1970s several legislative decisions and court cases mandated an end to the exclusion of women from male-dominated occupations in criminal justice agencies. The Civil Rights Act of 1964 and the Equal Employment Opportunity Act of 1972, prohibited discrimination on the basis of sex as well as race. Reed v Reed in 1971 specifically applied the equal protection clause of the Fourteenth Amendment to prohibit discrimination on the basis of sex.

By the 1980s approximately 6 percent of prison guards were women (Zimmer, 1986:1), nearly 10 percent of police officers were female (Martin, 1989:21) and 26 percent of all law degrees were awarded to women (Price and Sokoloff, 1982:373). While women had gained access to patrol in police work and were admitted as prison guards in male prisons, numerous researchers reported male resistance to and sexual harassment of women assigned in these traditionally male positions (e.g., Charles, 1981; Martin, 1979 and 1989; Petersen, 1982; and Zimmer, 1986 and 1989).

Summary

Daly and Chesney-Lind (1987:101) note that "the last decade has seen an outpouring of feminist scholarship in the academy . . . and that feminist thought has deepened and broadened." For the most part, however, criminology as a discipline has ignored this emerging scholarship on women and crime. The recent publication of articles on feminism and criminology in mainstream criminology journals (Daly and Chesney-Lind, 1987; Gelsthorpe and Morris, 1988; and Simpson, 1989) suggests a recognition of the existence of feminist criminology by scholars in the field but as Gelsthorpe and Morris (1988:103) suggest, "feminism is viewed as the property of 'others', 'outsiders' even."

Conflict Theory of Crime

While it is disturbing that leading criminologists have ignored women, it is especially difficult to understand how conflict theorists could totally neglect women. Men have been in positions of power to conduct research and to determine legal and criminal justice policies. Since conflict theory stresses that definitions of crime and the application of the label criminal are determined by the interests of those with economic and political power, this theory is the one most appropriate to explain the neglect of women by researchers and officials in the criminal justice agencies. It is ironic, therefore, that the male criminologists (e.g., Chambliss, Quinney, Taylor, et al., and Vold) who have dominated the conflict theoretical perspective have largely failed to consider the issues regarding women's changing roles as offenders, victims, and professionals.

In applying conflict theory to crime Vold stated:

> Many kinds of criminal acts must be recognized as representing
> primarily behavior on the front-line fringes of direct contact
> between groups struggling for the control of power in the
> political and cultural organization of society. On the surface, the
> offenses may seem to be the ordinary common-law ones
> involving persons and property, but on closer examination they
> often are revealed as the acts of good soldiers fighting for a
> cause . . . (Vold, 1979:292).

Vold indicates that violence, treachery and deceit may occur when
there is conflict of interests between groups, such as protest
movements, company management, and labor unions (Vold,
1979:293-95). Vold also introduced victimless crimes (e.g.,
gambling, vagrancy and begging, drunkenness, prostitution, and
drug law violations), organized crime and white collar crimes as
illustrations of criminal behavior that could better be understood
by using a conflict perspective.

More recent conflict theorists e.g., Chambliss and Seidman,
Quinney, Taylor et al., and Turk) have applied conflict theory to
explain crime in general instead of Vold's more narrow application
to specific crimes. These theorists assert that the crime producing
features of contemporary capitalism are bound up with the
inequities and divisions in material production and ownership.

Quinney (1969, 1970) and Chambliss and Seidman (1971) have
emphasized that criminal law is created and also interpreted by
particular men representing special interests, who have the power
to translate their vested interests into public policy. Although the
legal system is the most explicit form of social control in our society,
the law does not represent the norms and values of all persons in
our society. Instead, the governing process operates according to
the interests that characterize the socially differentiated positions.
The interest structure is characterized by an unequal distribution
of power and by conflict so that the higher a group's political or
economic position, the greater is the probability that its views will
be reflected in the laws (Chambliss and Seidman, 1971:473-74;
Quinney, 1969:26-27). For these authors, power and conflict are
inextricably linked in their conception of the interest structure.
Power, as the ability to shape public policy, produces conflict
between the competing segments. Conflict, in turn, produces
differences in the distribution of power.

The oppressed groups most frequently examined by conflict
theorists as victims of inequitable treatment by the criminal justice
system are the poor and minorities. The conflict perspective argues
that street crimes, most likely to be committed by minorities and
the poor, have been arbitrarily defined as crime. But the crimes

most likely to be committed by those with economic and political influence, white collar and professional crimes are legally protected from inclusion in criminal law (Reiman, 1990).

The failure of traditional criminologists and especially conflict theorists to include women results in biased research and inadequate theories of crime and criminal behavior. As Harris (1977:3) suggests, "general theories of deviance are no more than special theories of male deviance." Harris further argues that criminological theories should not only take the sex variable into account, but should start with it. Inclusion of gender/sex would greatly enrich the theoretical points in criminology.

Women, Crime and Conflict Theory

The history of scholarship on women in criminology presented above involves an increasing recognition of the hierarchical power relations between the sexes. This is especially reflected when one notes that the female offender was the first female participant in crime/criminal justice to be included. The female offender was followed by women victims and women workers in criminal justice. The early discussions of women offenders attempted to explain their deviance in superstitious and biological speculations. Victimization of women was either ignored or justified, and the woman was punished as property of the patriarchal family. Conflict theory has been expanded by feminists to include women among the powerless groups exploited by the capitalist system. Both the patriarchal structure and capitalism help maintain women in their subordinate positions.

The patriarchal societal structure in which men hold the positions of authority in our social institutions has a special impact on the role of women in both the private and public sector. Women have been in subordinate and oppressed positions throughout modern history. The concept of chivalry is used to explain the subservient role that women have held to men. "Chivalry" emerged in Europe during the middle ages to describe an institution of service rendered by crusading orders to feudal lords, to the divine sovereign, and to womankind. "Ladies" were special beneficiaries of the practice of chivalry as knights were sworn to protect female weakness (Moulds, 1978:417). While women have benefited somewhat from the chivalrous treatment, they have paid a price for this special treatment (Moulds, 1978). Chivalry has rendered women dependent and powerless to control their own lives.

However, Moulds contends that the differential power relationship between men and women is more accurately described as paternalism, which derives from a Latin-English kinship term that suggests a type of behavior by a superior toward an inferior resembling that of a parent to his child (Moulds, 1978:418). This paternalistic structure has established a power relationship between men and women that is most evident in the traditional patriarchal family system. Our culture has created a social system where the father dominates and all other members of the family, especially women, must submit to his will. Conflict theory, then, is central to understanding the power relationships between the sexes, which involves a dichotomy of sex roles. That is, most women are still being socialized into social roles as housewives and mothers, while men are socialized into occupations of authority and influence.

Furthermore, our sex role stereotyping of men into vocational roles and women into domestic roles has resulted in a criminal justice system that is dominated by men. As a result, criminal law has been codified by male legislators, enforced by male police officers and interpreted by male lawyers and judges.

As the ruling elite, male legislators are able to create laws to their own advantage. This is illustrated in traditional laws that make certain crimes sex specific. This has most often worked to the disadvantage of women. For example, historically legal codes made prostitution a punishable crime for women but provided legal protection for the male customer (Rafter and Natalizia, 1981:89-90). Also, the concept of wife as property of her husband has traditionally not provided legal protection for women against marital rape and wife battering (Rafter and Natalizia, 1981:88). As indicated in the Feinman chapter in this text, laws in several states (e.g., Pennsylvania, New Jersey, and Iowa) required women to receive longer sentences then men for the same crimes. There were also a few statutes that specified some crimes as male only offenses, e.g., statutory rape and voyeurism. One never makes reference to a "peeping Jane" but always a "peeping Tom." With the resurgence of the feminist movement in the 1960s, many of these laws have been changed to make them more gender neutral.

The recent acknowledgment of a feminist criminology is a reflection of the changing roles of women in relation to crime, the criminal justice system and academia. Feminist writers who continue to note the dominance of men in the criminal justice system and academia are now calling attention to the importance of extending our theories and research to include women of color and to examine crime beyond the western culture.

The chapters in the main body of this book will concentrate largely on the current status of women in various roles in the criminal justice system. The postscript will present a brief agenda for future research on women and crime.

Bibliography

Adler, Freda
    1975   *Sisters in Crime.* New York: McGraw-Hill.

Amir, Menachem
    1967   "Victim Precipitated Forcible Rape." *Journal of Criminal Law, Criminology, and Police Science* 58:493-502.

Baunach, Phyllis Jo
    1985   *Mothers in Prison.* New Brunswick, NJ: Transaction Books.

Berk, Richard L., Donileen R. Loseke, Sarah Fenstermaker Berk, and David Rauma
    1980   "Bringing the Cops Back In: A Study of Efforts to Make the Criminal Justice System More Responsive to Incidents of Family Violence." *Social Science Research* 9:193-215.

Blackstone Commentaries
    1768   445.

Bowker, Lee H.
    1978   *Women, Crime, and the Criminal Justice System.* Lexington, MA: Heath.

Bowker, Lee
    1982   "Police Services to Battered Women: Bad or Not So Bad?," *Criminal Justice and Behavior* 9:476-94.

Browne, Angela
    1987   *When Battered Women Kill.* New York: Free Press.

Brownmiller, Susan
    1975   *Against Our Will: Men, Women and Rape.* New York: Simon and Schuster.

Cavan, Ruth Shonle
    1962   *Criminology.* New York: Thomas Y. Crowell Company.
    1962   *Juvenile Delinquency.* New York: J. B. Lippincott Company.

Cameron, Mary Owen
    1964   *The Booster & the Snitch: Department Store Shoplifting.* New York: The Free Press of Glencoe.

Chambliss, William and Robert Seidman
    1971   *Law, Order, and Power.* Reading, MA: Addison-Wesley.

Chandler, Edna Walker
    1973   *Women in Prison.* New York: The Bobbs-Merrill Company, Inc.

Chapman, Jane Roberts
    1980   *Economic Realities and the Female Offender.* Lexington, MA: Heath.

Charles, Michael
1981 "The Performance and Socialization of Female Recruits in the Michigan State Police Training Academy." *Journal of Police Science and Administration* 9:209-23.

Clemmer, Donald
1965 *The Prison Community.* New York: Holt, Rinehart, and Winston.

Curran, Debra A.
1983 "Judicial Discretion and Defendant's Sex." *Criminology* 21:41-58.

Daly, Kathleen and Meda Chesney-Lind
1988 "Feminism and Criminology." *Justice Quarterly* 5:497-538.

Feinman, Clarice
1986 *Women in the Criminal Justice System.* New York: Praeger.

Freedman, Estelle B.
1981 *Their Sisters' Keepers: Women's Prison Reform in America, 1830-1930.* Ann Arbor: The University of Michigan Press.

Gelles, Richard J.
1974 *The Violent Home: A Study of Physical Aggression Between Husbands and Wives.* Beverly Hills, CA: Sage.

Gelsthorpe, Loraine and Allison Morris
1988 "Feminism and Criminology in Britain." *British Journal of Criminology* 28:93-110.

Giallombardo, Rose
1966 *Society of Women: A Study of a Women's Prison.* New York: Wiley.

Giordano, Peggy, Sandra Kerbel, and Sandra Dudley
1981 "The Economics of Female Criminality: An Analysis of Police Blotters, 1890-1976." Pp. 65-82 in Lee H. Bowker (ed.), *Women and Crime in America.* New York: Macmillan.

Groth, A. N., Ann W. Burgess, and Lynda L. Holmstrom
1977 "Rape: Power, Anger and Sexuality." *The American Journal of Psychiatry* 134:1239-43.

Hamilton, Mary E.
1924 *The Police Woman: Her Service and Ideals.* New York: Arno Press.

Harris, Anthony
1977 "Sex and Theories of Deviance: Toward a Functional Theory of Deviant Type-Scripts." *American Sociological Review* 42:3-15.

Harris, Mary Belle
1942 *I Knew Them in Prison.* New York: Viking.

Haskell, Martin R. and Lewis Yablonsky
1973 *Crime and Delinquency.* Chicago: Rand McNally.

Jolin, Annette
1983 "Domestic Violence Legislation: Am Impact Assessment." *Journal of Police Science and Administration* 11:451-56.

Klein, Dorie
  1981   "Violence against Women: Some Considerations Regarding Its
          Causes and Its Elimination." *Crime & Delinquency* 27:64-80.
Kuhl, Anna F.
  1985   "Battered Women Who Murder: Victims or Offenders." Pp.
          197-216 in Imogene L. Moyer (ed.), *The Changing Roles of
          Women in the Criminal Justice System: Offenders, Victims and
          Professionals*. Prospect Heights, IL: Waveland Press, Inc.
LaFree, Gary D.
  1981   "Official Reactions to Social Problems: Police Decisions in Sexual
          Assault Cases." *Social Problems* 28:582-94.
Laub, John H. and M. Joan McDermott
  1985   "An Analysis of Serious Crime by Young Black Women."
          Criminology 23:81-98.
Lombroso, Cesare
  1895   *The Female Offender*. London, England: Fisher Unwin.
Mahan, Sue
  1982   *Unfit Mothers*. Palo Alto, CA: R & E Research Associates, Inc.
Martin, Del
  1976   *Battered Wives*. San Francisco: Glide.
Martin, Susan
  1979   "*Police*women and Police*women*: Occupational Role Dilemmas
          and Choices of Female Officers." *Journal of Police Science and
          Administration* 7:314-23.
Martin, Susan E.
  1989   "Women on the Move?: A Report on the Status of Women in
          Policing." *Women & Criminal Justice* 1:21-40.
Moulds, Elizabeth
  1978   "Chivalry and Paternalism: Disparities of Treatment in the
          Criminal Justice System." *Western Political Quarterly*
          31:416-30.
Moyer [Simmons], Imogene
  1975   "Interaction and Leadership Among Female Prisoners."
          unpublished Ph.D. dissertation, University of Missouri, Columbia.
Moyer, Imogene L.
  1978   "Differential Social Structures and Homosexuality Among
          Women in Prison." *Virginia Social Science Journal* 13:13-19.
  1980   "Leadership in a Women's Prison." *Journal of Criminal Justice*
          8:233-41.
  1982   "Police Responses to Women Offenders in a Southeastern City."
          Journal of Police Science and Administration 10:376-83.
  1984   "Deceptions and Realities of Life in Women's Prisons." *Prison
          Journal* LXIV:45-56.
  1985   "Academic Criminology: A Need for Change." *American Journal
          of Criminal Justice* IX:197-212.

Moyer, Imogene L.
1986 "Gatekeepers for Academic Criminology: An Exploratory Study of the Status of Women." Proceedings of Twelfth International Improving University Teaching Conference. Heidelberg, Germany. 553-62.
Naffine, Ngaire
1987 *Female Crime: The Construction of Women in Criminology.* Boston: Allen & Unwin.
Nagel, Stuart and Lenore Weitzman
1971 "Women as Litigants." *Hastings Law Journal* 23:171-98.
O'Hare, Kate Richards
1923 *In Prison.* New York: Alfred A. Knopf.
Pagelow, Mildred Daley
1981 *Women Battering: Victims and Their Experiences.* Beverly Hills: Sage.
Petersen, Cheryl
1982 "Doing Time With the Boys: An Analysis of Women Correctional Officers in All-Male Facilities." Pp. 437-60 in Barbara Price and Natalie Sokoloff (eds.), *The Criminal Justice System and Women.* New York: Clark Boardman.
Pizzey, Erin
1974 *Scream Quietly or the Neighbors Will Hear.* Middlesex, England: Penguin.
Pollak, Otto
1950 *The Criminality of Women.* New York: A. S. Barnes and Company.
Price, Barbara Raffel and Natalie J. Sokoloff
1982 *The Criminal Justice System and Women.* New York: Clark Boardman.
Quinney, Richard
1969 *Crime and Justice in Society.* Boston: Little, Brown, and Company.
Quinney, Richard
1970 *The Social Reality of Crime.* Boston: Little, Brown and Company.
Rafter, Nicole and Elena Natalizia
1981 "Marxist Feminism: Implications for Criminal Justice." *Crime and Delinquency* 27:81-98.
Rasche, Christine E.
1974 "The Female Offender as an Object of Criminological Research." *Criminal Justice and Behavior* 1:301-21.
Reckless, Walter
1967 *The Crime Problem.* New York: Appleton-Century-Crofts.
Reiman, Jeffrey
1990 *The Rich Get Richer and the Poor Get Prison.* New York: Macmillan Publishing Company.

Robin, Gerald D.
1977   "Forcible Rape: Institutionalized Sexism in the Criminal Justice System." *Crime & Delinquency* 23:136-53.
Schrag, Clarence
1954   "Leadership among Prison Inmates." *American Sociological Review* February: 37-42.
Schwendinger, Julia R. and Herman Schwendinger
1983   *Rape and Inequality.* Beverly Hills, CA: Sage.
1984   "Rape, the Law, and Private Property." Pp. 42-56 in William J. Chambliss (ed.), *Criminal Law in Action.* New York: Wiley.
Shaw, Nancy Stoller
1982   "Female Patients and the Medical Profession in Jails and Prisons." Pp. 261-73 in Nicole Hahn Rafter and Elizabeth A. Stanko (eds.), *Judge, Lawyer, Victim, Thief: Women, Gender Roles, and Criminal Justice.* Boston: Northeastern University Press.
Shaw, Nancy S., Irene Browne, and Peter J. Meyer
1981   "Sexism and Medical Care in a Jail Setting." *Women and Health* 6, 1/2.
Simon, Rita
1975   *The Contemporary Woman and Crime.* Rockville, MD: National Institute of Mental Health.
Simpson, Sally S.
1989   "Feminist Theory, Crime, and Justice." *Criminology* 27:605-31.
Spender, Dale
1983   *Women of Ideas.* Boston: ARK Paperbacks.
Stanko, Elizabeth
1985   *Intimate Intrusions: Women's Experience of Male Violence.* Boston: Routledge & Kegan Paul.
Steffensmeier, Darrell
1978   "Crime and the Contemporary Woman: An Analysis of Changing Levels of Female Property Crime, 1970-1975." *Social Forces* 56:566-84.
Stone, Helen
1985   "The Changing Pattern of Female Crime: A Police Perspective." Pp. 54-75 in Imogene L. Moyer (ed.), *The Changing Roles of Women in the Criminal Justice System: Offenders, Victims, and Professionals.* Prospect Heights, IL: Waveland Press, Inc.
Straus, Murray
1973   "A General Systems Theory Approach to a Theory of Violence Between Family Members." *Social Science Information* 12:105-25.
Sullivan, Katharine
1956   *Girls on Parole.* Cambridge, MA: The Riverside Press.
Sykes, Gresham
1958   *The Society of Captives.* Princeton: Princeton University Press.

Taub, Nadine
   1983   "Adult Domestic Violence: The Law's Response." *Victimology*
           8:152-71.
Taylor, Ian, Paul Walton, and Jock Young
   1975   *Critical Criminology.* London: Routledge and Kegan Paul.
Totman, Jane
   1978   *The Murderess: A Psychosocial Study of Criminal Homicide.* San
           Francisco, CA: R & E Research Associates.
Turk, Austin
   1969   *Criminology and Legal Order.* Chicago: Rand McNally.
Visher, Christy A.
   1983   "Gender, Police Arrest Decisions, and Notions of Chivalry."
           Criminology 21:5-28.
Vold, George
   1979   *Theoretical Criminology.* New York: Oxford University Press.
Walker, Lenore
   1979   *The Battered Woman.* New York: Harper and Row.
Ward, David and Gene Kassebaum
   1965   *Women's Prison: Sex and Social Structure.* Chicago: Aldine.
Wilson, Nanci Koser
   1982   "Women in the Criminal Justice Professions: An Analysis of
           Status Conflict." Pp. 359-74 in Nicole Hahn Rafter and Elizabeth
           A. Stanko (eds.), *Judge, Lawyer, Victim, Thief.* Boston:
           Northeastern University Press.
Wilson, Nanci Koser and Constance M. Rigsby
   1975   "Is Crime a Man's World? Issues in the Exploration of
           Criminality." *Journal of Criminal Justice* 3:131-40.
Wright, Richard A.
   1987   "Are 'Sisters in Crime' Finally Being Booked? The Coverage of
           Women and Crime in Journals and Textbooks." *Teaching
           Sociology* 15:418-22.
Young, Vernetta D.
   1980   "Women, Race, and Crime." *Criminology* 18:26-34.
   1986   "Gender Expectations and Their Impact on Black Female
           Offenders and Victims." *Justice Quarterly* 3:305-27.
Zimmer, Lynn E.
   1986   *Women Guarding Men.* Chicago: The University of Chicago Press.
   1989   "Solving Women's Employment Problems in Corrections:
           Shifting the Burden to Administrators." *Women & Criminal
           Justice* 1:55-75.

Part I

Women Offenders and the Criminal Justice System

Introduction to Part I

A s indicated in Chapter One, research on women offenders and the criminal justice system historically has been very limited and/or based on traditional sex role stereotypes. Research on men has provided some support for the conflict perspective that sees crime as an arbitrary definition of behaviors that conflict with the vested interests of the segments of society (white, middle-class males) that have the power to shape public policy. While conflict theory has usually been applied to white collar and professional crimes by male offenders, it has recently been applied to definitions of crime involving women offenders.

As some feminists began to apply conflict theory to women, they (see Daly & Chesney-Lind, 1988; Jaggar & Rothenberg, 1984; and Simpson, 1989 for details of the various feminists theories) emphasized the oppression of women by a capitalist and patriarchal system. That is, these feminists suggest that capitalism produced a gendered division of labor in which women's production was for the consumption/use of the family and men's production was for market distribution. Through this economic/social division of labor, women became dependent on men who were the breadwinners. Eventually the patriarchal system based on capitalism developed with men as the heads of the family and every other social institution (e.g., education, religion, economics, politics etc.).

Because of the patriarchal system, women have been powerless to influence research projects on women in the criminal justice system. But the emergence of the civil rights and feminist movements have inspired some women to reconsider their traditional roles. As a result, some women have moved into professional positions that provide them the opportunity to influence research and policies concerning women in the criminal justice system.

The research and literature reviews presented in each of the following chapters on women offenders indicates, in a specific way, how cultural premises about women and sex role stereotyping of women's roles have influenced the perception and treatment of women by officials in the criminal justice system. In addition, the authors in this section examine new areas of research on women offenders as well as the changes involved in the processing of women offenders.

Chapter 2, "Patriarchy, Power Differentials, and Women

Offenders" by Whitson and Moyer, examines the changing roles of women offenders through a historical review of women offenders in the nineteenth and twentieth centuries. This chapter also explores the impact of the patriarchal structure on the criminal behavior of women, especially in the areas of prostitution and murder. Finally, wherever the literature allows, race and international issues are applied to explore the changing roles of women offenders.

The chapter, "Criminal Codes, Criminal Justice and Female Offenders: New Jersey as a Case Study," by Feinman points to the historical and cultural premises about the roles of adult and juvenile women in society. These roles have shaped the definitions of criminal behavior and sentencing in the New Jersey criminal codes. These sex specific laws were the work of male legislators. Feinman explores the influence of the women's movement on the recent revision of these codes and finds that conflict theory is quite applicable. These new gender neutral codes also provide Feinman with the opportunity to investigate the impact of the changing status of women on the treatment of women offenders in New Jersey.

Conflict theory suggests that, since most police officers are men, they have a double source of power: being men and also being officials of the criminal justice system. Speculations on the differential treatment of women offenders have been based on assumptions that officers have traditional attitudes toward women. According to this theory of chivalry, police give preferential treatment to women who display middle class standards of behavior, such as being polite, respectful and submissive, and harsh treatment to women whose behavior is gender inappropriate, such as being loud, disrespectful, and hostile. Moyer's chapter, "Police/Citizen Encounters: Issues of Chivalry, Gender, and Race," explores the emergence of research on police officers and on women offenders. It then presents a review of the few studies that have been conducted on police and women offenders. The chapter examines the impact of race and gender stereotypes and the differential treatment by police using the conflict perspective.

Kruttschnitt's " 'Female Crimes' or Legal Labels? The Effects of Deviance Processing Agents on Our Understanding of Female Criminality," questions the traditional explanations of women's crime by emphasizing the disparities between arrest offenses and conviction offenses. This chapter further explores a new area of research that raises questions about how the social profiles of women offenders might more accurately reflect actual female criminal behavior as well as influencing decisions made by criminal justice officials.

Conflict theory is applicable to any study of prisons because of the powerlessness of inmates, but it is especially appropriate for women inmates because of sex role stereotyping. Because of the paternalistic attitude toward women's prisons, the problems of women in prison have been largely ignored until recently. The chapter by Baunach, "Critical Problems of Women in Prison," describes programmatic inadequacies in women's prisons with special attention given to her own research on inmate mothers. Vocational training programs for women in prison are examined by Baunach in light of the changing social roles and needs of women offenders who return to society. She also provides several potential means of alleviating problems encountered by women offenders.

The failure of researchers to examine the needs of women offenders for vocational training programs is best explained by conflict theory. Sex role stereotyping has meant that administrators have assumed that rehabilitation involved simply preparing women to be good housewives and mothers. However, the current changes in the status of women have brought attention to the needs of women offenders for vocational skills. The chapter, "Project MET: A Community Based Educational Program for Women Offenders," by Fortune and Balbach reports on one of the first model employment training programs involving women offenders. The authors show the need for change in the way the system deals with reacclimating the female offender to society.

Rogers explores the impact of the patriarchal system on women on probation and parole in his chapter, "Probation, Parole, Power, and Women Offenders: From Patriarchal Parameters to Participant Empowerment." This chapter emphasizes the power differentials between women probationers and parolees and the officers who supervise them in the community. He presents a client empowerment model to help these women probationers and parolees obtain resources to enable them to gain greater control over their environment and to reach their goals.

Bibliography

Daly, Kathleen and Meda Chesney-Lind
    1988   "Feminism and Criminology." *Justice Quarterly* 5:497-538.
Jaggar, Alison M. and Paula S. Rotherberg (eds.)
    1984   *Feminist Frameworks*. New York: McGraw-Hill.
Simpson, Sally S.
    1989   "Feminist Theory, Crime, and Justice." *Criminology* 27:605-31.

Patriarchy, Power Differentials, and Women Offenders

Marian Whitson and Imogene L. Moyer
Indiana University of Pennsylvania

Introduction

One aspect of the late twentieth century women's movement has been an ever increasing abundance of scholarship on women by scholars who write from the women's perspective. The success of this research in various academic disciplines is evidenced in the establishment of Women's Studies Programs in major universities throughout the United States and in other countries. Courses on criminology are limited in Women's Studies programs, especially when compared to course offerings in the humanities and many other social sciences. Although there is a lack of consensus regarding the extent of the changes in women's roles in society and in crime, there is a general agreement among those conducting research on women offenders that the patriarchal society and the criminal justice system have limited women's power to make decisions and to act independently.

Some research on women offenders was conducted early in the nineteenth century, and history has recorded deviant/criminal activities of women dating back to at least the Civil War. Much of the nineteenth century research on women offenders was not acknowledged by criminologists until the 1970s (see Bowker, 1978; Rasche, 1974). Also, much of the attention given to women offenders in both the nineteenth and twentieth centuries has been sensationalized. The history of women offenders in the nineteenth century is mostly anecdotal documentation of the deviant activities of unusual women (e.g., robbery and cattle rustling), which trivializes and/or ignores the criminal activities of ordinary women whose crimes involved prostitution, child abandonment and neglect, and spousal homicide that resulted from battering.

During the late nineteenth and the twentieth century women's criminal behavior was largely ignored or attributed to their biological inferiority (e.g., Lombroso, 1893; Pollak, 1950). In the 1970s, criminologists began to speculate about the impact of the women's movement on women offenders. Adler (1975) hypothesized that during the 1970s women began to engage in more masculine types of offenses (e.g., robbery, burglary) as a result of the increasing opportunities, temptations, strains, and attention afforded them by the women's movement. This work was sensationalized nationally by the mass media. Studies, such as that conducted by Horney in 1978, which emphasized the increase in crimes committed by women, tended to support Adler's theory. While Simon (1975; 1981) concurred with Adler (1975) that the feminist movement was influencing changes in women's crime, Simon (1975:41) predicted increases in women's traditional property crimes, e.g., larceny, fraud and embezzlement, and forgery and counterfeiting.

While these works were refuted by later researchers (e.g., Daly, 1989; Feinman, 1985; Giordano, et al., 1981; Morris, 1987; Steffensmeier, 1980; and Steffensmeier and Allan, 1988), they brought the issue of women offenders to the forefront of Criminology and stimulated research on the topic. Morris (1987:73), however, states that the feminist movement had its greatest impact on white middle-class women, while the criminal justice system has its greatest impact on blacks and working-class women.

This chapter will examine the changing roles of women offenders as presented by historians and researchers from the nineteenth century through the twentieth century. The chapter will show that there has always been interest in women as prostitutes and as murderers. Therefore, there is more material available on these two types of offenders, especially in this century. It should also be noted that feminists have always viewed the crimes of women differently than mainstream scholars. This chapter also will provide information on minority women offenders whenever that information is available.

Women Challenge the Patriarchal Law

The feminist movement of the nineteenth century brought attention to the patriarchal rule of men over women as well as the inequality in the criminal justice system. Nineteenth century women were fighters for changes regarding women and the legal system. Women of the 19th century were classed either as criminal incorrigibles or morally "bad" whenever their activities deviated from stereotypically assigned roles. Despite public derision, these women activists continued to test the 19th century legal system and were influential in the establishment of legislative changes affecting women.

In 1848, women united at Seneca Falls, New York to generate recognition of woman's historic subjection to man (Beard, 1946; Dahlinger, 1918; Offen, 1989). They brought with them a list of grievances which summarized the "abuses and usurpations" of men over women (Beard, 1946:145). Women demanded a vindication from the common law rule subjecting absolute control of their person and property to the wills of men (Beard, 1946; Dahlinger, 1918; Offen, 1989).

Under common law, married women were not equal to men before the law (Beard, 1946; Dahlinger, 1918; Nowak, Rotunda and Young, 1983). Married women lacked the legal capacity to contract or convey property (Nowak, Rotunda and Young, 1983). Money earned by the wife became the husband's property (Dahlinger, 1918). The husband's superiority to his wife was such that the legal punishment for a wife killing her husband was more severe than for a husband killing his wife. If the husband were to kill his wife he might or might not be punished (Dahlinger, 1918:68). If the wife were to kill her husband, her punishment might be analogous to killing the king. So atrocious was the act, states Dahlinger (1918:68), that the wife was considered to have denied her husband conjugal affection, thus increasing the severity of the punishment. It was against such controls that women began to revolt.

Women who challenged the courts' right to declare male supremacy were not looked upon favorably by the majority. Through the efforts and sacrifices of women such as Caroline Norton, Mary Upton Ferrin, Isabella Beecher Hooker and Edith Lanchester (Beard, 1946; Hyde, 1951; Nowak, Rotunda and Young, 1983; and Rubinstein, 1986) married women won the right to inherit and bequeath property as could single women, to make a will without her husband's consent, and to have certain rights in the property of a husband dying intestate. Although the process was limited to particular states, by 1856 women of the Seventh National Women's Rights Convention reported that almost every northern state had modified its laws on married women and property (Beard, 1946:162).

However, women who challenged male preeminence and the patriarchal system were to some, both males and females, guilty of treason. Their actions, although not criminal in that they did not mandate imprisonment or arrest, were deviant for the times. Some women in this period, however, were briefly imprisoned for civil disobedience. Susan B. Anthony, for example, protested the denial of women's right to vote and was arrested for voting (Sachs and Wilson, 1978:68-69).

The fight for legal equality and recognition was not limited to the white community of the north. Paralleling the white society, the nineteenth century Negro community was also male dominated. Quarles (1969:177) states that the nineteenth century Negro community had fixed ideas about the role of women beyond the traditional categories of kitchen, church and school. Negro women, sensing the connection of gender politics to slavery, began to join their fight for racial equality with that of gender recognition. Jane Merritt and Mary A. Shadd, were two Negro women who openly voiced their disapproval of denying Negro women seats to annual abolitionists conventions (Quarles, 1969). Threatening to cause disruptions at these conventions, Merritt and Shadd were successful in gaining admission for women into the 1849 Ohio convention and the 1855 Philadelphia convention.

Other black women combined efforts to abolish slavery with efforts to combat patriarchy in the black community. While Sojourner Truth (Spender, 1983) is most famous for her speech, "Ain't I a Woman," which challenged the patriarchal attitudes toward black women, she also was active in the anti-slavery movement. Harriet Tubman, known as "Moses" for her underground anti-slavery activities, helped slaves escape to the North (Wesley & Romero, 1967). Tubman was able to pass through both Union and Confederate lines at will. Confederate soldiers, assuming she was a typical black female plantation worker, did not suspect her of gathering information to pass to the Union Army. The Union soldiers, recognizing her ability to obtain valuable information, permitted her in their camps. Her ability to deceive one army and help another contributed to her ultimate goal of freeing slaves. Tubman continued these activities despite the fact that rewards were offered for her life and there were many bounty hunters.

Although not as well known as Harriet Tubman, Mary Elizabeth Browser was also a Union ally. Mary Elizabeth, a former slave, was able to secure written and oral information regarding Confederate plans through her position as a servant in the home of Jefferson Davis (Wesley & Romero, 1967). Since she was thought to be illiterate, maps and letters were left open and she forwarded the information she obtained from these materials to a Northern plantation through another slave who visited the Davis' plantation.

Western Frontier and Women Offenders

While the women of the north challenged the patriarchal law and the women of the south fought for social justice and equality during the Civil War, women of the west were busy establishing their niche in the new wilderness. Not all of the women of the west were willing to settle as domestic caretakers. A variety of women ventured into the unsettled territory, many with characteristics uncommon to their gender (Beard, 1946; Dahlinger, 1918; Luchetti and Olwell, 1982; Lyons, 1969; Ray, 1972). Some carried guns, smoked cigars, played cards, established or worked in brothels, drank alcohol, and used abusive language.

The language used by Grace Newton, a leader of a gang of cattle rustlers, is thought to be responsible for her legal troubles as much as her actual deeds (Ray, 1972:31). On one occasion, the judge reprimanded Newton and adjourned the court until she could continue testifying like a lady (Ray, 1972).

Mary Jane Canary consumed large quantities of liquor. At the age of 16, she became active in crime, an area supposedly restricted to men. Changing her name to Calamity Jane, she became famous for her constant infractions with the law. Cursing, tobacco chewing, drinking alcohol, and gambling, normally associated with men, became part of her daily activities (Ray, 1972).

Flora Quick, a brothel owner, was also a horse thief. Known in the western territory as "Tom King," she was arrested numerous times for horse stealing (Ray, 1972). However, she was never jailed for more than a day or two. Some speculate that she received preferential treatment from the patriarchy because she was the owner of an establishment frequently inhabited by men.

Many women achieved their notoriety as offenders through their male companions. Etta Place, the female companion of the "Sundance Kid," assumed leadership of the all-male gang after the "Kid's" death until she left the country with Butch Cassidy (Ray, 1972). After escaping from years of being an abused spouse, Pearl Hunt entered a union with Joe Boot, a well-known stagecoach robber. A robbery of an Arizona stagecoach in 1898 netted Pearl and Joe $432.00 and five years in prison for Pearl, and thirty years for Joe (Ray, 1972). After her parole, Pearl began a stage tour as the "Arizona Bandit" (Ray, 1972).

Other women were killed as a result of their lawlessness. Myra Beth Shirley, the infamous "Belle Starr," was charged with horse stealing (Ray, 1972). She and her husband, Samuel, served twelve months for this conviction at the Detroit House of Correction. Upon her release, Belle continued to pursue her criminal activities in the disguise of a man (Ray, 1972). This disguise made it impossible for witnesses to render accurate descriptions. Fatally wounded by a rifle shot in the back, Belle died two days before her birthday.

Ella Watson, better known as "Cattle Kate," and her neighbor were hung on the assumption that they were cattle thieves (Ray, 1972:22). Kate was not an active participant in cattle rustling, but according to reports she was willing to accept stolen cattle as payment for a night with her (Ray, 1972). The vigilante group claimed that the hanging was an accident which occurred when they attempted to frighten Kate and the man into admitting that they had stolen the cattle (Ray, 1972). This contention is surprising, since according to recordings of Ray (1972:22) they were ordered to step off a boulder with a noose around their neck. Women of the western frontier were involved in a variety of criminal activities, including cattle rustling, horse stealing, gambling and robberies.

Prostitution Women's Oldest Criminal Offense

Prostitution has often been defined as the oldest and most universal of women's offenses. It also was probably the most noted female deviant behavior during the 19th century. The feminist movement (which included abolition, temperance, and women's rights) attempted both to help some women escape prostitution as a profession and to protect prostitutes from venereal disease. Feminists worked to pass laws mandating that prostitutes be under regular medical supervision. Despite the efforts of feminists to convince women to abandon prostitution, it remained the largest occupation for single women (Luchetti and Olwell, 1982).

According to Luchetti and Olwell (1982:35), prostitution began in earnest in the west during the gold rush. Prostitution in the west included orientals, brought to the United States as indentured slaves, whites, and Indians. Blassingame (1973) notes the prominence of prostitutes among the free mulattos, octoroons, pure Africans and other women in New Orleans during the nineteenth century, as well. Regardless of its origin, prostitution was not segregated to any specific geographical area, nor was it confined to any race.

Luchetti and Olwell (1982:31) state that prostitution was divided into three status classes by the latter part of the 1800s. The most profitable were the "class houses." Young women employed by the "madams" of the houses received substantial wages, in addition to room and board. Retention in the "class houses" was dependent upon the physical appearance of the women and the ability to retain clients (Luchetti and Olwell, 1982). Failure to maintain these standards resulted in their discharge from the establishment. If they were fortunate, they would find residence in a "second class house" (Luchetti & Olwell, 1982). Working in this house meant getting paid less but having more sexual encounters (Luchetti & Olwell, 1982). Women not accepted by or unable to maintain the quota of the "second-class houses" were reduced to the corrupted boarding houses and "cribs" (Luchetti & Olwell, 1982). A cramped room with a cot and a chair, the "cribs" were every prostitutes nightmare. With the streets as her arena and her pay fifty cents to a dollar for every trade, she became the victim of venereal diseases, physical attacks, and sometimes murder.

Frequently a woman was introduced to prostitution by a person she trusted. Her motivation was often a past due debt. Other times, submission or denial was directly linked to her continued survival. This was particularly true for the southern black female. In southern cities such as New Orleans, special institutions were established for sexual relations between white men and black women (Blassingame, 1973:17). It was common for a white man to offer a slave as a bed warmer to a male visitor, and for the master of the household to have fathered several children by his female property. Subject to the desire and control of white society, few black females were able to retain their virtue beyond the age of 13. Once the black female submitted to the sexual forces she was subjected to daily, she was then classified as promiscuous, a whore or prostitute. The fear of the consequences of not succumbing outweighed any future stigma.

In downtown New Orleans, casual liaisons with Negro women

were open and frequent (Blassingame, 1973). Negro prostitutes were not only desired, but preferred. Negro women were purchased by wealthy white men to serve as their concubines or bed partners. Yearly auctions often brought wealthy plantation owners into the city with the sole purpose of acquiring such women. The life of these slaves was usually more relaxed than that of the field slave or the slave girl born on the plantation and seduced later. Children born from the sexual union acquired the surname of the mother-slave. The father's race and prominence was disregarded (Blassingame, 1973).

It was not unusual for specific arrangements to be made between free Negro females and white males for the purpose of miscegenation (Blassingame, 1973). A system of prostitution, placage, resembled common-law marriages. A Negro woman who met the desires of the white man was courted and maintained in a home which the two of them shared, either constantly or periodically. The woman in a placage arrangement obtained financial security and was protected from the plantation's manual hardship, as well as the physical violence. Many of the placages were permanent, such as that between a white gentlemen and a Negro woman who remained together from 1796 until his death in 1845 (Blassingame 1973:18). Although many would view this arrangement as distinct from prostitution, it had much in common with prostitution.

Sexual contacts between black men and white women were less frequent. In addition to the lack of financial benefits afforded, an engagement if discovered by opposing whites, would result in the "fallen" woman being ostracized (Blassingame, 1973). However, white women were arrested annually for sexual involvement with slave men. Blassingame (1973:28) states that considering the opinion of their peers, the punishment was relatively light, usually a maximum of six months in jail.

While the white woman had power over the black man and the black woman, the black woman was powerless. She was a breeder for her owner, thus increasing his wealth through the sale of her children, his property. At the demand of her master, she became a sexual partner for any white male . . . If she had been designated to a bondsman (Blassingame, 1973:18), the slave was powerless to protect herself or her daughters from the sexual advances of white men, who considered every slave cabin a bordello (Blassingame, 1973). At the request of her mistress, she became the nursemaid and caretaker of her half brothers and sisters. Considering these factors, it is not surprising that free Negro women, although allowed to roam freely within the city of New Orleans, found it advantageous to hire themselves as concubines. The most beautiful of the slave girls and the free Negro women were hired by the month as concubines (Blassingame, 1973:18).

The various types of deviant/criminal behavior described above reflect the patriarchal, double standards about sex denoted in the madonna/whore duality discussed in Chapter One. This perspective of women, especially black women, has continued through the twentieth century and is reflected in the earliest social science theories and research studies. Women in the twentieth century continue to experience the powerlessness and exploitation in society and the criminal justice system that their nineteenth century counterparts did.

Twentieth Century Offenders

Prior to the 1960s, efforts to explain female crime relied on physical explanations such as those of Lombroso and Pollak. There were few studies of women offenders. Research in the 1970s was stimulated by the controversy over Adler's and Simon's predictions that women's crime was increasing as a result of the current women's movement.

Opponents of Adler contend that there is insufficient evidence to support the claim that women are moving into more masculine types of offenses. Today's females, according to Schur (1984:217), may exemplify a more liberated behavior but there is no support for the claim that the women's liberation movement had a direct influence on female contributions to crime. In fact, women's share of arrests for all crimes reported in the Uniform Crime Reports increased only 6-8 percent in the last thirty years.

Some argue that the Uniform Crime Reports appear to support the fact that the women's liberation movement had at a minimum, an indirect affect on the increase in female criminality. For instance, a review by Mann (1985) of a UCR report of 5,907 agencies, revealed that between 1975 and 1984 there was a 10.4 percent increase in female violent crimes and a 6.2 percent increase for property crimes.

Women Property Offenders

Research studies on property crimes in the twentieth century are limited to studies of Uniform Crime Reports by Feinman (1985) and Steffensmeier (1978) and of police records by Giordano, et al. (1981) who examined the claims of Adler (1975) and Simon (1975); an earlier study of shoplifting in Chicago by Cameron (1965); studies of white collar crime by Daly (1989) and Zeitz (1981); and finally a study (Fortune, et al., 1980) of female robbers in prison.

Several studies (Feinman,1985; Giordano, et al., 1981; and Steffensmeier, 1978) which examined secondary data on women's crime in general reported that a close examination of the property offenses found that women are committing these offenses less frequently than men, and that the increases that are reported are for petty crimes, such as credit card fraud, hotel fraud, and petty larceny.

Daly (1989:77) (from a study of a select group of women convicted of white-collar offenses in the U.S. Federal District Courts during the latter part of the 1970s) indicates that women do not comprise a large percentage of corporate white collar criminals. Daly (1989) further suggests that disagreements in the definition of white collar crime and the low number of women in positions of power in these areas account for some of the invisibility or absence of arrests for these crimes. She also notes that the notion that increased female involvement in crimes such as embezzlement, forgery and fraud is attributable to an increase in women in the labor force assumes that offenses are occupationally related. Chapman (1980) and Daly (1989) suggest that the increasing female share of UCR white collar arrests reflects women's economic and occupational marginality, not mobility.

The majority of the women offenders, according to Chapman (1980), Daly (1989), and Miller (1986) are young, single, poor mothers of several children who belong to a minority (most often black) and have a limited education and low occupational skills. Miller (1986:6) further states that the women street hustlers she interviewed in her 1979 study in Milwaukee had been involved in prostitution, petty property offenses, or drug offenses. This further supports Daly's (1989) assertion that these are not occupational crimes. These women are on the margin of society and perceive no other choices.

Zeitz (1981), like Daly (1989), studied women who committed white collar offenses (i.e., women who embezzle or defraud). Zeitz's (1981:23) study, however, was a study of women imprisoned at the California Institution for Women, which means they were somewhat different from the kinds of offenders examined by Daly (1989), Feinman (1985), Giordano, et al. (1981) and Steffensmeier (1978).

Zeitz's study was initially designed to replicate Cressey's (1953) report that embezzlers accept positions of trust in good faith but find they have a nonshareable problem. Their position of trust provides them the opportunity to embezzle; they start out "borrowing" money intending to pay it back. Then they rationalize "borrowing" more money on different occasions and finally get caught after the amount they have taken has increased to the point where they could never reasonably expect to pay it back.

Although Zeitz (1981) does not report the date for her research, she indicates that 45 percent of the prison population of women are convicted of theft, forgery, embezzlement, and fraud. Zeitz'(1981:24) study found two general types of women offenders. Women who appeared to meet Cressey's criteria were classified as "embezzlers" or "honest women who violated financial trust." All others in this sample were tentatively designated as "fraudulent operators" or "women who intended to steal or defraud" (p. 25). Zeitz (1981:25) book includes extensive interview data in which the women describe the events surrounding their crimes. Many of these women perceived themselves as having no choice. In some instances, they committed the crimes in desperate efforts to protect a loved one or to save a relationship (Zeitz, 1981:80-82).

Mary Owen Cameron's (1965) classic study of shoplifting conducted in Chicago in the 1940s included a sample from a major department store and a sample of shoplifting arrests from the Women's Court in Chicago (1964:24). Cameron (1964:39) reported two types of shoplifters. The first type are "snitches" or pilferers who bring shopping lists and steal merchandise for their own consumption. Ninety percent of shoplifters are "snitches" who are respected middle-class housewives who steal to supplement the family income (p. 56). The "boosters," who are usually men, are the more serious shoplifters who steal merchandise to sell. Cameron (1964:56) reports that "not over 10 percent of shoplifters in any department store are stealing to market the stolen merchandise."

Fortune, et al. (1980:319) reported a 1976 study of women offenders incarcerated in the Florida Correctional Institution at Lowell. Of the 174 inmates interviewed, 18.9 percent (n = 33) were for robbery. Fifty-eight percent of these robbers were young black women (p. 319). The need for money was the most motivating factor, followed by use of drugs and peer pressure (p. 321). Fortune, et al, (1981:322) found that 39 percent of the women committed robbery with male partners, 21 percent with female partners, 21 percent in mixed groups, and only 15 percent acted alone.

The authors developed a typology of robbers (p. 323). Situational robberies (15 cases) were committed due to circumstances external to the offender and there was no evidence of commitment to robbery as a continuing pattern. None of these women participated in planning the robbery. The second type of robbers were career robbers (18 cases). These women had extensive prior criminal records, which tended to include a history of robbery. This study is atypical of women offenders in other studies because they are incarcerated women. Furthermore, most of these women are accomplices in the offense and were motivated by a need for money and, in some instances, for drugs. Although the sample for this study is small, it provides a basis for more extensive or focused research on this type of offender.

The research on property offenders reported above suggests that even if there is some increase in the number of women property offenders, most of these women are petty offenders who perceive that they are in desperate situations without other choices. Thus, these studies do not support the projections of Adler (1975) or Simon (1975) that the women's movement and women's increased participation in the labor force are influencing women toward greater or traditionally male crimes.

Prostitution

The perspective of prostitution in the nineteenth century reflected the patriarchal double sex standards denoted in the madonna/whore duality discussed in Chapter One. This perspective of women is reflected in the earliest social science theories and research studies and has continued into the twentieth century.

Lombroso (1893:152) cited physiological abnormalities as the cause of female prostitution and suggested that it was quite natural for women to be impure. In 1923, Thomas also argued (in his study of prostitution in *The Unadjusted Girl*) that these girls, who come from poor homes and unstable families, have become demoralized, and, in some cases, are amoral.

In a similar view, Davis (1968:347-62) indicates that prostitution is "condemned . . . because it involves a high degree of sexual promiscuity. . . ." The prostitute is condemned because she "flaunts promiscuity by offering sexual favors in the market place . . ." (p. 351). Davis provides support for the feminist argument that the patriarchal society and justice system oppress women in statements that demonstrate a double sex standard. For example, he states that the customer is not punished by society because:

> Man is justified because of his natural sexual appetite but is not punished because he discharges important social and business relations. . . . He cannot be imprisoned without deranging society (p. 358).

Although he argues that women do not enter prostitution for economic reasons, he contradicts this position in the following statement:

> It is even true that some women physically enjoy the intercourse
> they sell. From a purely economic point of view, prostitution
> comes near the situation of getting something for nothing . . .
> the harlot's reward is not for labor, skill. . . . It is a reward for
> loss of social standing (p. 361).

The double sex standard found in the works of these early writers
demonstrates the hierarchical structure of the society that allows
those with power to exploit and punish those without power.
Studies of this type also have resulted in a number of stereotypes
and myths about prostitutes being man haters, oversexed, frigid,
self-destructive, or from the lower class.

Black and Jewish women are often stereotyped as whores. One
black woman who is not a prostitute said, "When I stand waiting
for a bus, especially in a white neighborhood, men passing assume
that I'm working. My color means "whore to them" (Delacoste and
Alexander, 1987:216). And in many countries (such as Netherlands,
France, and Germany) third world women are more likely to be
exploited in prostitution than native white women (Delacoste and
Alexander, 1987:217). These authors further suggest that Jews
have been identified as unchaste. "However, whereas black
unchastity is primarily attached to mythologies about black
women's sexual mysteries and black men's physical violence,
Jewish unchastity is primarily attached to myths about Jewish
women's sexual victimization and Jewish men's financial
conspiracies" (p. 217). Such racist mechanisms compound the
stigmatization of whores of color but they do not minimize the "dark
mark" branded on any prostitute.

Class and Power Structures

Following Davis' (1968) argument, there is a perceived class
difference between the prostitute and her customer. Prostitutes are
automatically placed in the lower class while customers are
assumed to be middle-or-upper class "pillars of society." James
(1982) suggests that our double sex standards are partially
responsible for this perceived class difference. James (1982:296)
argues that some behaviors in our society are considered acceptable
for men but not for women, e.g., standing on a corner alone at night
or soliciting sexual conversations with strangers. Prostitutes are
punished for violating sex-role stereotypes.

While society has labeled all prostitutes as lower-class (Davis,
1968; Heyl, 1979; and James, 1976 and 1982). James (1976) notes
in her study that 64 percent of streetwalkers reported their

childhood family's income as middle or upper class. Not only do prostitutes come from all walks of life and social classes but Heyl (1979) notes that there is a stratification among prostitutes. The lowest level of prostitute identified by Heyl (1979:197) is the street-walker, most of whom do originate in the lower class and have limited mobility among prostitutes. Middle-range prostitutes, who work away from the streets in houses, hotels, and massage parlors, charge middle-range prices while the highest level of prostitute is the independent call girl and convention or party girl.

Heyl (1979:199) applies sex stratification, economic status, and power differentials existing between men and women to examine the power and control that men have over prostitutes for each of the levels defined above. She notes (Heyl, 1979:200-201) that male police officers and pimps have political, physical, and psychological power over streetwalkers while pimps and businessmen have economic and consumer power over prostitutes in the two higher levels.

This system of sex stratification identified by Heyl is maintained through sex role stereotyping which is the core of the patriarchal power structure in both society and the justice system. The sex stratification system keeps women at the bottom of the economic structure and dependent on a traditional role in the patriarchal family structure for survival. Women at the bottom of the economic structure often see no alternative but to enter prostitution.

Those women whose behavior is not in accord with the sex role stereotypes are labeled deviant. Conflict theory, which states that those with economic and political power define the behavior of the powerless as a crime and differentially apply the label, is quite appropriately applied to the study of prostitution. Men define the behavior of women prostitutes as criminal and immoral but not the behavior of the male customers.

The Business of Prostitution

In contrast to the earlier stereotypes of prostitutes as manhaters or nymphomaniacs, more recent research indicates that prostitutes see themselves as businesswomen. Heyl (1979:207) quoted a prostitute as stating, "I am a business woman. I happen to work as a hooker. . . ."

Miller (1986:36) in her interviews with street hustlers in Milwaukee reports that "the major function of the deviant street network is to facilitate street hustling as an income-producing strategy. . . ." While network activity includes prostitution, petty larceny, forgery, credit card fraud, embezzlement, auto theft, drug traffic, burglary and robbery (p. 35), Miller (1986:126) notes that network women are most frequently arrested for prostitution and shoplifting.

Prostitutes are becoming much more vocal about their "right to work." Margo St. James was the first contemporary prostitute in the United States to speak out publicly for the rights of sex workers. In 1973 she founded a prostitutes' rights organization in San Francisco named COYOTE, an acronym for "Call Off Your Old Tired Ethics" (Pheterson, 1989:4). Pheterson also reports on prostitutes' rights organizations in other countries as well as two World Whores Congresses held in Amsterdam (1985) and in Brussels (1986). These Congresses addressed a variety of issues, including health, migration laws, and conflicts between feminists and prostitutes.

While prostitutes cited in Delacoste and Alexander (1987) and Pheterson (1989) are outspoken in their view that sex work is a legitimate occupation freely chosen by women, many feminists argue that prostitution exploits and degrades all women. Barry (1984:407-409) refers to prostitution as "female sexual slavery" and takes the feminist position that "prostitution is . . . economic exploitation caused by the lack of economic opportunities for women, the result of an unjust economic order." Barry further states that a major cause of sex slavery is the social-sexual objectification of women that permeates every patriarchal society in the world.

Legislation in the U.S.

Issues raised during the last two decades have called for a variety of legislative changes from legalization to decriminalization of prostitution. Several states, e.g., Illinois, New York, and Pennsylvania, have changed the criminal statutes to include customers of prostitutes; Nevada has made prostitution legal. However, the crime for customers has been defined as a less serious offense than prostitution, and legalization has resulted in severe restrictions on the personal lives of prostitutes.

Legalization.   In 1971 Nevada revised its statutes to make prostitution legal, except for two counties with a population of 200,000 or more and the Reno-Lake Tahoe area (Symanski, 1974:359). Although each county was allowed to establish its own rules to regulate the prostitutes, Symanski observes that the thirty-three legal brothels literally become prisons. In Ely County, for example, prostitutes must be twenty-one, obtain a work permit, be fingerprinted, photographed, and examined by a physician before commencing work (p. 362). Prostitutes' space and activities also are restricted. They are permitted outside the brothels, with a few exceptions, only between the hours of 10 a.m. and 6 p.m. Written regulations usually state that a "girl" may not be accompanied by a male escort in town. In many counties, they are not allowed to have friends or family in town (p. 371-72). Obviously, most prostitutes are not in favor of this type of legalized prostitution.

Decriminalization. New York was one of the first states to "decriminalize" prostitution. In 1961, the prostitution statutes in New York applied only to women and included sentences up to three years. A new law, which became effective September 1, 1967, decriminalized prostitution by reducing it to a violation (not a crime) with a maximum penalty of fifteen days or $50.00 fine. This law also made it a violation to patronize a prostitute (Roby, 1976:30-34). Since the police could no longer use officers as decoys to solicit prostitutes, arrests and prosecution became much more difficult.

Roby (1976) provides excellent documentation of the strong opposition to the new law by the New York City police. During a "clean-up" of the city between August 20 and September 30, 1967, the police made 2400 arrests (Roby, 1976:41-42). This was only two hundred less arrests in six weeks than the number of prostitution arrests during the first six months of the year. The judge dismissed many of the loitering charges as illegal. Furthermore, the police simply refused to enforce the law against patronizing prostitutes. Only 6 percent of arrests and .8 percent of convictions were for patronizing a prostitute (Roby, 1976:43).

By the fall of 1969, a conservative legislature passed a bill that upped the maximum penalty to ninety-one days or a $500.00 fine (Sheehy, 1980:116). Once again, prostitution was defined as a misdemeanor and a crime. In a study of law enforcement of prostitution in Buffalo for 1977-1980, Bernat (1984:105-107) reports that police failed to arrest patrons of prostitutes even though the 1978 law made both prostitution and patronizing a misdemeanor.

Thus, the efforts to legalize or decriminalize prostitution have minimally benefitted the prostitutes. In recent years, activist prostitutes are calling for the decriminalization of prostitution. They are not asking for a reduction of the crime or sentence but for a complete removal of the act from the criminal statutes (Delacoste and Alexander, 1987; Pheterson, 1989). These prostitutes argue that prostitution is an occupation and should not be treated as a crime.

Violent Crimes

Although the general public and some uninformed students often assume that murder is a typical crime for women, evidence from crime statistics and research studies indicate that murder is somewhat of an anomaly for women (Simpson, 1991:115) both in the United States and in other countries. Wolfgang's (1958:32) analysis of 588 criminal homicides in Philadelphia (1948-1952) found that 24 percent of the victims were female and 18 percent of the offenders were female. Browne (1987:10) and Goetting (1988:3) report that less than 15 percent of arrests for homicide in this country are females. These data suggest that patterns for women's violent crime have not changed much over the years. Browne (1987:9) further notes:

> Nearly one-fourth of the nation's homicide victims in 1984 were related to their assailants; 4,408 murders in that one year were committed by family members. The rate of homicide among families in the United States is higher than the rate for *all* homicides in countries such as England, Denmark, and Germany.

Characteristics of the Female Violent Offender

Most researchers (Goetting, 1988; Mann, 1988 and 1990; Totman, 1978; Weisheit, 1984; Wilbanks, 1982; and Wolfgang, 1958) have found that women murderesses are intersexual and intraracial; they kill men within their own race. In his analysis of case files for 460 female homicide offenders in a women's prison covering the years 1940-1983, Weisheit (1984:476) reported finding:

> . . . a nonmonotonic pattern with regard to race over time. While the white female offender is more common in the 1949-1966 time period, the proportion of offenders who are black are similar for both time periods.

Goetting's (1988:4) study of police records in Detroit for female homicide arrests in 1982 and 1983 and Mann's (1988:42) study of female murderesses from police records in six major U. S. cities both report a "preponderance" of black women offenders. Browne (1987:20) was the only researcher to report a high (66) percentage of white women murderesses. Browne's was an interview study of forty-two women who were charged with a crime in the death or serious injury of their mates. She had a more select population, since her study was conducted while she was a part of a consultant team at Walker & Associates in Denver, Colorado (p. 197, footnote, 32).

Regardless of time period or method of research study, women homicide offenders were most likely to be both black and unemployed (Goetting, 1988:7; Mann, 1988 and 1990:47; Weisheit, 1984:479). Weisheit (1984:479) further reported that more than 70 percent of the prison records in his study contained no information about the offender's primary source of income. Where the information was available, Weisheit reported that most were on public assistance, followed by private household work, service work (such as waitressing), and prostitution. In Mann's (1990:181) study, 70.5 percent of the black subjects were unemployed. She further states:

> The national rates of unemployment, underemployment and overrepresentation in lower status jobs among American Blacks, particularly Black women, and the finding here that the Black women who killed appear to be from the lower economic strata, suggest a link between economic status and homicide. . . . the data strongly suggest that the combined disadvantages of being poor, Black, and female create a degree of life-style stress that contributes to homicide (Mann, 1990:182).

Simpson (1991:116) also suggests that the higher rates of homicide and aggravated assault among black females may be because "black females appear to respond differently to conditions of poverty, racism, and patriarchy than their class, gender, and race counterparts." Simpson (1991) makes a strong argument for the correlation between economic inequality with its increasing marginalization and social isolation of underclass blacks and high levels of criminal violence. One must recognize the importance of the correlation between economics and homicide for black women as presented by Mann (1988; 1990) and Simpson (1991). However, the conflict perspective, which argues that those with economic and political power (white males) define the circumstances under which violence is defined as a crime and also differentially enforce the laws on violence, is also crucial to our understanding of race and violent crime. This perspective is presented most cogently by Reiman in his book, *The Rich Get Richer and the Poor Get Prison*.

These women are in their early thirties, which is somewhat older than most male murderers (Mann, 1988:4; Weisheit, 1984:477; and Wilbanks, 1982:65). Weisheit (1984:477) also reports that female homicide offenders during the 1981-1983 period were five and one-half years younger than the women in the earlier period. This finding, he argues, is consistent with the argument that changes in female roles will have the greatest impact on crime committed by younger offenders.

While most murders by women are intrafamily in which women kill their spouses (Browne, 1987:20; Totman, 1978:33; Ward, Jackson, and Ward, 1980:183; and Wolfgang, 1958:260), recent studies by Mann (1988; 1990) and Weisheit (1984) report some variation in marital status for their populations of women. According to Mann (1988:43-44):

> . . . The most frequent marital status was common-law. Combining common-law status with married, divorced, separated, and widowed status (not by crime) . . . the women who killed in domestic encounters were more likely than the nondomestic female killers to have ever married or have common-law status. Conversely, women who killed in nondomestic situations were predominantly single compared to domestic killers. . . .

Weisheit (1984:480) introduces an interesting dimension of marital status and living arrangements through "indicators of independence and autonomy." An application of this perspective suggests dependency on the part of the domestic homicide group and more freedom, independence, and autonomy among the nondomestic, single homicide group.

Several research studies (Goetting, 1988:7; Mann, 1988:45; and 1990:183; and Totman, 1978; 39-40) reported previous arrests for the homicide offenders . . . While arrest records were not available for all women in these studies, Mann (1990:183) reports that 54.9 percent of the black women for whom arrest histories were found had some type of criminal history. She also reported that "black women who kill have more extensive criminal histories than do their non-Black counterparts."

Circumstances of the Offense.   Most female homicide offenders commit their offenses in the home and not on the street or in public places (Browne, 1987; Totman, 1978; Ward, Jackson, and Ward, 1980; Weisheit, 1984; Wilbanks, 1982; and Wolfgang, 1958). While Wolfgang (1958:124) reported most women killed their victims in the kitchen (29.4 percent) or the bedroom (25.7 percent), Mann (1990:185) reported that 36.1 percent of homicides in the present study occurred not inside the home but on the porch, in the driveway, or in the street, "where the victim had either been chased from the home or encountered on the way in."

There is agreement among most researchers (Browne, 1987; Goetting, 1988; Totman, 1978; Weisheit, 1984; Wilbanks, 1982;

and Wolfgang, 1958) that women who kill act alone and in self-defense after a long history of violent interpersonal tensions with the victim. Wolfgang (1958:124) introduced the concept of victim-precipitation and suggested that, "In many cases the victim has most of the major characteristics of an offender. In many cases two potential offenders come together in a homicide situation and it is probably only chance which determines which becomes the victim and which is the offender." Kuhl (1985:200-201 and 210-11) has argued that the "battered woman syndrome" applies to women who, after extensive histories of battering, have become isolated, dependent women who can perceive no alternative and believe that they are in imminent danger of serious bodily injury or death.

Although Mann (1988 and 1990) does not totally reject the "battered women syndrome," she indicates that the women in her sample are not dependent, helpless women but had previous histories of arrest for violence and had preplanned the murder. Mann (1988:48) supports her argument by stating that, since these women are single and not financially dependent on the men they kill, they could have left the battering situation. Other research (e.g., Kuhl, 1985 and Totman, 1978) has demonstrated that one does not have to be financially dependent or married to be emotionally dependent. Mann's findings are based on research from police records and contradict the findings of Browne (1987), Kuhl (1985), and Totman (1978) who indicate that their interview data provide evidence for a self-defense or battered women syndrome for these women who kill.

Conclusions

Undoubtedly, as Mann (1988:49) suggests, additional empirical research on women as offenders must continue if advancement is desired in this area. In addition, the historical exclusion of women of color and third world women as offenders and victims has done little to enhance the understanding of these groups in the area of criminology. The exclusion of these women means that the discipline of criminology is incomplete. The actions and treatment of women continue to be measured by the male yardstick (Cain, 1990:2). The continued isolated illustration of women in academic disciplines, such as criminology, is but one example that women continue to be considered only in their differences from the male (Cain, 1990).

If gender equality is to be achieved in criminology and women offenders are to be given a central place in our theories, research, and publications, the patriarchal system that has sustained male dominance in our society and in criminology must cease to control our discipline. This is not to imply that we must overlook the important work of mainstream criminology. However, if we are to be successful in identifying and understanding those entities that continue to contribute to the criminal behavior of women, feminist theory and research must be accepted and integrated as an essential part of mainstream criminology.

Bibliography

Adler, Freda
  1975   *Sisters in Crime: The Rise of the New Female Criminal.* New York: McGraw-Hill.
Adler, Freda, (ed.)
  1981   *The Incidence of Female Criminality in the Contemporary World.* New York: New York University Press.
Barry, Kathleen
  1984   "Female Sexual Slavery." Pp. 405-16 in Alison M. Jaggar and Paula S. Rothenberg, eds., *Feminist Frameworks.* New York: McGraw-Hill.
Beard, Mary
  1941   *Woman as a Force in History: A Study in Traditions and Realities.* New York: Macmillan Co.
Bernat, Frances P.
  1984   "New York State's Prostitution Statute: Case Study of the Discriminatory Application of a Gender Neutral Law." *Women and Politics* 4:103-20.
Blassingame, John W.
  1973   *Black New Orleans: 1860-1880.* Chicago: University of Chicago Press.
Bradwell v Illinois
  1873   183 U.S. 130
Browne, Angela
  1987   *When Battered Women Kill.* New York: Free Press.
Cain, Maureen
  1990   "Towards Transgression: New Directions in Feminist Criminology." *International Journal of the Sociology of Law* 18:1-18.
Cameron, Mary Owen
  1964   *The Booster & the Snitch: Department Store Shoplifting.* New York: Free Press.
Carlen, Patricia, (ed.)
  1985   *Criminal Women: Autobiographical Accounts.* Billing and Sons.

Chapman, Jane Roberts
  1980   *Economic Realities and the Female Offender.* Lexington MA: Lexington Books.
Cloward, Richard A. & Ohlin, Lloyd E.
  1962   "Illegitimate Means and Delinquent Subcultures." Pp. 255-57 in Marvin E. Wolfgang, Leonard Savitz and Norman Johnston (eds.), *The Sociology of Crime and Delinquency.* New York: John Wiley & Sons, Inc.
Cressey, Donald
  1953   *Other People's Money.* Glencoe, IL: Free Press.
Dahlinger, Charles
  1918   "The Dawn of the Women's Movement: An Account of the Origin and History of the Pennsylvania Married Woman's Property Law of 1848." *Western Pennsylvania Historical Magazine,* 1.
Daly, Kathleen
  1989   "Gender Varieties in White-Collar Crime." *Criminology* 27:769-93.
Daly, Kathleen and Meda Chesney-Lind
  1988   "Feminism & Criminology," *Justice Quarterly* 5:497-538.
Davis, Kingsley
  1966   "Sexual Behavior." Pp. 322-72 in Robert K. Merton and Robert A. Nisbet (eds.), *Contemporary Social Problems.* New York: Harcourt, Brace & World, Inc.
Delacoste, Frederique and Priscilla Alexander
  1987   *Sex Work: Writings by Women in the Sex Industry.* Pittsburgh: Cleis Press.
Edwards, Anne R.
  1989   "Sex/gender, Sexism and Criminal Justice: Some Theoretical Considerations." *International Journal of the Sociology of Law* 17:165-84.
Feinman, Clarice
  1986   *Women in the Criminal Justice System.* New York: Praeger.
Fortune, Eddyth P., Manuel Vega, and Ira J. Silverman
  1980   "A Study of Female Robbers in a Southern Correctional Institution." *Journal of Criminal Justice* 8:317-25.
Fox-Genovese, Elizabeth
  1988   *Within the Plantation Household: Black and White Women of the Old South.* Chapel Hill: University of North Carolina Press.
Giordano, Peggy, Sandra Kerbel, and Sandra Dudley
  1981   "The Economics of Female Criminality: An Analysis of Police Blotters, 1890-1976." Pp. 65-82 in Lee Bowker (ed.), *Women and Crime in America.* New York: Macmillan.
Goetting, Ann
  1988   "Patterns of Homicide Among Women." *Journal of Interpersonal Violence* 3:3-20.
Hellerstein, Erna, Leslie Hume, and Karen Offen
  1981   *Victorian Women: A Documentary Account of Women's Lives*

in Nineteenth-Century England, France and the United States. Stanford University Press.

Heyl, Barbara
1979   "Prostitution: An Extreme Case of Sex Stratification." Pp. 196-210 in Freda Adler and Rita Simon (eds.), *The Criminology of Deviant Women*. Boston: Houghton Mifflin Company.

Hindelang, Michael
1981   "Variations of Sex-Race-Age- Specific Incidence Rates of Offending." *American Sociological Review* 46:461-74.

Hooks, Bell
1981   *Ain't I a Woman: Black Women and Feminism*. Boston: South End Press.

Horney, Julie
1978   "Menstrual Cycles and Criminal Responsibility." *Law and Human Behavior* 2:25-33.

Hull, Gloria T., Patricia Bell Scott, and Barbara Smith
1982   *All the Women are White, All the Blacks are Men, But Some of Us are Brave*. New York: Feminist Press.

Hyde, Montgomery
1951   *Cases that Changed the Law*. Melbourne: Hinemann.

Inciardi, James, Alan Block, and Lyle Hallowell
1977   *Historical Approaches to Crime: Research Strategies and Issues* 57: Sage Publications.

In re Lockwood
1894   154 U.S. 117

James, Jennifer
1976   "Motivations for Entrance into Prostitution." In Laura Crites (ed.), *The Female Offender*. University of Alabama Press.

James, Jennifer
1982   "The Prostitute as Victim." Pp. 292-314 in Barbara Raffel Price and Natalie J. Sokoloff (eds.), *The Criminal Justice System and Women*. New York: Clark Boardman.

Jones, Ann
1980   *Women Who Kill*. New York: Fawcett Columbine.

Jones, Jacqueline
1986.   *Labor of Love, Labor of Sorrow/Black Women, Work and the Family from Slavery to the Present*. New York: Vintage.

Kuhl, Anna F.
1985   "Battered Women Who Murder: Victims or Offenders." Pp. 197-216 in Imogene L. Moyer, ed., *The Changing Roles of Women in the Criminal Justice System: Offenders, Victims, and Professionals*. Prospect Heights, IL: Waveland Press.

Laub, John H.
1983a   "Patterns of Offending in Urban and Rural Areas." *Journal of Criminal Justice*, II: 129-143.
1983b   "Urbanism, Race and Crime." *Journal of Research in Crime and Delinquency*, 183-198.

Laub, John H. and M. Joan McDermott
1985   "An Analysis of Serious Crime by Young Black Women." *Criminology* 23: 81-98.

Lerner, Gerda
  1977   *The Female Experience: An American Documentary.*
       Indianapolis, IN: Bobbs-Merrill Educational Publishing.
Lewis Diane K.
  1977   "A Response to Inequality: Black Women, Racism and Sexism."
       Signs: Journal of Women in Culture and Society. 3: 339-361.
Lombroso, Caesare
  1895   *The Female Offender.* London, England: Fisher Unwin.
Luchetti, Cathy and Carol Olwell
  1982   *Women of the West.* Antelope Island Press.
Lyon, Peter
  1969   *The Wild, Wild West.* Funk & Wagnells.
"Madison Woman Freed"
  1890   March 1, *Chicago Tribune* Microfilm.
Mann, Coramae Richey
  1988   "Getting Even? Women Who Kill in Domestic Encounters."
       Justice Quarterly 5: 33-51.
Mann, Coramae Richey
  1990   "Black Female Homicide in the United States." *Journal of
       Interpersonal Violence* 5: 176-201.
Miller, Eleanor M.
  1986   *Street Woman.* Philadelphia: Temple University Press.
Nowak, John E., Ronald Rotunda, and Nelson Young
  1983   *Constitutional Law Hornbook* 2nd Edition. St. Paul: West
       Publishing.
Nussbaumer, Beverly
  1976   "The Female Felon: A Study of Factors Related to Increased
       Female Crime." Unpublished master thesis, Indiana University
       at Pennsylvania, Indiana, PA.
Offen, Karen
  1988   "Defining Feminism: A Comparative Historical Approach." *Signs:
       Journal of Women in Culture and Society* 14:123-46.
Pheterson, Gail
  1989   *A Vindication of the Rights of Whores.* Seattle: Seal Press.
Quarles, Benjamin
  1969   *Black Abolitionist.* New York: Oxford Press.
Ray, Grace
  1972   *Wiley Women of the West.* Texas: The Waylor Co.
Roby, Pamela
  1976   "Politics and Criminal Law: Revision of the New York State Penal
       Law on Prostitution." Pp. 28-50 in George F. Cole (ed.), *Criminal
       Justice: Law and Politics.* Belmont, CA: Duxbury Press.
Rubinstein, David
  1986   *Before the Suffragettes, Women's Emancipation in the 1890s.*
       New York: St. Martin's Press.
Sachs, Albie and Joan Hoff Wilson
  1978   *Sexism and Law.* New York: The Free Press.

Schur, Edwin M.
   1984   *Labeling Women Deviant: Gender, Stigma and Social Control.*
          New York: Random House.
Sharpe, May Churchill
   1928   *Chicago May: Her Story.* Forward by Henry J. Nelson. New York:
          Mccaulay.
Sheehy, Gail
   1980   "The Economics of Prostitution." Pp. 223-37 in Susan K.
          Datesman and Frank R. Scarpitti (eds.), *Women, Crime and
          Justice.* New York: Oxford University Press.
Simon, Rita J.
   1975   *The Contemporary Woman and Crime.* Rockville, MD: National
          Institute of Mental Health.
   1976   "American Women and Crime." Pp. 18-37 in Lee H. Bowker (ed.),
          Women and Crime in America. New York: Macmillan Publishing.
Simpson, Sally S.
   1990   "Caste, Class, and Violent Crime: Explaining Differences in
          Female Offending." *Criminology* 29: 115-37.
Smart, Carol
   1977   "Criminological Theory: Its Ideology and Implications Concerning
          Women." *British Journal of Sociology* 28:89-100.
Spender, Dale
   1982   *Women of Ideas.* Boston: ARK Paperbacks.
Steffensmeier, Darrell J.
   1980   "Assessing the Impact of the Women's Movement in the Handling
          of Adult Criminal Defendants." *Crime and Delinquency,*
          July:344-57.
Steffensmeier, Darrell J. and Emilia Andersen Allan
   1988   "Sex Disparities in Arrest by Residence, Race, and Age: An
          Assessment of the Gender, Convergence/Crime Hypothesis."
          Justice Quarterly 5: 53-80.
Symanski, Richard
   1974   "Prostitution in Nevada." *Annals of the Association of American
          Geographers* 64:357-77.
Thomas, William I.
   1923   *The Unadjusted Girl.* New York: Little, Brown, & Company.
Totman, Jane
   1978   *The Murderess: A Psychosocial Study of Criminal Homicide.* San
          Francisco: R and E Research Associates, Inc.
Townsey, Roi Dianne
   1982   "Black Women in American Policing: An Advancement Display."
          Journal of Criminal Justice 10:455-69.
Ward, David., Maurice Jackson, and Renne E. Ward
   1980   "Crimes of Violence by Women." Pp. 171-91 in Susan K. Dates
          and Frank R. Scarpitti (eds.), *Women, Crime and Justice.* New
          York: Oxford University Press.

Weisheit, Ralph A.
  1984   "Female Homicide Offenders: Trends Over Time in an Institutional Population." *Justice Quarterly* 1:471-89.
Wesley, Charles Harris and Patricia W. Romero
  1967   *Negro Americans in the Civil War: From Slavery to Citizenship.* New York: Publishers Co.
Wilbanks, William
  1982   "Murdered Women and Women Who Murder: A Critique of the Literature." Pp. 151-80 in Nicole Hahn Rafter and Elizabeth A. Stanko (eds.), *Judge, Lawyer, Victim, Thief: Women, Gender Roles and Criminal Justice.* Boston: Northeastern University Press.
Wolfgang, Marvin
  1958   *Patterns in Criminal Homicide.* Philadelphia: University of Pennsylvania Press.
Young, Vernetta D.
  1980   "Women, Race and Crime." *Criminology* 18:26-34.
Zeitz, Dorothy
  1981   *Women Who Embezzle or Defraud: A Study of Convicted Felons.* New York: Praeger.

chapter 3

Criminal Codes, Criminal Justice and Female Offenders
New Jersey as a Case Study

Clarice Feinman
Trenton State College

Historically state and federal criminal codes for adults and juveniles have discriminated against females both in the definitions of crime and delinquency and in the sentencing process. The emergence of the civil rights and feminist movements in the 1960s inspired the creation of state and federal task forces and new legislation to eliminate sex-based discrimination. The passage of the 1964 Civil Rights Act Title VII and the Equal Rights Amendment by Congress motivated many states to remove sex-based discrimination from their statutes. Following this national trend, New Jersey in the 1970s ratified the national Equal Rights Amendment and proceeded to revise its statutes. As a result, the New Juvenile Code and the New Jersey Code of Criminal Justice (known as 2C) went into effect in 1974 and 1979 respectively. The codes eliminated gender based discrimination in the definition of crime and delinquency and in the sentencing process. Although it is still too early to evaluate the extent to which the administration of justice will carry forth the goals of the new codes as they apply to criminal and delinquent adults and juvenile females and males, evidence already exists that the administration of the juvenile code in respect to status offenses (acts that would not be considered criminal if committed by adults, e.g., truancy, incorrigibility) has not eliminated sex-based discrimination.

The purposes of this paper are to point out the historic cultural premises about women and girls and how those premises helped shape the approach taken by the criminal justice system in New Jersey. We will also examine the extent to which traditional concepts affected the treatment of juvenile and adult females in both the definitions of delinquent and criminal behavior and in the sentencing process. Finally, this paper will evaluate the impact of the New Juvenile Code and the New Jersey Code of Criminal Justice (hereafter referred to as 2C) on juvenile and adult females in both areas.

Impact of Traditional Attitudes on Criminal Codes and Female Offenders

Stereotypes concerning females, so obvious in criminal codes, reflect traditional attitudes towards females and their role in society that date back to Greek and Roman pagan mythology and Judeo-Christian theology (Feinman, 1980; Pomeroy, 1975; Smith, 1970). As a result of these attitudes, women were stereotyped either as madonnas, life-producing mothers who have to be protected and prevented from falling off their pedestals, or as whores, temptresses who use their sexuality to destroy men and therefore have to be punished and restored to true womanhood. In both cases, the treatment of females was for their own good as well as for the good of society. Therefore, men categorized women and girls according to the degree to which they fit these roles and established codes of expected behavior for females and codes to control and punish nonconforming females. Men who wrote and interpreted these codes believed, as did the Illinois Supreme Court in the Bradwell case in 1869, "That God designed the sexes to occupy different spheres of action, and that it belonged to men to make, apply, and execute the laws . . ." (Kanowitz, 1973:44).

These beliefs are evident in the laws and court decisions concerning females. For example, women could enter into certain areas of life only under carefully controlled circumstances for their own good. This was true for employment where the principle of classification by sex was reinforced in *Muller v. Oregon* in 1908 when the U.S. Supreme Court declared constitutional protective labor legislation for females. Basing his decision on the traditional values that a woman's maternal role and sexual cycle made her dependent on men, Justice Brewer stated, "That woman' s physical structure and the performance of maternal functions place her at a disadvantage in the struggle for subsistence is obvious" (Kanowitz, 1973:47).

If womanhood and motherhood had to be protected in the labor market, it followed that they had to be protected from the sordid facts of life in society. Thus laws singling out females as a "vulnerable class" requiring protection were passed making it a crime for men to use vulgar and obscene language in the presence of females and excluding women from jury duty. In 1966, the Mississippi Supreme Court upheld the state law excluding women from jury duty on the grounds that, "The legislature has the right to exclude women so they may continue as mothers, wives, and homemakers, and also to protect them [in some areas they are still upon a pedestal] from the filth, obscenity and noxious atmosphere that so often pervades a courtroom during a jury trial" (Kanowitz, 1973:59).

Just as the purity and delicacy of womanhood and motherhood had to be protected from the evils of the world, the offending female had to be punished. The crime of prostitution, for example, a crime traditionally and legally for females only, symbolized the "legal embodiment" of stereotypes concerning females and their proper sexual and social roles (Brown et al., 1977:66; Feinman, 1980:2-7). As the sexually destructive whore, the prostitute posed a threat to her own safety and also to the safety of man, family and society.

Whether to protect virtuous females or to punish female offenders, laws and court decisions have had a common basis: the traditional perception of the dual nature of females and the belief that they had to be protected and/or punished for their own good. This became particularly apparent in criminal codes wherein a double standard of justice based on a double standard of sexual morality existed resulting in harsher treatment for adult and juvenile females in the criminal justice system.

For example, until the New Jersey Code of Criminal Justice (2C) and the New Juvenile Code went into effect in the 1970s, adult and juvenile females were singled out as a special class, based solely on sex, for differential definitions of criminal and delinquent behavior and for sentencing, presumably for their own good. Prior to September 1979 when the new criminal code for adults, 2C, went into effect, certain crimes applied only to women either as victims or perpetrators. Crimes such as rape, abduction, seduction and carnal abuse held that defilement of a woman's chastity or virtue constituted a crime and only women could be the victims of these offenses. However, the criminal code required that the female victim corroborate the evidence to prove that she had, in fact, been a victim. This "statutory reluctance" to accept the verbal testimony of a "defiled" female resulted in the need for the victim to prove that she had led a chaste and virtuous life prior to the crime against her. Thus while the criminal code appeared to protect females, in practice, it made the victim bear the burden of proof that the crime had taken place and in essence it protected the accused men (Jacobs, 1979:35-36; N.J.S.A. 2A:85-1, et seq.).

New Jersey's sentencing procedures prior to 1979 also singled out females for disparate treatment, often resulting in longer sentences for women than for men even if both had committed similar crimes under similar circumstances. Sentencing statutes for females over sixteen years of age required that, except for manslaughter or murder, they had to receive a reformatory indeterminate to five year sentence unless the statutory maximum for that offense was less than five years. In such cases they had to receive the maximum statutory sentence. In addition, if the statutory maximum for the offense was more than five years, the court could give the convicted women a longer indeterminate sentence to that minimum. In all cases, incarcerated women were not eligible for work credits, continuous orderly deportment credits, nor were they eligible for parole by the State Board of Parole as were incarcerated men. On the other hand, men sixteen to thirty years of age could receive either a reformatory indeterminate sentence or a prison minimum-maximum sentence, and the judge could set the maximum at less than the statutory limit.

Sentencing disparity rested on the belief, as stated in *State v. Costello*, that "female criminals were basically different from male criminals, that they were more amenable and responsive to rehabilitation and reform — which might, however, require a longer period of confinement in a different type of institution — and that, therefore, the legislature could validly differentiate between sexes with respect to the length of incarceration and the method of the determination thereof" (*State v. Costello*, 1971:334, 344).

In *State v. Costello* in 1971, New Jersey Supreme Court Justice Hall reviewed the differences in sentencing between males and females as stated in the New Jersey sentencing statutes. Mary Costello, aged thirty-nine, convicted for bookmaking and operating a gambling resort, received an indeterminate to five year sentence and was sent to serve her term at the Women's Correctional Institution at Clinton, the only secured facility for females over the age of sixteen in New Jersey. Her release date had to be determined by the Board of Managers of the Institution; a date based on the degree to which the Board believed she had been rehabilitated. She had no right to have time off for good behavior and work credits. A male, convicted of a similar crime under similar conditions, would have received a minimum of one year to a maximum of two years with his release date determined by the Board of Parole. With good behavior and work credits, he could have been eligible for parole in four months and twenty-eight days. Costello could have been obliged to remain at Clinton for the full five years if the Board of Managers felt that the time was needed for her reformation. The most significant difference was, in effect, that women could receive longer sentences than men for similar crimes. The State Supreme Court held that, "These distinctions, in essence, form the basis of defendant's claim of denial of equal protection because of discrimination on the basis of sex" (*State v. Costello*, 1971:343).

Finally, in 1973, the State Supreme Court in *State v. Chambers* rejected the rationale that females were more amenable to rehabilitation and required a longer period of incarceration. Justice Sullivan, speaking for the Court, declared that statutory provisions for sentencing female offenders to an indeterminate sentence when a similarly situated male would receive a minimum-maximum term were unconstitutional in that they violated the equal protection clause of the Fourteenth Amendment (*State v. Chambers*, 1973:287-300). As a result of the Court's decision in *State v. Chambers*, discriminatory sentencing against women offenders ended, in practice. However, it was not until the new code, 2C, went into effect in September 1979 that sex discrimination in sentencing disappeared from the criminal statutes.

The treatment of juvenile females in the juvenile justice system reflected the same attitudes and stereotypes that affected adult females. Although the juvenile justice code differed from that for adult offenders, the female juvenile also faced harsher treatment in the system than juvenile males, and the rationale was the same as for adults; the treatment was for their own good. Before the implementation of the New Juvenile Code in March 1974, no differentiation was made between status offenders and delinquent youths and both were incarcerated together in secure facilities. Status offenses are acts that are unique to juveniles and would not be a crime if committed by an adult, such as truancy, running away from home, drinking and incorrigibility. Delinquent behavior includes those acts that would be a crime if committed by adults. The old juvenile code permitted the arrest, adjudication and punishment both for delinquent and status offenders.

Interest in status offenders in New Jersey stems from the early nineteenth-century when judges, legislators and reformers voiced concern about children growing up without a proper family structure. This concern for children who were truant, who smoked, drank, or were homeless paupers in need of special care resulted in legislation to establish a State Home for Boys in Jamesburg in 1867 and a State Home for Girls in Trenton in 1871 (Dannefer and DeJames, 1979:15-16).

In keeping with traditional attitudes concerning the dual nature of females, the juvenile justice system assumed a paternalistic stance in dealing with young girls to protect them against their own sexuality and from defiling themselves. Although fewer girls than boys were arrested each year, a disproportionate number of juvenile females were arrested for status offenses. Of all status offenders arrested, a disproportionate number of girls were held in detention centers prior to their court hearings and a disproportionate number of them were incarcerated for an indeterminate term at the State Home for Girls. For example, in 1973, 44 percent of all female status offenders were in custody whereas only 24 percent of all male status offenders were in custody. To further illustrate the paternalistic attitude of the courts in matters of female morality, both female status and delinquent offenders were questioned about their sexual experiences and examined for virginity and venereal disease. Often it was their sexual behavior that determined whether or not they would be incarcerated (Jordan, 1979; 3-17).

Juvenile females suffered both from inequities in the justice system and from the double standard of morality imposed upon females by society. Studies conducted in New Jersey in the 1970s show that parent-signed complaints more often involved daughters. Parents are more likely to ask the courts to control and confine their daughters, especially if they are sexually active. As such, the juvenile court and other juvenile justice agencies are forced to involve themselves in the enforcement of female adolescent morality (Dannefer and DeJames, 1979:xx, xxviii).

Until the 1970s juvenile and adult female offenders in New Jersey received harsher treatment in the justice system than their male counterparts. Traditional attitudes concerning the proper role and place of women and girls in society permeated New Jersey's criminal codes and criminal justice system, and any treatment given to female offenders was considered to be for their own good.

Impact of the New Criminal Codes on Female Offenders

Inequities in the justice system that negatively affected adult and juvenile females have been recognized and new criminal codes have been implemented. These reforms resulted from efforts made by women's groups, civil rights groups and legal reformers since the 1960s. The civil rights struggle in the 1960s, seeking to gain equality under the law for black people, triggered subsequent movements to gain full equality for females under the law. As a result of the 1964 Civil Rights Act Title VII and its 1972 amendments, the courts had to consider a myriad of sex discrimination cases involving females. This resulted in many sweeping changes, not least of which were those affecting the criminal justice system.

In New Jersey, the Commission to Study Sex Discrimination in the Statutes was created on July 6, 1978 when Governor Brendan T. Byrne signed P. L. 1978 c.68. The Commission, chaired by State Senator Wyona Lipman, is responsible for reviewing all state statutes and for proposing revisions of any statutes containing sex-based classification. The Commission is currently examining Criminal Justice statutes. The Commission is one of the results of efforts made by women lawyers and feminists in New Jersey since the 1940s. In 1947, the New Jersey Bar Association Committee to Study the Status of Women recommended that no distinction be made in the statutes based on sex and urged the passage of a state and national Equal Rights Amendment. The Committee, made up of women lawyers, argued that women had no security under the law as the courts had set precedents in upholding discriminatory laws directed at women. The recommendations of the Committee were not incorporated in the 1947 New Constitution of New Jersey. Women had to wait until the 1970s to succeed in getting legislation passed that would end the pattern of sex-based discrimination in the statutes.

In addition to efforts made by women in New Jersey to achieve equality under the law, national pressures for equal rights and civil rights encouraged Governor Richard Hughes to establish, in January 1968, the New Jersey Commission to Study Crime. As a result of the Commission's findings, a new criminal code was proposed in the State Legislature in 1975. The legislation passed in August 1978 and went into effect on September 1, 1979 as the New Jersey Code of Criminal Justice, Title 2C of the New Jersey

Statutes, replacing the Title 2A code of 1951. The new code, commonly referred to as 2C, removed almost all references to gender in discussing victims or perpetrators and in the sentencing process in an effort to make definitions of criminal behavior and the sentencing process gender neutral.

The problems in achieving gender neutrality in 2C can be seen specifically in Chapter 14 dealing with "Sexual Offenses" and Chapter 34 dealing with "Public Indecency" (N.J.S A. 2C:14-1 through 7; N.J.S.A. 2C:34-1 through 5). Included under Chapter 14 are sexual assault, sexual contact, lewdness and admissible evidence. The word "actor" is used in lieu of perpetrator, but unfortunately the gender word "he" is used but not "she." For example, "An actor is guilty of aggravated sexual assault if he commits an act of sexual penetration with another person ..." (N.J.S.A. 2C:14-2a) and "A person commits a disorderly persons offense if he does any flagrant lewd and offensive act ... (N.J.S.A. 2C:4-4). Included under "Public Indecency" in Chapter 34 are prostitution and obscenity. For example, "A person commits a petty disorderly persons offense if he hires a prostitute to engage in sexual activity with him ..." (N.J.S.A. 2C: 34-le; N.J.S.A. 2C:34-4b). This implies that a man is the buyer of sexual services but a woman is not. The use of the gender word "he" may in the future be challenged in the courts on the basis of sex discrimination as it provides opportunities to discriminate between male and female offenders and victims by offering a legal loophole.

A case that tested the gender neutral intent of 2C was won by a woman defendant in Monmouth County in the summer of 1980. She received a summons from a police officer for sun bathing bare breasted on the public beach. The case was argued on the basis of sex discrimination because men sun bathing bare breasted did not receive a summons. Pointing to Chapter 14 in 2C to prove her case, she noted that the words "breast of a person" listed under "intimate parts" of the body was gender neutral (N.J.S .A. 2C:14-le). Consequently, Monmouth County should either make all males cover their breasts in public or permit females to go uncovered. She won her argument (Mitchell, 1980).

Despite these few references to gender which could lead to discrimination against males or females, the new criminal code, 2C, represents a significant improvement over the old, particularly in areas of sexual offenses and sentencing. Assumptions and stereotypes concerning women have, for all practical purposes, been eliminated from the criminal statutes.

Unfortunately, the New Juvenile Code did not result in eliminating discriminatory practices against juvenile female status offenders. The history of the juvenile justice system in New Jersey parallels national developments. Undifferentiated treatment of juveniles and adults continued from the Colonial Era to the mid-nineteenth century. Responding to reform efforts of the "save the children" movement, the New Jersey legislature, as stated earlier, established a State home for Boys in 1867 and one for girls in 1871. This movement culminated in the development of a separate juvenile justice system. In 1903, New Jersey created a separate juvenile court with specially designated juvenile justice judges. The first comprehensive juvenile justice law, "The Juvenile and Domestic Relations Court Law," adopted in 1929, specified all juvenile offenses, placing delinquent and status offenses in a single category and provided for the same methods of disposition and punishment for both types of offenders. Therefore, juveniles, males and females from eight to eighteen years of age, could be institutionalized for status offenses, such as truancy and running away, as well as for delinquent offenses such as stealing or manslaughter (Dannefer and DeJames, 1979:15-16).

The Gault decision in 1967 required due process guarantees for juvenile delinquents, but not for status offenders. As a result of this decision, a national movement emerged to adopt legislation to differentiate between delinquent and status offenders and to provide procedures for their differential treatment. Governor William Cahill called for major revisions in the juvenile justice system. In January 1971 the Juvenile Delinquency Committee of the New Jersey Bar Association submitted a proposal to the Governor to reform the juvenile justice code. The law was signed by Governor Cahill on December 14, 1973 and the New Juvenile Code went into effect on March 1, 1974. The most significant features of the new code included differentiation between delinquent and status offenders. It established the category of Juveniles in Need of Supervision, JINS, for status offenders. In addition, the new code provided for different methods of dealing with delinquent and status offenders by the justice system (Dannefer and DeJames, 1979; 21-23; N.J.A.S. 2A:4-44, 45).

The code defined delinquent offenses as those that would be a crime if committed by an adult (N.J.S.A. 2A:4-44). Status offenses are defined as acts that would not be a crime if committed by an adult, but are "unique" to juveniles who: a) are habitually diso-bedient to parent or guardian; b) are ungovernable or incorrigible; c) are habitually truant from school; and d) have committed an offense or violated a statute or ordinance applicable only to juve-niles. In addition, the new code prohibited the placement of a JINS offender in detention or a correctional facility (Dannefer and DeJames, 1979:24-25, xx-xxviii; N.J.S.A. 2A:4-62).

A report of the Task Force on the Juvenile Code concluded that female juveniles more than male juveniles had been adversely affected by the previous code. These findings were corroborated by a study conducted on female offenders for the New Jersey Advisory Commission on the Status of Women (Jordan, 1979:7-18). Specifically, the New Juvenile Code had a greater impact on JINS girls than boys. Prior to the new JINS designation and disposition statutes, most of the juvenile status offenders committed to secure institutions were females. Of the juveniles incarcerated six months prior to the implementation of the new code, no status offenders were at the State Home for Boys in Jamesburg, and 14 percent of the boys at the Training School for Boys at Skillman were there for status offenses. But 67 percent of the girls at the State Home for Girls in Trenton were sent there for status offenses. As a result of the new code, the JINS offenders were released from the institution. Since so few girls remained at the State Home for Girls, and since, historically, the overwhelming number of incarcerated juvenile females were status offenders, the State Department of Corrections no longer felt the need for the State Home for Girls. The delinquent girls are currently housed in a cottage at Skillman, the juvenile male facility, and in community-based residences (Dannefer and DeJames, 1979:xx).

The removal of juvenile female status offenders from secure facilities appears to be a positive result of the new code. However, the deinstitutionalization of JINS females has resulted in "hidden incarceration" rather than freedom. JINS offenders are usually placed under the supervision of the Division of Youth and Family Service, DYFS, for placement in a "structured environment" for care and for their own good. Due to the double standard of justice based on the sexual double standard, JINS females are more likely than JINS males to be arrested and come before the courts, and are more likely to be referred by the courts for agency care and supervision than are JINS males. In addition, parents are more likely to sign a complaint warrant against incorrigible daughters requiring the courts to place them with DYFS (Dannefer and DeJames, 1979:xxii-xxvi).

It is important to understand that, as a result of the 1967 Gault decision, delinquent juveniles are guaranteed due process protection in the juvenile justice system whereas status offenders have no such protection. Therefore, when female or male status offenders are "placed" in a residential or foster home, they must go because the courts refer them and they have no legal protection against such placement. In addition, status offenders are "placed" by DYFS for an indeterminate period of time, whereas delinquent juveniles receive an indeterminate sentence to a maximum of three years except for murder or manslaughter. Furthermore, sentenced delinquents are eligible for parole and usually serve about fifteen months.

JINS offenders are more harshly treated than delinquents in New Jersey in that they have no legal protection against "hidden incarceration." As most of the JINS offenders are females, the system proves to be more punitive towards females than males. According to the Task Force on the Juvenile Code, "Female JINS receive more stringent treatment than male JINS," whereas delinquent girls receive "consistently more lenient treatment than male delinquent offenders" (Dannefer and DeJames, 1979:xxv). The Task Force concluded that, "juvenile justice agencies mirror the traditional family which has always exerted greater control over the behavior of its daughters than its sons, especially in regard to adolescent sexuality" (Dannefer and DeJames, 1979:xxxviii).

Conclusion

For juvenile female offenders, discrimination continues to exist both in the definition of punishable behavior and in the disposition process. The juvenile justice system continues to expect girls to conform to socially valued behavior; they are expected to be sexually pure and obedient daughters. If they do not conform they are treated more stringently than girls who commit crimes. Parents also expect this behavior from daughters and willingly hand them over to the state for punishment and control. The courts, acting for the state and society as a whole, assume the parental role to protect girls for their own good.

Under the new criminal codes implemented in the 1970s, adult and juvenile females who commit crimes have won the right to due process and equal sentencing with males. JINS females and males have yet to achieve due process rights. JINS females, in particular, continue to be the victims of a justice system that is permeated with traditional cultural values and stereotypes concerning female behavior, categorizing them as either madonnas or whores.

The feminist and civil rights movements resulted in the elimination of gender based discrimination in New Jersey's new criminal codes for adults and juveniles. However, these movements have failed to eliminate stereotypes concerning the proper role of females in society. This is most evident in the treatment of male status offenders in New Jersey.

Bibliography

Brown, Barbara, Ann Freedman, Harriet Katz and Alice Price
   1977   *Women's Rights and the Law.* New York: Praeger.
Dannefer, Dale and Joseph DeJames
   1979   *Juvenile Justice in New Jersey: An Assessment of the New Juvenile Code.* Trenton, NJ: Department of Human Services, Task Force on the Juvenile Code.
Feinman, Clarice
   1980   *Women in the Criminal Justice System.* New York: Praeger.
Jacobs, Cynthia M.
   1979   "Women Offenders in New Jersey." *New Jersey Lawyer* 35-37.
Jordan, Judith A.
   1979   "Female Offenders in New Jersey: Compilation of Information on Program Needs and Priorities." Trenton, NJ: New Jersey Advisory Committee on the Status of Women. Unpublished report.
Kanowitz, Leo
   1973   *Sex Roles in Law and Society: Cases and Materials.* Albuquerque, NM: University of New Mexico Press.
Mitchell, Gary
   1980   Interview with Attorney, Public Defender's Office. Trenton, NJ.
New Jersey Statutes Annotated
   1951   Title 2A Administration of Civil and Criminal Justice.
New Jersey Statutes Annotated
   1974   Title 2A Administration of Civil and Criminal Justice.
New Jersey Statutes Annotated
   1979   Title 2C New Jersey Code of Criminal Justice.
New Jersey State Supreme Court
   1971   *State v. Costello,* 59.
New Jersey State Supreme Court
   1973   *State v. Chambers,* 63.
Pomeroy, Sarah B.
   1975   *Goddesses, Whores, Wives, and Slaves: Women in Classical Antiquity.* New York: Schocken.
Smith, Page
   1970   *Daughters of the Promised Land: Women in American History.* Boston: Little, Brown Co.

chapter 4

Police/Citizen Encounters
Issues of Chivalry, Gender and Race

Imogene L. Moyer
Indiana University of Pennsylvania

Prior to the 1970s, there was little research on either police officers or women offenders. The sparsity of research on women offenders can be explained by the dominance of men in criminology who excluded gender from their studies of offenders. The lack of research on police officers resulted from the positivists of the nineteenth and twentieth centuries (e.g., Durkheim, 1933; Merton, 1939; Shaw and McKay, 1929) who were concerned primarily with individual differences and causes of crime. These theorists concentrated on answering questions such as what's wrong with the offender and/or the offender's environment. The interactionist theoretical perspective and the feminist movement in the 1960s focused on both police officers and women offenders. This chapter will examine the development of interest in both police behavior and the woman offender, as well as the more recent concern with police decisions involving gender and race.

Research on Police Officers and
on Women Offenders

Research on Police Officers

The interactionist theoretical perspective (e.g., Becker, 1963; Lemert, 1967) emerged in the 1960s and emphasized the arbitrary definitions of deviance/crime as well as societal reactions to offenders. The interactionists rejected the positivists' causation theories of criminal behavior and stressed that it is the process of society's response to the initial deviant act which lead to the emergence of a criminal career.

The research agenda of criminologists in the 1960s and early 1970s, therefore, changed from the criminal to the various representatives of the criminal justice agencies, such as police officers. Since police officers are the front line representatives of the criminal justice system, they make important screening decisions that affect societal response to the initial deviant act of the offenders. Reiss (1974) states that the police control decisions concerning the discovery and investigation of crimes because they use discretion in investigation. They decide who to stop, question, and search as well as make decisions regarding arrests, warrants, and booking of offenders. Goldstein (1980:85) asserts "that full enforcement of deviance is not a realistic expectation." He argues that "selective law enforcement" is necessary for the criminal justice system to function. Skolnick's (1975) research verifies Goldstein's assertions. Skolnick found that police see themselves as "competent craftsmen" able to determine guilt and to perceive accurately which citizens pose a dangerous threat to society. Police are in a position to control many decisions about how criminal laws are enforced. Several early research studies show that extralegal factors, such as race, social class and demeanor often affect how some police choose to process male offenders. (Black and Reiss, 1970; Lundman, 1974; Piliavin and Briar, 1964; and Skolnick, 1975).

Research on Female Offenders

At the same time that scholars with an interactionist perspective were focusing on the role of police officers in influencing whether a deviant act would be a single aberration or the start of a criminal career, the feminist movement raised questions about the role of women in society. As with the nineteenth century feminist movement, feminists during the 1960s questioned and examined the hierarchical, patriarchal structure of society and the institutionalized sexism in the treatment of women throughout the American society. The drive for women's rights and equality in a male dominated society brought about a closer examination of the processing and treatment of women in the criminal justice system.

Efforts to explain the low crime rate of women (10 percent of all arrests reported in the Uniform Crime Reports in the 1950s and 16 to 18 percent of all such arrests in the 1980s) led to a great deal of speculation about the nature of women as well as about the treatment of women by officials in the criminal justice system. Three major models developed to examine the impact of gender on the processing of women offenders by the police. The first model indicates that gender is not a factor in the treatment of women; the second model suggests that women receive preferential or chivalrous treatment; the third argues that women are treated punitively. The last two models reflect the madonna/whore duality discussed in chapter one that views the male role as one of protector of good women and punisher of bad women.

With regard to the first model, many states have revised their statutes and implemented policies so that gender cannot legally be a factor in how women are processed by the justice system. This chapter will explore whether these revisions in the law have been successful in attaining equality of treatment for women offenders.

The chivalrous model has received the most attention, largely because women have low official crime rates. According to some scholars (Simon, 1975 and Steffensmeier, 1980), the low crime rates for women are because police are less apt to arrest women. The police compare women offenders to other women they know — namely their wives and mothers — whom they could not imagine behaving in a criminal or a dangerous way. They may also view women as "less capable than men of committing criminal acts" (Steffensmeier, 1980:350). Cavan (1962:32) suggests the sex differences in crime "seem related to the different roles of men and women and the different social worlds in which they live. . . . Often there is actual participation of women in crimes but of a type that does not lead to arrest."

The most frequent interpretation (Cavan, 1962; Haskell and Yablonsky, 1973; Pollak, 1950; and Reckless, 1961) of the chivalrous model is that criminal justice officials provide women with preferential treatment because they want to protect them. Cavan (1962:32), for example, states:

> Finally, even in crime a certain degree of chivalry prevails. Some people dislike to report a woman criminal to police and police

are more likely to release women or to turn a young woman over to her parents or a social agency than would be true for boys and men.

It should be noted that there was little, if any, research to support any of these early claims of chivalry. In fact, some scholars suggest that if chivalry exists, it would not apply equally to all women. Middle-class and white women would benefit more than lower class and minority women. Klein (1973:10 and 13) observes:

> Chivalry is a racist and classist concept . . . reserved for the women who are least likely ever to come in contact with the criminal justice system: the ladies, or white middle-class women.

The third model suggests that gender impacts the decisions of criminal justice officials in a negative way. That is, police and other justice officials are more apt to punish women offenders. Women who fail to behave as pure women and violate traditional sex role stereotypes by committing deviant/criminal acts are punished more severely.

Historically, several states (e.g. Pennsylvania, New Jersey, and Iowa) had laws requiring women who were convicted of certain crimes to receive longer sentences than males convicted of the same crimes (Feinman, 1985; Temin, 1973). The rationale given by court officials for these longer sentences was the "rehabilitation" provided by the prison. An examination of women's prisons, however, suggests that there are few rehabilitation programs available to women.

Another example of the continued discrimination against women is the differential enforcement of the prostitution laws. Even in states that have made it a crime to be a customer of a prostitute, the police have refused to enforce the law against male customers (see Bernat, 1984 and Roby, 1976). Also, the statutes provide for shorter sentences for customers than for prostitutes.

Some research supports the idea that chivalrous treatment works to the disadvantage of juvenile girls who commit status offenses. Chesney-Lind (1978) argues that juvenile girls, who violate gender norms, receive more punitive responses from police than male juvenile offenders. She states:

> Clearly, at the level of the decision to arrest, studies of police behavior do not support the contention that officers ignore all female delinquent acts. Rather, they may be selectively arresting those young women who are acting out sexually or those who are behaving in nontraditional ways while ignoring those they suspect of criminal misconduct (Chesney-Lind, 1978:179).

In Chapter Three of this book, Feinman reports that discrimination for juvenile girls continues in New Jersey even after revision of the legal code which removed references to gender. These girls are still expected to be sexually pure and obedient daughters. If they do not conform they are treated more stringently than girls who commit crimes.

Police/Citizen Encounters: the Gender Issue

In the 1970s feminists began to challenge the conflict theorists for their failure to consider women as a powerless group. This included a criticism of the early police studies (e.g., Black and Reiss, 1970; Goldstein, 1980; Lundman, 1974; Piliavin and Briar, 1964; and Skolnick, 1966) because they did not include gender in their research. Although most early studies of police decisions to arrest ignored gender, a few studies, such as DeFleur (1975: drug arrests in Chicago) did mention women briefly. While most of her article concerned only male offenders, she does state:

> Also, there was a tendency not to arrest females as often as males, if they behaved in expected, stereotypical ways. During drug raids females often cried, claimed to have been led astray by men, or expressed concern about the fate of their children. These behaviors were successful and the females were seldom processed (DeFleur, 1975:101).

Police Attitudes Toward Feminism and Female Offenders

One of the earliest studies to consider the police decision-making process and its relationship to gender (Stone, 1985:57) was conducted in 1978. It explored attitudes of police officers toward feminism, police perceptions of female felons, and police attitudes toward the use of discretion in dealing with female felons. The sample was limited to fifteen police officers from rural and urban areas of north and south Louisiana who had a minimum of five years experience on the police force. Despite its small sampling, this research makes an important contribution to criminology not only because of the pioneer nature of the study but also because of the creative effort to explore police attitudes.

Stone (1985:58) used a modified form of a questionnaire constructed by Kirkpatrick (in 1936) to measure attitudes toward feminism which focused on occupational, domestic and social role identities for women in contemporary society. A five point Likert scale was employed to measure occupational attitudes for statements such as, "Women should have the right to compete with men for all kinds of jobs," or "Regardless of sex, there should be equal pay for equal work," (Stone, 1985:70). Examples of statements to measure domestic attitudes of police officers include, "The husband should be regarded as the legal representative of the family in all matters of law," and "Married women should be able to give or withhold sex as they choose" (Stone, 1985:72). Attitudes toward social roles of women were measured by statements such as, "Women should be allowed to keep their maiden names after they marry," and "A girl standing in a crowded bus has a right to expect a man to give up a seat to her" (p. 73-74).

Analysis of police responses to this 34-item questionnaire revealed that, "Although there was no indication of a well-defined positive or negative bias in the police response to the questionnaire, more support was expressed for 'liberated' domestic roles than for 'liberated' occupational or social roles for women" (Stone, 1985:60). Among the findings from informal interviews with the same police officers was the acknowledgement by the majority of officers that their use of discretionary powers in the past may have protected some female felons from arrest. While this phenomenon was attributed to the perception of some officers that women are the "weaker" sex, one officer commented that more and more police officers were realizing that women were capable of criminal activity (Stone, 1985:61). Although the findings of this study must be treated cautiously because of the small sample and the specific region of the country, the research does present an interesting and unique perspective of police attitudes toward women that may influence their arrest decisions.

Police/Citizen Encounters:
Issues of Gender and Race

Several studies (Krohn, et al., 1983; Moyer, 1982; Moyer and Hopper, 1982; Visher, 1983; and Wilbanks, 1986.) conducted research on police/citizen encounters and gender between 1976 and 1983. These studies used a variety of methodologies, including analysis of official arrest data (Krohn, et al., 1983; Wilbanks, 1986;), completion of questionnaires by police officers (Moyer, 1982), and field observations (Moyer and Hopper, 1982; Visher, 1983). Each of these methods provides a different type of information. The official arrest data used by Krohn et al., and by Wilbanks are secondary data based on what police record about the offender and the circumstances of the offense. The vignettes or hypothetical events used by Moyer (1982:377) "closely approximate a real-life, decision-making situation." Both the official records and the vignettes tell the researchers more about what police think they should do and/or say they do than about the actual decisions they make as they encounter citizens. Field observations conducted by Moyer and Hopper and by Visher provide information about what police actually do. Regardless of the methods for obtaining the data, these studies reported few gender differences in police arrest decisions.

In response to the chivalry claim that women were receiving preferential treatment by police officers, Moyer (1982:377) conducted an exploratory study of police decisions. A questionnaire containing five different vignettes (or hypothetical situations) was administered to 584 officers and detectives in four different police departments and a police academy in a large metropolitan area in one Southeastern state during September 1978-August 1979. The hypothetical episodes were constructed to measure the effects of type of offense, sex of offender, race of offender, and demeanor of the offender on the decisions made by the police. The study found that officers were most influenced by the type of offense. Demeanor was the second most important variable in determining police decisions but sex alone and race alone were rarely used by police officers in making decisions about offenders (Moyer, 1982:379). Moyer's (1982:382) research did find that the interaction of type of crime and demeanor were more important for women than for men in influencing police decisions. While the research provides only limited support for the chivalry claim, it does give criminologists information about the training police received in this state that emphasized making decisions based on legal criteria so as not to violate offender rights. This information is important for researchers to understand police decisions.

Two field observation studies (Moyer and Hopper, 1982 and Visher, 1983) were conducted in order to explore the actual behavior of police officers as compared to what the police officers said they would do in Moyer's (1982) survey study. While the study by Moyer and Hopper (1982) was much smaller than the study by Visher (1983), there were some similarities between the two studies.

Visher (1983) was the first researcher to report a large field observation study that concentrated on the impact of gender on police decisions. The study conducted in 1977 involved trained citizens riding on 900 patrol shifts in twenty-four different police departments in the St. Louis, Rochester, and Tampa-St. Petersburg metropolitan areas (Visher, 1983:11). Although the field researchers in Visher's (1983:12) study observed 5688 police-citizen encounters, her analysis focused on the behavior of police officers and their encounters with 785 males and females who were suspects of criminal offenses or violations of public order. In addition to type of offense and gender, Visher's study included demeanor, race, and age. Of the 643 males and 142 females in this sample, 20 percent of the male suspects and 16 percent of the female suspects were arrested (p. 22).

While Visher (1983:19) reported that "offense type is a powerful predictor of arrest for males and females," she also found that age, race, and demeanor have a greater impact on police decisions for females than for males. She states:

> The impact of age for female suspects is probably related to different gender expectations for younger and older women. Police officers adopt a more paternalistic and harsher attitude toward younger females to deter any further violation of appropriate sex-role behavior. . . . Young, black, or hostile women receive no preferential treatment, whereas older, white women who are calm and deferential toward the police are granted leniency (Visher, 1983:15 and 23).

Visher's study reports selective chivalrous treatment by the police.

In 1981, Moyer and Hopper (1982) completed 144 hours of exploratory field observations in police patrol cars in a large metropolitan police department in the Midwest. Although the researchers conducted a systematic sample of all police shifts and every day of the week, the observations were heavily weighted in the 3:00 to 11:00 p.m. shift on Friday and Saturday nights in order to maximize the number of police-citizen encounters observed.

The patrol car observations by Moyer and Hopper (1982) provided data on 159 police-citizen encounters, involving interaction between police officers and a variety of citizens including alleged offenders, victims, complainants, and bystanders. There were 97 offenders (20 females) for whom police made arrest decisions (Moyer and Hopper, 1982:7). Of these offenders, police arrested 26 percent of the men and 32 percent of the women. Field observations provided only minimal differences in the police decisions to arrest men and women. While the officers hesitated on a couple of occasions to arrest women with children, they also were observed to give preferential treatment (did not arrest) a male offender whose brother was on the police force.

Although the numbers of women were very small in the Moyer and Hopper (1982:11) study, 33 percent of the 16 white women were arrested as compared to fifty percent of the four nonwhite women. They further reported that all women in their small sample were observed to have a cooperative and positive demeanor.

While Moyer (1982) and Moyer and Hopper's (1982) studies seem to provide more support for the first model discussed earlier in this paper that suggests that police do not differentiate by gender in making arrest decisions, they report some support for differential treatment of women based on race and demeanor. The Visher (1983) study suggests that chivalry and leniency may be granted to older white women but that young women, especially black and hostile ones, receive harsher treatment from the police.

The selective chivalrous treatment of women by the police reported by the field observation studies is also supported by studies using data from official police records (Krohn, et al., 1983 and Wilbanks, 1986). Krohn et al. (1983:418) reported an examination of data on police referral for juvenile and adult males and females for birth cohorts (those born in 1942, 1949, and 1955) in the three time periods. While Krohn et al. found evidence that the proportion of female offenders arrested tended to increase over time for most types of offense (p. 423), the data also suggest that sex differences in police dispositions are greater among whites than nonwhites. Evidence for sex bias in the disposition of juvenile offenses (e.g., incorrigibility and sexual promiscuity) are treated in a paternalistic fashion and the authors found that this pattern did not show signs of declining by the late 1960s (Krohn et al., 1983:431).

The Wilbanks (1986:520) study of a representative sample of all felony cases processed by the police in California in 1980 found that the odds of being arrested varied dramatically by sex, age, and race. The odds of being arrested ranged from a high of 1 in 42 for black females, age 20-29 to a low of 1 in 667 for white females 70 years and older.

In sum, while Moyer (1982) found no difference in police decisions based on race alone or sex alone, all the research studies (DeFleur, 1975; Krohn, et al., 1983; Moyer, 1982; Moyer and Hopper, 1982; Visher, 1983; and Wilbanks, 1986) of police-citizen encounters reported some support for the chivalry model of treatment. Visher (1983:21) summarizes these findings as follows:

> In sum, some females will receive lenient treatment at the hands of criminal justice personnel because they display appropriate gender behaviors and characteristics; other females who violate traditional sex-role expectations will not receive leniency.

Except for the studies of prostitution (Bernat, 1984 and Roby, 1976) in New York where police refused to support new laws that made it a misdemeanor to be a customer of a prostitute and research that shows punitiveness toward juvenile girls who violate traditional sex norms (e.g., Chesney-Lind, 1978), there is little evidence for the punitive model.

There have been few studies of police decisions as they pertain to women offenders. The studies that we have use a variety of methodologies with numerous limitations and mixed findings. Perhaps, these findings reflect a diversity of responses to female offenders but certainly no conclusions can be reached without more research. This research will not be forthcoming until granting agencies recognize the importance of understanding the female offender and begin funding these research projects.

Bibliography

Becker, Howard
  1963   *Outsiders—Studies in the Sociology of Deviance.* New York: Free Press.
Bernat, Frances P.
  1984   "New York State's Prostitution Statute: Case Study of the Discriminatory Application of a Gender Neutral Law." *Women and Politics* 4:103-20.
Black, Donald and Albert Reiss
  1970   "Patterns of Behavior in Police and Citizen Transactions." Section 1 in Field Surveys 3: Studies in Crime and Law Enforcement in Major Metropolitan Areas, Volume 2. Report of research submitted to President's Commission on Law Enforcement and Administration of Justice. Washington, DC: U. S. Government Printing Office.
Cavan, Ruth Shonle
  1962   *Criminology.* New York: Thomas Y. Crowell Company.
Chesney-Lind, Meda
  1978   "Young Women in the Arms of the Law." Pp. 171-196 in Lee H. Bowker, *Women, Crime, and the Criminal Justice System.* Lexington, MA: Lexington Books.
DeFleur, Lois B.
  1975   "Biasing Influences on Drug Arrest Records: Implications for Deviance Research." *American Sociology Review* 40:88-103.
Durkheim, Emile
  1933   *The Division of Labor in Society.* New York: Macmillan.
Feinman, Clarice
  1985   "Criminal Codes, Criminal Justice and Female Offenders: New Jersey as a Case Study." Pp. 41-53 in Imogene L. Moyer (ed.), *The Changing Roles of Women in the Criminal Justice System: Offenders, Victims, and Professionals.* Prospect Heights, IL: Waveland Press.

Goldstein, Joseph
1980   "Police Discretion not to Invoke the Criminal Process: Low-visibility Decisions in the Administration of Justice." Pp. 81-100 in George Cole (ed.), *Criminal Justice: Law and Politics*. Belmont, CA: Wadsworth Publishing Company.
Haskell, Martin R. and Lewis Yablonsky
1973   *Crime and Delinquency*. Chicago: Rand McNally.
Klein, Dorie
1973   "The Etiology of Female Crime: A Review of the Literature." *Issues in Criminology* 8:3-30.
Krohn, Marvin D., James P. Curry, and Shirley Nelson-Kilger
1983   "Is Chivalry Dead? An Analysis of Changes in Police Dispositions of Males and Females." *Criminology* 21:417-37.
Lemert, Edwin
1967   *Human Deviance, Social Problems, and Social Control*. Englewood Cliffs, NJ: Prentice Hall.
Lundman, Richard J.
1974   "Routine Police Arrest Practices: A Commonwealth Perspective." *Social Problems* 22:127-44.
Merton, Robert K.
1938   "Social Structure and Anomie." *American Sociological Review* 3:672-82.
Moyer, Imogene L.
1982   "Police Responses to Women Offenders in a Southeastern City." *Journal of Police Science and Administration* 10:376-83.
Moyer, Imogene L. and Donald Hopper
1982   "A Field Study of Police Decisions: Do Race, Sex, and Demeanor Make a Difference?" A paper presented at the American Society of Criminology.
Piliavin, Irwin and Scott Briar
1964   "Police Encounters with Juveniles." *American Journal of Sociology* 70:206-14.
Pollak, Otto
1950   *The Criminality of Women*. New York: A. S. Barnes & Company.
Reckless, Walter C.
1961   *The Crime Problem*. New York: Appleton-Century-Crofts.
Reiss, Albert
1974   "Discretionary Justice." Pp. 679-699 in Daniel Glaser (ed.), *Handbook of Criminology*. Chicago: Rand McNally.
Roby, Pamela
1976   "Politics and Criminal Law: Revision of the New York State Penal Law on Prostitution." Pp. 28-50 in George F. Cole (ed.), *Criminal Justice: Law and Politics*. Belmont, CA: Duxbury Press.
Shaw, Clifford R. and Henry D. McKay
1929   *Delinquent Areas*. Chicago: University of Chicago Press.

Simon, Rita J.
  1975   *The Contemporary Woman and Crime*. Rockville, MD: National
         Institute of Justice.
Skolnick, Jerome
  1975   *Justice Without Trial: Law Enforcement in a Democratic
         Society*. New York: John Wiley.
Steffensmeier, Darrell
  1980   "Assessing the Impact of the Women's Movement on Sex-Based
         Differences in the Handling of Adult Criminal Defendants." *Crime
         and Delinquency* 26:344-57.
Stone, Helen
  1985   "The Changing Pattern of Female Crime: A Police Perspective."
         Pp. 54-75 in Imogene L. Moyer (ed.), *The Changing Roles of
         Women in the Criminal Justice System: Offenders, Victims, and
         Professionals*. Prospect Heights, IL: Waveland Press.
Temin, Carolyn
  1973   "Discriminatory Sentencing of Women Offenders: The Argument
         for ERA in a Nutshell." *American Criminal Law Review* 11:
         355-373.
Visher, Christy A.
  1983   "Gender, Police Arrest Decisions, and Notions of Chivalry."
         Criminology 21:15-28.
Wilbanks, William
  1986   "Are Female Felons Treated More Leniently by the Criminal
         Justice System?" *Justice Quarterly* 3:517-29.

chapter 5

"Female Crimes" or Legal Labels?

Are Statistics About Women Offenders Representative of Their Crimes?

Candace Kruttschnitt
University of Minnesota

Statement of the Problem

Changes in the gender ratio of official crime statistics have produced numerous attempts to account for an assumed increase in the law-violating behavior of women (Adler, 1975; Giordano and Cernkovich, 1979; Norland and Shover, 1977; Rans, 1978; Simon, 1975; Steffensmeier, 1978; Weis, 1976). Although some scholars acknowledge the problems in using official crime statistics (Rans, 1978; Simon, 1975), most have assumed that such data give us a fairly accurate picture of female crime.

The accuracy of this picture, however, can be questioned on many

81

levels. For example, it is well known that arrest rates represent only a fraction of all crimes known to the police. Moreover, crimes known to the police represent only a fraction of all offenses actually committed (U.S. Department of Justice, 1976:13). Similarly, because of the courts' reliance on plea bargaining, conviction data may have little bearing on the actual charges which were brought against criminal defendants (e.g., Buckle and Buckle, 1977:161; Hagan, 1975:543; Sudnow, 1965, 262). Although these points are not new, they have been largely ignored with regard to female offenders. Instead of addressing how the criminal justice system selectively identifies a population of women, scholars have generally taken the identified population as a basis for etiological perspectives on female crime.

This work is concerned with demonstrating that official statistics on female crime may be misleading indicators of the actual conduct of women. The primary focus of this study is not, however, quantitatively verifying or attacking the validity of Uniform Crime Reports (e.g., Hindelang, 1978; Skogan, 1974). Instead, in a qualitative manner, both arrest and conviction data and the women behind these data are examined to see how factors other than official conduct might affect the final conviction. The ultimate aim of this work, then, is twofold: implicitly, it attempts to question the current theories regarding women offenders that are based on official crime statistics and, explicitly, it presents an alternative method of approaching and explaining the criminal adjudication of women.

Data and Methodology

A stratified random sample of females convicted of assault, petty theft, forgery and drug law violations was drawn from the files of an adult probation department in a middle-sized county in northern California (N = 942).[1] The data encompass the calendar years 1971-1976. While the main function of probation is postdisposition supervision, this department also prepares the presentence investigation which provides a wealth of information on the factors surrounding a woman's illegal activity. As will become apparent, then, these data provide valuable insights into the nature of female crime.

Although probation data supply one of the best bases for assessing the quality of female crime, it is also important to examine other relevant deviance processing data. By so doing we can broaden the scope of the study suggesting how both police and prosecutors shape our images of women offenders (see also, Moulds, 1980:289). Accordingly, the analysis begins with a comparison of national arrest statistics on female offenders.

Findings

In order to discover patterns of legal behavior in response to female offenders, we begin by juxtaposing arrest and conviction data. Since Table 1 contains information from national arrest statistics on women, the natural comparison would be with national conviction statistics. The 89 U.S. District Courts annually publish national conviction statistics. Unfortunately these data include some offenses which are largely unique to men (e.g., violation of the selective service act). California and Ohio also publish annual conviction statistics which are broken down by sex of the offender. These data, however, reveal information on only those women who are convicted in superior courts. Since superior courts deal almost entirely with felony convictions, it was felt that juxtaposing such conviction data to an unspecified set of arrest data would be invalid. Accordingly, Table 1 utilized the conviction data from this study, thus contrasting data from one county in California to statistics on the entire country. It should be noted, however, that these conviction statistics are generally quite representative of overall California statistics (Kruttschnitt, 1979:33-34) and, in turn, that the crime statistics produced by California are fairly representative of the national crime statistics (Simon, 1975:57).

Examining Table 1, we find that there is a substantial degree of discrepancy between the offenses for which women are convicted and the offenses for which they are arrested. Specifically, women are arrested most frequently for such offenses as theft, drunkenness, disorderly conduct, drug law violations, and assaults. In contrast three of the top five offenses for which women are convicted — forgery, fraud, and drunken driving do not appear on the most frequent arrest list. Three possible, and interrelated, explanations for this disparity in the data are 1) visibility of conduct; 2) deviance processing priorities; and, 3) plea bargaining.

The first explanation as to why arrests and convictions differ refers to aspects of the crime itself. Of the five offenses listed under the arrest column, two involve highly visible forms of conduct: drunkenness and disorderly conduct. Since these offenses are more easily detected, both by the public and by law enforcement officials, than fraud or forgery, it is no surprise that they comprise a higher percentage of female arrests. As Black (1970: 737) points out:

Table 1
Rank Order of the Top Five Offenses
For Which Women Were Arrested and Convicted 1972

Arrest[1]	(Percent)	Conviction[2]	(Percent)
Larceny-theft	(19)	Larceny-Theft	(25)
Drunkenness	(10)	Drugs	(23)
Disorderly Conduct	(8)	Forgery	(11)
Drugs	(7)	Fraud	(8)
Assaults	(4)	Drunken Driving	(8)

1. Source: Kelley, 1972 (Uniform Crime Reports).
2. Source: Based on the data for this study.

> Some of the more common felonies, such as burglary and auto theft, generally involve stealth and occur when the victim is absent; by the time the crime is discovered, the offender has departed. Other felonies such as robbery and rape have a hit-and-run character, such that the police rarely can be notified in time to make an arrest at the crime settings. Misdemeanors, by contrast, more often involve . . . crimes that are readily audible or visible to potential complainants and . . . proceed in time with comparative continuity.

Thus, some of the properties of crime make felony offenders less visible and more difficult to arrest than misdemeanor offenders. Even though in most jurisdictions the law compensates for this discrepancy by allowing the police to make a felony arrest with less evidence, the visibility of an offender's act no doubt has some influence on the likelihood of, and hence frequency of, arrest.

This explanation is not limited to female offenders in that drunkenness, drunk driving and disorderly conduct are also the offenses for which males are most frequently taken into custody. However, the generally higher frequency of arrests for men may in fact be related to sex-based differences in conduct. For instance, data on the circumstances of drug arrests suggest that males tend to use marijuana in visible settings, such as on the street or in a car, where they are especially vulnerable to arrest. Women, by contrast, are more likely to use marijuana in a private residence where they are more frequently cushioned from arrest (Bowker, 1978:202-3). Nevertheless, since males are also arrested significantly more often than females for such "nonvisible" crimes as burglary and robbery (Simon, 1976:45), this explanation does not account for all sex-based variation in arrest rates. The few data we have on the effect of a defendant's sex on the decision to arrest provide no definitive answer as to whether such discrepancies reflect discriminatory police practices. Studies indicate both that the offender's sex has no effect on police behavior (Moyer and White, 1981:375), and that women exhibiting stereotypic female demeanor are not arrested as often as men (Bowker, 1978:203).

A second explanation for the disparity between arrests and convictions relates to concerns about evidence and, more generally, deviance processing priorities. Prior research shows that, regardless of the offender's sex, the strength of evidence in a case—as measured by eyewitness testimony, recovered stolen property and either statements by the victim or a defendant's confession—and the legal seriousness of the crime are given the greatest weight in the decision to prosecute (Bernstein et al., 1977a:747-51; Myers and Hagan, 1979:446-47). These factors are most likely to turn private matters into public ones (Myers and Hagan, 1979:439), creating new official data. In other words, given a pool of arrest data, the availability of evidence should sift out a selective group of cases for prosecution and conviction. Women offenders are frequently arrested not only for larceny-theft and drugs but also for the crimes of forgery, fraud and drunken driving (see Table 1). Larceny-theft arrests for women are generally shoplifting arrests (Steffensmeier, 1978:48)—offenses that may include both eyewitness identification and recovery of stolen property. Similarly, drunken driving involves an eyewitness and, as is true of drug cases, may include the testimony of experts such as the arresting officer. However, by contrast to these crimes, fraud and forgery usually occur without a victim or reporting officer's immediate knowledge and therefore make gathering evidence more difficult. In these instances, we would assume that the legal system is showing a preference for directing its energies toward those acts which are statutorily deemed most serious (e.g., Blumberg, 1967).

Finally, a third possible explanation is that plea bargaining affects arrest and conviction data. A prosecutor, for instance, could include a number of situationally relevant offenses (Sudnow, 1965:256-59) in an assault indictment in order to increase the chances that a woman will bargain for a charge reduction. As such, the woman who is charged with assault, disturbing the peace and drunken driving pleads guilty on the latter charge in order to avoid chancing a guilty verdict on the assault charge at trial. The outcome of this process is simply that, as with males (Buckle and Buckle, 1977:115), there may be little parity between the offenses for which females are arrested and the offenses for which they are convicted. Unfortunately, only a few studies report quantitative data on the influence of gender on the likelihood of a negotiated plea (Bernstein et al., 1977b; Crites, 1978; Sterling and Haskins, 1980). Moreover, these studies suggest no definitive pattern: one study finds women are more likely than men to have their charges reduced and two others find that sex has no effect on the magnitude of the reduction in charge severity (Nagel and Hagan, 1982:125-27). Thus, since the available evidence, albeit limited, suggests that plea bargaining affects the dispositions of males and females in the same fashion, a female defendant's actions may ultimately have little or no bearing on the crime(s) for which she is convicted.

In sum, a woman's chances of being processed through the criminal courts may be affected not only by her actual conduct but also by the various organizational properties of the law enforcement system. Specifically, one might expect that such factors as the probability of detection, or the contingencies of plea bargaining may play a greater role in determining the invocation of law than actual criminal conduct itself.[2]

This section of the chapter will present a detailed examination of conviction statistics. Specifically, both the nature of women's activities and their social profiles are presented for the offense categories of assault, petty theft, forgery and drug law violations. We present an alternative analysis to the three legal areas explored above.

Table 2 presents a breakdown of the offenses encompassed in the crime categories above and the relative frequency of women's participation in the respective offenses. Two things are readily apparent from this table: 1) Except for petty theft, women are committing a number of very different forms of criminal conduct within each of these offense categories; 2) There is a broad range of legal consequences in the types of criminal activities. However, by examining the activities of women in each crime category, and the social characteristics of the women themselves, some patterns of conviction may emerge.

Assault

The assault offense category encompasses such diverse behaviors as displaying a deadly weapon and assault with intent to commit murder. Thus, for example, both the woman who shoots her employer after being fired and a female drunkard who attacks the police officer arresting her for disturbing the peace are included in this offense category. It should be apparent, then, that a number of these offenders originally may have been charged with offenses

Table 2
Distribution of Convicted Women Within Four Selected Offense Categories for the Years 1972-1976

Offense Category	Percent
Assault	
Assault with intent to murder	2
Assault with deadly weapon	24
Assault of peace officer	29
Child beating	9
Shooting at dwelling	3
Simple assault/battery	30
Displaying deadly weapon	3
Total Percent	100
Total No.	(115)
Petty theft	
Petty theft with prior	5
Petty theft	95
Total Percent	100
Total No.	(286)
Forgery	
Passing forged notes or possessing forged checks	40
Fictitious checks	1
Nonsufficient funds (checks)	27
Nonsufficient funds (checks-misdemeanor)	4
Use of others' credit card	2
Forged credit card	23
Theft of credit card	3
Total Percent	100
Total No.	(214)
Drug Law Violations	
Possessing narcotics/dangerous drugs	31
Selling narcotics/dangerous drugs	16
Possession narcotics/dangerous drugs for sale	2
Possession drugs with prior	3
Visiting where drugs are present	5
Possessing/producing marijuana	24
Selling marijuana	4
Possessing marijuana for sale	2
Drug without prescription	4
Forged prescription	9
Total Percent	100
Total No.	(327)

as diverse as homicide and disturbing the peace. Although it is difficult to pinpoint the common denominator among assault offenders, some similarities do exist among these women. Specifically, these similarities can be found by examining their social profiles rather than their conduct. As can be seen in Table 3, the largest percentage of blacks is found in the assault category. More of the assault offenders were in the middle income category than were petty theft, forgery, or drug offenders. In addition, the victims of these women also follow somewhat of a pattern: they are most frequently known to or involved with the offender.

Petty Theft

The activities of petty theft offenders contrast sharply with those of assault offenders; there is a striking absence of diversity of conduct encompassed within this category (see Table 2). In one sense these women are, in fact, a rather homogeneous group. In a large number of cases, the criminal behavior simply represents a minor theft and an adventure to the youthful women involved:

> I went to a [department store] to buy a coworker a birthday present. Since [Martha] was choosing the gift, I started looking at dresses. I saw a pretty dress and decided to steal it because another girl had told me of a fool proof [sic] way to steal and had never gotten caught. So I did it.[3]

However, in another sense, many of these women are more than just petty theft offenders. Specifically, in a number of cases their thefts indirectly involve other criminal conduct. A probation officer's description of one such offender succinctly portrays this behavioral repertoire:

> [Nancy] is twenty-nine years old. In the past, she has been very dependent and passive, often a tool used by her common-law husband. With one exception, all of the past thefts have involved the stealing of liquor, most likely for sale so that [Steve's] heroin habit could be supported.

Similarly, the following account illustrates how a defendant's own drug addiction was disguised by the conduct for which she was apprehended:

> My old man and I were strung out. I was pregnant and twenty-three years old in the month of March or April when he and I were in a [department store] walking out with a sewing machine. He was carrying it to the door until we were caught. He dropped the sewing machine and ran. I couldn't run because I was eight months pregnant and so he got away. So, they gave me the rap.

Table 3 Percentage of Women in Each Category According to Various Social Characteristics

Offence	Race				Income[1]				Marital Status[2]			
	White	Black	Other	(N)	Low	Middle	High	(N)	Married	Divorced or Separated	Single[3]	(N)
Assault	51	45	4	(115)	50	37	13	(115)	26	42	32	(98)
Petty Theft	54	29	17	(286)	56	27	17	(286)	32	31	37	(233)
Forgery	58	38	4	(214)	75	18	7	(214)	21	50	29	(178)
Drugs	79	17	4	(327)	73	19	8	(327)	26	39	35	(262)

Offence	Victim-Offender Relationship[4]				Male Intimate's Prior Record		
	Intimate	Friend[5]	Stranger	(N)	Prior Record	No Record[6]	(N)
Assault	38	43	19	(74)	23	77	(108)
Petty Theft	—	—	—	(—)	12	88	(278)
Forgery	11	17	72	(116)	24	76	(208)
Drugs	—	—	—	(—)	28	72	(321)

[1] The categorization of income into the groups of low ($0-$400), middle ($401 to $700) and high ($701 or above), was based on the 1975 estimates for poverty level and the mean income for females by selected characteristics in California (U.S. Bureau of the Census, 1978). The poverty level for a three-member household in 1975 was $257 per month; hence, $400 or less was deemed a low income. During that year, the average personal income of females between the ages of 24 and 53 in California was $564 per month; as a result, over $400 but not more than $700 was delineated as a middle income level.

[2] Widows, and those women involved in common law relationships were excluded.

[3] Never married.

[4] The victim was an organization in all but sixteen of the petty theft cases and drugs, of course, is a victimless offense.

[5] Includes defendants' neighbors and acquaintances.

[6] Includes if no recent male in her life.

In attempting to ascertain why many of these women were convicted of a petty theft rather than for the sale of stolen goods or as accessories, their social profiles provide little help: these women come from a variety of racial and economic backgrounds (see Table 3). The nature of their victims, however, does appear to be consistent. In all but sixteen offenses, the victim was a business organization, ranging in scale from a department store to a small grocery market. One might conclude that in the case of petty theft offenders, the nature of the victim rather than any particular set of social attributes predicts the offense for which the defendant is convicted (see, also, Black, 1976:95).

Forgery

The forgery offense category contains an array of activity. Consider first, the woman who forges with a credit card. This conduct usually includes larceny, most often from a total stranger but in some instances from an employer:

> I used a credit card from the company I worked for. I took a large cut in salary going to the company with the promise that I would be up to my old salary within six months, with a raise at three months. Three months came and went with no raise . . . so I started to use one of the credit cards for gas going back and forth to work, as I felt that they were pulling a dirty deal with me.

Possessing forged checks is also a very common occurrence among these women; such behavior often includes a form of embezzlement. The following is a paradigm case:

> Well at [this company] I worked with thousands of pay checks on a computerized system. I was in charge of disbursing them . . . the checks were signed with the legitimate signature and were blank . . . all you would have to do is put in the name and amount. I stole one of these checks with the intent to cash it.

And finally, by cashing checks with insufficient funds, a large percentage of these women steal from merchants:

> As I have stated, my husband was a totally disabled veteran and died quite suddenly and left me with just one month's rent. Upon his death all payments of the checks stopped . . . . Thinking I would receive . . . checks made out to me to replace my late husband's, I made out checks to [the] market for food.

In sum, these women are performing a variety of behaviors, all of which were deemed forgeries. One could examine the legal codes and attempt to determine to what degree their various activities approximate legal prescriptions. However, one can also look to their location in social life to see if there are similarities among these women which might explain their convictions for the same offenses. For instance, a sizeable proportion of these women are black and either separated or divorced. In these two respects they are remarkably similar to assault offenders. However, as Table 3 shows, their social profiles do differ from those of assault offenders in two other ways. First, forgers rarely victimize someone they know. Second, whereas half of the assault offenders can be classified as falling into a middle or upper-income bracket, only a quarter of the forgers could be similarly classified.

Drugs

Finally, those women who are convicted of drug law violations are also engaging in a wide variety of behavior. First, the majority of these women are accessories and few actually engage in the sale of narcotics on their own:

> I had a boyfriend. At the time I met him he only drank. About two months later he was doing dope, only occasionally but then it got worse and worse. Finally, he quit a $200 a week job with no employment, and started to deal to support his habit. By this time, I thought I loved him. I also started doing dope with him.

Women who are "along for the ride" also constitute the majority convicted of marijuana drug law violations:

> At the time this all happened, my boyfriend [Mike] was living with me. . . . I was coming from the bathroom when the policeman came to the door . . . he said he smelled grass. . . . The officer started demanding to know who was in the other room. I told him there was no one. . . . He pushed me aside and opened the door. There was a pipe on the stove. I never thought anything of it . . . because [Mike] had about six pipes. Then he picked it up and said it smelled like grass. . . . Then the officer informed me I was under arrest.

Only one other form of criminal conduct occurs relatively frequently within this drug offense category—forgery. These forgers are generally not interested in monetary gain, but instead forge a prescription as a result of a drug dependency, often not even their own:

> Right after I was married, my husband was using drugs and I was desperate to help him kick. He needed something to sleep.

> The doctor gave me twelve Nembutals and I knew this wouldn't
> help. So, like a fool, I added a zero on the end.

One could say that some forgers and heroin addicts are labelled as drug law violators because their conduct is, in fact, related to obtaining or using illegal substances. Again, however, by examining the social characteristics of these women, another reason for their being classified within one particular offense category is suggested. By comparison to other female offenders, the vast majority of these women are both white and somewhat more likely (relative to other types of offenders) to have been involved with a man who has a prior criminal record (see Table 3).

Thus, delineation of the actual conduct involved in the offense categories chosen for this study reveals not only a broad range of behavioral repertoires among these offenders, but also some rather concrete portraits of the women themselves. Moreover, a close examination of the activities of these women reveals that the offense category does not necessarily represent the behavior involved: a petty theft conviction may disguise a drug habit and, similarly, an assault conviction may well stem from alcohol addiction. Clearly, then, what is labelled as a particular type of legal violation may in actuality involve several other dimensions of criminal behavior. Therefore, one can only posit that a conviction for one specific offense in large part may mask much of the actual behavior of those adjudicated in our criminal justice system.

Discussion

From the foregoing analyses, it seems that the legal system responds to a number of different forms of conduct in the same way. Similarly, it also seems that certain characteristics of these offenders are more common to a crime category than the crimes within the category. In particular, the defendant's race and income bracket, the respectability of her associates and the nature of relational distance to the victim, all seem to be associated with her official conduct.[4] It is especially interesting to note the offense-specific findings regarding the relationship between the defendant and the victim: again, victims of assault offenders are most frequently intimates or friends, victims of petty theft offenders are generally large business organizations and, finally, victims of forgers are commonly strangers. Since numerous studies have shown that legal outcomes are affected by the relationship between litigants, regardless of whether the case is a criminal or civil matter (e.g., Black, 1976; Bonn, 1972; Macaulay, 1963; Sarat, 1976), it seems probable that this variable also would predict offenses leading to conviction.

Suggesting that a woman's social location affects her offense of conviction, is not, however, unique to this study. For example, in a national study of women's correctional programs, some of the social characteristics of female inmates were classified by crime categories. From this analysis, it appears that, by comparison to other ethnic groups, black women are predominantly convicted of crimes of violence (murder, robbery, assault), Hispanic women of burglary, and white and Indian women of fraud and forgery (Glick and Neto, 1977). In addition, studies of plea bargaining have also shown that, rather than strictly legal criteria, a set of procedural regularities, including the social biographies of both the victim and the defendant, suggests offense of conviction (e.g., Buckle and Buckle, 1977; Mather, 1979). Sudnow (1965:259) explains this process as follows:

> In the course of routinely encountering persons charged with "petty theft," "burglary," "assault with a deadly weapon," "rape," "possession of marijuana," etc., the Public Defender gains knowledge of the typical manner in which offenses of given classes are committed, the social characteristics of the persons who regularly commit them, the features of the setting in which they occur, the types of victims often involved, and the like.

Finally, it also should be noted that the relationship between a defendant's social profile and the legal system is not limited to postarrest procedures. Those variables which contribute to an individual's social status also affect policemen's decisions to write official reports on incidents (Black, 1970) and their decisions to arrest (Black, 1971; Piliavin and Briar, 1964). As such, just as the crime for which a woman is convicted may have little to do with her actual behavior, so also might the crime for which she is arrested. Simply put, regardless of a woman's conduct, what she is ultimately arrested and adjudicated for may depend more upon her race, her income, who her victim is and various other aspects of her social profile, than upon any specific legal violation. Consequently, inferences should not be made concerning the actual rate or type of illegal conduct of women from these conviction statistics; instead, what can be inferred are typical social biographies of offenders in respective offense categories.

Conclusion

For years the underrepresentation of women in official crime statistics contributed to the belief that there existed a lack of material to justify research on female criminality. Despite an occasional study of women offenders questioning the validity of official statistics (e.g., Pollak, 1950; Radzinowicz, 1937; Smart, 1976), most research still relies on such official data (e.g., Adler, 1975; Rans, 1978; Simon, 1975). Consequently, it should not be surprising to find that as official crime rates show female arrests on the upswing, research in the area of female criminality is also on the upswing.

Precise information regarding the amount and nature of women's criminal conduct can probably never be known. The data presented in this study reflect only the number of women who have been defined as deviant regardless of their actual behavior. In juxtaposing their conduct with the offenses for which they are convicted, this study has attempted to suggest some of the ways in which conviction statistics in particular, and crime statistics in general, might not be representative of female offenders' behavior. Although the idea that official crime statistics are misleading indicators of the quantity and quality of crime is not novel, it seems to have been overlooked with regard to women offenders. As such, this work has attempted to point out how explanations for trends in female criminality which are based on questionable data, as a result, may also be questionable. In so doing, it is an attempt to improve the research currently being conducted on women in crime and also to contribute to those works which study legal behavior (e.g., Black, 1976; Mileski, 1971; Sarat, 1976). This study also represents a contributory endeavor in proposing that women's social characteristics may be important in the sanctioning process. Future research, interested in predicting and explaining trends in female crime, might, then, be directed toward examining the degree to which the social profiles of women in general have changed and the degree to which law is responding to such changes.

Endnotes

*I would like to thank the National Institute of Mental Health for financial support. Appreciation should also be extended to Richard Petronio, James Inverarity, Kelly Weisberg and Tom Hart for their comments on an earlier draft of this paper.

[1] The data for this paper were drawn from a larger study on the court processing of female defendants (Kruttschnitt, 1979).

[2] These points are best exemplified in Donald Black's (1970:737) study of the police and David Sudnow's (1965:256-59) study of a public defender's office.

[3] The names utilized throughout this study, for purposes of quoting from probation records, are fictitious.

[4] With regard to the concept of relational distance, see Black (1970:740-42).

Bibliography

Adler, Freda
  1975   *Sisters in Crime.* Prospect Heights, IL: Waveland Press, Inc. Reprinted 1985.
Bernstein, Ilene N., William R. Kelly and Patricia A. Doyle
  1977a   "Societal Reaction to Deviants: The Case of Criminal Defendants." *American Sociological Review* 42:743-55.
Bernstein, Ilene N., Edward Kick, Jan Leung and Barbara Schulz
  1977b   "Charge Reduction: An Intermediary Stage in the Process of Labelling Criminal Defendants." *Social Forces* 56:362-84.
Black, Donald
  1970   "Production of Crime Rates." *American Sociological Review* 35:733-48.
  1971   "The Social Organization of Arrest." *Stanford Law Review* 23:1087-1111.
  1976   *The Behavior of Law.* New York: Academic Press.
Blumberg, Abraham S.
  1967   *Criminal Justice.* Chicago: Quadrangle.
Bonn, Robert L.
  1972   "The Predictability of Nonlegalistic Adjudication." *Law and Society Review* 6: 563-78.
Bowker, Lee H.
  1978   *Women, Crime and the Criminal Justice System.* Lexington, MA: D. C. Heath.
Buckle, Susan R. and L. G. Buckle
  1977   *Bargaining for Justice.* New York: Praeger.
Crites, Laura
  1978   "Women in the Criminal Court." Pp. 160-75 in Winifred Hepperle and Laura Crites (eds.) *Women in the Courts.* Williamsburg, VA: National Center for State Courts.
Giordano, Peggy C. and Stephen A. Cernkovich
  1979   "On Complicating the Relationship Between Liberation and Delinquency." *Social Problems* 26:467-81.
Glick, Ruth M. and Virginia V. Neto
  1977   *National Study of Women's Correctional Programs.* Washington, DC: Government Printing Office.

Hagan, John
  1975   "Parameters of Criminal Prosecution: An Application of Path
         Analysis to a Problem of Criminal Justice." *Journal of Criminal
         Law and Criminology* 65:536-44.
Hindelang, Michael
  1978   "Race and Involvement in Common-law Crimes." *American
         Sociological Review* 43:93-109.
  1979   "Sex Differences in Criminal Activity." *Social Problems*
         27:143-56.
Kelley, C. M.
  1972   *Crime in the United States: Uniform Crime Reports-1972.* U.S.
         Department of Justice, Washington, DC: Government Printing
         Office.
Kruttschnitt, Candace
  1979   The Social Control of Women Offenders: A Study of Sentencing
         in a Criminal Court. Unpublished Ph.D. dissertation, Yale
         University.
Macaulay, Stewart
  1963   "Non-contractual Relations in Business: A Preliminary Study."
         American Sociological Review 28:55-67.
Mather, Lynn
  1979   *Plea Bargaining or Trial? The Process of Criminal Case
         Disposition.* Lexington, MA: D. C. Heath.
Mileski, Maureen
  1971   "Courtroom Encounters: An Observational Study of a Lower
         Criminal Court." *Law and Society Review* 5:473-536.
Moulds, Elizabeth F.
  1980   "Chivalry and Paternalism: Disparities of Treatment in the
         Criminal Justice System." Pp. 277-99 in Susan K. Datesman and
         Frank R. Scarpitti (eds.), *Women, Crime and Justice.* New York:
         Oxford.
Moyer, Imogene L. and Garland F. White
  1981   "Police Processing of Female Offenders." Pp. 366-77 in Lee H.
         Bowker (ed.), *Women and Crime in America.* New York:
         Macmillan.
Myers, Martha A. and John Hagan
  1979   "Private and Public Trouble: Prosecutors and the Allocation of
         Court Resources." *Social Problems* 26:439-51
Nagel, Ilene and John Hagan
  1982   "Gender and Crime: Offense Patterns and Criminal Court
         Sanctions." Pp. 91-144 in Norval Morris and Michael Tonry (eds.),
         Crime and Justice Vol. IV. Chicago: University of Chicago Press.
Norland, Stephen and Neal Shover
  1977   "Gender Roles and Female Criminality: Some Critical
         Comments." *Criminology* 15:67-87.

Piliavin, Irving M. and Scott Briar
  1964   "Police Encounters with Juveniles." *American Journal of Sociology* 69:206-14.
Pollak, Otto
  1950   *The Criminality of Women.* Philadelphia: University of Pennsylvania.
Radzinowicz, L.
  1937   "Variability of the Sex-Ratio of Criminality." *Sociological Review* 29:76-102.
Rans, Laurel
  1978   "Women's Crime: Much Ado About . . . ?" *Federal Probation* 42:45-49.
Sarat, Austin
  1976   "Alternatives in Dispute Processing: Litigation in Small Claims Court." *Law and Society Review* 10:339-75.
Simon, Rita J.
  1975   *Women and Crime.* Lexington, MA: D. C. Heath.
Skogan, Wesley G.
  1974   "The Validity of Official Crime Statistics: An Empirical Investigation." *Social Science Quarterly* 55:25-38.
Smart, Carol
  1976   *Women, Crime and Criminology: A Feminist Critique.* London: Routledge and Kegan Paul.
Steffensmeier, Darrell J.
  1978   "Crime and the Contemporary Woman: An Analysis of Changing Levels of Female Property Crime, 1960-1975." Pp. 39-59 in Lee H. Bowker (ed.), *Women and Crime in America.* New York: Macmillan.
Sterling, Joyce S. and Mary Haskins
  1980   "Plea Bargaining: Responsive Law or Repressive Law." Paper presented at the annual meeting of the American Sociological Association.
Sudnow, David
  1965   "Normal Crimes: Sociological Features of the Penal Code in a Public Defender Office." *Social Problems* 12:255-76.
U.S. Bureau of Census
  1978   Current Population Reports. Consumer Income Money and Poverty Status in 1975 of Families and Persons in the U.S. and the West Region by Divisions and States, Series P-60, No. 113. Washington, DC: Government Printing Office.
U.S. Department of Justice
  1976   Criminal Victimization in the United States: A National Crime Survey Report. Washington, DC: Government Printing Office.
Weis, Joseph
  1976   "Liberation and Crime: The Invention of the New Female Criminal." *Crime and Social Justice* 6:17-27.

chapter **6**

Critical Problems of Women in Prison*

Phyllis Jo Baunach
U.S. Department of Justice, Washington, D.C.

Until recently, the problems confronting incarcerated women offenders have been largely ignored. The massive ten volume report issued in 1967 by the President's Commission on Law Enforcement and the Administration of Justice made no mention of women offenders (Murton and Baunach, 1973:543). The Department of Labor Manpower Administration devoted only about one half of a page of its 113 page report dealing with research efforts in correction to incarcerated women because those offenders "did not play a major role in the offender projects" (McArthur, 1974:8).

The primary reason that women offenders of all ages have been neglected is that there are so few of them in American jails and prisons. Surveys in 1970 indicated that only one in seven persons arrested (FBI, 1970:12) and only one in ten persons incarcerated

---

* This article originally appeared in the first edition of this text. Several editorial changes were made for the second edition.

(National Prisoner Statistics, 1972:6) was a woman over 18 years old. Some authors suggested in the mid-1970s that these statistics remained accurate (Simon, 1975:108).

More recent figures indicate that the percentage of women incarcerated in the United States increased from 4.4 percent to 5.7 percent (Bureau of Justice Statistics, 1990). Immarigeon and Chesney-Lind (1991:5-6) argue that:

> Women have been hit hard by our nation's punitive policies. In recent years, female populations in jails and prisons have increased disproportionately to the increase in women's involvement in serious crime. The U.S. Bureau of Justice Statistics (BJS) reports that the average daily population of women confined in local jails rose by 82 percent between 1984 and 1988. The number of men in jail increased by 44 percent during this period . . . . In 1979, there were 12,005 women in our nation's prisons. By 1988, that number had grown to 32,691, an increase of 172 percent.

Thus, despite the fact that there are fewer women than men incarcerated in American jails and prisons, the number of women incarcerated is rising dramatically. Therefore, the needs of incarcerated women must be understood in order to deal more effectively with this increasing population. With these points in mind, this chapter will describe conditions of confinement, programmatic inadequacies, and potential means of alleviating problems encountered by women offenders.

The Conditions of Women's Confinement

Unlike prisons for men, many women's prisons resemble college campuses, rather than fortress penitentiaries.[1] Often, there are no gun towers, no armed guards and no stone walls or fences with concertina wire strung on top. Neatly pruned hedges, well-kept flower gardens, attractive brick buildings and wide paved walkways greet the visitor's eye at women's prisons in many states. Often these institutions are located in rural, pastoral settings which may suggest tranquility and well-being to the casual observer.

However, placid external appearances are not indicative of the psychological environment of incarceration from an inmate's perspective. The freedom of movement and choice of daily activities we take for granted may be nonexistent in a prison setting. Regulations formulated by those in authority guide the inmate's life. Close personal contacts may be forbidden to minimize the potential development of homosexual relationships. However, these restrictions may limit the formation of more acceptable interpersonal relationships as well. Security requirements dictate searching letters, packages and incoming inmates for contraband. After a brief "incarceration" in the Women's Detention Center in Washington, D.C., journalist Jessica Mitford perceived prison life as "planned, unrelieved inactivity and boredom . . . no overt brutality but plenty of random, largely unintentional cruelty" (Mitford, 1973:27).

The lack of autonomy, the loss of identity, and powerlessness create an exaggerated dependency upon those in authority for incarcerated women. Burkhart's descriptions suggest that reactions to this environment may entail despondency, frustrations, heightened tensions, anxiety and apathy. As one inmate said:

> You start losing your identity when you get locked up. You stop seeking things, you stop doing things for yourself, you stop looking for things. You feel nothing's gonna be all right again . . . (Burkhart, 1973:120).

Two major problems confronting incarcerated women are the loss of love and family and the lack of meaningful training programs.

The Loss of Love and Family

Perhaps one of the most serious problems faced by incarcerated women is separation from their loved ones. Anecdotal and limited statistical evidence suggests that one of the greatest concerns of confined women is their children (Click and Neto, 1977:116). In their study of the women at the California Institution for Women (CIW) at Frontera, Ward and Kassebaum found that 43 percent of the women incarcerated for less than six months, 42 percent of the women incarcerated for six months to a year, and 38 percent of the women incarcerated for more than a year responded that the most difficult aspect of adjustment to prison was the absence of home and family (Ward and Kassebaum, 1965:120). At the time they conducted their study, the authors noted that problems of the separation of women from their children were especially felt among the women at CIW, as 59 percent of them had minor children and 68 percent were mothers (Ward and Kassebaum, 1965:15). More recently, the National Study of Women's Correctional Programs reported that of approximately 6,300 incarcerated women studied in fourteen states, 56.3 percent had one or more dependent children living with them prior to incarceration (Click and Neto, 1977:116).

Inmate-mothers are especially concerned about the custody and care of their children during their confinement. Children most often stay with their maternal grandmothers. Other caretakers include the child's father or other relatives. However, incarcerated mothers express the most satisfaction when children are placed with their maternal grandmothers and when they have participated in the decision as to where the child will live. Involvement in the decision-making process to place children gives inmate-mothers some peace of mind that their children will live in safe surroundings. Moreover, in placing children with maternal grandmothers, inmate-mothers feel sure that they will encounter minimal difficulties in taking the child back after release (Baunach, 1984).

Children may, however, be placed in foster homes or put up for adoption if suitable alternatives are unavailable. This might occur if the woman's mother is not a viable placement; if the child's father cannot be located or is in prison himself; or if there are no other relatives to care for the child. In the long run, this separation may severely damage the family relationship (Female Offender Resource Center, 1976:12; LEAA Task Force on Women, 1975:5). Moreover, sometimes the careful arrangements made by women prior to incarceration for the care of their children may be reversed by authorities who "know what is best" for the child's welfare. For instance, a black inmate in Washington state had procured placement for her eight children with white members of her congregation. Despite the inmate's efforts, and the help of her Christian friends, a young social worker decided that the children should be placed with black families. The inmate objected that her children would be happier with white friends than with black strangers, and responded, "They're not like kittens where you give half the litter away" (O'Brien, 1974:3).

Incarcerated mothers are burdened not only with the stigma associated with imprisonment but also with the knowledge that their own behavior has caused the separation from children. The psychological consequences experienced by these women often are very severe (Lundberg, et al. 1975). For instance, mothering seems to be an 'axis of self-esteem" (Lundberg, et al., 1975:36) for incarcerated women. The separation generates feelings of emptiness, helplessness, anger and bitterness, guilt and fear of loss or rejection by the children. DuBose (1975:8) similarly found that with prolonged separation, mothers feared that children might establish bonds of affection more closely with caretakers than with their mothers. Moreover, mothers feared that teenage children who stayed with elderly grandparents would be arrested because supervision was inadequate.

Baunach (1984) studied the effects of the separation from their children on 138 inmate mothers incarcerated in prisons in Washington state and Kentucky. Her findings revealed that regardless of race or age, women expressed guilt and shame that they committed crimes which separated them from their children. Moreover, for any women drug users, incarceration was the first extended time period they were not using drugs and had an opportunity to consider the effects of their behavior upon their children. Many wondered how they would remain "clean" once released and reunited with their children. Other women were bitter and angry at "the system" because they had pled guilty or because they felt that they had been convicted unfairly. These women thus felt that the separation from their children was unjust.

Most of the women with older children indicated that their children knew that their mothers were locked up for "being bad." Some mothers wanted this situation to serve as an example to their children of what would happen if they, too, broke the law. In addition, many mothers told their children where they were, because these mothers preferred to have a "straight relationship" with their children. On the other hand, women with very young children often did not tell their children that they were in prison because they felt the children were too young to understand or would suffer negative reprisals from playmates (Baunach, 1984).

The emotional pains of separation may be especially acute for women who are pregnant when incarcerated. These women bear their children in the prison maternity ward or at a nearby hospital and within a short time are compelled to give them up, possibly to foster parents or adoption agencies. One effect of this separation may be severe depression, shock, or loss of self-esteem.[2]

In addition, although varying among institutions, visitation policies and procedures determine the extent to which a woman can maintain contact with her children. Sometimes, this contact is minimal. For example, the Washington, D.C. Citizen's Council issued a report in 1972 which noted, among other things, that women at the Washington, D.C. Detention Center had only two one-hour visits each week. Moreover, there had been no provisions made for the mothers, who comprised some 86 percent of the inmate population to visit with their children (Murton and Baunach, 1973:548).

It must be noted that whether or not an inmate-mother should retain or relinquish her parental rights to her child(ren) during or following incarceration involves both moral and legal decisions which in some ways may overlap. From a legal perspective, Palmer (1972) argued that incarceration, per se, does not provide adequate evidence that a parent is unfit. Rather, he suggested that the courts should consider additional factors, such as the woman's relationship to the offspring prior to incarceration and the causal relationship between the criminal act and the mother's ability to perform her parental role. With these points in mind, judges would be better able to determine the mother's parental fitness and to decide whether or not the child(ren) should be placed in her custody after her release.

A further argument raised along these lines was that legislative guidelines limit the extent to which the courts may modify their procedures for deciding parental fitness. Guidelines currently consider the best interests of the child(ren), but simultaneously treat the issue of parental fitness inequitably. Established standards such as nonsupport, child abuse, neglect, desertion, drunkenness, adultery, mental illness and incarceration have been regarded as manifestations of the abandonment of parental responsibilities and their justification for the termination of parental rights. The author pointed out that these interpretations are erroneous and that a reassessment of the standards is required (Palmer, 1972).

The court's consideration of a mother's criminal act and subsequent incarceration as voluntary relinquishment of her parental rights was decided in re: Jameson (1967). In this case, the court held that the mother knew prior to committing the act that she would be incarcerated for it if convicted. Palmer challenged this justification as illogical, since the woman's intention may have been to obtain money or food with no intention of getting caught. Furthermore, he noted, if she wished to abandon her child, the woman probably could have devised alternative means which would not have been detrimental or discomforting to herself.

The author suggested that imprisonment in and of itself does not constitute abandonment. Rather, additional factors, such as parental neglect and withholding affection should be used to substantiate claims of abandonment. Given this background, Palmer recommended legislative reform, such as allowing an inmate to live with her children (under two years old) in prison, in conditions conducive to positive interaction; devising "mother release" programs to enable inmate-mothers to stay with their children in the community; and reforming visitation practices to allow for more relaxed visits in less security-oriented surroundings.

With respect to legislation, a few states have legislation allowing children under two years old to live with their mothers in prison; however, this practice is not currently used regularly. In addition, there has been a growing concern for the legal rights and rehabilitative needs of inmate-mothers and their children. This concern was reflected in a California lawsuit regarding an inmate-mother's right to have her children live with her in prison. The suit, however, was denied in court. Arguments raised included the effects that the prison environment and procedures could have on the child and the potential effects of the child's presence on the prison and other inmates (La Point, 1977:13-14; Shepard and Zemans, 1950).

Baunach (1984) explored some of the inmates' attitudes toward allowing children to stay in the prison for short periods of time (i.e., all day or overnight). Regardless of whether or not they have children of their own, women in prison tend to respond favorably to the presence of children. Many women indicated that they try to "clean up their language and behavior" when children are present, and enjoy watching or playing with children. However, to date, there has been no research on the effects on the children of being in a prison with mothers for short or long periods of time.

Lack of Meaningful Training Programs

Since the social roles of women in our culture traditionally have been oriented toward homemaker and mother, incarcerated women usually have been trained to assume these roles upon release. Thus, training programs for women offenders include feminine hygiene, makeup application, cosmetology, home decorating, sewing, gardening, cooking, nursing and other domestic services. In addition, some institutions offer training programs which include business courses, such as typing, bookkeeping or key punch.

The National Study of Women's Correctional Programs found that the most frequently offered training programs in the jails and prisons studied included clerical skills, cosmetology, and food services. In addition, six prisons provided training in key punch; two prisons offered graphic arts and one prison offered training in banking through the Chase Manhattan Bank. However, in the latter program only four of 365 incarcerated women were involved in the program (Click and Neto, 1977:73).

Although the Manual of Correctional Standards suggests that incarcerated women should be taught a marketable skill, as Burkhart points out, the manual "gets back to reality when it states: 'Perhaps the largest number of inmates are placed in work assignments necessary for maintaining the institution'" (Burkhart, 1973:296). Just as are incarcerated men, women inmates are required to drive garbage trucks, operate lawn mowers, cook, clean, wash clothes, and haul heavy sacks of supplies to keep the institution running. In addition, women offenders often provide a cheap labor force in prison industries which make goods for their own institutions or for other agencies.

Although work of this nature sometimes has been considered as "on-the-job-training" programs, the likelihood that women will be employed in similar positions upon release is minimal. In fact, the machinery employed in prison industries is often outdated and not used commercially outside the prison (Burkhart, 1973:294). Therefore, women cannot transfer acquired skills to jobs even if they are able to secure employment upon release. One inmate described the limitations of programs at the Women's Detention Center in Washington, D.C. as follows:

> Vocational training programs? There's eight old broken-down typewriters somewhere in the building. I don't know if anybody ever uses them, though. Or you can go down to group theory. But who wants it? A bunch of us [and] . . . our deprived lives? (Mitford, 1973:19).

Although there may be deficiencies in the programs provided for male inmates in this country, male inmates are afforded better opportunities to learn meaningful, marketable skills during incarceration than their female counterparts. A recent General Accounting Office study (1980) points out that in comparison with men, women inmates have "unequal access" to available training facilities. One reason cited for this discrepancy is that male inmates may have the opportunity to transfer between institutions within the state or within the federal prison system and may thus take advantage of a variety of programs. Confined women, on the other hand, have little opportunity to transfer to other facilities that might offer training programs because there are none (General Accounting Office, 1980:12). For instance, in one state, GAO researchers observed that there were eighty-five correctional facilities in sixty-seven counties. Women were housed in only one primary institution and four halfway houses (General Accounting Office, 1980; 15).

Further, the study reported a wide disparity in the number and types of training programs provided for male and female inmates. In one state visited in the study, the researchers noted that women housed in a single facility could learn keypunch and food services; men housed in one of the two prisons in the state could participate in thirteen vocational and on-the-job training programs. These programs included welding, auto body repair, drafting, computer programming, medical lab assistance and X-ray technician. Similarly, the other prison for men in the state had eleven such programs (General Accounting Office, 1980:18).

Within the federal prisons, men have had better access than

women to industries which provide both a training and work environment and an hourly wage. Of eighty-four industrial operations, male offenders may take part in eighty-two. However, women offenders may participate in only thirteen; eleven of these programs for women are located in co-correctional facilities and thus are available to male offenders as well (General Accounting Office, 1980:19).

In recent years, the GAO report noted that the federal prison system has, however, made some attempt to improve the training opportunities for women inmates. The Federal Women's Reformatory at Alderson now has programs for women inmates in apprenticeship trade areas credited by the U.S. Department of Labor. What the report did not mention, but what is needed to assess the effectiveness of this effort, is careful research on the extent to which women graduates of this program are better equipped to and actually do pursue training and work opportunities following release.

Where Do We Go From Here?

The conditions and problems of women's confinement outlined previously suggest a need to explore alternatives to the traditional modes of dealing with women offenders. Recognizing the deficiencies of the current system, the National Advisory Commission on Criminal Justice Standards and Goals urged all states to "reexamine" and "readjust" their "policies, procedures and programs" to make them "more relevant to the problems and needs of women." Among other things, the Commission has argued for a comprehensive evaluation of women offenders' needs in each state, and the development of adequate diversion and alternative programs in community centers (National Advisory Commission on Criminal Justice Standards and Goals, 1973:378).

If a woman has a job and some source of emotional support, it may be more beneficial to her and less costly to the state or county to keep her at home and require restitution or community service. The Des Moines Project, cited a few years ago by the National Institute of Justice as an Exemplary Project, affords one such possibility. For women requiring more secure placement, live-in residential halfway houses may provide an appropriate alternative. When it was operative, Project ELAN in Minneapolis, Minnesota enabled both women and their children to live together in a community setting. For live-in programs, requiring women to pay at least part of their costs for room and board would assist in defraying the program costs. This is especially important since, given the number of women served, many community programs may be as expensive as prisons (Click and Neto, 1977:181).

However, whether women are incarcerated in detention centers, prisons, or community facilities, the environment and relationships with others are important in determining the attitudes of the offender when she is released. Adherence to the old medical model which suggests that offenders are "sick and must be cured" prior to release means that things must be done to or for the offender rather than with her.

An alternative approach to this traditional medical model is participatory management. In this approach, inmates are given an opportunity to develop responsible decision-making skills (Murton, 1975). The underlying assumption is that despite the type of offense, sex, or age of the offender, a person who has committed a crime has demonstrated her lack of behaving responsibly toward herself or others. Therefore, one of the most valuable activities is to engage in making decisions about her own life while she is incarcerated. If incarcerated women are taught only to conform to institutional rules for several months or years, it should be no surprise that they cannot adequately handle difficulties that arise after they are released.

In this approach, the superintendent strives to provide an environment conducive to the growth and development of offenders, one in which inmates may learn respect for themselves and others. Yet the superintendent does not coddle the inmates or relinquish her authority over the institution to them. Rather, she involves staff and inmates jointly with her in making decisions that affect the institution. Areas of decision-making might, for instance, include jointly developing rules that govern curfews, noise level or even inmate discipline.

One way in which this involvement may be brought about is by the creation of staff-inmate councils where staff and inmates elect peers to discuss matters of importance to them both. Inclusion of staff in the councils is important to assist in reducing the "We-They" syndrome characteristic of prison life. Working together for common goals would enable each group to see the other in a different light.

Everyone should be able to vote or run for office. Enabling women and staff to elect council members also entails their responsibility for the people elected. Therefore, if they are dissatisfied with the council's work, they may elect new people at the next election or they may run for office themselves. Realizing that their decisions will affect their own well-being in the institution, women (and staff) may feel a vested interest in the process (Baunach 1981).

Whether or not this type of participatory management could be introduced into a prison or community facility, of course, depends upon the interest and willingness of the superintendent or director to do so. However, the literature indicates that at least four prisons in different parts of the world and at different time periods successfully developed participatory management for male offenders (Murton and Baunach, 1973; Baunach, 1981). If men are capable of developing and engaging in participatory management, then women can do equally as well. In addition, careful documentation of the council's evolution and evaluation of its effectiveness must be done to indicate the process others might use in developing similar approaches and the ways it might be improved.

Another way in which women with children might be given a chance to develop responsible decision-making skills is to involve them in dealing with their children on a routine basis prior to release. Mothers who plan to reunite with children upon release (as most do), need the opportunity to interact with them during incarceration. Mothers need to learn their own strengths and weaknesses as a parent by accepting this important responsibility. Moreover, they need to determine if they really want to be mothers and if they are able to handle problems of discipline, demands, and routine care for children. Parental responsibility entails far more than simply showing off a child to others or sitting together during regular visiting hours.

Some states (i.e., Minnesota, Nebraska, Tennessee, Kentucky, Washington, New York, California) allow children to stay overnight with mothers in prison. However, in developing this type of program, care should be taken to ensure that the welfare of both mother and child are considered. For some women, having the responsibility of children may make it more difficult to deal with their own problems. Thus, even the decision allowing inmate mothers to be involved with their own children during incarceration should be made jointly with the inmate-mothers. Many women feel that unless they want to be with their children, they will be viewed as "bad mothers" by those around them. In fact, many of these women may feel insecure as mothers and fear they could not handle the responsibilities adequately. Thus, parenting programs such as those at the Kentucky Correctional Institution for Women, Minnesota Correctional Institution for Women or Purdy Treatment Center (Washington) may be helpful. Some of these programs attempt to combine textbook information with actual interactions with children.

Finally, a need exists to identify and examine more systematically particular issues pertaining to women offenders. For instance, research on the long range effects of the separation on children or the possible impacts of involvement with the mother in a prison setting need to be determined before live-in programs in prison are created extensively.

Careful research should address the problems encountered by women of all ages from the time of arrest and processing through the courts, through the time served in detention centers or prisons or on probation or parole. Studies, such as that by Kruttschnitt (1982) which suggests that sentencing may be affected by both sex and economic dependency status of the defendant, need to be expanded and refined. In-depth analyses of specific problem areas such as sentencing will provide valuable information which may be useful to administrators and practitioners in planning and developing appropriate programs designed to meet the needs of women offenders as effectively and efficiently as possible.

Endnotes

The views in this chapter are those of the author and do not reflect the policies or opinions of the Bureau of Justice Statistics or the U.S. Department of Justice.

[1] The published National Study of Women's Correctional Programs identified four designs among the sixteen women's prisons studied: four prisons had a complex of buildings each with one or more functions, surrounding a central administration building; two had a single building which housed all the functions of the prison; six had a campus design which included a group of buildings each with a separate function and grassy areas within which inmates might move; one had a cottage design which consisted of several small buildings that look like multiple-family dwellings; and three had designs which were variations of these four basic designs (Glick and Neto, 1977:20-25).

[2] Tom Murton, former Warden of the Arkansas prison system, reported the incident of a woman inmate who gave birth to a child while incarcerated. Murton reported that immediately following the baby's birth, the welfare department planned to put the baby up for adoption. The impact on the inmate was "semi-shock and depression." Murton, however, retrieved the child and for a short time, at least, the child lived with foster parents who worked at the prison and lived directly adjacent to the prison grounds on the "free line." Thus, the inmate-mother responded positively to the brief chance she had to maintain contact with the newborn child before she voluntarily surrendered the baby to the welfare department (Murton and Hyams, 1969:170-181).

Bibliography

Baunach, Phyllis Jo
  1984 *Mothers in Prison*. New Brunswick: Transaction.
  1981 "Participating Management: Restructuring the Prison Environment." Pp. 196-218 in D. Fogel and J. Hudson (eds.), *Justice as Fairness*. Cincinnati, OH: Anderson Publishing Company.
Bureau of Justice Statistics Bulletin
  1990 "Prisoners in 1989." Washington, D.C.: Department of Justice.
Burkhart, Katheryn
  1973 *Women in Prison*. New York: Doubleday and Company, Inc.
DuBose, D.
  1975 "Problems of Children Whose Mothers are Imprisoned." New York: Institute of Women's Wrongs.
Federal Bureau of Investigation
  1970 *Crime in the United States: 1970*. Washington, D.C.: U.S.Department of Justice.
Female Offender Resource Center
  1976 *Female Offenders: Problems and Programs*. Washington, D.C.: American Bar Association.
General Accounting Office
  1980 *Women in Prison: Inequitable Treatment Requires Action*. Washington, D.C.: U.S. General Accounting Office.
Glick, Ruth and Virginia Neto
  1977 *National Study of Women's Correctional Programs*. Washington, D.C.: National Institute of Law Enforcement and Criminal Justice.
Immarigeon, Russ and Meda Chesney-Lind
  1991 *Women's Prisons: Overcrowded and Overused*. Washington, D.C.: National Council on Crime and Delinquency.
Kruttschnitt, Candace
  1982 "Women, Crime and Dependency: An Application of the Theory of Law." *Criminology* 19 (4):495-513.
La Point, Velma
  1977 "Child Development During Maternal Separation: via Incarceration." Washington, D.C.: NIMH (unpublished).
LEAA Task Force on Women
  1975 The Report of the LEAA Task Force on Women. Washington, D.C.: Law Enforcement Assistant Administration.
Lundberg, O., A. Scheckley and T. Voelkar
  1975 "An Exploration of the Feelings and Attitudes of Women Separated From Their Children due to Incarceration." Masters thesis. Portland: Portland State University.
McArthur, Virginia
  1974 *From Convict to Citizen: Programs for the Woman Offender*. Washington, D.C.: U.S. Department of Labor.

Mitford, Jessica
  1973   *Kind and Usual Punishment.* New York: Alfred A. Knopf.
Murton, Thomas O.
  1975   *Shared Decision-making as a Treatment Technique in Prison Management.* Minneapolis: Murton Foundation for Criminal Justice.
Murton, Thomas O. and Joe Hyams
  1969   *Accomplices to the Crime: The Arkansas Prison Scandal.* New York: Grove Press, Inc.
Murton, Thomas O. and Phyllis Jo Baunach
  1973   "Shared Decision-making in Prison Management: A Survey of Demonstrations Involving the Inmate in Participatory Management." Pp. 543-573 in M. G. Herman and M. G. Haft (eds.), *Prisoners Rights Sourcebook.* New York: Clark Boardman Company.
  1973   "Women in Prison." *The Freeworld Times* 2 (June-July).
National Advisory Commission on Criminal Justice Standards and Goals.
  1973   *Corrections.* Washington, D.C.: U.S. Department of Justice.
National Prisoner Statistics
  1972   *Prisoners in State and Federal Institutions for Adult Felons.* Washington, D.C.: U.S. Department of Justice.
O'Brien, Lois
  1974   "Women in Prison." *The Freeworld Times* 3 (March).
Palmer, D.
  1972   "The Prisoner-mother and her Child." *Capital University Law Review* 1:127-44.
Shepard, Dean and Eugene Zemans
  1950   *Prison Babies.* Chicago: John Howard Association.
Simon, Rita
  1975   *Women and Crime.* Lexington, MA: D.C. Heath and Company.
Ward, David and Gene Kassebaum
  1965   *Women's Prison.* Chicago: Aldine Publishing Company, Inc.

chapter 7

Project *Met*
A Community Based Educational Program for Women Offenders

Eddyth P. Fortune and
Margaret Balbach

In a study attempting to determine the status of women's correctional programs in the United States, Glick and Neto (1977) ascertained that only one woman for every ten in prison or jail was involved in a community-based program. They further pointed out that there were basically three types of community-based programs for women: work-release centers, which involved only about two percent of convicted women; halfway houses; and drug and alcohol treatment programs. A review of the data presented by Glick and Neto on the number of programs existing in the states they studied suggests a dearth of community programs for women offenders.

The National Council on Crime and Delinquency (NCCD, 1976) has made the recommendation that:

> Community based correction programs should be established for offenders (women) convicted for economic or property related offenses (p. 30).

In its policy statement on the female offender, NCCD recommended that "where appropriate, efforts should be made to allow the offender to serve time in the community . . . [utilizing] community correction models which can serve the dual role of penalizing the offender while utilizing resources and services in the community . . ." (NCCD, 1976:30-31).

The scarcity of community-based programs for women offenders appears to be reflected in the lack of literature and the lack of empirical data on the topic. The need for more research has been emphasized repeatedly and as indicated by Glick and Neto (1977), among the many areas where more research needs to be conducted, is the need to find out who are the women offenders in community based programs and what are more effective ways to employ community services. In one of the earlier studies of modern day women offenders, Hendrix (1972) recommended more emphasis on community-based corrections using more diversionary treatment ". . . whereby women can maintain contact with their children and family and receive counseling, job training, job placement, medical assistance, and other services . . ." (p. 42). These recommendations are supported in much of the literature on women offenders (Glick and Neto, 1977; Hendrix, 1972; Lehtinen, 1977; McArthur, 1974; Miller, 1977; Price, 1977; U.S. Department of Labor, 1976, 1977).

Repeatedly, the literature describes the woman offender as typically poor, undereducated, untrained in a job skill, and a minority member who is frequently a mother and the sole supporter of her children (Glick and Neto, 1977; U.S. Department of Labor, 1976). Although it appears that many programs which are briefly described in the literature have attempted to address the needs of this population, rarely does the literature reflect the details of these programs. Information often neglected includes the characteristics of the participants, the methods for determining the needs of participants, implementation and outcome of the programs (McArthur, 1974; Miller, 1977; U.S. Department of Labor, 1976).

Further, many of the programs discussed focused on educational and vocational opportunities within prisons. McArthur (1974) described the details of a report on correctional vocational training which indicated that of sixty-six training programs for prisoners, eight involved females. In a national survey, the Yale Law Review reported that a male prison had an average of ten vocational programs, whereas the average number of programs in women's institutions was 2.7 (Arditi et al., 1973). An additional complication is that many of the vocational programs in women's institutions focused mostly on the kinds of jobs the offenders had held prior to incarceration, or, worse, they focused on the needs of the institution.

Frequently, the training offered involved clerical, cosmetology, nurses aids, food services, janitorial services—but rarely were programs offered in financially rewarding fields (Glick and Neto, 1977; McArthur, 1974; North, 1977; Sorensen, 1978; U.S. Department of Labor, 1976). It is important to note that while Glick and Neto (1977) found 43 percent of the women offenders had had previous vocational training, it was typically in these traditional, low paying fields. In addition to vocational training, academic education is a problem area for the woman offender. Glick and Neto (1977) found that only 40 percent of the women offenders in their study had at least a high school education. Further, it was found that educational level was directly related to ethnic group in that blacks, who constituted 50 percent of the incarcerated female population, had the lowest levels of education.

Sorensen (1978) also found that, while basic survival skills were needed by all of the women offenders in her study, literacy level was directly related to the complexity of the level of additional skill training needed. For instance, while most subjects reported they could save very well and were able to determine if a purchase was a bargain, 80 percent were dysfunctional in mathematical skills.

It also is important to consider the attitudes toward work, sex role and occupations. Glick and Neto (1977) concluded that women offenders had a positive attitude toward working, but that they supported the traditional sex roles whereby women were mothers and men the primary breadwinners. Glick and Neto also concluded that while the offenders reported that "nontraditional jobs for women are all right, they strongly endorsed high status, white collar jobs . . ." tending to reject the skilled trades jobs. Other studies have reported similar findings. Both Fortune (1978) and Sorensen (1978) found that women offenders tend to prefer traditional female occupations and white collar jobs above the skilled trades jobs.

Despite the fact that many incarcerated women indicate a preference for traditional jobs, there has been a good deal of emphasis placed on attempts to offer vocational training in women's correctional institutions and with apparently some level of success (Herman, 1979; North, 1977). Herman (1979) indicated that among the problems to be overcome in firmly incorporating these types of programs is the need to increase the interest of women offenders in these areas and to establish transition methods whereby the women participating in nontraditional vocational training can, when released, carry these skills into the community.

It seems to make sense that such training opportunities should be incorporated at the community level also. While a major portion of women are on probation, there are fewer programs designed to assist them in the community (U.S. Department of Labor, 1976). The cost of incarceration is much higher than the cost of probation (NCCD, 1976). Yet it appears that, for the most part, only women who are incarcerated can benefit from programs directed at substantial improvement of their economic status. Even if the cost of community-based programs was added to the cost of probation, it is likely that the combined costs would still be less than the cost of incarceration. And even if the cost of alternative programs is greater, the NCCD (1976) pointed out that it is the goal of correctional objectives to meet the individual offender's needs and not just custodial services that are important.

Impetus for Project *Met* (Model Employment Training)

As pointed out by Glick and Neto (1977), the availability of federal funding has given a great deal of impetus for the development of programs for women offenders. Project *Met* was no exception. This project, conducted by women faculty at a large state university located in a large rural county in the midwest, was created in response to what appeared to be a critical need of women offenders, i.e., better employment training and opportunities for women offenders in the community setting.

The proportion of women on probation in the area was almost three times the national average and a large number of these women were unemployed. As of February 1980, the number of probationers in the jurisdiction was 479. Women constituted 33 percent of this population whereas nationwide, women constituted only slightly more than 10 percent of those persons on probation (Simon, 1980; U.S. Department of Justice, 1979).

A review of the history of the jurisdiction revealed that, while there had been two CETA funded projects which addressed the needs of women in developing job application skills and securing employment for displaced homemakers, there had never been any formal, or informal, program designed to develop job training opportunities for women offenders and ex-offenders (Cicciu, 1980). The current unemployment rate was 7 percent, with about 45 to 50 percent of these unemployed being women. Of great value, too, would be gainful employment of the women on probation (Davidson, 1980).

Three factors were considered to contribute to the local unemployment situation. First, the number of manufacturers in the area is limited; second, the skills of the unemployed are limited. And finally, there is great difficulty in matching available jobs with what skills the unemployed do possess (Illinois Bureau of Employment Security, 1980). The lack of programs for women offenders seemed to add to the dilemma for these individuals.

Method

Objectives

The hypothesis to be tested by this research was: could women who have proven unsuccessful at the low-skill service jobs traditionally held by women respond to job training in skills normally associated with male-dominated occupations, such as automobile repair, small engine repair, photographic processing and landscape care?

The goal of the research was to determine if it was reasonable to design a training program for women having the following combination of problems: 1) currently under probation or parole supervision; 2) currently unemployed; 3) previous work experience (if any) limited to unskilled, dead-end type jobs such as motel maids, general janitorial cleaners, clerks in fast food service businesses, sales clerks, etc.; and 4) unsuccessful in holding even these low-skill jobs.

Approach

A model employment training program incorporating these goals was designed by three women faculty at the university. The name of the program was: Model Employment Training Program for Women Offenders in Predominantly Male-Oriented Occupations: Project *Met.*

Client Selection

The sixteen-week project, which was funded by CETA through the Governor's Special Grant/Governor's Youth Program, began with the identification of twenty women offenders on probation or parole in a large rural county in the midwest. The county's probation agency and the local office of the state's Adult Parole services identified those women under their supervision who were currently unemployed and who indicated an interest in receiving the training to be provided in this project.

Initial eligibility (according to CETA guidelines) was determined. Eligible women were interviewed by the project directors to determine specific needs for occupational training, based upon the following criteria: employment history, previous vocational training, and stated interest in obtaining skill in a nontraditional occupation. Each participant would be receiving a weekly allowance while in the project in conformity with CETA guidelines. All qualified women were given a battery of standardized tests of intelligence, achievement, personality and vocational interest.

Program Design and Implementation

The sixteen-week project focused on two major areas: basic skills (writing, mathematics, reading, typing and job application) and vocational training (photography, landscape care, automobile repair, and small engine repair). At the onset of the project, participants were asked to rank the areas of proposed vocational training in the order of most interest to least interest. Group and individual counseling, as well as several mini-projects (battered women's discussion group, field trip to a women's correctional institution, a charm class, and a conference on corrections), were also included.

Activities were organized in the following general format: 1) the first and sixteenth weeks were scheduled for pre- and post-testing; 2) weeks two and three concentrated on basic skills (writing, mathematics, job application skills and typing); 3) during the fourth week and thereafter, basic skills and vocational training components were separated into half day sessions, i.e., basic skills in the morning and vocational training in the afternoon or vice versa; 4) group counseling sessions were scheduled for once a week and individual counseling, as needed. Other activities, such as the battered women's discussion group, the charm class and the trip to the women's correctional institution, were scheduled periodically throughout the sixteen weeks. Weekly staff meetings also were scheduled to provide staff an opportunity to determine student progress, discuss problems, and assess the need for continuing or revising planned activities.

Tests and Evaluation

A testing program was originally included in the project for three reasons: 1) to aid in selecting from a pool those participants who would be most likely to experience success; 2) to use the results in dealing with participants during the course of the project; and 3) to establish a data base that would help in the design of similar programs in the future.

The specific questions to be investigated were:

1) Are members of this group characterized by certain variables that distinguish them from the average female population?

2) Which variables predict those participants who would remain with the program until it was concluded?

3) Which variables predict general success for participants in the program?

4) Which variables predict specific success (i.e., success in landscaping, automobile repair, etc.)?

The tests used for this project were: 1) 16PF; 2) CAQ-Clinical Analysis Questionnaire; 3) Minnesota Vocational Interest Inventory; 4) Gordon Occupational Checklist; 5) Tennessee Self Concept Scale; 6) Standard Progressive Matrices (Raven's); and 7) California Personality Inventory.

The norms used are for the total female population, except in the case of the Minnesota Vocational Interest Inventory. Since there are no female norms for this survey, scores were examined relative to the groups under consideration in this project, i.e., which women scored highest on the "Outdoors" scale and how high are the scores compared to male norms.

The questions of predicting general and specific success were not dealt with at this time because to do so would require many more cases in the study.

After pre- and post-testing were completed, the results were compared to records of behavior-based staff observations and to the results of tests of a clinical psychologist.

The testing procedures were designed, administered and interpreted by Dr. Elizabeth Harris, Associate Professor of Psychology and Director of Measurement and Evaluation Services. In addition, Dr. Margaret Waimon, Assistant Professor of Psychology, was employed as the project's staff psychologist, and was to accompany the women in all of their activities to monitor and record their behaviors. Women were also used in instructional and administrative roles as often as possible to serve as female role models. However, male instructors were included to provide a realistic heterogeneous environment.

The first meeting between the staff and participants was arranged as an informal gathering to provide an opportunity for everyone to become acquainted and to allow the staff to explain the project in depth to the participants. This meeting was held at mid-morning and in a lounge where an atmosphere of friendly, social interaction was potentially possible.

Results

The original number of participants intended to be served was twenty. The number beginning the program was actually fifteen. However, of these, only twelve women completed the test battery which was administered during the week designated for pre-testing. Of these twelve, five remained with the program until its conclusion, two never attended, four dropped out of the program for various reasons of their own, and one was dismissed because of a behavior problem. Three other women joined later, but were dismissed for behavior problems one day before they were scheduled to pre-test.

It was decided that post-testing would be administered to all who participated in the project, even if it was only briefly and initially, as in the pre-testing, in order to compare the women who completed the project with those who dropped out.

It was immediately obvious that sophisticated multivariate statistical procedures could not be used even for the original group of nine, which later was reduced to five. However, a decision was made to continue collecting data since it could be used for descriptive purposes, and some simple inferential statistics such as t-tests could be analyzed. In addition, analyses of the data could provide clues to assist with subsequent projects and could be combined with data collected in the future.

Test Results

Two variables (from the sixteen PF scales) that appear to characterize the entire group of women on probation versus the general female population are: 1) Group Dependency, and 2) Willingness to Experiment. Group Dependency was outstanding in that four of the five participants completing the entire program attained sten (standard score with a mean of 5.5 and standard deviation of 2.0) scores of one. The California Personality Inventory yielded mean scores for all groups on both pre-tests and post-tests that were below the population means, except for the variable, Femininity, where all groups scored above the population mean. The women scored low on traits such as Responsibility, Social Maturity, Self-Control, Achievement, Motivation, Self-Acceptance, Sociability and Intellectual Efficiency.

Both Intelligence and Self-Concept means were generally below the population means, but within the average range. The results on these tests were found to agree essentially with the clinical reports.

Variables on the pre-tests that discriminate between women who remained in the program versus women who started and subsequently dropped out are Self-Acceptance, Social Adequacy, Femininity, Feelings of Personal Worth, Intellectual Efficiency, Sociability, Experimenting, and Self-Image. In all cases the means for women who remained were higher than for those who dropped out.

Equally as important in analyzing the results of the project is identifying characteristics of the participants who showed a statistically significant difference between pre-testing and post-testing. Correlated t-tests showed significant differences on Healthy Self-Criticism (Tennessee Self-Concept), Self-Assurance, Tender Mindedness, Femininity, and Self-Control, all increasing closer to the population mean. In most cases, means for dropouts, as well as participants, move closer to population means.

The results of the Minnesota Vocational Inventory which was administered as part of the pre-testing program showed that, as a group, the women who remained in the program did not score high on any of the nontraditional female vocational scales. They scored highest on Office Work, Sales Work and Health Services scales. Other test scores and experience with the program indicate that the MVI is providing generally valid information.

For women participants, scores on the CAQ were within normal range, the highest being a sten of seven on paranoia. Dropouts were not especially high on any CAQ variables, but did score between seven and eight on four variables: paranoia, high psychopathic deviation, schizophrenia, and compulsiveness. Results of the individual psychological reports and experience with the women in the program indicate that the CAQ is an appropriate testing instrument for screening purposes.

In response to the pre-test question related to the order in which subjects were to indicate primary areas of interest, photography was ranked first while small engine repair was rated least interesting. Automobile repair and landscape care were ranked fairly even in level of interest.

Observations and Discussion

The First Meeting Between Staff and Participants

At this first, informal meeting, the women sat quietly and apart from each other. Attempts by the staff to converse with individuals were met with non-hostile, but superficial and closely guarded, responses. It appeared that, at that particular point, the major motivation for the women's participation was the opportunity to earn some money immediately.

The Pre-testing Period

Contrary to the women's behavior exhibited during the first meeting, the testing period was marked by their excessive noisiness, exaggerated laughter, and at times, argumentative interactions. Much of the behavior was interpreted as defensiveness and was supported by their frequent responses of inadequacy or discomfort during the testing period. It was during this period, however, that a foundation of trust with the staff was established. They were frequently assured that they were not expected to know "everything," and that the tests were not for the purpose of "judging them." They did, therefore, after the initial reactions, begin working on the instruments with more of an attitude of willingness to cooperate.

Basic Skills

On the whole, response to their basic skills training provided in the program was poor. Most of the women scored fairly low in these skills but attempts to improve these areas through instruction proved difficult. Writing was provided through the university's Writing Skills Center and although some program participants made progress, their progress was minimal during the sixteen week project. Reading was conducted through the Reading Study Skills Center with each participant working with reading instruction interns (graduate students) on a tutorial basis. Again, while some of the women showed reading improvement, overall progress was slow. A major factor contributing to the lack of progress was the lack of attendance at these class sessions. Despite the fact that the women were paid for attendance, they were frequently absent or if in attendance for these sessions, exerted minimal efforts. The same held true for mathematics instruction, and, while also true for typing and job application skills, the latter was an area (aside from the vocational classes) in which these women appeared to have the greatest responsiveness. Although these women did not become proficient typists as the result of this training, they did achieve basic typing knowledge such as the keyboard and basic operation of the typewriter. Speed building was the area in which these women proved unresponsive and disinterested.

Photography

Behaviors exhibited during this segment of the program were very diverse. The disruptive behavior described in the testing period carried over into the lecture portion of the course. Early assignments were accomplished without regard to instructor expectations or appropriate student behavior. When the women were dealt with on a more individualized basis, however, such as during film development, the level of interest and cooperation tended to increase. Defensiveness again was demonstrated when they were expected to display their pictures for evaluation. As the course work progressed, much of the earlier behavior noted seemed to subside. The women began to work as a group. They showed a higher degree of cooperation with one another and took greater interest in each other. They became more willing to experiment with new ideas and to express themselves more openly.

It was during this segment of the program that an event occurred which may have had significant impact on the project and on the participants as a cohesive group. By this time (the fourth week of the program), three of the original twelve participants had been terminated and three new participants had been admitted to the program. The crisis occurred during the fifth week when four of the women—the three new participants and one of the original participants—were involved in an altercation which left one woman injured from a stab wound and two others charged with the offense. Because of the seriousness of this event, the four who were involved were terminated from the project.

It is important to note that of the four, three were new to the project. The entire staff had had little or no opportunity to interact with the new participants nor to communicate to them that this was a program that was "safe" and the staff "trustworthy." Although the incident was quite alarming to everyone, the staff felt that it might have very well contributed to the cohesion which later developed within the group. The women realized for the first time that someone could be dropped from the program for disciplinary reasons. Some expressed concern that the project itself might be terminated if additional incidents occurred. Within a few days after the incident, two more participants withdrew. It was later learned that each of these individuals had become involved in new illegal activities.

Automobile Repair

During the first few sessions of this activity, the participants exhibited behaviors similar to that shown at the beginning of the program. It can be assumed that this behavior is displayed anytime these women would enter a new, perhaps somewhat threatening, situation. In addition, the enthusiasm shown for this topic was not as great as that for the photography training. Instructional activities, such as lectures and movies, frequently encountered behaviors related to boredom or disinterest. Attendance in this activity also became an indicator of interest and general attitude toward the subject. Those who were more regular in attendance showed a greater willingness to assist others or displayed a higher ability in the subject.

Other subtle changes were also beginning to occur within the group. More student-like behaviors began to develop in the majority of participants. In addition to an observable increase in self-control, there was also an ability to admit to not knowing something, without the previous degree of defensiveness. Individual personalities also began to emerge and the women were more willing to reveal differences, as well as communicate more personal information.

Landscape Care

As with the previous segments, there was an initial breakdown of behavior at the beginning of the landscape care segment. The activities involved in this subject, however, were so obviously uninteresting to the women that the instructor revised the course plan and incorporated floral design arrangements and greenhouse management into the curriculum rather than the outdoor landscape care. Having made this revision, the instructor was then able to capture the interest and attention of the participants and reverse the counterproductive activities into a rewarding experience for them. It was during this part of the program that the participants began to demonstrate a sense of pride in their accomplishments. This was demonstrated both in their group interactions and in their utilization of their newly acquired skills in their private lives.

Other marked changes in behavior occurred during this segment. More socially acceptable behavior began to emerge. They began to be more polite to each other and staff; they were able to accept critiques of their work with less defensiveness; attendance improved greatly; overall involvement increased — they forgot to take breaks; they began to show some enthusiasm for learning; and they assumed responsibility for cleaning up without being told.

A significant activity occurred during this segment. A group of mentally retarded adults from a local center was brought to the

greenhouse for the women to teach them how to pot plants. The
response was overwhelming. The women acted in an extremely
positive manner, demonstrating confidence, patience and total
cooperation.

Small Engine Repair

The last class offered in the project was small engine repair. As
anticipated from their earlier responses when they were asked to
rank the courses to be offered, this subject was the one for which
the women showed the least interest. In spite of the lack of interest,
however, they behaved in a manner that indicated self-control and
greater maturity than they had demonstrated at the beginning of
the program. The most important change in behavior was that the
women exhibited greater student-like behavior than before and a
greater ability to tolerate frustration. Keeping a notebook, taking
notes and referring to the notes when necessary — all for the first
time during the project — showed a degree of self-discipline that was
very different from the behavior shown at the start of the project.
The fact that they attended class at all and worked on what was
required, in spite of an extreme lack of interest, indicated growth
and increased maturity.

Other Activities

Of these activities scheduled into the program as one-time events,
such as the battered women's discussion group, the charm class
and the trip to the women's correctional institution, the last
appeared to have the greatest impact.

The trip to the women's correctional institution was scheduled
for an all day trip. Both staff members and participants were in
attendance. There had been prior arrangements made with the
warden of the institution to structure activities for the *Met*
participants in such a way as to provide them with some insight
into what being in a prison was really like. Shortly after the *Met*
group entered the facility, the staff and participants were separated
into two groups, with the staff members being given a traditional
tour of the institution and the participants being "admitted" as
"inmates" for the day. The women were searched as an entering
inmate would be, taken to living quarters, assigned jobs to
complete, and escorted from one area to another as would a regular
inmate. They were informed of the rules they were to follow and
of the consequences if they did not. (It should be noted that no one

violated any rules established for the day.) They were also given opportunities to interact with the residents; however, they refrained from any interaction except during a "safe" group setting scheduled for the afternoon and attended by the entire *Met* group, both staff and participants.

There was a marked difference in the women's attitudes and behavior after this experience. Comments by the participants indicated that this was the most valuable experience in the *Met* project. They also suggested that this be included in all such programs as *Met*.

Conclusions and Recommendations

Given the small sample size of this group, only tentative conclusions can be made. However, the basic premise of this study, that women of this particular background will respond to training in skills normally associated with male-dominated occupations, appears to be, at least in part, discounted. While the women grew to accept and to cooperate in the training in auto mechanics and small engine repair, not all responded to these traditionally male courses with the same uniformity of positive response and with the degree of pleasure exhibited in doing the traditionally female work such as floral design, plant care, and teaching the mentally retarded adults.

In light of the women's behavior, as reported in faculty staff observations and based on the results of the testing, it is suggested that traditional female vocational training be considered as at least part of future course offerings in projects of this nature. Based on their behavior and responses to the different segments of this program, there are indications that these women had a strong alliance to the traditional feminine roles in work and in socializing, as was remarkably demonstrated by their unanimous and overwhelmingly positive response to the classes in floral design, plant care and in teaching the mentally handicapped adults. Since these attitudes are the same as reported by other research, it would seem important to examine closely the type of training typically offered women offenders and strengthen training programs which offer more marketable skills with the greatest financial rewards. Although participation in nontraditional areas may be limited at the present time, they should not be excluded.

Even though these women expressed an initial interest in the nontraditional training offered, their attitudes toward traditional female roles won out over nontraditional work in successful completion of the training. It is suggested that perhaps a different approach be taken in offering nontraditional training to women with this background than has been attempted previously. Past efforts, including this project, seem to approach the woman offender with the "here it is, come and get it" perspective. What appears to be needed is an intermediate component that deals with increasing the woman's awareness of the benefits of such occupations and her acceptance of female participation in such occupations. Although she may view her role as secondary to the male in the family, the facts are that she is often the primary supporter of the family and needs to have opportunities equal to the male functioning in the primary position. Unless she is provided the chance to change her attitudes toward the female role, she may continue the frustration of raising a family on less adequate resources by maintaining employment in the lower paying traditional female occupations.

Of additional importance in offering community-based vocational programs for women offenders should be the following considerations. First, adequate testing is essential to determine the individual's aptitudes, capacities and interests. Second, the assessment of basic skills should be incorporated, and highly rewarding experiences should be provided to motivate participation in these areas. When possible, basic skills should be included as well-integrated parts of the vocational training to promote the sense of relevance to the vocational skills being taught. Third, the length of the program and the sequence of the activities should be carefully considered. It is essential that the training be offered in a well-organized manner so that the subject matter is not concentrated into too short a time frame. However, caution should be exercised to avoid the other extreme. That is, too lengthy a time frame could create the possibility of a loss of interest and boredom. Finally, participating staff should be provided with training on the female offender to orient them to the needs of this offender group and provide insight into the problems of dealing with this population. Included should be an orientation in the behaviors typical of this population and methods for dealing with problems which might arise when working with these students.

In conclusion, it is important to stress that women comprise a fast growing segment of the U.S. prison population. It appears that community-based projects such as *Met* could provide real assistance to society as well as to individual women. To provide the woman with opportunities to increase her earning potential as well as her self-assurance before she becomes part of the prison population could prove of great benefit for society.

Note

* The authors acknowledge and give special thanks to those faculty
involved in this project. Special credit is given to Mary Kay Huser, who
acted as co-director and fiscal officer for the project. Also, a special note
of gratitude is given to Elizabeth Harris who directed all testing, and to
Margaret Waimon, the project's staff psychologist, both of whom were
major contributors to the final report submitted to the State of Illinois,
Department of Commerce and Community Affairs, Employment and
Training Services Division.

Bibliography

Arditi, Ralph, Frederick Goldberg, Jr., M. Martha Hartle, John H. Peters,
and William R. Phelps
  1973   "The Sexual Segregation of American Prisons." *Yale Law
          Journal* 82:1229-73.
Cicciu, Gary
  1980   McLean County, Illinois CETA—Personal Interview,
          Bloomington, Illinois.
Davidson, B.
  1980   Research Analyst of the Research and Analysis Subdivision of the
          Illinois Bureau of Employment Security—Personal Interview.
          Bloomington, Illinois.
Fortune, Eddyth P.
  1978   Vocational Profiles of Female Offenders Incarcerated in a
          Southern Correctional Institution. A paper presented at the
          Annual Meeting of the American Society of Criminology. Dallas,
          Texas.
Glick, Ruth M. and Virginia V. Neto
  1977   National Study of Women's Correctional Programs. Washington,
          D.C.: National Institute of Law Enforcement and Criminal Justice,
          Law Enforcement Assistance Administration.
Hendrix, Omar
  1972   *A Study in Neglect: A Report on Women Prisoners.* New York:
          The Women's Prison Association.
Herman, Alexis M.
  1979   "If She Were a Carpenter: Nontraditional Apprenticeships for
          Women in Prison." *Corrections Today* 41:24-5, 28, 38, 56.
Illinois Bureau of Employment Security
  1980   "Nonagricultural Wage and Salary Employment Estimates."
          Labor Trends. Bloomington, Illinois. SMSA.
Lehtinen, M. W.
  1977   "Women's Corrections: Problems and Future Prospects."
          Quarterly Journal of Corrections 1:34-39.

McArthur, Virginia A.
1974   *From Convict to Citizen: Programs for the Woman Offender.*
Washington, D C: District of Columbia Commission on the Status
of Women.
Miller, E. E.
1977   "Woman Offender and Community Corrections," in E. E. Miller
and M. R. Montilia, (eds.), *Corrections in the Community—
Success Models in Correctional Reform.* Reston, VA: Reston
Publishing Company, Inc.
National Council on Crime and Delinquency
1976   *Recommendations: The Female Offender—Policy Statement.*
Washington, D C: U.S. Department of Justice.
North, D. S.
1977   "Women Offenders—Breaking the Training Mold." *Manpower*
7:13-19.
Price, Ray
1977   "The Forgotten Female Offender." *Crime and Delinquency*
23:101-8.
Simon, Kenneth
1980   Director, McLean County, Illinois Court Services—Personal
Interview and Agency Data.
Sorensen, Virginia
1978   Women in Prison—Educational and Vocational Needs
Assessment. Unpublished Master's thesis, Governor's State
University.
U. S Department of Justice
1979   *Source book of Criminal Justice Statistics—1978.* Washington,
D.C.: National Criminal Justice Information and Statistics Service,
Law Enforcement Assistance Administration.
U. S Department of Labor
1976   *Female Offenders—Problems and Programs.* Washington, D.C.:
American Bar Association.
U.S. Department of Labor
1977   Employment Standards Administration, Women's Bureau.
Employment Needs of Women Offenders—A Program Design.
Washington, D.C., Pamphlet No. 13 by E. Denison.

chapter 8

Probation, Parole, Power, and Women Offenders

From Patriarchal Parameters to Participatory Empowerment

Joseph W. Rogers
New Mexico State University

"The neglect of the concept of power" claims Yeheskel Hasenfeld (1987:470), "is common to most helping professions." Such negligence seems no less true of probation and parole, which is addressed here regarding female offenders. This chapter recognizes not only a social conflict approach but also the feminism depicted by Charlotte Bunch (1981) as "transformational politics." Operating at a dual level embracing both personal and social change, it promotes individual and collective involvement and liberation. Carolyn Morell (1987:147-48) describes its overarching idealism as follows:

> The broad goal of feminism is not limited to the elimination of
> dominant-subordinate relationships between sex groups but

aims at the dismantling of all permanent power hierarchies in which one category of humans dominates or controls another category of humans. Therefore, feminism aims at a complete method of releasing human power and social power for the welfare of all.

This chapter will discuss the importance of client empowerment for women probationers and parolees as follows: (1) the female component of probation and parole; (2) roles of probation and parole officers *vis-a-vis* clients; (3) creation of a client-empowerment model for female offenders; and (4) conclusion.

Probation and Parole: The Female Component

Today there are approximately 3.5 million persons under some form of community correctional supervision, thus approaching 2 percent of our adult population in jail, in prison, on probation, or on parole (Bureau of Justice Statistics, December, 1989: Front cover). Many of these probationers and parolees are women. In fact, the rate for women being sent to jail and prison has increased more rapidly than that of men in some recent years. During 1989 some 2 million women were arrested with over 25,000 becoming prison inmates. From 1983 to 1987, the number of women incarcerated increased 53 percent in contrast to 31 percent for men (Bureau of Justice Statistics, Multiple Sources, 1986-1989). Jails not only serve as penal sanctions but as holding facilities pending court disposi- tions, transfer to correctional institutions, or transfer to another jurisdiction. According to the Bureau of Justice Statistics (1988:49), of 100 *felony* court sentences in 1985, 45 would be given prison terms; 7 would receive jail time only; and 48 (the modal category) would be placed on probation (26 probation only; 22 probation with jail time).

Because there are over 2.25 million people on probation, its crucial role in corrections is evident. Moreover, should the 7 percent annual rate of increase continue, the number of probationers will double to 4.5 million within ten years.

Data also are available for parolees. Two *differences* are striking: (1) while the 7 percent of persons on parole are women, this is *less* than the proportion on probation (16.1 percent); however, (2) the 1986-87 comparison of *annual increase* of female parolees (18.8 percent) far exceeds the 6.8 percent growth rate of female proba- tioners, a rate so high that the 1987 number of women parolees (24,096) would double in just four years should it continue! During

1986 alone more than 17,000 women were conditionally released to some form of community supervision, while another 3,721 were unconditionally released (e.g., sentence expiration or commutation).

In summary, a substantial number of women reside in the community under correctional supervision: about 310,000 on probation; approximately 25,000 on parole. These numbers are increasing at an annual growth rate of 7 percent for female probationers, and 19 percent for women parolees; the overwhelming bulk (95 percent) of both categories are under state supervision. When one compares these 335,000 cases with a single-day combined count of 52,000 incarcerated women in jails and prisons, their significance is pronounced.

Probationers are drawn from the pool of convicted offenders who are sentenced to a period of supervision in the community with the understanding that violators of probation will be returned to the court for reconsideration and probation may be revoked. In contrast, the parole decision is usually made by a parole board/commission after the person has served a portion of her/his prison sentence. Parolees, therefore, are drawn from a smaller number of women. Parolees who fail to comply with regulations of supervision may be returned to the parole board/commission for reconsideration. If parole is revoked, the offender is returned to prison to complete the sentence.

As discussed in chapters one and two, researchers (e.g., Erez, 1988; McCarthy and McCarthy, 1984; Pollock-Byrne ;1990; Renzetti and Curran, 1989; Steffensmeier, 1980; Weisheit and Mahan; 1988; and Wolfe, Cullen, and Cullen; 1984) have found that women offenders are predominantly petty property offenders who are young, minorities, poor, undereducated, vocationally unskilled, unmarried, and mothers of one or more children. Since surveys of prison populations (e.g., Glick and Neto, 1977; Pollock-Byrne, 1990) have reported similar population characteristics, clients for probation and parole are likely to be black or Hispanic, poorly educated, occupationally disadvantaged, unmarried, and the mother of at least one child.

Probation/Parole Officer Roles

There are a number of excellent discourses and typologies (e.g., Allen, et al, 1985; Glaser, 1969; Ohlin, Piven, and Pappenfort, 1956; O'Leary and Duffee, 1971; and Tomaino, 1975) that examine what officers emphasize as important in supervision of probationers and parolees. Two classic typologies delineate 4 or 5 models of officers with variations of high or low emphasis on the person or the community (O'Leary and Duffee; 1971) and rehabilitation or control (Tomaino, 1975).

For example, the ideal model for O'Leary and Duffee (1971) would be high on concern for the person and high on concern for community change. This would not only assist women offenders as persons to effect changes in their lives but would involve efforts to improve the social environment surrounding them. Tomaino's typology identifies an ideal officer who seeks to integrate the often conflicting concerns for community protection (control) and offender welfare (rehabilitation). This means the officer stresses goals rather than personality traits. The officer and the offender work together to create conditions enabling the latter to succeed. Underlying this role preference is the notion that persons are more likely to be "rehabilitated" when they internalize expected behavior and can exert adequate self-control.

Unfortunately, many women offenders may never encounter such idealism in the real world of corrections. In his study of probation officers in two California counties, John Rosecrance (1985; 1988) found probation officers worked in a system dominated by routinization, organizational maintenance, and the officers' fear of criticism. To make matters worse, Whitehead and Gunn (1988) found in their research in New York, Indiana, Connecticut, and Pennsylvania that both job dissatisfaction and "burnout" were widespread among some 400 probation/parole employees. Many of their concerns centered on administrative and court-related problems, similar to findings about police-officer job stress.

The officers found in Rosecrance's (1985; 1988) study more accurately reflect O'Leary and Duffee's (1971) restraint type officer who is low on emphasis on the person and low on emphasis on the community. This person is concerned with rule maintenance, bureaucratic efficiency, and public opinion. High risks are avoided in favor of tight and prompt law enforcement.

The roles that probation and parole officers play *vis-a-vis* their clients can and do make a difference in outcomes (see Gendreau and Andrews, 1989). We should never underestimate the importance of everyday decisions—both large and small—that may seriously affect individual futures. For this reason we cannot allow the professional demise described above by Rosecrance (1985; 1988) to become commonplace. When this happens, the officers suffer occupational "burnout" which has been aptly described by Maslach (1978:56) as:

. . . the gradual loss of caring about the people they work with. Over time they find that they simply cannot sustain the kind of personal care and commitment called for in the personal encounters that are the essence of their job.

Toward a Client Empowerment Model

The assertion that "a mind is a terrible thing to waste" applies to anyone whose opportunity to succeed is suppressed. As with many minority groups, we too often underestimate the potential locked inside female offenders. In the first edition of this anthology, Rogers (1985:148) argued for the importance of the voice of women inmates whom he found to be empathetic, inquiring, sensitive, perceptive, and intelligently discriminating. The degrading stereotypes of imprisoned women needed to be challenged and defeated by further research. As reported above, many of these women are poorly educated and occupationally disadvantaged. The suggestion by Moyer [Simmons] and Rogers (1970:74) that role ambiguity may partially explain high violation rates for young women parolees is easily understandable. Given maturity and more clearly defined roles, such women may better discover more satisfying and secure lives in the community.

Modern social conflict theorists, including contemporary feminists have addressed such maladies, pointing to persistent patriarchy as one link in the chain of female subjugation. Janet A. Nes and Peter Iadicola (1989:14) define patriarchy as "the institutionalized system of male dominance and control over women. Originally based on biological differences, patriarchy currently depends on ideology, law, and violence (such as rape and spouse abuse) for its survival." A key word here is "institutionalized" which underscores the intergenerational and pervasive nature of the problem.

Such entrenchment, as Sara E. Kestenbaum (1977) and other advocates of women's liberation have long promoted, must be addressed by programs (e.g., employment) that encourage the return of female offenders to mainstream society. To be sure, the argument here is not simply one of idle blame on a single factor or our institutional past. As Kathleen Daly (1989) has demonstrated in her study of two court systems (New York and Seattle) multiple variables are involved, at least in criminal court decisions. Arguing that neither the male-centered conflict, labeling perspectives, nor the paternalism thesis sufficiently explain the logic of court decision making, Daly calls for more research on "how familial-based justice practices are classed, raced, and gendered (p. 186)." As we remain sensitive to vestiges of patriarchy, we must maintain awareness about continuing controversies. Nor should we assume, of course, a single united front of feminism when Eric Plutzer's (1988) research exposes us to some of the ideological diversity and differential commitment among women (also see Nes and Iadicola, 1989).

Social work as a profession (to which we shall link probation and parole for our purposes here) is currently exploring feminist perspectives. For instance, Morell (1987:147) modifies Ruth Smalley's (1967) definition of social work slightly, but significantly. (Morell's changes in parentheses):

> The underlying purpose of all social work (feminism) effort is to release human power in individuals for personal fulfillment and social good, and to release social power for the creation of the kinds of society, social institutions and social policy which make self-realization (self-determination) most possible for all men (people).

Reacting to oppression based on membership in some category or group (rather than based on personal qualities), Morell (1987:148-50) calls for social work integration through a feminist approach in which "cause *is* function." By this she means that purpose and process are inseparable and must proceed in a unified direction not only to reformulate practice models but to resist those social conditions that burden people.

Congruent with the above, Hasenfeld (1987:469) argues that the effectiveness of social work practice is predicated on the enhancement of the power resources of clients and workers. Defining power as an integral component of social work practice, Hasenfeld (1987:470-71) identifies four major sources of that power: (1) the power of *expertise* derived from access to and command of special knowledge; (2) *referent* power or persuasion emanating from interpersonal skills, especially the capability to develop empathy, trust, and rapport with clients; (3) *legitimate* power — an appeal to dominant cultural values and authoritative norms; and (4) most importantly of all, power exercised through organizational control of resources and services to be dispensed to clients. Such power is reinforced, states Hasenfeld, by the fact that clients must relinquish a measure of personal control over their own fate to the agency when aid is sought. For court attached probation and parole agencies, the additional power of law, court orders, and conditions of community release must be added as a fifth form.

Given the authority and explicitly delineated control over

probationers and parolees, inequality of power between clients and officers becomes a fundamental assumption. In contrast to many other social agencies where clients voluntarily seek the assistance of social workers, persons on probation and parole must be viewed as commonly reluctant, involuntary subjects under surveillance of assigned monitors, albeit friendly, empathetic counselors. This recognition (or concession) need not deter us from developing a client empowerment model from a feminist perspective, a task to which we now turn.

A Client Empowerment Model
A Tentative Proposal for Women on Probation and Parole

[E]mpowerment is a process through which clients obtain resources—personal, organizational, and community—that enable them to gain greater control over their environment and to attain their aspirations (Hasenfeld, 1987:478-79).

Hasenfeld's (1987:479) four principal courses of action to enhance individual empowerment are applicable to women offenders as well as to general social service clients if adapted as follows:

(1) reduce probationer and parolee need for particular resources and services (e.g. enable the person to obtain meaningful work and to become financially self-supporting).

(2) increase the range of alternatives through which needs can be met (e.g. introduce working mothers to preschool and low cost child care services allowing more freedom for work and education).

(3) increase client value to the community in which they live (e.g. encourage offenders to serve in voluntary roles in such groups as Alcoholics Anonymous, Co-Dependency sessions, or Parents Anonymous for Child Abusers).

(4) reduce agency alternatives within the key option of providing needed resources and services (e.g. collective advocacy of the short and long range merits of offender reintegration over recidivism and reincarceration).

Operating at three levels, worker-client, organizational, and policy, officers and their agencies must be sensitive to and informative about such matters as (a) rights and responsibilities; (b) education, training, and job opportunities; (c) effectively meeting the clients' basic needs; (d) developing personal and interpersonal skills; (e) effectively handling stress; (f) establishing linkages to new friendship networks; (g) identifying and locating multiple sources of information, expertise, and independence; and (h) avoiding the familiar "we-they" syndrome where officers and clients are perceived as mutual enemies.

It is also appropriate to ask whether programs should take into account differential roles or needs of the female offenders. Belinda and Bernard McCarthy (1984:282) answer affirmatively:

> In regard to their problems and needs, criminal offenders are more alike than different. They need education, job training and placement, and counseling to be self-sufficient and to resolve various personal problems. Female offenders do have special needs, however, simply because the roles they tend to occupy in society are different from those held by males. Because women have children, they have special pressures and responsibilities; the financial demands and the all-encompassing managerial and emotional task of child rearing must be met. Regardless of the manner in which these obligations are performed, women with children must find the means to support themselves and their children.

In a cogent analysis, the McCarthys (1984:282-83) remind us that most female offenders are ill prepared for the world of work, particularly for those positions needed to provide adequate support for a family. Why is this? At least five reasons are relevant: (1) many women, especially those in the "extremely disadvantaged segments of society," are seldom encouraged to excel academically, much less to gain a basic education. (2) Such individuals commonly view life in dead-end fashion, captives of an "endless procession" of menial jobs. (3) Routes outward and upward, through semi-skilled or skilled employment, are generally perceived as "mysterious, arduous, and risky" ventures. (4) For many of these women, personal achievement may pose a threat to their interpersonal relationships with significant male figures. (5) Many of them continue to be taught dependent behavior patterns while, conversely, failing to learn ambition, discipline, and other characteristics to get ahead. Accordingly, women offenders need to learn how to become confident, independent, educated, and employable—sufficiently so, to enable them to earn a living to support themselves and their children.

Table 1 details facilitation of client empowerment as a means of achieving goals and making good choices. In this model, probation and parole officers must balance the restraints of legal and organizational requirements with the role expectations rooted in a feminist perspective and a transition of power to one's clientele.

Table 1
A Tentative Client-Empowerment Model for Women
on Probation and Parole*

Dimensions	Feminist Perspectives
Selected Aspects and Assumptions	Although males and females may be deemed similar, some feminists perceive women as more caring and spiritual; men more individualistic and power seeking. Patriarchy is widespread and reinforced by many social institutions, thus giving rise to gender inequality, even oppression. Race and sex are illegitimate discriminators which benefit males in particular. Sex-role socialization promotes female acceptance of their subjugation and secondary positions. Although some women should become more like men . . . more assertive, competitive, individualistic and possessing the same privileges, more radical feminists argue that men should become more like women with positive values and attitudes transcending traditional male-female dichotomies.
Problem Identification and Assessment	Recognize individual shortcomings, including those stemming from malsocialization, noting any linkages to gender related dominance. Identify structure-related difficulties and the interaction between client deficiencies and access to opportunities. Search for institutional network support. Assess these in terms of types and degree, listing priorities and availability of social psychological and institutional supports.
Treatment Goals and Strategies	Basic goals include enhancement of individual and collective awareness of appropriate roles for women to remove structural blockages to advancement, to establish a support network, and to empower clients through available, meaningful choices. Beyond consciousness-raising of one's potential as a woman, an array of strategies may be utilized — casework, family therapy, psychotherapy, group treatment, community acceptance and change client advocacy (ombudspersons), etc.

* An adaptation of Tables 1 and 2 from James A. Nes and Peter Iadicola, "Toward a Definition of Feminist Social Work: A Comparison of Liberal, Radical, and Socialist Models," *Social Work*, Vol. 34, No. 1 (January 1989):12-21. This adaptation draws primarily on their portrayal of a liberal feminist model but combined with selected views from radical feminism.

Conclusion

The participatory empowerment of women probationers and parolees has numerous benefits. Not only does such an approach present a correction to negative stances steeped in paternalism and patriarchy, but it includes a constructive format of alternatives to criminal recidivism. Simultaneously this stance reiterates the importance of individual, organizational, community, and societal considerations on behalf of the worthy goal of a law abiding citizenry reaching for a higher level and quality of life. No one, particularly this author, claims such ideals would be easy to achieve; however, our professional literature increasingly seems to be exploring ways and means of enhancing client autonomy and female identity (for example see De Voe, 1990; Dovidio, Allen, and Schroeder, 1990; McBride, 1990).

In the process, we must remain cognizant of what Sue Mahan (1984) has described as the "imposition of despair" characteristic of so many women in prison. Replacing the alienation of such women with the aims of participatory empowerment represents a worthy cause on behalf of a criminal justice system and the persons flowing through it.

Bibliography

Allen, Harry E., Chris W. Eskridge, Edward J. Latessa, and Gennaro F. Vito.
   1985   *Probation and Parole in America.* New York: Free Press.
Bunch, Charlotte
   1981   *Feminism in the 80's. . . Facing Down the Right.* Denver, CO: Inkling Press.
Bureau of Justice Statistics
   1988   *B.J.S. Data Report, 1987.* Washington, DC: U.S. Department of Justice.
Bureau of Justice Statistics
   1989   *Correctional Populations in the United States, 1986.* Washington, DC: U.S. Department of Justice.
Bureau of Justice Statistics
   1987   *Correctional Populations in the United States, 1985.* Washington, DC: U.S. Department of Justice.
Bureau of Justice Statistics
   1987   *Jail Inmates, 1986.* Washington, DC: U.S. Department of Justice.
Daly, Kathleen
   1989   "Neither Conflict Nor Labeling Nor Paternalism Will Suffice." Intersections of Race, Ethnicity, Gender, and Family in Criminal Court Decisions." *Crime and Delinquency* 35:136-68.

De Voe, Doug
  1990   "Feminist and Nonsexist Counseling: Implications for the Male
          Counselor." *Journal of Counseling and Development* 69:33-36.
Dovidio, John F., David A. Schroeder, and Judith L. Allen
  1990   "Specificity of Empathy-Induced Helping: Evidence for Altruistic
          Motivation." *Journal of Personality and Psychology* 59:249-60.
Erez, Edna
  1988   "The Myth of the New Female Offender: Some Evidence from
          Attitudes toward Law and Justice." *Journal of Criminal Justice*
          16:499-509.
Gendreau, Paul and D.A. Andrews
  1989   "What the Meta-Analyses of the Offender Treatment Literature
          Tells Us About What Works." Unpublished paper.
Glaser, Daniel
  1969   "The Effectiveness of a Prison and Parole System." Indianapolis,
          IN: Bobbs-Merrill.
Glick, R. and V. Neto
  1977   *National Study of Women's Correctional Programs.* Washington,
          DC: U.S. Government Printing Office.
Hasenfeld, Yeheskel
  1987   "Power in Social Work Practice." *Social Service Review*
          61:469-83.
Kestenbaum, Sara E.
  1977   "Women's Liberation for Women Offenders." *Social Casework*
          (February):77-83.
Mahan, Sue
  1984   "Imposition of Despair: An Ethnography of Women in Prison."
          Crime and Justice 7:101-29.
Maslach, C.
  1978   "Job Burn-out: How People Cope." *Public Welfare* 36:56-58.
McBride, Martha C.
  1990   "Autonomy and the Struggle for Female Identity: Implications for
          Counseling Women." *Journal of Counseling and Development*
          69:22-26.
McCarthy, Belinda Rodgers and Bernard J. McCarthy
  1984   *Community-Based Corrections.* Monterey, CA: Brooks/Cole.
Morell, Carolyn
  1987   "Cause *Is* Function: Toward a Feminist Model of Integration in
          Social Work." *Social Service Review* 61:144-54.
Moyer [Simmons], Imogene and Joseph W. Rogers
  1970   "The Relationship Between Type of Offense and Successful
          Postinstitutional Adjustment of Female Offenders." *Criminology*
          7:68-76.
Nes, Janet A. and Peter Iadicola
  1989   "Toward a Definition of Feminist Social Work: A Comparison of
          Liberal, Radical, and Socialist Models." *Social Work* 34:12-21.

Ohlin, Lloyd E., Herman Piven, and D.M. Pappenfort
1956 "Major Dilemmas of the Social Worker in Probation and Parole." *National Probation and Parole Association Journal* (2):21-25.
O'Leary, Vincent and David Duffee
1971 "Correctional Policy: A Classification of Goals Designed for Change." *Crime and Delinquency* 17:373-86.
Pollock-Byrne, Joycelyn M.
1990 *Women, Prison, and Crime.* Pacific Grove, CA: Brooks/Cole.
Plutzer, Eric
1988 "Women's Support of Feminism." *American Sociological Review* 53:640-49.
Renzetti, Claire M. and Daniel J. Curran
1989 *Women, Men and Society: The Sociology of Gender.* Boston, MA: Allyn and Bacon.
Rogers, Joseph W.
1989 "The Greatest Correctional Myth: Winning the War on Crime through Incarceration." *Federal Probation* 53:21-28
Rogers, Joseph W.
1985 "Women Inmate Views on Parole: A Belated Report." Pp. 129-52 in Imogene L. Moyer (ed.), *The Changing Roles of Women in the Criminal Justice System.* Prospect Heights, IL: Waveland Press.
Rosecrance, John
1988 "Maintaining the Myth of Individualized Justice: Probation Presentence Reports." *Justice Quarterly* 5:235-56.
Smalley, Ruth
1967 *Theory for Social Work Practice.* New York: Columbia University Press.
Steffensmeier, Darrell J.
1980 "Sex Differences in the Pattern of Adult Crime, 1965-1977: A Review and Assessment." *Social Forces* 57:566-84.
Tomaino, Louis
1975 "The Five Faces of Probation." *Federal Probation* 39:42-45.
Weisheit, Ralph and Sue Mahan
1988 *Women, Crime, and Criminal Justice.* Cincinnati, OH: Anderson.
Wolfe, Nancy T., Frances T. Cullen, and John B. Cullen
1984 "Describing the Female Offender: A Note on the Demographics of Arrest." *Journal of Criminal Justice* 12:483-92.
Whitehead, John T. and Susan Gunn
1988 "Probation Employee Job Attitudes: A Qualitative Analysis." *Crime and Justice* 9:143-64.

Part II

Women Victims and the Criminal Justice System

Introduction to Part II

T he resurgence of the feminist movement in the 1970s along with the development of the victim's rights movement brought recognition to the plight of the victim. Prior to this era, unless the victim was considered as precipitating, initiating or criminally provoking the offender, little notice was given to the victim's relevance in criminal proceedings. With the renewal of the feminist movement came the recognition of the needs of the female victim. However, the majority of the empirical research focusing on the victim remained concentrated on males, unless the incident was classed as female oriented, such as rape, spouse abuse, and incest. Recently, both qualitative and quantitative studies have begun to incorporate women in the analysis of victim causation, victim-offender relationships and gender differences in victimization frequencies (Bowker, 1979, 1981; Elias, 1984, 1986; Karmen, 1984; Mann, 1988, 1990; NCS, 1985, 1987).

The Concept of Victimology

Victimology, as a subdiscipline of criminology, was developed by traditional male criminologists (Mendelsohn, 1963; von Hentig, 1948; and Wolfgang, 1958). It is characterized by an investigation of and concentration on the victim of a crime, including the victim-offender relationship, the ways in which the victim might share at least some of the responsibility for the criminal act, and the utilization of the results to assess the amount of crime committed (Weis and Borges, 1973:74). While the concept of victim-precipitated crimes may be applied to many different kinds of unlawful acts, it is most readily applied to those crimes which are directed toward women. This is clearly illustrated in Amir's study of rape in Philadelphia. He states: "In a way, the victim is always the cause of the crime . . ." and "If the victim is not solely responsible for what becomes the unfortunate event, at least she is often a complementary factor" (Amir, 1967:493).

These perceptions of victims of crime have flourished in a patriarchal family system. In such a system, the men are established in positions of authority as heads of the family and as officials in the criminal justice system, while most women are located in positions as subordinates. This differential power between men and women is reflected in the early statutes that made women the property of male family members. Men were also in positions of authority to interpret the laws and to establish the procedures for enforcement and prosecution of violators of the laws. Conflict theory is, thus, applicable to the treatment of women who are victims of violent and domestic crimes by male offenders. The concept of victimology as applied to crimes such as rape, spouse abuse, and incest works to the advantage of men.

Current Responses to the Concept of Victimology

Skogan, Lurigio and Davis (1990:7) report that crime will either touch most Americans or affect the lives of a friend, relative or acquaintance. The probability is greater among some groups than among others, just as fear of crime varies for different groups. Braungart and Hoyer (1982:62) and Toseland (1982:205) report that older black women living alone in a large urban area who are in poor health or who have recently been victims of crime are most apt to express fear of crime. Toseland (1982) further states that fear of crime appears to be greatest among those who are relatively powerless to do anything to prevent victimization.

The victimization studies reported in the National Crimes Surveys provide data for the following major offenses: rape, robbery, assault, larceny, burglary, and theft. These data indicate that men are subjected to personal crimes of theft at a rate about 25 percent higher than women and to violent crimes at nearly twice the rate suffered by women (Bowker, 1981:160). However, crimes of theft with contact are slightly more likely to be committed against women, and rape victimization statistics are dominated by women. While Karmen (1984:59-64) indicates that men are mugged and robbed twice as often as women, women are more likely than men to resist robbers, to be physically injured during robberies, and to call the police when they are victimized by robbers.

However, some women are more likely to be victimized than others. Groups with inferior education, inferior housing, high unemployment rates and low income, not only have higher arrest rates for crimes and violent acts than other groups, but also experience higher victimization frequencies (U.S. Department of Justice, 1985, 1987). Persons most likely to be victims of violence are nonwhite, lower-class individuals (Elias, 1986). For example, the frequency of victimization of blacks is seven times higher for assaults and twenty-five times higher for robberies with assaults

than the same offenses committed against whites (Elias, 1986).
Victimization rates for black women, sixteen to nineteen years of
age, are higher than they are for men in general (Bowker, 1981:161).
Karmen (1984:59-64) reports that married men and women have
lower victimization rates than divorced and separated people. In
addition, Bowker (1981:165) found that divorced or separated
women are more likely than married women to be victims of rape,
robbery, assault, and theft. These data, however, are based on
official survey data and may not include many incidents of victimization of women in the home.

Unemployed women whose activities are primarily restricted to
the home may indicate higher victimization frequencies of spousal
abuse than employed females (Bowker, 1979; Pirro, 1982; Radford,
1987). Pirro (1982:352) further notes that physical violence occurs
between members of the same family more often than it does be·
tween any other category of individuals. The isolation and restric-
tion of a woman within her home often increases her dependence
on the man—thus making it easier for the woman to be assaulted
and abused in the privacy of the home (Radford, 1987). However,
females within the work force may have a higher victimization
frequency of sexual harassment, sexual abuse, discrimination,
assault and robbery (Lynch, 1987; Maume, 1989; Radford, 1987).

There is reason to believe that under some conditions victimization experiences may facilitate criminal behavior (Pirro, 1982;
Singer, 1986). Children, by witnessing violence between their
parents or through continued physical punishment, learn early that
violence is an acceptable means of problem-solving (Pirro, 1982).
The socialization of traditional sex roles may also contribute to
victimization. The traditional concept of masculinity is one of
dominance and power, while femininity is conceived as passive and
submissive (Adler, 1985). As young people begin to learn about
sexuality through socialization into stereotypical sex roles by peers
and/or adults, they learn to accept their roles of male power and
aggressiveness and female inferiority and submissiveness (Adler,
1985; Manle and Hirschel, 1988). Role identification through
socialization is visible by the increase in the frequency of reported
criminal offenses against females. Indeed, the frequency rate would
be even higher if certain crimes did not go unreported by the
victims.

Crimes of rape, spouse abuse, and incest have been the topics of
most of the research on women victims. Traditionally, research on
women who are victims of rape, spouse abuse, and incest was
conducted by male criminologists who viewed these women as
contributing to the crime. The past decade has witnessed the return

of the victim as a necessary entity in the criminal justice system. Although much of the interest is in the form of securing victims' cooperation in the apprehension and conviction of offenders, the interest has contributed significantly to recognition of the needs and rights of victims. Concern for the innocent victims of violent crimes took the form of advocacy of victims' compensation statutes in the 1960s (Skogan, Wesley, Lurigio and Davis, 1990; Smith, Sloan and Ward, 1990). By the 1970s state politicians had introduced and gained financial support for victim assistance programs, under the probing of grass-root victim advocacy groups (Skogan, et al., 1990).

Feminist groups in particular have helped to sensitize people to the issues of rape, spouse abuse, and sexual abuse of children. Rose (1977:75) credits the women's movement with bringing the issue of rape to the public's attention. Similarly Tierney (1982:207) notes that wife beating became an object of media attention and government policy because of the development of a social movement and the changing roles of women in society. MacFarlane (1978:81) reports that "growing interest and social action on behalf of battered children over the past ten years have highlighted an even more distasteful form of child victimization: sexual abuse of children." Interest in the victimization of women through sexual harassment has increased recently as more women move into traditional male occupations especially in criminal justice agencies. This book will concentrate on past and current research in these areas.

New Research on Women Victims and the Criminal Justice Systems

Research during the last decade has drawn attention to the "revictimization" of women victims of rape, spouse abuse, and incest by officials in criminal justice agencies. While a few of these research studies have included an examination of the treatment of these victims by officials of criminal justice agencies, most studies have concentrated on the general myths and problems involving these women victims.

The chapters in this section concentrate on the roles of women victims in the criminal justice system. Most importantly, all of these chapters focus on the issues from the perspective of the women who are the victims of these crimes. The conflict perspective is quite evident in these chapters. The dominance of men in the criminal justice system has resulted in the neglect of women victims of rape,

spouse abuse, incest, and sexual harassment. Since male legislators, police officers, prosecutors, and judges readily identified with
male offenders, male officials often assumed that some incidents
were private, domestic affairs or that the women precipitated the
crime in some way. These chapters will point to some changes in
the laws and policies and will present issues regarding the validity
of some of the current assumptions and practices within the
criminal justice system.

The chapter by Goodstein and Lutze, "Rape and Criminal Justice
System Responses," applies feminist theories to examine rape as
a social problem. The authors point to the myths about rape and
rape victims as well as exploring community and criminal justice
system responses to rape victims. While changes in the law and
criminal justice policies have become official, this chapter suggests
that many of the myths and the sex role stereotypes are still
widespread.

In the chapter, "Perceptions of Woman Battering: A Review of
the Literature and an Empirical Test of Law Enforcement Officers,"
Belknap applies conflict theory to explore issues of the patriarchy
and power differentials in the context of myths about battered
women. A unique feature of this chapter is the discussion of
battering within lesbian relationships. This is an important
contribution to the literature; historically, criminology has failed
to examine issues regarding lesbians in any roles in the criminal
justice system. Belknap also includes research studies on battering
across racial and ethnic groups as well as a cross-cultural study.
Finally, she reports the results of her own research study of police
perceptions of battering.

Schwartz and Miller in their chapter, "Dealing with Child Sexual
Assault: The Victim, The Offender, and Society," explore the myths
and controversies concerning the effects of child sexual abuse on
the victim and the most appropriate way to deal with the abusers.
The chapter also examines issues regarding the child victim/witness
in the criminal courtroom. Finally, these authors point to the patriarchal society that legitimizes male dominance in the home and
allows the man in the family to get away with battering, rape, and
child sexual abuse.

The last chapter in this section. "Sexual Harassment in the
Criminal Justice System," by Erez and Tontodonato discusses the
development of the concept of sexual harassment that emerged as
women entered nontraditional occupations, particularly in criminal
justice agencies. The authors suggest that sexual harassment, like
rape or domestic violence, is a phenomenon in which cultural

stereotypes and beliefs about gender roles have resulted in the widespread acceptability of the victimization of women.

All of these chapters were written to examine the changing status of women victims and the influence of the criminal justice system's responses to women victims. They also raise important issues and questions for future research regarding the responses of officials in criminal justice agencies to these women victims.

Note

I am grateful to Marian Whitson for her assistance in the survey of the literature and in the writing of the first draft of this Introduction to Part II.

Bibliography

Adler, Christine
   1985   "Sexually Aggressive Behavior." *Crime and Delinquency* 31:306-31.
Amir, Menachem
   1967   "Victim Precipitated Forcible Rape." *Journal of Criminal Law, Criminology, and Police Science* 58:493-502.
Bowker, Lee H.
   1979   "The Criminal Victimization of Women." *Victimology: An International Journal* 4:371-84.
   1981   *Women and Crime in America*. New York: Macmillan Publishing Company.
Braungart, Richard G. and William J. Hoyer
   1980   "Age, Sex, and Social Factors in Fear of Crime." *Sociological Focus* 13:55-66.
Elias, Robert
   1984   *Victims of the System: Crime Victims and Compensation in American Politics and Criminal Justice*. New Brunswick, NJ: Transaction Books.
   1986   *The Politics of Victimization: Victims, Victimology and Human Rights*. New York: Oxford University Press.
Karmen, Andrew
   1984   *Crime Victims: An Introduction to Victimology*. Monterey, CA: Brooks/Cole Publishing Company.
Lynch, James P.
   1987   "Routine Activity and Victimization at Work." *Journal of Quantitative Criminlogy* 3: 238-300.
MacFarlane, Kee
   1978   "Sexual Abuse of Children." Pp. 81-109 in Jane Roberts Chapman and Margaret Gates (eds.), *The Victimization of Women*. Beverly Hills, CA: Sage Publication.

Mann, Coramae Richey
    1988   "Getting Even? Women Who Kill in Domestic Encounters."
          Justice Quarterly 5:33-46.
    1990   "Black Female Homicide in the United States." *Journal of*
          Interpersonal Violence 5:176-201.
Mannle, Henry W. and J. David Hirschel
    1988   *Fundamentals of Criminology.* Englewood Cliffs, NJ: Prentice
          Hall.
Maume, David Jr.
    1989   "Inequality and Metropolitan Rape Rates: A Routine Activity
          Approach." *Justice Quarterly* 6: 513-29.
Mendelsohn, B.
    1963   "The Origin of the Doctrine of Victimology." *Excerpta*
          Criminologica: 239-44.
Pirro, Jeanine
    1982   "Domestic Violence: The Criminal Court Response." *New York*
          State Bar Journal: 352-57.
Radford, Jill
    1987   "Policing Male Violence—Policing Women." Pp. 30-46 in Jalna
          Hanmer and Mary Maynard (eds.), *Women, Violence and Social*
          Control. Atlantic Highlands: Humanities Press International, Inc.
Rose, Vicki
    1977   "Rape as a Social Problem: A Byproduct of the Feminist
          Movement." *Social Problems* 25:75-89.
Singer, Simon
    1986   "Victims of Serious Violence and their Criminal Behavior:
          Subcultural Theory and Beyond." *Victims and Violence* 1:1-71.
Skogan, Wesley G., Arthur J. Lurigio, and Robert C. Davis
    1990   "Criminal Victimization" Pp. 7-23 in *Victims of Crime: Problems,*
          Policies, and Programs. Newbury Park, CA: Sage Publications.
Smith, Brent L., John J. Sloan and Richard M. Ward
    1990   "Public Support for the Victims Rights Movement: Results of a
          Statewide Survey." *Crime and Delinquency* 36:488-502.
Tierney, Kathleen
    1982   "The Battered Women Movement and the Creation of the Wife
          Beating Problem." *Social Problems* 29:207-20.
Toseland, Ronald W.
    1982   "Fear of Crime: Who is Most Vulnerable?" *Journal of Criminal*
          Justice 10:199-209.
U.S. Department of Justice
    1985   "Criminal Victimization in the United States, 1983: A National
          Crime Survey Report." Washington, D.C.: Bureau of Justice
          Statistics.
    1987   "Criminal Victimization in the United States, 1985: A National
          Crime Survey Report." Washington, D.C.: Bureau of Justice
          Statistics.

Von Hentig, Hans
  1948   *The Criminal and His Victim: Studies in the Sociobiology of Crime.* New Haven: Yale University Press.
Weis, Kurt and Sandra Borges
  1973   "Victimology and Rape: The Case of the Legitimate Victim." *Issues in Criminology* 8:71-113.
Wolfgang, Marvin
  1958   *Patterns in Criminal Homicide.* Philadelphia: University of Pennsylvania Press.

chapter 9

Rape and Criminal Justice System Responses

Lynne Goodstein and Faith Lutze
The Pennsylvania State University

The societal concerns of the 1960s and 1970s focused national attention on the social discontent experienced by racial/ethnic minorities and women. Inspired by the civil rights movement, women began to conceptualize their problems as the result of societal treatment of women as a class. One of the problems identified early in the growth of the feminist movement was sexual violence against women. Both activists and researchers mobilized to the task of dealing with sexual violence. Activists concentrated on change directed at governmental institutions and society in general, while researchers attempted to define the problem, its scope, and to investigate possible solutions.

The early 1970s brought with them new understandings of the biased attitudes and beliefs surrounding rape victims and offenders, attitudes crossing gender and racial boundaries. Activists and researchers discovered that women were being victimized by male sexual violence with little response from the criminal justice system

(Giacopassi and Wilkinson, 1985; Russell, 1974), except in instances where black men were accused of raping white women. In this instance, the system could be brutal to the offender (LaFree, 1989; Russell, 1974; Walsh, 1987; Williams and Holmes, 1981).

As the women's movement gathered strength and fought injustices perpetrated against women by the community as well as the criminal justice system, rape became a catalyst for change. Feminists initiated community groups which pressured governmental leaders for legal mandates and policy changes. Significant changes in law and policy have occurred in the ensuing two decades (Berger, Searles and Neuman, 1988; Loh, 1981), yet women continue to be victims of male sexual violence at an alarming rate.

The Extent of the Problem

The rate of rape has often been difficult to measure due to underreporting by victims to the police and police failure to recognize victim's accounts as rape. Recent studies, however, have reported alarming rates of rape. In 1987 the National Crime Survey (NCS) estimated that 1.3 women in 1,000, age 12 and over, had been victimized during that year. Women of color were more likely to be victimized than white women (1.8 and 0.5 percent, respectively) and 49.6 percent of victims of completed rape knew their attackers (Flanagan and Jamieson, 1988).

The National Crime Survey which relies upon one member of the household to answer for all residents and does not specifically question respondents about rape victimization, undoubtedly underrepresents the incidence of rape. More reliable figures have been produced through surveys of women, in some cases randomly selected from circumscribed populations. In 1978 Russell (1984) conducted a survey of 930 adult female San Francisco women residents 18 years or older. She found that 44 percent of the respondents reported having been victimized by attempted or completed rape during their lifetimes. Only eight percent of the total number of rapes, completed or attempted, had been reported to the police.

Several studies have been performed on college student populations, all of which demonstrate alarmingly high rates of rape. In 1957 and again in 1977, Kanin (1957; 1984) surveyed college men and women and found that a consistent 25 percent of college women reported having suffered attempted or completed rape. In the early 1980s Mary Koss performed a study of 3,187 college and university women at 32 institutions of higher learning, systematically selected to represent the general college student population. Respondents were asked to indicate whether, since the age of 14, they had been forced to have sexual intercourse against their will. The word "rape" was not used in the questions to avoid missing the "unacknowledged victims." Koss, as reported in Warshaw (1988) reported statistics similar to Kanin's for women's experience with completed (15.3 percent) and attempted (11.8 percent) rape. Of those victims, 84 percent knew their attacker and 57 percent of the rapes or attempted rapes occurred on dates.

While data on the extent of rape may have improved in the last two decades, efforts to explain causes of rape are still speculative and the source of disagreement among theorists.

Theories of Rape

Why do men rape? While numerous theories exist, they can be subsumed into two general categories: (1) psychological or physiological models and (2) sociocultural models. The first model assumes that rapists are driven to rape by either psychological or physiological conditions which are abnormal and differentiate sexual offenders from "normal" males. The second model focuses on social and cultural conditions conducive to the perpetration and acceptance of sexual violence, which may affect any male.

Psychological and Physiological Theories of Rape

Early theorists relied heavily upon psychological explanations of rape. They proposed that men who rape are psychologically maladjusted and suffer from various emotional disorders (Lottes, 1988; Williams and Holmes, 1981). Studies which purportedly demonstrated these theories used psychological tests, intelligence scales, physical measurements, childhood experiences, dreams, and genetic analyses of rapists to test for abnormalities (Check and Malamuth, 1985).

Other theorists attribute men's proclivity to rape to innate physiological characteristics. Males, with higher levels of hormones such as testosterone, (also linked to aggression) are viewed as being incapable of controlling their sexual desires (Ellis, 1989; Lottes, 1988). Some theorists, notably sociobiologists, view males' biological role as propagating the species. Moreover, males, with the potential of fathering large numbers of children throughout their lifetimes, are viewed as being motivated to have sex with multiple partners in order to increase the likelihood that their genetic material will be continued into the next generation. Males who do not have access to legitimate sexual outlets, for instance those who lack the skills to find appropriate mates, are likely to rape. (Ellis, 1989).

Both of these theories have come under criticism for a number of reasons. First, most research attempting to identify psychological or physiological abnormalities among rapists has been based upon populations of convicted rapists confined in penitentiaries. As proportionately few rapists ever come to trial and fewer are imprisoned, (Sheffield, 1987; Temkin, 1986), research data from this population of extreme cases are likely to offer a misleading picture of the characteristics of actual rapists. Moreover, even with such unrepresentative samples, clinical studies have not found much support for psychological explanations of rape (Check and Malamuth, 1985; Lottes, 1988). Second, feminists argue that these theories suggest that rapists are qualitatively different from "normal" males. They present rapists as isolated, mentally deranged individuals who attack female strangers by surprise, apparently rejecting the possibility that rape occurs among acquaintances (Williams and Holmes, 1981). Thirdly, by attributing rape to psychological or physiological causes, these theories appear to absolve perpetrators of responsibility for their offenses. Rapists are characterized as not in control of their sexuality and thus not accountable for their behavior. By characterizing rapists and sexual violence as abnormal, deviant, and infrequent, these theories appear to deny the much more prevalent forms of sexual aggression which occur in more socially normal contexts among individuals previously acquainted (Williams and Holmes, 1981). Feminists have interpreted these theories as justifications for socially accepted male sexual aggression (Griffin, 1982) and fault them for failing to account for social and cultural factors influencing male behavior (Williams and Holmes, 1981).

Sociocultural Explanations of Rape

Rather than concentrating on pathological characteristics of the offender, sociocultural explanations of rape focus on the nature of gender roles in contemporary culture, especially as they pertain to sexual behavior. Gagnon and Simon (1973) coined the term "sexual scripts" to account for "normal" sexual interactions which involved the male as the dominant aggressor, the female as the passive gatekeeper. Supporters of sociocultural explanations of rape argue that "rape occurs in cultures characterized by other forms of violence, that rape is largely an act of male domination, and that rape results from social inequities between the genders" (Lottes, 1988:194).

Interestingly, early sociocultural explanations fell prone to the same type of absolving of rapists' responsibility as the psychological and physiological models. Instead of sexual violence being attributed to uncontrollable male behavior, male accountability was reduced by attributing rape to "victim precipitation," resulting from women's wearing provocative clothing or being out alone at night (Amir, 1971). However slanted these views were, they helped to introduce sociocultural explanations of rape into the mainstream of rape analysis.

Sociocultural explanations have received considerable attention among anthropologists and cross-cultural researchers. For example, Sanday (1981) has demonstrated that not all cultures foster sexual violence against women to the same degree. Moreover, the degree to which a society allows rape is related to the women's general status within that culture. "Rape prone," as opposed to "rape free," societies, view women as inferior to males in terms of power, authority, and decision making ability (Sanday, 1981; Lottes, 1988). These societies also experience higher rates of interpersonal violence, and toughness, aggression, risk-taking, and a casual attitude toward sexuality are evident among males. Recent studies (Costin, 1985; Costin and Schwartz, 1987) of rape in the United States, England, Israel, and West Germany have arrived at similar conclusions. These studies, focusing on disparities between gender roles, have also been cited in attempts to account for high rates of rape in black communities in North America (Costin, 1985; Costin and Schwartz, 1987).

The high rates of rape in African American communities have been attributed by some researchers to the cultural value placed on male aggression (Amir, 1971; LaFree, 1980a). Other studies suggest that black intraracial rape reflects an acting out of the stereotypes of the white majority culture, which "reinforces" the notion that blacks engage in sexual aggression (Curtis, 1976). At this time, relatively little is known of the specific dynamics through which gender and race interact to determine black sexual victimization. Most recent work on rape has focused upon analyses of the effects of the white patriarchal culture on sexual violence.

Feminist Theories of Rape

Some feminist theorists point to the sexual domination of women by men as a primary means through which male power is perpetuated and fostered under a patriarchal system (MacKinnon, 1982). For this reason, considerable attention has been given by feminists to developing a theoretical analysis of sexual violence. Patriarchy refers to the social organization of male dominance which "regulates women to the private realm of family and men to the public sphere of the economy, politics and state" (Caringella-Macdonald, 1988a). The women's position is not only private, it is socially inferior, creating conditions which lead to the creation of rape myths and sex role stereotypes and result in sexual exploitation (Rose, 1977). By linking sexual victimization to the social condition of patriarchy, feminists have further redefined rape not as a crime of uncontrollable sexual passion but one of power and control over women (Brownmiller, 1971; Griffin, 1986). Feminists therefore conclude that if the power of men and women in all spheres (political, domestic, economic, social) were equal, society would be rid of rape.

Early feminist work was based upon anecdotal stories and case studies, often uncovered at feminist sponsored "speakouts." These events, occasionally transcribed and published (Connell and Wilson, 1974), gave women opportunities to share experiences of victimization with one another in a supportive, nonvictim-blaming setting. More recently, studies using conventional social science methodologies have yielded findings consistent with the feminist standpoint. Burt (1980), for example, demonstrated the significant extent to which persons subscribe to "rape myths" and "adversarial sexual beliefs." In a study of cultural myths and supports for rape she found that over half of her respondents agreed that, "If a girl engages in necking or petting and she lets things get out of hand, it is her own fault if her partner forces sex on her" and "Women who get raped while hitchhiking get what they deserve" (p. 223). More generally, this and other studies (Cann, Calhoun, Selby, & King, 1981; Deitz, 1982; Deitz, 1984; Klemmack & Klemmack, 1976) suggested that substantial proportions of United States citizens, male and female, hold beliefs that make it difficult for victims of sexual aggression to be believed, to not be held responsible for their victimization, and to obtain justice. These beliefs have been characterized as "rape myths", which include the following: (1) rape is purely a sex crime; (2) women who are careful can avoid rape; (3) women secretly want to be raped; (4) rapists are usually strangers; (5) women who dress provocatively or act seductively are asking to be raped, and get what they deserve; (6) when rape is inevitable, women should relax and enjoy it; and (7) many women falsely accuse men of rape (Burt, 1980; Burt and Albin, 1981; O'Reilly, 1984).

How do these assumptions about women come about? Theorists point to sex role socialization as the process through which boys come to understand their impending social power and internalize attitudes and behaviors which enable them to exert it. Correspondingly, girls learn of their "place" in relation to men. In our society women are expected to be weak, dependent, inferior and submissive; men are expected to be strong, independent, superior and domineering (Russell, 1974). These expectations about gender roles in general bear heavily upon the development of rape myths and the manifestation of sexual aggression. Men feel it is their "sexual entitlement" to attempt to dominate women and to obtain sex regardless of the desires of their partners. Women are reluctant to be too assertive around men for fear of being perceived as unfeminine or embarrassing their partners, so they may not speak up when their partners make unwelcome advances. These assumptions and communication problems may lead to rape among acquaintances.

Recent studies have begun to substantiate the linkage between conventional gender socialization and the subscription to rape myths (Burt, 1980; Acock and Ireland, 1983; Fischer, 1987; Giacopassi and Dull, 1986). One team of researchers has shown that persons who embody traditional gender roles regard rape as more the woman's fault, believe rape myths, and view the rape victim as experiencing more pleasure and less pain, compared with those of less traditional beliefs (Muehlenhard and McNaughton, 1988). Perhaps most importantly, the more males embody conventional sex roles, the more they indicate a willingness to rape. Check and Malamuth (1985, p.353) found that "men with more stereotyped sex-role beliefs were more likely to indicate that they might commit rape," and in another study these men agreed that they would rape if they could be assured that no one would know (Muehlenhard and MacNaughton, 1988). For women, conforming to conventional gender roles leads to beliefs that "leading men on justifies rape" (Muehlenhard and MacNaughton, 1988, p. 77). Others have shown that those with traditional views of gender believe that sex is an adversarial process, in which the man or the woman could win, but not both (Burt, 1980).

Both race and sex are important in shaping beliefs about rape. Giacopassi and Dull (1986) found race differences on the acceptance of rape myths, with black males more accepting of rape myths and stereotypes than any other grouping. Williams and Holmes (1981) compared Anglos, blacks, and Mexican Americans on their acceptance of rape myths. In terms of traditionality, Mexican Americans scored highest, blacks scored close behind, and Anglos were found to be the least traditional. Another study concerning date rape showed Hispanics to hold more traditional attitudes than "majority" subjects, although attitudes were also found to differ among Hispanics according to gender and their degree of assimilation into the dominant culture (Fischer, 1987).

It is interesting to note such racial/ethnic differences in traditionality, as these discrepancies may affect victim recognition of rape, rates of reporting to the police, and victim recovery rates. We know that the vast majority of rape is intraracial (Flanagan and Jamieson, 1988). If women of color accept more traditional gender roles, they may be less likely to acknowledge that a rape has been committed against them. If they do report the rape to the police, the women may be faced with fellow minority officers who disbelieve their claims. Finally, community institutions responsible for dealing with rape's aftermath may also discount the seriousness of victimizations of women of color, resulting in the victims receiving inadequate post-rape support services. Williams (1984) describes this process, which she argues as being more likely to occur to women victims of color, as "secondary victimization."

The link between traditionality and rape supportive attitudes has been well established. What is known about the next logical link, that between rape supportive attitudes and actual instances of sexual victimization? Do men who subscribe to rape myths rape women with greater frequency? Are conventionally feminine women more likely to be raped? Unfortunately, little research exists on the relationship between rape supportive attitudes and rape proneness. What is available, however, supports this link. For example, in a study of convicted rapists, researchers found that, compared to noncriminals, rapists are more alienated, have greater hostility to women, and are more likely to have a diagnosis of antisocial personality disorder (Scott and Tetreault, 1986). These researchers conclude that "rape is related to sexual stereotyping and conservative attitudes toward women" (p. 379).

Research on nonconvicted date rapists also points to the impact of rape supportive beliefs on men's proclivity to rape. When asked to account for why they had forced a date to have sex against her will, over 90 percent of a sample of college males attributed the sexually offensive incident to the fact that their companions had sexually aroused them and that alcohol was involved (Kanin, 1984). Interestingly, in 68 percent of the incidents where consensual sex play was reported prior to the rape, the woman had stipulated the maximum level of sexual activity in which she was willing to engage. These findings suggest that many of the men who were admittedly involved in date rapes blamed the incident at least partly on the woman's behavior.

Findings concerning acceptance of sex role stereotypes and support of rape myths suggests that traditional attitudes concerning sex and gender roles still exist in our society. Considering that our criminal justice system is a reflection of the greater society, it is reasonable to anticipate that the criminal justice system will embody many of the attitudes and responses to rape displayed in society in general (LaFree, 1980b).

Community Response to Rape

The goal of changing community responses to rape was undertaken by feminists primarily as a grass roots effort in the early 1970's (Temkin, 1986; Walker and Brodsky, 1976). Women began meeting in small groups and sharing their experiences concerning relations with men and sexuality. Strikingly, many of these experiences involved some form of coerced or unwanted sexual activity (Connel and Wilson, 1974; Largen, 1976). Despite the magnitude of victimization that was uncovered in these consciousness raising sessions and speakouts, it became clear that few of these experiences had ever been brought to the attention of the criminal justice system. Moreover, among women who had reported their victimizations to the police and proceeded through the courts, there was grave dissatisfaction with the system's response. Laws and courtroom procedures appeared to be favoring the rapist rather than the victim; the police were accused of treating victims harshly; treatment by medical personnel responsible for collecting evidence was crude and often inadequate (Caringella-MacDonald, 1988b; Temkin, 1986)

In response to the failure of the criminal justice and social service systems to address the needs of victims of sexual assault, community groups were organized and began a two-pronged approach in advocating for change. First, feminist groups organized around the task of helping the victim personally (Rose, 1977). Hotlines and crisis centers were established to assist rape victims with both short and long term services (Largen, 1976). The focus of these services was decidedly feminist. The term "rape victim" was later discarded for "rape survivor," to suggest the woman's ability to overcome the devastation of victimization and reassume control over her life. Counseling, both crisis and longer term, was primarily delivered by nonprofessional sexual assault survivors who had successfully dealt with their own victimization and had undergone extensive training in lay-counseling. The first priority of these centers was the well-being of the woman rather than prosecution of offenders. Should women chose to prosecute, however, counselors would accompany them through all the stages of the investigative and judicial process (Rose, 1977). Many centers also offered self-defense courses to provide women with the confidence and skills to ward off future attackers.

Antirape advocates' second approach focused on the judicial and criminal justice systems. Activists recognized that in order to bring about justice for rape victims, women would have to be willing to prosecute their rapists. Current laws and police procedures at that time were challenged. Suggestions were made for legal and procedural reform.

The Criminal Justice System's Response to Rape

Prior to the rape reformers' campaign to focus public attention on sexual victimization, the criminal justice system's track record on the support of rape victims was poor. Unless a woman was viewed as a victim of a classic "real rape" (Estrich, 1987), that is sexual victimization perpetrated in a violent fashion by a stranger in which the woman physically resisted to the extreme, she did not receive impartial justice through the system (see LaFree, 1980b). If she was raped by an acquaintance or her husband, she was not usually considered to be a victim. In the same vein, if a man accused of rape did not fit the stereotype of a mentally deranged, desperate and violent rapist, a conviction was also unlikely. Even rape victims whose cases were consistent with the "real rape" stereotype met with many obstacles. Their word was often questioned by police officers and investigators, their prior sexual history inevitably brought into the trial; as "witnesses" to the government's case, they were forced to endure the often tedious and drawn out process with no personal advocate, attorney or counselor.

Rape and the Law

Feminists brought attention to rape laws which institutionally reflected acceptance of rape myths concerning many aspects of sexual assault (Cobb and Schauer, 1974; Largen, 1976; LeGrand, 1977). They argued that the laws protected the defendant and questioned the victim's integrity to the point that women were afraid to prosecute their attackers (Lowe, 1984; Minch, Linden and

Johnson, 1987). Their assumption was that until laws were changed, attitudes of police, courts and society as a whole would prevent rape victims from being treated fairly (LeGrand, 1977). Legal reformers, many of them feminist lawyers, law students, and members of local, state and national organizations against sexual violence, sought to remove biases which they believed adversely influenced the outcomes of rape cases. To some extent they have been successful; in some cases, their efforts have been found to have backfired (Estrich, 1987).

What is the legal definition of rape? The traditional, common law definition, which remains the core of most rape statutes today, is: sexual intercourse with a woman who is not the man's wife, by force or threat of force, against her will and without her consent. The definition is straightforward; it says nothing about the victim's past sexual experiences, about her relationship to the rapist (except that they cannot be married), about whether the victim was physically harmed in other ways, in addition to the rape itself. Yet, in the processing cases through the criminal justice system and in applying conventional practices of rape investigation and prosecution, these factors may be crucial to the outcome of the cases.

Schwartz and Clear (1980) note that "American law has developed obstacles to the prosecution of an alleged rape that are unmatched in other types of crime." They argue that prosecution is obstructed by a number of elements of law, including such means as "demanding corroboration by physical evidence of one or more elements of the crime, demanding that the victim prove resistance to her attacker, forcing the victim to prove lack of consent, and allowing the defense to enter into evidence the victim's previous sexual history" (p. 131). Let us review some of the legal obstacles to successful rape prosecutions and consider changes wrought by rape reformers.

The Consent Standard

One such obstacle has been the standard by which women have had to prove nonconsent. For a woman to prove that she did not consent to forced intercourse, traditionally she would have had to attempt to fight off her attacker as hard as she could, to demonstrate "utmost resistance" (Estrich, 1987). This standard appears to be based upon the value of chastity and the fact that women were expected to defend it, almost to their deaths if necessary. Failure to demonstrate this level of resistance could lead to an acquittal. Indeed, this is the case in a classic rape trial which occurred at the turn of the century in Wisconsin. The victim, a sixteen-year-old neighbor of the accused, testified that upon returning from her grandmother's she was accosted by the defendant, tripped to the ground and raped. Crushed by his weight, she indicated that she tried as hard as she could to get away; she screamed as hard as she could, but he put his hand on her mouth until she "was almost strangled." The initial guilty decision was reversed on appeal to the State Supreme Court on the ground that the victim had not adequately demonstrated her nonconsent. To quote the Court, "there must be the most vehement exercise of every physical means or faculty within the woman's power to resist the penetration of her person" (Brown v. State, as cited in Estrich, 1987).

The reality of the experience of rape for most women belies this belief. The "utmost resistance" standard has very little to do with the normal reaction of most rape victims. Indeed, the resistance requirement probably reflects the projected reactions of men who wrote the standard to the prospect of rape. Moreover, in no other type of criminal victimization, even when the victim is seen as cooperating with the attacker, such as when a victim gives his possessions to an armed robber, is failure to exercise "utmost resistance" viewed as a justifiable defense.

The "utmost resistance" standard was replaced by the "reasonable resistance" standard by the 1950's and 1960's in most states. Nevertheless, in considering cases for prosecution even today, the responses a victim makes to the sexual assault continue to be scrutinized. Victims who are able to demonstrate nonconsent through the existence of physical signs of struggle, e.g. bruises, torn clothing, lacerations, etc. would be perceived by prosecutors as having more "winnable" cases than victims whose resistance was expressed through purely verbal means.

The Rules of Evidence in Rape Cases

A second area which has demanded reform concerns the rules governing proof of rape. Victims of rape, more than victims of any other crime, may be faced with observers who question their accounts and doubt that a crime has actually been committed. Thus, victims may be placed in the position of having to defend their stories to disbelievers, creating the impression that they, rather than their rapists, are being tried. Suspicion of the veracity of rape victims' accounts harks back to the Biblical story of Potiphar's wife, who seduced Joseph and then claimed to her husband that she had been raped. It is reflected in the famous statement made hundreds of years ago by the English Lord Chief Justice Matthew Hale, who warned that rape is a charge "easily to be made and hard to be proved and harder to be defended by the party accused, tho' never so innocent" (Hale, 1971). Indeed, this statement has been the basis for cautionary instructions given to juries routinely in contemporary rape cases (Estrich, 1987).

This predisposition to disbelieve the victim has led to certain standards in rape cases which rarely hold in judicial proceedings of other types of offenses. A prolonged time interval between the sexual assault and its reporting, for example, can be one element which raises a flag inviting scrutiny. Lack of corroboration has also been used as the basis for the dismissal of a rape case, purely on the grounds that it is too easy for women to fabricate a rape story. From the victim's standpoint, a delay in reporting a rape victimization is quite normative, especially in cases of acquaintance rape (Warshaw, 1988), and it is obvious that eyewitnesses are rarely available to substantiate the victim's account.

A typical example of a case in which unreachably high standards of proof are set may involve a victim and assailant who know each other. In one case a victim met two men in a bus station. They made aggressive advances to her in the bus station and offered to take her to her destination. Instead of waiting to take the bus, she consented to their offer. While in their vehicle, the two men hit her and forced her to have intercourse with them. Following the assault she remained in their presence until they reached her destination; one man then called a cab for her. The woman did not call the police until after a friend inquired why she had not been on the bus (Baker v. Commonwealth, as cited in Estrich, 1987).

This case contains many elements common to acquaintance rape cases which may be interpreted by third parties, e.g. judges, jurors, etc. as grounds for disbelieving that a rape has taken place. Generally in acquaintance rape cases, the issue is not whether intercourse occurred, but whether it was consensual. In this case, numerous elements of the woman's conduct — tolerating public sexual advances from two men, accepting a ride, failing to attempt an immediate escape following the sexual aggression, allowing the man to call a cab, failing to report the event to the police prior to discussing it with a friend — may suggest, especially to rape myth subscribers, that the incident may have not been pleasant for the woman, but that it was not rape.

Another element which traditionally has been admissible as evidence in rape cases is the sexual history of the woman. This information was viewed as relevant to the case because it was assumed that a sexually experienced woman would be less likely

to resist a man's advances than would a virgin. In addition to calling
consent into question, it was assumed that sexual experience would
undermine the credibility of a victim's testimony concerning the
extent of force or violence used by the assailant.

The setting of such high, sometimes unreachable, evidentiary
standards, coupled with the allowance of information concerning
the victim's, but not the accused's, sexual past, sets the stage for
women to experience humiliation and intimidation in the
courtroom. Indeed, the insistence of the court on the fulfillment of
these standards often leaves women feeling "twice traumatized,"
once by the rapist, once by the criminal justice system.

The Definition of and Penalties for Rape

Another problematic area of rape law has been the definition of
the crime and the corresponding penalty structure. According to
the common law, rape was limited to sexual intercourse by a man
against a woman. This definition omitted numerous other types of
coercive and violent sexual behaviors, those not involving
intercourse (e.g. forced fellatio, insertion of objects into the vagina,
etc.), and discounted cases when the sexes of the two parties
involved were not male perpetrator/female victim.

Some critics objected to the legal name of the crime itself; rape
carried with it connotations of sex and being a sexual crime. Critics
reasoned that victims may be more reluctant to report their
victimization to the authorities because of their shame of being
involved in this type of offense. Moreover, the emphasis on the
sexual nature of the offense shifted attention away from the reality
of rape for victims; they did not experience rape as sex at all but
as a violent insult to their physical and psychological persons.

Finally, the traditional penalty structure for rape had been harsh,
comparable to only the most serious crimes against the person:
homicide and kidnapping. Indeed, until the 1960's many states
could impose the death penalty or life imprisonment for rape
(Babcock, Freedman, Norton and Ross, 1975). The concern was that
penalty structures that were too harsh could dissuade jurors from
convicting defendants when an imbalance existed between the
defendant's degree of culpability and the punishment prescribed
by law.

Efforts Toward Rape Reform

Rape reformers, sensitive to the real hardships suffered by victims because of the unreasonable standards of evidence, have focused much of their attention on creating a courtroom climate more friendly to the victim. The rules of corroboration requiring the victim's testimony be substantiated by other forms of evidence are no longer applied. The use of the victim's sexual history in the trial is also restricted in most states (Cobb and Schauer, 1974; Searles and Berger, 1987). Many states have rejected the requirement that a rape must be reported immediately after its occurrence to be legitimate.

Most states have undergone broad scale revisions of the definitions, gradations of offenses, and penalty structures for rape as well. A number of states have replaced the term rape with "criminal sexual assault" to emphasize that rape is a violent crime rather than an instance of uncontrolled sexual passion. Since assault is "by definition, something to which the victim does not consent" (Bienen, 1980:182), attention is presumably diverted away from questions of victim consent and to issues of rapist coercion and force. The definition of the crime has also been broadened in many jurisdictions to extend beyond the tra- ditional penile-vaginal intercourse to include oral and anal pene- tration, sexual penetration with objects, and, in some cases, touching of intimate body parts (Berger, Searles and Neuman, 1988).

Finally, many reformed rape or sexual assault statutes include gradations of the offense which specify varying degrees of seriousness based on elements such as the amount of coercion, use of a weapon, relationship between the victim and attacker, and age of the victim (Berger, Searles and Neuman, 1988). Penalties, in turn, are linked to the various grades of offense seriousness.

The range and extent of rape law reforms implemented over the past two decades are impressive and substantial testaments to the determination and commitment of rape reform activists. The simple passage of so many reforms should be hailed as a triumph of feminist imagination in the legal arena. As Estrich (1987:57) notes, "this is the good news. The bad news is that looks can be deceiving." Assessments of the impact and extent of rape law reforms suggest that change has not always been as wide-ranging or thorough as it may appear. Moreover, legal reform can go only so far in altering policies dependent upon individuals to carry them out. Observers of the courts in the era of post rape law reform find that ingrained suspicions of women victims and protective attitudes towards male defendants persist (Lowe, 1984; Daane, 1988).

Impacts of Rape Reform Legislation

Several studies have been designed to assess the extent and impact of rape reform legislation. Searles and Berger (1987) conducted a national study of state rape statutes to determine the extent to which these laws embody provisions they define as "feminist" versus "traditional." They conclude that one-third of the states retain the most traditional definition, while less than one-fifth have adopted the most feminist conceptualization. Overall, they report that legal reforms have been piecemeal and that traditional and feminist provisions may even coexist in the same statues (Berger, Searles and Neuman, 1988).

Moreover, certain areas of rape law continue to be dominated by prereform era thinking. Possibly the most important of these is the exclusion of marital rape from rape laws in most jurisdictions (Bumiller, 1987; Searles and Berger, 1987). While reported cases of marital rape tend to be particularly violent and brutal, husbands who rape their wives are still totally exempt from prosecution in some states (Caringella-MacDonald, 1988b). Other states trivialize marital rape by making it a separate crime or by defining it as a lesser degree felony or misdemeanor. Even those states which have marital rape statutes rarely prosecute cases.

Several major studies have addressed the impact of rape reform legislation on the processing of cases. Information such as the percentage of rape complaints resulting in arrests, rates of charging defendants with rape, and rates of convictions and pleas was gathered. Evaluating the 1974 Michigan law, the earliest law and the one used as a model for legal reform in other states, Marsh, Geist and Caplan (1982) found that the law did not lead women to report more rapes and did not alter the decision making strategies of prosecutors in evaluating their potential success in taking a case. They conclude that "the law has very little impact on the system's approach to sexual assault cases" (p. 65). Loh's (1981) study of the Washington statute further demonstrates the minimal impact of rape reform legislation on case processing. There were no changes in the overall rates of convictions, pleas or charging, although the new gradations of the crime led to the more accurate labeling of convicted offenders as "rapists" rather than "assaulters." Those convicted of rape also received more certain, although no more severe, punishment.

Considering the passion and effort expended by rape reform activists, their failure to have a major impact on rape case processing may be viewed as disappointing at the least. Yet it is important to recognize that law reform simply reflects new concepts on a printed page. The key to effective change lies with the individuals who carry out the laws. As Loh (1981:49) remarks, "Legislative reform is necessary but not sufficient for effective enforcement of the criminal law. As important as the formulation of legal rules is their day-to-day discretionary implementation by the criminal justice officials." Over time, it is likely that these reforms may subtly help to erode rape myth supportive attitudes of courtroom personnel and ultimately lead to greater justice for victims.

The Police and Rape

Police response to rape may be the most crucial link in the chain to ensure fair treatment for rape victims. The police officer is the first representative of the criminal justice system the reporting victim encounters; the quality of her contact with the police officer may color her perception of the entire prosecution process. The main concern is whether officers understand and adhere to the new rules of evidence and new definitions of rape in many jurisdictions. They must realize that the victim's prior sexual conduct, her demeanor during the offense, and her relationship to the accused is no longer relevant except in special instances. If officers apply previous standards, the treatment of victims may go unchanged despite reforms in the law.

The past two decades have witnessed considerable change in the response of police departments to sexual victimization. With the support and encouragement of women's centers, many police departments have implemented training programs to sensitize officers to the concerns of rape victims (Burgess and Holmstrom, 1979; O'Reilly, 1984; Chappel and Singer, 1977; Feild, 1978). In addition, new policies and programs have been implemented in attempts to provide better services to rape victims. Some of the strategies include: (1) involvement of citizen advocates at each step of processing through the system (Amidon and Wagner, 1978; Wood, 1973); (2) special units to investigate only sexual assault cases (Galton, 1975; LaFree, 1981); (3) hiring of more women officers (Bohmer and Blumberg, 1975; Wood, 1973)); and (4) changing public opinion by using police in the role of rape prevention specialists.

Little is known about the effects of these efforts, as many were never studied and some were relatively short-lived (Daley and Chesney-Lind, 1988). Anecdotal evidence from those who work with rape victims, however, suggests that some of these innovations have been significant in improving the climate for victim treatment and, therefore, for prosecution. Cooperation between police departments and rape crisis units has contributed to increased chances for convictions and decreased victim trauma to the victims (Berger, et al., 1988). The creation of special sexual assault units has led to reduced rates of unfounding, or declaring that an offense had not actually occurred (LaFree, 1981). Finally, some research has been performed on the introduction of women into sexual assault investigations. Overall, women officers are not found to be more effective in handling rape victims than men (Chappel and Singer, 1977; Galton, 1975; O'Reilly, 1984). This may not be surprising; as women police officers, they have been "schooled just like the male officers to be mistrusting and incredulous" and are expected to function like their male peers in a male-dominated, hierarchical organization. It might be safe to predict that response to rape victims is more a matter of training than that of gender.

These innovative programs have begun to have an impact on officers' attitudes, as demonstrated in research by LeDoux and Hazelwood (1985). They reported that police officers exhibited sensitivity to the plight of rape victims, disagreeing vehemently with the statement that rape victims deserve to be raped. Yet even these more "enlightened" officers manifested signs of rape myth subscription. The officers indicated that they were suspicious of victims who met certain criteria, such as having had previous willing sex with the assailant or dressing and acting in a provocative manner. In general, police officers have also been found to hold more traditional rape attitudes than other social service providers. In a study of how to reduce rape, views of social service workers focused on changing social norms, while views of criminal justice workers emphasized curtailment of potential victims' behavior (Feldman-Summers and Palmer, 1980). In another study conducted on crisis counselors, police, citizens, and convicted rapists, patrol officers' views of rape were more similar to the rapists than to counselors (Feild, 1978).

In summarizing police responses to rape, it is important to note that many of the studies utilized data collected in the late 1970s and early 1980s and that changes may have occurred subsequently. Nevertheless, it appears that while there has been real progress in the establishment of police policies, procedures and programs to aid rape victims, many officers continue to reflect traditional values which may inhibit adequate response to sexual victimization.

The Prosecutor's Response to Rape

The prosecutor is hailed as one of the most influential actors in the criminal justice system and is responsible for the crucial decision of dismissing reported rape cases or continuing them to trial. More than any other actor, the prosecutor is also responsible for implementing the reforms in the rape laws discussed earlier.

Little is known of prosecutors' attitudes to rape cases. It is known that substantial proportions of cases reported to the police and referred to the district attorney's office for prosecution are dismissed before they reach trial or plea. For example, in a study of prosecutors in Michigan after the rape reform law was enacted, Caringella-MacDonald (1984) found that almost two-thirds of all cases coming to the prosecutor's attention were lost prior to the trial or plea stage. In part, the willingness of prosecutors to give up on cases may be less a reflection of their personal views than of their assessments of the likely response of a judge or jury to the case. Nevertheless, if prosecutors decide to drop cases for which the evidence suggests that a crime has been committed because they are perceived as less "convictable," the interests of rape victims are not protected.

In one of the rare studies of prosecutors, Jeffords (1984) provided them with several hypothetical instances of marital rape. Surprisingly, prosecutors reported that they would press maximum charges in 63.6 percent of the cases with minor injury and 71.2 percent of the cases with serious injury. They were reluctant to prosecute in any marital case, however, until it was determined that: the victim was willing to proceed with criminal charges; there was sufficient corroborative evidence; and the victim was intending to, or had already made, arrangements to live apart from the defendant. These conditions again reflect not the defendant's but the victim's behavior and underscore the fact that women are unlikely to receive full benefit from the system unless they have been involved in a classic stranger rape.

Juries and the Treatment of Rape Cases

Advocates intent upon improving the climate of rape trials for victims may be viewed as having the fewest opportunities where jurors are concerned. Considering the support for rape myths in society at large, juries, who tend to be older and more middle class than would be representative of the general public (Kalven and Zeisel, 1966), may be even more likely to embody those myths.

Hence it is not surprising that studies have found bias among juries in their consideration of rape cases.

In jury trials, it is the twelve jurors, uneducated on the fine points of law, often embracing conservative and conventional attitudes and presuppositions about human behavior, who will ultimately determine the guilt or innocence of the defendant. In cases which are straightforward (in rape cases, this involves the classic, violent stranger rape), jurors' predispositions about gender roles or rape myths are for the most part irrelevant. However, in cases where the defense attorney attempts to make an issue of consent, jurors' general attitudes about gender roles, sex, and rape may influence their decisions concerning guilt or innocence of the defendant. Jurors' rape myth supportive attitudes may come into play when they are presented with cases in which the facts are muddier, such as those which include one or more of the following elements: (1) the victim's prior involvement with the defendant; (2) her "provocative" conduct prior to the alleged rape; (3) her "risky" behavior by accepting a ride or going to the defendant's apartment; (4) her intoxication by alcohol or drugs; (5) her social status, relative to the man's; and (5) the presentation of the alleged rapist as a man of good moral character.

Indeed, a recent study demonstrates that jurors' social attitudes are less relevant in clear-cut cases than in those in which rape myths may be involved. Reskin and Visher (1986:423) report that "while jurors were influenced by extralegal factors, these effects were largely limited to weak cases in which the state presented little hard evidence." In strong cases jurors tended to ignore the personal characteristics of the victim and defendant, with the exception of whether or not they thought the victim exercised sufficient caution. In weak cases, "Jurors were more likely to believe in a defendant's guilt if he were unemployed or seemed unattractive, and more likely to exonerate him, if, by their standards, the victim had behaved carelessly or was of poor moral character" (p. 435).

LaFree's work (LaFree, 1989; LaFree, Reskin and Visher, 1985) also attests to the importance of sex role stereotypes in juror decision making. He reports that jurors "were clearly influenced by testimony about victims' life-styles. Any evidence of drinking, drug use, or sexual activity outside marriage led jurors to doubt defendants' guilt, as did any prior acquaintance between victim and defendant" (LaFree, 1989:226). Hence, while it might have been the goal of the rape reformers to shift attention away from the victim's behavior to that of the rapist, evidence of juror decision making suggests that scrutiny of the victim's behavior, at least in so-called "weak" cases, persists.

Conclusion

Significant advances in the treatment of rape victims by the criminal justice system have occurred in the last two decades. These advances, however, have not come easily nor have they been a panacea for rape victims. While palpable successes can be noted at both the community and institutional levels, public support for rape myths and traditional sex role stereotypes is still widespread, as are obstacles to "victim friendly" investigation and prosecution of rape cases.

Over the past two decades there has been a virtual explosion of knowledge on rape and sexual assault. Yet we are far from possessing the whole picture. There is little information about the relationship between rape supportive attitudes and the proclivity to rape, for example. If this link could be conclusively established, intervention programs aimed at changing attitudes could be developed for rape prevention. Currently, our knowledge of rapists' attitudes relies primarily upon populations of convicted felons, a group hardly representative of rapists in general. Recently, there has also been an overconcentration of research on college populations. The expansion to more diverse populations would significantly assist researchers in learning about rapists' attitudes, motivations, and behaviors.

Research must once again focus on how the criminal justice system is dealing with rape. Many of the studies reviewed, even though published in the 1980s, are based on data collected during the mid to late 1970s. The 1970s were a time of great social change. Observations made by researchers in this context may be less applicable to the more conservative climate of the 1980s and 1990s. There is also a dearth of information concerning institutional programs such as police and prosecutor training to deal with rape and campus date rape awareness/prevention.

There is a need for more comparative research, within and across jurisdictions of the criminal justice system, across racial and ethnic groups, and cross-culturally. The "criminal justice system" which responds to rape victims consists of numerous local and state systems. Each "system" is comprised of various components, e.g. police, courts, and corrections. More research must be done on the extent of change in rape case processing and system response across jurisdictions, within jurisdictions, and across the various components. We cannot assume the extent of overall advances in rape case handling when so few jurisdictions and components have been analyzed.

Comparative research which investigates the interactive impact of racism and sexism on sexual victimization is also sorely needed. Conventional research on rape and minorities often fails to take the realities of racism and classism into account when findings are interpreted. This may lead to misinterpretations and misrepresentations of the reality of rape as it is experienced among populations of people of color.

Finally, the burgeoning field of research on sexual violence has rarely encompassed non-North American or non-European populations and cultures. The pathbreaking work of Robin Morgan (1984) and her colleagues in documenting the realities of women's lives in nations around the globe underscores the critical problem of sexual violence for women in numerous non-Western countries. It is time for researchers to apply their theoretical perspectives and methodological skills, in collaboration with local researchers, to problems of rape and victimization in developing countries.

Only when stranger rape, date/acquaintance rape, and marital rape are given equal consideration by the community and governmental authorities will women victims be in positions of being justly treated. If the current status of rape reform and the treatment of rape victims in this country are a reflection of the status of women in society, then women continue to face an uphill battle.

Bibliography

Acock, Alan C. and Nancy K. Ireland
    1983   "Attribution of Blame in Rape Cases: The Impact of Norm Violation, Gender, and Sex-role Attitude." *Sex Roles* 9(2):179-93.
Amidon, Harold T. and Terry A. Wagner
    1978   "Successful Investigation and Prosecution of the Crime of Rape: A Descriptive Model." *Journal of Police Science and Administration* 6(2):141-56.
Amir, Menachem
    1971   *Patterns in Forcible Rape*. Chicago: University of Chicago Press.
Babcock, Barbara, Ann Freedman, Eleanor Norton and Susan Ross
    1975   *Sex Discrimination and the Law*. Boston: Little, Brown, and Co.
Berger, Ronald J., Patricia Searles, and Lawrence W. Neuman
    1988   "The Dimensions of Rape Reform Legislation." *Law & Society Review* 22(2):329-57.
Bienen, Leigh
    1980   "Rape III-National Developments in Rape Reform Legislation." *Women's Right Law Reporter* 6:170-213.

Bohmer, Carol and Audrey Blumberg
  1975   "Twice Traumatized: The Rape Victim and the Court."
         Judicature 58(8):391-99.
Brownmiller, Susan
  1975   *Against Our Will: Men, Women and Rape.* New York: Simon and
         Schuster, Inc.
Bumiller, Kristin
  1987   "Rape as a Legal Symbol: An Essay on Sexual Violence and
         Racism." *University of Miami Law Review* 42:75-91.
Burgess, Ann W. and Lynda L. Holmstrom
  1979   *Rape: Crisis and Recovery.* Bowie, MD: Robert J. Brady Co.
Burt, Martha R.
  1980   "Cultural Myths and Supports for Rape." *Journal of Personality
         and Social Psychology* 38(2):217-30.
Burt, Martha R. and Rochelle S. Albin
  1981   "Rape Myths, Rape Definitions, and Probability of Conviction."
         Journal of Applied Social Psychology 11(3):212-30.
Cann, Arnie, Lawrence Calhoun, James W. Selby and Elizabeth H. King
  1981   "Rape: A Contemporary Overview and Analysis." *Journal of
         Social Issues* 37(4):1-3.
Caringella-MacDonald, Susan
  1984   "Sexual Assault Prosecution: An Examination of Model Rape
         Legislation in Michigan." *Women and Politics* 4(3):65-82.
  1988a "Parallels and Pitfalls: The Aftermath of Legal Reform for Sexual
         Assault, Marital Rape, and Domestic Violence Victims." *Journal
         of Interpersonal Violence* 3(2):174-89.
  1988b "Marxist and Feminist Interpretations on the Aftermath of Rape
         Reforms." *Contemporary Crisis* 12:125-44.
Chappel, Duncan and Susan Singer
  1977   "Rape in New York City: A Study of Material in the Police Files
         and its Meaning." Pp. 245-71 in Duncan Chappell, Robley Geis,
         and Gilbert Geis (Eds.), *Forcible Rape: The Crime, the Victim,
         and the Offender.* New York: Columbia University Press.
Check, James V. P. and Neil Malamuth
  1985   "An Empirical Assessment of Some Feminist Hypotheses About
         Rape." *International Journal of Women's Studies* 8(4):414-23.
Cobb, Kenneth and Nancy Schauer
  1974   "Michigan's Criminal Assault Law." *Journal of Law Reform*
         8:217-359.
Connell, Noreen and Cassandra Wilson (Eds.)
  1974   *Rape: The First Sourcebook for Women.* New York: New
         American Library.
Costin, Frank
  1985   "Beliefs About Rape and Women's Social Roles." *Archives of
         Sexual Behavior* 14(4):319-25.

Costin, Frank and Norbert Schwarz
  1987   "Beliefs About Rape and Women's Social Roles: A Four-Nation
          Study." *Journal of Interpersonal Violence* 2(1):46-56.
Curtis, Lynn A.
  1976   "Rape, Race and Culture: Some Speculations in Search of a
          Theory." Pp. 117-34 in Marcia J. Walker and Stanley L. Brodsky
          (Eds.), *Sexual Assault: The Victim and the Rapist*. Lexington,
          MA: Lexington Books.
Daane, Diane M.
  1988   "Rape Law Reform: How Far Have We Come?" *The Prison
          Journal* LXVII(2):3-10.
Daly, Kathleen and Meda Chesney-Lind
  1988   "Feminism and Criminology." *Justice Quarterly* 4(4):497-538.
Deitz, Sheila R., Karen T. Blackwell, Paul C. Daley and Brenda J. Bentley
  1982   "Measurement of Empathy Toward Rape Victims and Rapists."
          Journal of Personality and Social Psychology 43(2):372-84.
Deitz, Sheila R., Madeleine Littman, and Brenda J. Bentley
  1984   "Attribution of Responsibility for Rape: The Influence of Observer
          Empathy, Victim Resistance, and Victim Attractiveness." *Sex
          Roles* 10(3):261-80.
Ellis, Lee
  1989   *Theories of Rape: Inquiries Into the Causes of Sexual
          Aggression*. New York: Hemisphere Publishing Corporation.
Estrich, Susan
  1987   *Real Rape*. Cambridge, MA: Harvard University Press.
Feild, Hubert S.
  1978   "Attitudes Toward Rape: A Comparative Analysis of Police,
          Rapists, Crisis Counselors, and Citizens." *Journal of Personality
          and Social Psychology* 36(2):156-79.
Feldman-Summers, Shirley and Gayle C. Palmer
  1980   "Rape as Viewed by Judges, Prosecutors, and Police Officers."
          Criminal Justice and Behavior 7(1):19-40.
Fischer, Gloria J.
  1987   "Hispanic and Majority Student Attitudes Toward Forcible Date
          Rape as a Function of Differences in Attitudes Toward Women."
          Sex Roles 17(1/2), 93-101.
Flanagan, Timothy and Katherine Jamieson (Eds.)
  1988   *Sourcebook of Criminal Justice Statistics*. U.S. Department of
          Justice, Bureau of Justice Statistics: Washington DC: USGPO.
Gagnon, John H. and William Simon
  1973   *Sexual Conduct: The Social Sources of Human Sexuality*.
          Chicago: Aldine Publishing Company.
Galton, Eric R.
  1975   "Police Processing of Rape Complaints: A Case Study." *American
          Journal of Criminal Law* 4(1):15-30.

Giacopassi, David J. and Thomas R. Dull
  1986   "Gender and Racial Differences in the Acceptance of Rape Myths within a College Population." *Sex Roles* 15(1/2):63-75.
Giacopassi, David and Karen Wilkinson
  1985   "Rape and the Devalued Victim." *Law and Human Behavior* 9:367-83.
Griffin, Susan
  1982   "Rape: The All-American Crime." Pp. 223-39 in Barbara R. Price and Nicole J. Sokoloff (Eds.), *The Criminal Justice System and Women*. New York, NY: Clark Boardman Company, Ltd.
  1986   *Rape: The Politics of Consciousness* (3rd. Ed.). San Francisco: Harper & Row, Publishers.
Hale, Matthew
  1971   *The History of the Pleas of the Crown.* London: Professional Books.
Jeffords, Charles R.
  1984   "Prosecutorial Discretion in Cases of Marital Rape." *Victimology: An International Journal* 9(3-4):415-25.
Kalvin, Harry and Hans Zeisel
  1966   *The American Jury.* Boston: Little, Brown, & Co.
Kanin, Eugene J.
  1984   "Date Rape: Unofficial Criminals and Victims." *Victimology* 9:95-108.
Kanin, Eugene J.
  1957   "Male Aggression in Dating-courtship Relations." *American Journal of Sociology* 63:197-204.
Klemmack, Susan H. and David L. Klemmack
  1976   "The Social Definition of Rape." Pp. 135-47 in Marcia J. Walker and Stanley L. Brodsky (Eds.), *Sexual Assault: The Victim and the Rapist.* Lexington, MA: Lexington Books.
LaFree, Gary D.
  1980a   "The Effect of Sexual Stratification by Race on Official Reactions to Rape." *American Sociological Review* 45:842-54.
  1980b   "Variables Affecting Guilty Pleas and Convictions in Rape Cases: Toward a Social Theory of Rape Processing." *Social Forces* 58(3):833-50.
  1981   "Official Reactions to Social Problems: Police Decisions in Sexual Assault Cases." *Social Problems* 28(5):582-94.
  1982   "Male Power and Female Victimization: Toward a Theory of Interracial Rape." *American Sociological Review* 45:842-54.
  1989   *Rape and Criminal Justice: The Social Construction of Sexual Assault.* Belmont, CA: Wadsworth Publishing Company.
LaFree, Gary D., Barbara F. Reskin and Christy A. Visher
  1985   "Jurors' Responses to Victims' Behavior and Legal Issues in Sexual Assault Trials." *Social Problems* 32(4):389-407.

Largen, Mary A.
1976 "History of the Women's Movement in Changing Attitudes, Laws, and Treatment Toward Rape Victims." Pp. 69-73 in Marcia Walker and Stanley Brodsky (Eds.), *Sexual Assault*. Lexington, MA: D.C. Heath and Company.

LeDoux, John C. and Robert R. Hazelwood
1985 "Police Attitudes and Beliefs Toward Rape." *Journal of Police Science and Administration* 13(3):211-20.

LeGrand, Camille E.
1977 "Rape and Rape Laws: Sexism in Society and Law." Pp. 67-86 in Duncan Chappell, Robley Geis, and Gilbert Geis (Eds.), *Forcible Rape: The Crime, the Victim, and the Offender*. New York: Columbia University Press.

Loh, Wallace D.
1981 "Q: What Has Reform of Rape Legislation Wrought? A: Truth in Criminal Labelling." *Journal of Social Issues* 37(4):28-52.

Lottes, Ilsa L.
1988 "Sexual Socialization and Attitudes Toward Rape." Pp. 193-220 in Ann W. Burgess (Ed.), *Rape and Sexual Assault II*. New York: Garland Publishing, Inc.

Lowe, Marion
1984 "The Role of the Judiciary in the Failure of the Sexual Offenses (Amendment) Act to Improve the Treatment of the Rape Victim." Pp. 67-88 in June Hopkins (Ed.), *Perspectives on Rape and Sexual Assault*. London: Harper & Row, Publishers.

MacKinnon, Catherine A.
1987 *Feminism Unmodified: Discourses on Life and Law*. Cambridge MA: Harvard University Press.

Marsh, Jeanne, Alison Geist and Nathan Caplan
1982 *Rape and the Limits of Law Reform*. Boston: Auburn House Publishing, Co.

Minch, Candice, Rick Linden and Stuart Johnson
1987 "Attrition in the Processing of Rape Cases." *Canadian Journal of Criminology* 29(4):389-404.

Morgan, Robin (Ed.).
1984 *Sisterhood is Global*. Garden City, NY: Anchor Books.

Muelenhard, Charlene L. and Jennifer S. MacNaughton
1988 "Women's Beliefs About Women Who 'Lead Men On'." *Journal of Social and Clinical Psychology* 7(1):65-79.

O'Reilly, Harry J.
1984 "Crisis Intervention With Victims of Forcible Rape: A Police Perspective." Pp. 89-103 in June Hopkins (Eds.), *Perspectives on Rape and Sexual Assault*. London: Harper & Row, Publishers.

Reskin, Barbara F. and Christy A. Visher
1986 "The Impacts of Evidence and Extralegal Factors in Jurors' Decisions." *Law and Society Review* 20(3):423-38.

Rose, Vicki M.
  1977   "Rape as a Social Problem: A Byproduct of the Feminist Movement." *Social Problems* 25(1):75-89.
Russell, Diana H.
  1974   *The Politics of Rape: The Victim's Perspective.* New York: Stein and Day.
  1984   *Sexual Exploitation: Rape, Child Sexual Abuse, and Workplace Harassment.* Beverly Hills, CA: Sage Publications Inc.
Sanday, Peggy R.
  1981   "The Socio-Cultural Context of Rape: A Cross-Cultural Study." *Journal of Social Issues,* 37(4):5-27.
Schwartz, Martin, and Todd Clear
  1980   "Toward a New Law on Rape." *Crime and Delinquency* 26(2):129-51.
Scott, Ronald L., and Laurie A. Tetreault
  1986   "Attitudes of Rapists and Other Violent Offenders Toward Women." *The Journal of Social Psychology* 127(4):375-80.
Searles, Patricia, and Ronald J. Berger
  1987   "The Current Status of Rape Reform Legislation: An Examination of State Statutes." *Women's Rights Law Reporter* 10(4):25-43.
Sheffield, Carole J.
  1987   "Sexual Terrorism: The Social Control of Women." Pp. 3-19 in Jo Freeman (Ed.), *Women: A Feminist Perspective.* Mountain View, CA: Mayfield Publishing Company.
Temkin, Jennifer
  1986   "Women, Rape and Law Reform." Pp. 16-40 in Sylvana Tomaselli and Roy Porter (Eds.). *Rape.* New York: Basil Blackwell.
Walsh, Anthony
  1987   "The Sexual Stratification Hypotheses and Sexual Assault in Light of the Changing Conceptions of Race." *Criminology* 25(1):153-73.
Warshaw, Robin
  1988   *I Never Called it Rape.* New York: Harper & Row, Publishers.
Williams, Joyce E.
  1984   "Secondary Victimization: Confronting Public Attitudes About Rape." *Victimology: An International Journal* 9(1):66-81
Williams, Joyce E. and Karen A. Holmes (Eds.).
  1981   *The Second Assault: Rape and Public Attitudes.* Westport, CT: Greenwood Press.
Wood, Pamela L.
  1973   "The Victim in a Forcible Rape Case: A Feminist View." *The American Criminal Law Review* 11:335-54.

chapter 10

Perceptions of Woman Battering

Joanne Belknap
University of Cincinnati

Identifying the Battering of Women as a Social Problem

Until the 1970s, very little was known about battered women and their batterers. This is not because battering was nonexistent or less common prior to the 1970s. Rather, the abuse of women by their intimate male partners was considered unimportant or even acceptable by those with power. Moreover, the problems of woman battering were minimized and deemed as unimportant by society, the media, and even the criminal justice system. "In the 1950s and 1960s, cases of women being killed by abusive husbands were rarely recognized for what they were. Headlines such as 'Husband

Goes Berserk and Shoots Estranged Wife,' masked the reality, and we will never know how many battered women died" (Schecter, 1982).

Historically, many laws have even legalized some forms of woman battering. The "rule of thumb," established by early British Common Law, allowed husbands to beat their wives with rods no larger than the thickness of their thumbs. In 1864, North Carolina's "curtain rule" stated that the police could only "interfere" with a husband's actions toward his wife (go beyond the curtain of the home) when his actions resulted in the permanent injury of his wife (Tong, 1984:128). Finally, the "stitch rule," arresting only if an injury required stitches, was in effect until recently in many places (Stanko, 1985:113; Tong, 1984:135).

Edwards (1987:14-15) views the 1970s as a "critical decade" in the modern history of women, particularly regarding the awareness of male violence against women. She attributes the identification of male violence against women to classic texts of modern feminism (e.g., Millet, Firestone, etc.) and to the feminist analyses conducted by women actively working on behalf of female victims in shelters for battered women and rape crisis centers. Despite work by feminists in the eighteenth and nineteenth centuries (Abigail Smith Adams, Susan B. Anthony, and Elizabeth Cady Stanton), woman battering was not labeled as a social problem until recently. (For a lengthier historical analysis of the early battered women's movement see Dobash and Dobash, 1979 and Pleck, 1983.)

Defining the Intimate Abuse of Women
by their Male Intimates

"Woman battering" includes the physical, sexual, and psychological abuse of a woman by her (usually male) intimate partner. "Brutality is not necessarily confined to hitting, pushing, and pulling out hair. Its extreme, yet not infrequent, forms often leave women severely scarred, physically and emotionally" (Schecter, 1982:14). Originally, this behavior has been defined as simply "domestic violence," "spouse abuse," or "wife abuse." Such labeling ignores the fact that most intimate violence is conducted by men against women (Berk, Berk, and Loseke, 1983; Browne, 1987) and that a substantial amount of battering occurs among nonmarried or dating couples (DeMaris, 1990; Erez, 1986; Lane and Gwartney-Gibbs, 1985; Makepeace, 1981; 1986; 1989). Furthermore, considerable evidence exists regarding women being abused by their ex-husbands and ex-boyfriends (Erez, 1986; Russell, 1984).

Why Does Battering Occur?

Chapter One discussed conflict theory and the patriarchal society as explanations of the victimization of women. Conflict theory was expanded to include women in the "powerless" category; society was characterized as patriarchal where men have control over women within the home (the private sphere) as well as outside of the home (the public sphere). Men are often viewed as the dominant force both in the private sphere ("breadwinners," the protectors, and the ones who discipline) and in the public sphere (congresspersons, judges, and police officers). Men generally hold the policy-making and decision-making positions. If how a man treats his wife or girlfriend is viewed as his "right" and his "business," or if police officers fail to view woman battering as a serious crime worthy of arrest, or if judges do not deem the abuse worthy of a conviction or punitive sentence, assaults against women proceed undeterred. One study found that the police tend to view masculinity as involving a natural biological dominance of men over women, which in turn defines battering as somewhat normal (Hatty, 1989:81). Moreover, if the officers take action, it will only be if the men guilty of abuse "resort to individual strategies such as threatening the officer with physical violence" (1989:84).

Some say that "men batter because they can." That is, because there is no social or criminal justice system response telling them not to batter. Some researchers have also suggested an intergenerational transfer of violence theory. This theory maintains that males growing up in battering homes "learn" to become batterers, and females growing up in battering homes "learn" to become battering victims. Stated another way, children learn from their parents' abusive behavior to become victims or offenders in battering relationships later in life. One study of college students' dating violence found that "parental fighting enhanced the likelihood both that men assaulted their girlfriends and that women were assaulted by their boyfriends" (DeMaris, 1990:228). Interestingly, reports of parental fighting increased the likelihood of black men stating they abused their girlfriends, while parental fighting decreased the likelihood of white men stating they abused their girlfriends (1990:226).

The greatest motivation behind battering is *power*. Battering, then, is an expression of power. As such, it is more likely to occur when the relationship is less equal. Because heterosexual relationships have a "built in" power imbalance—that of gender inequality—it is not surprising that battering is more likely to occur in these relationships than in lesbian and gay relationships (see, for example, Brand and Kidd, 1986:1307).

The Frequency of Woman Battering

Although studies report variations in the rates of woman battering, it is clear that this phenomenon occurs in epidemic proportions. Some experts report that as many as half of all women will be victims of battering by males over the course of their lifetimes (Mills and McNamar, 1981). More recent studies have found that "courtship" or dating violence occurs to between one-fifth and one-third of college students. One study found that violence was common and more severe among "first date" and "living together" couples than in relationships defined as "casual dating," "steady dating," and "engaged" (Makepeace, 1989).

Walker's Cycle of Violence Theory

Psychologist Lenore Walker is credited not only with helping to bring the plight of battered women into the public eye but also with developing the "Cycle Theory of Violence." From her experiences treating battered women, she perceived a pattern evident in many battering relationships. This pattern consisted of three phases which usually recurred (with escalating frequencies and degrees of violence) during the course of the relationship.

The first phase is referred to as the "tension building" stage. During this point both persons in the relationship are aware of an uneasiness between them. If battering has occurred before, the victim is often aware that this tension will likely be released in the form of violence against her. Walker (1979) found that many battered women tried to dissipate the tension and avoid the violence which they feared was inevitable. Walker (1979:59) reports that this is a very anxiety producing time for the victim. She wonders if the "second shoe" is going to drop, how she might keep herself and her children safe, and what she should do if it does occur again.

Phase one ends when the violent outburst erupts and phase two, the "acute battering incident," occurs. This is usually the briefest phase in the cycle. It can occur at any time or place, but usually the batterer is "careful" to keep his abusive behavior hidden from the public. Walker (1979:61) claims that "[i]t is not uncommon for the batterer to wake the woman out of deep sleep to begin his assault." If the police are involved at all, they are usually called during this phase. However, if the battering has not stopped before the police arrive, it often stops with their arrival.

After the acute battering incident, the cycle usually moves into phase three: "reconciliation." During this period the batterer usually tries to convince the victim that he is genuinely sorry and promises it will never happen again. This is the only phase which allows any semblance of calmness. Although the batterer may indeed be sorry, it is evident that he has a severe problem in choosing to control his violence. Frequently he is persuasive not only to the victim but also convinces himself that he is never going to do this again. This is easier for both of them to believe at the beginning of a battering relationship.

Once battering is established as part of the relationship, many victims (understandably) lose any sense of self-determination and belief in their abilities to escape. "Over time, the first phase of tension building becomes more common and loving contrition, or the third phase, declines" (Walker, 1983:43). At this point, since the batterer has the victim in a state of fear for her life, reconciliatory behavior is no longer necessary to ensure that she will not leave him. Threats to kill her if she leaves are usually sufficient to keep her from leaving, since she has every reason to believe he will carry out his threat.

Walker (1979) claims that once the cycle starts it usually continues until something occurs to stop it. In rare cases it ends either because the batterer decides to stop (on his own or through counseling) or because of the threat of actions by the criminal justice system. Again, this is very unlikely. Also unlikely, but possible, is that the battering will end because the offender voluntarily leaves the relationship. Unfortunately, he often moves on to another relationship where he continues his abuse. Although some battering stops when the victim leaves the relationship, in other cases this has been found to cause even more severe battering. A final possibility to the end of the battering relationship is the death of the victim and/or the offender. Frequently these deaths are part of the battering relationship. For instance, the batterer kills the victim in yet another battering incident, the victim kills the batterer in self-defense, or the batterer kills the victim and himself. Not surprisingly, statistics indicate that the homicide victims of violent intimate relationships are more likely to be women than men (Walker, 1983b:102).

Myths about Battered Women

Not only is the frequency with which woman battering occurs poorly acknowledged but most people are also unaware of the dynamics behind battering. The remainder of this chapter will discuss some perceptions of battering and report the findings of a study on law enforcement officials' perceptions of these myths, as well as their perceptions of "domestic violence" in general.

Myth #1: If battered women didn't like being battered, they would leave.

Probably the question most frequently asked of battering victims and persons working to help battered women is "Why do battered women stay?" This line of questioning eclipses the responsibility issue and implies that asking "why women stay" is more important than asking "why men batter." Furthermore, focusing on the victim often results in absolving the offender of his wrongdoing and blames the victim for being abused. Finally, asking why victims stay ignores the fact that many women do leave battering relationships (see Strube and Barbour, 1984). Given the shame this society attributes to battering victims, battered women survivors do not tend to publicize their victimizations. Consistent with conflict theory, Carlson (1987:173) found that "women have come to be viewed as deviant in the domestic violence encounter." In fact, one study found that police believe victims who stay in battering relationships do so out of "a lack of intelligence, a lack of psychological strength, masochism, and psychopathology" (Hatty, 1989:83) Such an approach denies "the sadistic behavior of the violent men and the degree to which women abhor the abuse" (1989:86).

There are many economic, social, and psychological reasons why it is difficult for battered women to leave abusive relationships. *Economic* factors make it extremely difficult for women to leave battering relationships. Stanko (1985:57) states that "important practical" reasons such as financial support, shelter, even access to the ability to earn a living many times rest with the husband/ boyfriend. Getting out is almost as bad as staying in the relationship." The workplace is often sex segregated reflecting "the differential status of men and women, since women's jobs tend to be subordinate to men's and typically offer less prestige and pay" (Epstein, 1988:136). *Social* factors also make it difficult for women to leave abusive relationships. Marriage is often viewed as a commitment "'til death do us part," regardless of the abuse suffered at the hands of the husband. Keeping a marriage (or relationship) together is frequently viewed as a duty and the *woman's* responsibility. Many battering victims report pressure from their in-laws or even their own parents to "work things out." People may ask what *she* is doing to "cause" the abuse. Research has also found that women who violate sex-role norms by wanting an equal relationship or maintaining their own careers are often punished by their batterers (Carlson, 1987:176).

Bates (1990) examines the added pressure that African-American women face in leaving unhealthy heterosexual relationships. "As African Americans, our strong family values encourage us to have a male in the home, or if we're single, at least to have one around. Add children to the equation, and the inducement to tolerate behavior that would otherwise be unacceptable becomes even more powerful" (1990:62). She goes on to explain how African-American women are aware of the pressures of the outside world on black men which make them feel emasculated and oppressed. Black women are under significant pressure to serve as a "buffer" between African-American men and the racist and oppressive outside world. The motivation for black women to stay in unhealthy heterosexual relationships with black men is further compounded by the small number of black men compared to black women: "If men seem in scarce demand, then the man you have may seem like a valuable commodity" (1990:62).

Richie (1985:40) states: "Too many blacks still think this [the battering of women in the black community] is a divisive issue which should not be aired in public." She goes on to examine the "trap of loyalty" in divulging violence against women in the black community when there already exists a great deal of negative information about blacks and black families, but concludes: "While it remains critical that black people continue actively struggling against racism and discrimination, it must not be done at the physical and psychological expense of black women. We have paid our dues and black men must be held responsible for every injury they cause" (1985:43).

Coley and Beckett (1988) discuss the problems black women face in accessing services for battered women. For instance, they suggest that the racial and economic oppression that black women experience (relative to white women) may inhibit the black women from self-disclosure in integrated counseling sessions for battered women, due to pressures of loyalty to the black community (1988:490). In order to help women of color leave battering relationships, it is necessary for shelters to enhance their physical environments to make them culturally comfortable for the battered women and their children (e.g., dolls of different races and children's and adults' reading materials and decorations reflecting multicultural values). A multiracial shelter may be many women's first integrated living experience (1988:486).

Similarly, Renzetti (1989) discusses the problems battered lesbians face in leaving abusive relationships. First, similar to black women, lesbians may not perceive existing sources to be available to them, and in fact, they may not be (1989:160). The few battered lesbians in her study who contacted women's shelters and hot lines found them to be of little or no help. Furthermore, law enforcement officials were even less helpful than shelter and hot line workers, and the batterers were rarely challenged (1989:161). Another effect of societal homophobia was that many lesbian victims of battering could not turn to their parents for support or help, since their parents were not aware of their sexual preference. Not surprisingly, counselors and friends of the lesbian victims were their most supportive allies.

There are also *psychological* restrictions to leaving an abusive relationship. Often, women have lost any sense of self-determination after living in the "combat zone" of an abusive relationship. The role of **fear** cannot be too heavily emphasized. A battered woman has every reason to believe her batterer's threats to harm or kill her (or their children or her parents) if she leaves. After all, she is the one who has directly experienced his violence. Walker (1979:62) reports from her work with battered women that "[t]he one feeling that consistently comes across is the futility of trying to escape."

A final and important inhibitor to women leaving violent relationships is the lack of adequate responses by the criminal justice system. This is not to say that there are no criminal justice system actors who attempt to and are successful in helping battered women. However, there is considerable evidence implicating a lack of response on the part of the criminal justice system. The police have historically been trained to "mediate" or simply "keep the peace" in "domestic violence" calls. This fails to treat battering as an offense and gives the message to the victim and offender that this type of abusive behavior is legally acceptable.

Research published in the 1980s claimed that arrested batterers were less likely to continue their abuse at a later date than those batterers who were not arrested (Sherman and Berk, 1984; Berk and Newton, 1985). More recent research has challenged whether arrest is effective in deterring battering (Dunford, Huizinga, and Elliot, 1990). While the "jury is not in" as to the effect of arrest on the deterrence of battering, it is important to note that violent behaviors which represent breaking the law should in fact be treated as crimes, regardless of the deterrent effect. Rowe (1985:866) points out that a mediation approach to battering is faulty in that it encourages a focus on the *victim* and what she may have done to "cause" the violence, rather than focusing on the offender as responsible. Since the findings in the 1980s suggested that arresting batterers helps deter future battering, many police departments have implemented arrest policies, requiring officers to arrest in cases where they believe battering has occurred (Cohn and Sherman, 1986). Unfortunately, research attempting to establish how effectively such arrest policies are carried out by line officers has found that police frequently *still* fail to arrest even when they are mandated to do so (Ferraro, 1989; Lawrenz, Lembo, and Schade, 1988). It is important to remember that no matter how distasteful or frustrating it is for police officers to respond to battering calls, it is part of their job.

Regrettably, the small percentage of battered women whose cases make it to court, do not tend to fare any better by this aspect of the criminal justice system than they do in dealing with the police (Atkins and Hoggett, 1984; Blodgett, 1987; Carlson, 1987; Crites, 1987; Tong, 1984). This is especially apparent when comparing battering men who murder their wives or girlfriends to battered women who murder their husbands or boyfriends: "Men who murder women for their irritating, humiliating or unfaithful behavior are somehow understood; women's actions can lead men to lose control. Women, on the other hand, unless provoked beyond endurance—beaten and threatened over years—are expected to retain control" (Stanko, 1985:89).

Myth #2: Battering is a way of life for persons in lower classes and statuses.

Many people tend to think of battered women as intrinsically different from women who are never battered — as though there is some inherent quality of these women that makes them victims and distinguishes them from "mentally healthy" nonvictims. Certainly many people, including criminologists, have offered explanations for why some women end up in battering relationships. The explanations range from low self-esteem to being too independent. These "rationales" support Lerner's Theory of the Just World: people like to think of violence as being nonrandom; thus, certain people are likely or even deserving victims, while others (such as themselves) are safe from harm. Adherence to such a belief serves as a psychological "security blanket" but does little to explain why, for example, women from all backgrounds are victims of battering.

> In spite of psychiatry's determined efforts to convince us otherwise, battered women are not all the same, nor do they fit into any one personality type; they are as varied as any random group of women in the population. This frightening fact helps explain the readiness with which we distance ourselves from battered women and label them as different (Schechter, 1982:16).

Atkins and Hoggett (1984:128) state that "there is a long-standing belief among legal writers that the lower orders take a certain amount of violence for granted." The racist and classist assumptions that battering is more "acceptable" among persons of lower socioeconomic statuses is played out in a number of ways. First, there is the assumption that battering is not as harmful or worrisome for poor women or African-American, Hispanic, or other women of color than it is for wealthier Anglo women. Thus, police are less likely to respond adequately to help the more socio-economically disadvantaged women than their white, wealthier counterparts (Stanko, 1985:112). This is certainly not to suggest that police always respond appropriately to middle- and upper-class white women victims. Tong (1984:170) claims that police training supports such racist myths and implies that "there is no reason to rush to the aid of a black woman who is being battered by her husband, for she and he are just 'working things out of their systems.'" Therefore, it is not surprising that some studies have found police more likely to arrest when middle- or upper-class victims request arrest than for their lower-status sisters (Ferraro, 1989:67; Smith and Klein, 1984:477). On the other hand, that black rapists have been treated significantly more harshly than white rapists only reinforces a black battered woman's reluctance to seek police protection (Tong, 1984:171). While wishing police protection, the black woman victim is also often concerned that the police may respond with more force (even brutality) than what would be necessary to deter her black batterer.

Furthermore, African-American victims are probably less likely than white victims to seek shelter services and more likely to turn to medical care systems and the informal support of friends and family (see Coley and Beckett, 1988:484). Because many black battering victims believe that shelters are for white victims, it is necessary to increase awareness of the shelters with the black community (1988:88).

Myth #3: Battered women often do something to provoke the violence.

As mentioned previously, another myth which receives substantial support is the belief that battered women somehow "ask for" or deserve the abuse they receive. Obviously, this is a very victim-blaming stance. This is not to suggest that people in healthy intimate relationships never experience frustration and anger toward their partners. What is significant is how individuals choose to respond to their anger and frustration toward their partners. In short, *violence is never an acceptable response unless it is in self-defense.*

While some batterers try to explain their abusive behavior by offering an action or inaction on the victim's part, most of the time the victim's behavior is irrelevant. One study of victims found that they could identify the batterers' behaviors "leading up to a violent episode." The women felt that the violence was not only unprovoked but that they had tried to avoid the attack through excessive compliance and passivity or through attempting to divert the batterers' attention (Hatty, 1989:85). *Excuses* are denials of responsibility and *justifications* are denials of wrongdoing (Ptacek, 1988). Excuses include "losing control," or being drunk or frustrated, while justifications include "shortcomings" on the victim's part, ranging from not being a good cook to being unfaithful. Batterers are more likely to blame the victims for "making" them violent (use justifications), than they are to use excuses (Dutton, 1988:86). It is important to acknowledge that using "losing control" as an excuse for battering is entirely unacceptable. These batterers usually manage not to "lose control" when they are angry at their bosses, or in public places. They also usually hit their victims in places which will be less apparent to the public. Thus, simply claiming they "lose control" is a cop out.

A study of Australian police officers suggests that it is not only the batterer and the families of the victims and offenders who focus on the victim's "nonconforming" behavior as "justifications" for battering (Hatty, 1989). This research found that the officers view the women's role in "producing" the violence in three separate ideological constructs. The first construct is related to discussion under myth one. Specifically, police view the victim's adherence to traditional gender behaviors as reflecting *her* responsibility in the battering. "The police conceptualize any departures from the accepted standards of mothering and housekeeping as contributory factors towards violence" (Hatty, 1989:78). This nontraditional behavior, however, would also include infidelity, drinking alcohol in male company, and going out alone at night. The second construct has to do with police believing that the victim "provoked" the violence through her own aggressive behavior, such as "nagging" or "taunting" (1989:80). Finally, police officers viewed victims of battering as "psychologically abnormal" or "psychologically disturbed," who drove their husbands to abusing them (1989:80).

Myth #4: In most battering relationships, the women beat up on the men as much as the men beat up on the women.

A final myth concerned with battering is the concept that men are battered by women, or that "violent relationships" are "mutually combative" (both parties contribute equally to the violence in the relationship). While battering does exist in heterosexual relationships where the male is the victim and the woman is the batterer, ninety-five percent of the battering cases are men battering women (Berk et al., 1983; Browne, 1987:8). Moreover, men are not only more likely to batter than women, but women are more likely to use violence only in self-defense during beatings and women are more likely than men to receive serious injuries (Berk et al., 1983; Loving, 1980; Oppenlander, 1982; Saunders, 1988; Schwartz, 1987). This is not surprising in a patriarchal culture such as our own which allows men much more power than women in the work force, the media, the military, and in the home.

Method for Police Study on Perceptions of Woman Battering

The discussion thus far on the myths and perceptions of woman battering suggest the need to understand the degree to which police officers subscribe to the myths. Hatty (1989:87) states: "Clearly, a comparison between police constructions of male violence and women's experiences of this violence indicates that the two are, in fact, diametrically opposed." For these reasons, the original research presented in the remainder of this chapter was conducted. It is an attempt to determine the degree to which police support myths surrounding woman battering.

The author distributed a survey to 324 law enforcement officials in a large midwestern metropolitan area. The surveys were distributed at roll calls in a manner designated to approach representative sampling. Comparisons with the approximately 70 percent of officers who did not take part in the study shows that there were no real demographic differences between those who participated in the study and those who did not. Table 1 describes the sample as 87 percent Anglo, largely from working and middle-class backgrounds; most were patrol officers (73 percent) from the city police department (85 percent) and from the county sheriff's department (15 percent), and the survey was fairly equally divided between shifts. The mean age of the respondents was 36.8 years old, and the mean years of experience was 12.4 years. Sixty-five percent of the sample had completed at least some college courses.

While the survey was composed of numerous sections and questions, this chapter will examine those questions attempting to assess police officials' perceptions of battering (particularly regarding the myths listed above) and questions about the officers' interest in responding to battering calls and their perceived rewards from this aspect of their job. The following Likert scale statements (to which the officers reported their degree of agreement) from the survey were used in this analysis. (Original numbers have been retained.)

1. In the long run, it is best for a battered woman to work things out and stay with her husband/boyfriend.
5. Sometimes the woman really has it coming to her, and the husband is justified in losing his temper and hitting her.
8. It is not worth putting much energy into situations involving domestic violence, since the victim always returns to the abuser.
10. In most cases of domestic violence, the woman batters the man as much as he batters her.
11. Domestic violence is usually more a problem in lower-class neighborhoods than in middle- or upper-class neighborhoods.
12. I used to care about the victim in domestic violence cases, but now I've lost interest.
13. If a battered woman really didn't like it, she would leave her husband/boyfriend.
17. In some cases, such as a woman cheating on her husband/ boyfriend, I can understand why he would beat her up.
24. Some people feel like the battered woman really deserves being abused. Others believe she never deserves her abuse. How about you? How often do you believe she deserves the abuse she received?

Table 1
Description of the Sample[a]

Characteristic	N	Distribution	%	(n)
Race	309	white	87.1	(269)
		African-American	12.9	(40)
Age	304[b]	21-30	19.7	(60)
		31-35	20.7	(63)
		36-40	31.6	(96)
		41+	28.0	(85)
Sex	313	male	93.6	(293)
		female	6.4	(20)
SES	308	poor	10.4	(32)
		working class	38.6	(119)
		middle-class	44.2	(136)
		upper-middle class+	6.8	(21)
Education	302	high school	35.8	(108)
		2 years of college	21.2	(64)
		between 2 and 4 years of college	22.5	(68)
		college degree+	20.5	(62)
Rank	308	patrol officer	73.4	(226)
		specialist	12.3	(38)
		detective	2.3	(7)
		sergeant	8.8	(27)
		lieutenant	1.3	(4)
		other	1.9	(6)
Years Experience[c]	304	less than three	14.1	(43)
		3-7	13.5	(41)
		8-14	26.6	(81)
		15-20	33.2	(101)
		21+	12.5	(38)
Department	317	county	15.5	(49)
		city	84.5	(268)
District	308	one	23.1	(71)
		two	13.0	(40)
		three	17.5	(54)
		four	20.5	(63)
		five	26.0	(80)
Shift	290	first	31.4	(91)
		second	32.8	(95)
		third	35.9	(104)

[a] Percentages may not total 100.0 because of rounding.
[b] The mean age was 36.8 years.
[c] The mean number of years of experience was 12.4 years.

27. Spouse abuse is precipitated by a wife's s nagging or similarly annoying behavior.
30. As one of the aspects of a police officer's job, how rewarding is working with domestic violence cases?

Findings of the Police Survey

This section will report the findings from the survey distributed to the 324 law enforcement officers. Table 2 summarizes the frequencies of the officers' responses to the various Likert questions representing battering myths presented earlier. Additionally, this section will discuss any significant demographic differences between the officers based on age, race, sex, class background, rank, years of experience, and departmental affiliation (county sheriff or city police). Significant demographic differences between the officers are not reported in the tables, only in the text. There were no significant differences based on shift, district, and educational attainment.

Regarding the myths surrounding victims staying in the relationship and "liking it," this survey found that three-fourths of the officers disagreed that it is best for a woman to stay in a battering relationship and "work things out" with her husband or boyfriend (Question 1). White officers (79 percent) were more likely than black officers (70 percent) to disagree with this ($x^2 = 15.52$, $p = .02$). One quarter of the officers agreed with the statement that victims always return, so there is not much use in putting energy into the problem (Question 8). The county sheriffs (63 percent) were more likely than the city officers (45 percent) to disagree with this ($x^2 = 6.32$, $p = .04$).

Few officers (5 percent) agreed that sometimes the victims deserve the abuse and the husband was justified in hitting her (Question 5). Ranking officers (86 percent) were more likely than nonranking officers (61 percent) to disagree with this ($X^2 = 11.08$, $p = .01$), and the sheriffs (80 percent) were more likely than the city officers (62 percent) to disagree ($x^2 = 5.80$, $p = .05$). When the question was modified to include the "provocation" of a victim's infidelity, the percent of officers agreeing that the husband is justified jumped to almost one in five officers (17 percent, Question 17). Almost four-fifths of the officers reported that victims never deserve the abuse, while one-fifth believe that battering victims deserve abuse in at least occasional instances (Question 24). Ninety-six percent of the officers believe that the victims' behavior, such

Table 2

Frequency Responses to Likert Scale Questions[a]

Likert Item	N	Strongly Agree % (n)	Agree % (n)	Undecided/ Neutral % (n)	Disagree % (n)	Strongly Disagree % (n)	— X
1. victim should stay	322	0.6% (2)	4.0% (13)	18.6% (60)	45.7% (147)	31.1% (100)	4.03
5. victim deserves abuse	322	0.6 (2)	4.3 (14)	11.8 (38)	47.5 (153)	35.7 (115)	4.13
8. victims always stay	321	2.8 (9)	22.7 (73)	26.2 (84)	43.0 (138)	5.3 (17)	3.25
10. partners are mutually combative	323	1.9 (6)	12.1 (39)	24.5 (79)	54.8 (177)	6.8 (22)	3.53
11. Domestic violence is class issue	323	4.1 (13)	25.7 (83)	14.6 (47)	46.1 (149)	9.6 (31)	3.32
12. Lost interest in domestic violence	321	2.2 (7)	9.3 (30)	16.5 (53)	59.8 (192)	12.1 (39)	3.70
13. Victim would leave if didn't like it	322	5.0 (16)	21.4 (69)	18.3 (59)	45.3 (146)	9.9 (32)	3.34
17. in some cases domestic violence is justified	321	1.2 (4)	15.9 (51)	18.3 (59)	50.8 (163)	13.7 (44)	3.60

	N	All of the Time	Most of the Time	Some of the Time	Only Occasionally	None of the Time	— X
24. does victim deserve abuse?	319	0.3 (1)	0.6 (2)	5.6 (18)	14.7 (47)	78.7 (251)	4.71
27. wife's behavior causes abuse	318	0.0 (0)	8.8 (28)	62.9 (200)	24.2 (77)	4.1 (13)	3.24

	N	One of Most Rewarding	Fairly Rewarding	Somewhat Rewarding	Rarely Rewarding	Never Rewarding	— X
30. Rewards of domestic violence cases	321	0.6 (2)	1.9 (6)	14.6 (47)	61.4 (197)	21.5 (69)	4.01

[a]Percentages may not total 100.0% because of rounding.

as "nagging," precipitates at least occasional battering incidences (Question 27). The black officers were more likely than the white officers to view the victim's behavior as causing the abuse ($x^2 = 8.03$, $p = .02$).

Fourteen percent of the officers agreed with a statement suggesting that men and women are "mutually combative" in battering relationships, and one-quarter were undecided (Question 10). Almost one-third of the officers believe that battering is more prevalent among the lower-class (Question 11). It is interesting to note that black officers (75 percent) were more likely than white officers (53 percent) to disagree with this ($x^2 = 6.75$, $p = .03$), and that city officers (78 percent) were more likely than county officers (51 percent) to disagree ($x^2 = 12.49$, $p = .01$).

This study was also interested in generating information on officers' satisfaction in handling battering calls. It is encouraging that although about one-tenth of the officers agreed that they had lost interest in responding to battering calls, the majority (72 percent) had not (Question 12). This was particularly true for those at the beginning and end of their careers in terms of years of experience (less than three years and more than 14 years), and least likely for those in the middle range of years of experience ($x^2 = 16.27$, $p = .04$). One-fifth of the officers, however, believed that working with "domestic violence" cases was "never rewarding" and an additional three-fifths found it "rarely rewarding." Thus, less than one-fifth of the officers found responding to battering calls even "somewhat" rewarding (Question 30). Policewomen were more likely than policemen to view these calls as rewarding ($x^2 = 9.50$, $p = .01$).

These findings suggest that while numerous officers do not support victim-blaming and many battering myths, a substantial number are uninformed concerning the reality of the complex dynamics involved in battering relationships. This seems to be particularly apparent concerning myths surrounding class differences in battering relationships and victims leaving and staying in battering relationships. It is also apparent that there are significant differences between departments based on such demographics as age, sex, experience on the force, rank and particularly race and departmental affiliation. This has important implications for hiring and training practices as well as the subcultures of the departments.

While it is understandable that law enforcement officers may get frustrated in responding to the battering calls and that most do not find it rewarding, at least most reported not losing interest in these cases. It is also important to remember when interpreting these findings, that these are the officers' *reported* attitudes. It is possible that some of them reported what they thought they "ought" to believe or what they thought the researcher perceived as the "correct" responses.

Conclusions

Woman battering occurs with a high degree of regularity to a broad spectrum of women. We need a social and systematic response to battering to help victims leave abusive relationships. While some police officers' responses to a questionnaire suggest an understanding of battered women's plight, a substantial proportion of the officers were unaware of the complexities of woman battering and why leaving an abusive relationship is difficult. One-quarter of the officers agreed with a statement that there was no point in "putting much energy" into woman battering calls since the woman always returns. Research shows that victims often leave, if not after the first battering incident, then at some later point. There was considerable support among the officers for the perception that victims exhibit some behavior which causes the abuse. This victim-blaming approach fails to recognize that no behavior justifies violence (unless it is in self-defense). Furthermore, one-third of the officers believed that battering is more prevalent among the lower classes, although research has not found this to be true. As we learn more about battering and develop more strategies to combat it, we can hope for a society and criminal justice system which will be less tolerant of all woman battering.

Bibliography

Atkins, S. and B. Hoggett
  1984   *Women and the Law*. New York: Basil Blackwell.
Bates, Karen Grigsby
  1990   "Never Can Say Good-Bye: A Bad Relationship Can Be Hard to Leave." *Essence Magazine*, February:61-62.
Berk, Richard A. and P. J. Newton
  1985   "Does Arrest Really Deter Wife Battery? An Effort to Replicate the Findings of the Minneapolis Spouse Abuse Experiment." *American Sociological Review* 50, 2:253-62.

Berk, R. A., S. F. Berk, D. R. Loseke, and D. Rauma
  1983   "Mutual Combat and Other Family Violence Myths," pp. 197-212,
          in David Finkelhor, Richard J. Gelles, Gerald T. Hotaling, and
          Murray A. Straus (eds.), *The Dark Side of Families*. Beverly Hills,
          CA: Sage.
Blodgett, Nancy
  1987   "Violence in the Home." *American Bar Association Journal*, May
          1:66-69.
Brand, Pamela A. and Aline H. Kidd
  1986   "Frequencies of Physical Aggression in Heterosexual and Female
          Homosexual Dyads." *Psychological Reports* 59:1307-13.
Browne, Angela
  1987   *When Battered Women Kill*. New York: Free Press.
Caldwell, Mayta A. and Letitia A. Peplau
  1984   "The Balance of Power in Lesbian Relationships." *Sex Roles* 10,
          7/8: 587-599.
Carlson, Bonnie E.
  1987   "Wife Battering: A Social Deviance Analysis," pp. 172-96 in
          Josefina Figueira-McDonough & Rosemary Sarri (eds.), *The
          Trapped Woman: Catch-22 in Deviance and Control*. Newbury
          Park, CA: Sage.
Cohn, Ellen B. and Lawrence M. Sherman
  1987   "Police Policy on Domestic Violence, 1986: A National Survey."
          Crime Control Reports, No. 5, March.
Coley, Soraya M. and Joyce O. Beckett
  1988   "Black Battered Women: Practice Issues." *Social Casework*
          3:483-90.
Crites, Laura L.
  1987   "Wife Abuse: The Judicial Record," pp. 38-53, in Laura L. Crites
          and Winifred L. Hepperle (eds.), *Women, the Courts, and
          Equality*. Newbury Park, CA: Sage.
DeMaris, Alfred
  1990   "The Dynamics of Generational Transfer in Courtship Violence:
          A Biracial Exploration." *Journal of Marriage and the Family*
          52:219-31.
Dobash, R. Emerson and Russell Dobash
  1979   *Violence Against Wives*. New York: Free Press.
Dunford, Franklyn W., David Huizinga, and Delbert S. Elliot
  1990   "The Role of Arrest in Domestic Assault: The Omaha Police
          Experiment." *Criminology* 28, 2:183-206.
Dutton, Donald G.
  1988   *The Domestic Assault of Women*. Boston: Allyn and Bacon.
Edwards, Anne
  1987   "Male Violence in Feminist Theory," pp. 13-29 in Jalna Hanmer
          and Mary Maynard (eds.), *Women, Violence, and Social Control*.
          Atlantic Highlands, NJ: Humanities Press International.

Epstein, Cynthia Fuchs
1988   *Deceptive Distinctions: Sex, Gender, and the Social Order*. New Haven, CT: Yale University Press.

Erez, Edna
1986   "Intimacy, Violence, and the Police." *Human Relations* 39, 3:265-81.

Ferraro, Kathleen J.
1988   "Policing Woman Battering." *Social Problems* 36, 1:61-74.

Hatty, Suzanne E.
1989   "Policing and Male Violence in Australia," pp. 70-89 in Jalna Hanmer, Jill Radford, & Elizabeth A. Stanko (eds.), *Women, Policing, and Male Violence*. London: Routledge.

Lane, Katherine E. and Patricia A. Gwartney-Gibbs
1985   "Violence in the Context of Dating and Sex." *Journal of Family Issues* 6, 1:45-59.

Lawrenz, Lembo and Schade
1988   "Time Series Analysis of the Effect of a Domestic Violence Directive on the Number of Arrests per Day." *Journal of Criminal Justice* 16:493-98.

Loving, N.
1980   *Responding to Spouse Abuse and Wife Beating: A Guide for Police*. Washington, DC: Police Executive Research Forum.

Makepeace, James K.
1981   "Courtship Violence Among College Students." *Family Relations* 30:97-102.
1986   "Life Events and Courtship Violence." *Family Relations* 32:101-9.
1989   "Dating, Living Together, and Courtship Violence," pp. 94-107 in Maureen A. Priog-Good and Jan E. Stets (eds), *Violence in Dating Relationships*. New York: Praeger.

Mills, B. G. and M. L. McNamar
1981   "California's Response to Domestic Violence." *Santa Clara Law Review*, 21:1-21.

Oppenlander, Nan
1982   "Coping or Copping Out." *Criminology* 20, 3-4:449-65.

Pleck, Elizabeth
1983   "Feminist Responses to 'Crimes against Women,' 1868-1896." *Signs: Journal of Women in Culture and Society* 8, 3:451-70.

Ptacek, James
1988   "Why Do Men Batter Their Wives?", pp. 133-157 in Kersti Yllo and Michele Bograd (eds.), *Feminist Perspectives on Wife Abuse*. Newbury Park, CA: Sage.

Renzetti, Claire M.
1989   "Building a Second Closet: Third Party Responses to Victims of Lesbian Partner Abuse." *Family Relations* 38:157-63.

Richie, Beth
1985   "Battered Black Women: A Challenge for the Black Community." *The Black Scholar* :40-44.

Rowe, Kelly
  1985   "The Limits of the Neighborhood Justice Center: Why Domestic
          Violence Cases Should Not be Mediated." *Emory Law Journal*
          34:855-909.
Russell, Diana E. H.
  1984   *Sexual Exploitation: Rape, Child Sexual Abuse, and Workplace
          Harassment.* Beverly Hills, CA: Sage.
Saunders, D. G.
  1988   "Wife Abuse, Husband Abuse, or Mutual Combat? A Feminist
          Perspective on the Empirical Findings," pp. 90-103 in Kersti Yllo
          and Michele Bograd (eds.) *Feminist Perspectives on Wife Abuse.*
          Newbury Park, CA: Sage.
Schechter, Susan
  1982   *Women and Male Violence.* Boston: South End Press.
Schwartz, Martin D.
  1987   "Gender and Injury in Spousal Assault." *Sociological Focus* 20,
          1:61-75.
Sherman, Lawrence W. and Richard A. Berk
  1984   "The Specific Deterrent Effects of Arrest for Domestic Assault."
          American Sociological Review 49:261-72.
Smith, D. A. and J. R. Klein
  1984   "Police Control of Interpersonal Disputes." *Social Problems* 31,
          4:469-81.
Stanko, Elizabeth
  1985   *Intimate Intrusions: Women's Experience of Male Violence.*
          Boston: Routledge & Kegan Paul.
Strube, M. J. and M. L. Barbour
  1984   "Factors Related to the Decision to Leave an Abusive
          Relationship." *Journal of Marriage and the Family*, 837-44.
Tong, Rosemarie
  1984   *Women, Sex, and the Law.* Totowa, NJ: Rowman & Allanheld.
Walker, Lenore E.
  1979   *The Battered Woman.* New York: Harper & Row.
  1983a   "The Battered Woman Syndrome Study," pp. 31-48 in David
          Finkelhor, Richard J. Gelles, Gerald T. Hotaling, and Murray A.
          Straus (eds.), *The Dark Side of Families.* Beverly Hills, CA: Sage.
  1983b   "Victimology and the Psychological Perspectives of Battered
          Women." *Victimology* 8, 1-2:82-104.

chapter 11

Dealing With Child Sexual Assault
The Victim, the Offender, and Society

Martin D. Schwartz

Ohio University

Jody A. Miller

University of Southern California

Nearly 15 years ago a massive research and publication interest in forcible rape forced us to take a careful look at rape laws and criminal justice system practices. Slowly we began to realize that the law and justice system were a part of the problem itself; at the very least, the system gave the force of law to a series of myths and "old husbands' tales" (Schwartz and Clear, 1980). In the 1980s, another surge of interest, research, public debate and publication occurred, this time on child sexual assault.

Unfortunately, things were easier with forcible rape, where there was at least general agreement between researchers, reformers and the criminal justice system that the goal of rape law was to convict and punish as many stranger rapists as possible. Since quite a number of studies had pinpointed the extent to which the justice system was operating from false presumptions and myths (cf. Katz and Mazur, 1979), the problem for reformers was the relatively simple one (in theory, not necessarily in practice) of removing such myths and anti-victim elements from the criminal law (Caringella-MacDonald, 1988). Unfortunately, what was too often ignored in order to achieve this general agreement was that a tremendous amount of forcible rape takes place within the confines of the family (Schwartz, 1982; Schwartz and Slatin, 1984; Finkelhor and Yllo, 1985).

In the case of child sexual abuse, the problem is even worse: most of the abuse takes place within the family, yet we continue to ignore it. Incest "is still the least talked-about form of child sexual abuse" (Crewdson, 1988:81), despite the fact that "intrafamily sexual abuse, particularly by fathers, stepfathers, and older brothers, is clearly the most pressing priority, both because of its prevalence and its devastating impact" (Finkelhor et al., 1988:260). We have spent the past decade engaged through the media in a series of moral panics over sexual abuse in day care (Finkelhor et al., 1988), missing children (OJJDP, 1988), murdered abducted children (OJJDP, 1989b), and the supposed problem of overreaction to false reports (Zegart, 1989). None of these problems are as relatively important as incest.

Just as with forcible rape, researchers have discovered that we are handicapped by widespread belief in myths about child sexual abuse. Many of these myths parallel rape myths, including the ideas that victims are seductive and manipulative and that women and children lie and therefore cannot be trusted as witnesses. Also like rape, the crime normally occurs when only the victim and the offender are present (MacMurray, 1989). Physical evidence is unavailable in most cases without penetration; even those cases must be reported immediately or the evidence will be useless. Thus, the lack of witnesses, the lack of corroborating evidence, and the common belief that child witnesses and their mothers are incompetent, unreliable or not credible, limits the number of cases which can go to trial (Whitcomb, 1985). Cases of father-daughter incest are particularly susceptible to these prejudices. Charges may be dropped because the prosecutor does not want to put small children on the witness stand. If the incest causes the marriage to dissolve, the father can demand joint custody and have it enforced by a court which points out that there has never been a conviction for sexual abuse (Crewdson, 1988). Even where there is a conviction, there has been great debate over whether treatment or punishment is the appropriate response. These issues will be dealt with later in this chapter.

Perhaps there are more male victims and female offenders in child sexual abuse than has often been presumed. However, we argue that the abuse of girls by older male family members is the most common and most serious form of abuse. Given a lack of space to cover all aspects of the problem, the victimization of girls by men will be the primary concern here.

Facts and Myths About Child Sexual Assault

Characteristics of the Event

A common myth is that child sexual assault is most often committed by a stranger, or at least a childcare worker or someone else outside the family. We not only continue to warn children about taking candy or rides from strangers, but in some areas we've terrorized an entire generation of children with stories about the abduction, rape and murder of children by strangers, particularly near schoolyards. Fortunately, these acts are in fact relatively rare. Unfortunately, molestation by a relative or family member is the most prevalent type of abuse (Russell, 1986).

The presumed incest frequency taught for many years in medical, mental health and psychology courses was Weinberg's (1955) estimate of one case for each one million persons in the population. However, there have been a number of recent surveys; roughly a quarter to a third of all females and a tenth or more of all males report some form of sexual abuse as a child (Peters et al, 1986; Crewdson, 1988). Finkelhor and Lewis (1988) estimate from a randomized self-report survey of men in the general population that men commit 90 percent of child sexual abuse; that between five and ten percent of all men have committed such acts; and that approximately 22 percent of all children are in some way victimized. Child sexual abuse usually does not involve only one incident. Researchers have reported figures ranging from 46 to 79 percent of child victims reporting that it happened more than once (Risin and Koss, 1987). In fact, MacMurray (1989) found that 13 percent of the victims in his study of reported child sexual abuse were abused for over five years.

Although many think that child sexual assault is more common among older and more developed children, researchers have always found very young children to be victims as well. Siegel et al. (1987) reported the mean age of first assault for victims of ongoing assault to be 8.5; while Moyer (1989) found that 31 percent of her sample of abused children in western Pennsylvania were under the age of 10; and MacMurray's study of prosecution files showed that 37 percent of the victims were under age 5.

There has been little research produced with a primary focus on race, but what has been done has "consistently failed to find any black-white differences in rates of sexual abuse" (Finkelhor and Baron, 1986:53). For example, one of the more instructive studies was a national poll conducted by the Los Angeles Times which found no differences in the rates of incest victimization among whites and blacks (Crewdson, 1988). More typically, there are some contradictions in the literature. Siegel et al. (1987), for example, reports a rate in Los Angeles almost three times higher for whites than for Hispanics. Russell (1983) on the other hand, found rates for Hispanics were slightly higher than for the general population, while rates for Asian and Jewish women were significantly lower. Interestingly, one strong racial difference was found by Morrow and Sorell, who did not look at rates, but found that "being nonwhite was related to lower self-esteem, greater depression, and higher frequency of negative behaviors" (1989:681).

Unfortunately, there have been few other studies which have focused on race or ethnicity, and there are excellent reasons to be wary of statistics gathered from official agencies. Finkelhor (1987:233) notes that "it is well recognized that officially reported cases constitute only a small proportion of all occurring cases and even of all cases known to professionals." Hampton and Newberger (1988) found that of all of the cases of child abuse and neglect they examined, 60 percent of the cases involving white children were reported to the Child Protective Service agencies. It was noted that 74 percent of the cases involving black children and 91 percent of those involving Hispanic children were reported. As they note: "If child abuse reporting is as biased by class and race as these data suggest, then there is clearly a need for a critical review of the *system* as well as the *process* of reporting" (1988:22, emphasis in original).

Incest Families

The behavior most researchers consider the most victimizing and traumatizing is father/daughter incest (Finkelhor et al., 1988). Russell (1986), who conducted one of the most widely respected random sample victim surveys, estimates that perhaps 4.5 percent of girls may be victims. Other research shows there are some common features of these cases. Most often the victim is not forcibly raped (although this does happen) but rather is misled or coerced into the sexual activity (see, e.g., Siegel et al., 1987:1150). Further, incest tends to occur in families where there are already existing serious problems. Both the father and the daughter commonly have poor social relations with the mother. While this is not always true, often the mother is either absent from the home or does not play the "traditional" role of homemaker, sexual partner and mother (Butler, 1978). In mainstream literature, the father/daughter incest is almost invariably blamed on the wife, who by refusing to play her "proper" role causes the incest by virtually forcing her husband to look elsewhere for sexual gratification. She then allows the incest to occur because it allows her to continue to shirk her "duties" (see, e.g., Justice and Justice, 1979; Weiner, 1964; Weinberg, 1955).

Unfortunately, these authors never found evidence for these assertions (Wattenberg, 1985). Because health providers assumed that mothers have the responsibility for protecting children, they were quick to blame the mother for problems the children encountered. The fathers, having no responsibility, were assigned less blame. A major contribution of feminist theorists has been to examine the family and note the tremendous power a patriarchal society has given to men. Men are in positions of power so that through violence they can require the submission of all family members (Wattenberg, 1985). In fact, a large percentage of incestuous fathers are also wife abusers (Paveza, 1988; Truesdell et al., 1986). Even the mother who may be aware of the incest is often in a subservient dependent position, believing that she does not have the power to intervene. The traditional socialization of women into passive, submissive roles allows the abuser to exert his dominance.

Male socialization also plays a role: "Child sexual abuse is . . . a predominantly male behavior, and can . . . be plausibly analyzed as having roots in the social construction of masculinity" (Finkelhor and Lewis, 1988:73). One aspect of this is the oversexualization of needs. Because boys' socialization discourages emotional dependency and encourages autonomy, sex often becomes the one acceptable outlet for men to meet their emotional needs. This can lead to sexual abuse when men are unable to separate sex from other distinct emotional needs. In addition, most men learn early to sexualize subordination. These men perceive smallness, youthfulness and vulnerability as sexually attractive and inexperience, dependency, acquiescence and helplessness as desirable qualities.

As a result, some men sexualize children, who have all of these traits. Further, Finkelhor and Lewis argue, many restraints exist which may make it difficult for men to develop empathy for children. These restraints include male devaluation of and their exclusion from, child care and their "alienation from their own childlike vulnerabilities" (1988:75).

One additional problem which we need to begin to explore is the seemingly high rate of sexual victimization within families by older children. Much of what we have been labeling as noncoercive sexual experimentation by relative equals may in fact be more serious. Because cases are commonly dropped when the offenders are young themselves (MacMurray, 1989), we evidently have not noticed that a significant percentage of all sex offenders, particularly victimizers of younger children in the same family, may be adolescents or even children themselves (Bethea-Jackson and Brissett-Chapman, 1989; Johnson, 1988; Crewdson, 1988; Davis and Leitenberg, 1987). We still know too little about this phenomenon, as "available evidence suggests that the problem is being discovered at a rate that exceeds our current ability to adequately define the problem" (Pierce and Pierce, 1987:362).

The Effect of Child Sexual Abuse on Victims

Developing concrete evidence that incest and child sexual assault cause significant harm has been difficult because a number of traditional clinical researchers have claimed that such experiences are not particularly damaging to the child's personality development (Bender and Blau, 1937; Gagnon, 1965; Gentry, 1978; Henderson, 1983; Kaufman et al., 1954; Kilpatrick, 1986; Landis, 1956; Lukianowicz, 1972; Lustig et al., 1966; Schultz, 1973; Sloane and Karpinski, 1942; Yorukoglu and Kemph, 1966). Swan (1985) recently argued in a reputable social work journal that not only do children seduce their fathers to get attention, but they also try to gain control over adults.

Unfortunately, some researchers have twisted their data to report that incest is a positive experience for children. For example, Nelson (1986) found reports showing that if the relationship was noncoercive it was remembered as a positive experience. Unfortunately, a reconstruction of her tables makes it clear that most of the male aggressors reported the experience as positive, and most of the female victims reported the experience as negative, a point she seems to have missed.

Despite such convoluted attempts to argue that child sexual

abuse is not a serious problem, the solid weight of the evidence is on the side of serious mental health impairment in a significant number of victims. Finkelhor and Browne (1988) argue that empirical, rigorous literature based on community studies confirms the results of many clinical studies that child sexual abuse victims are more likely than others to have such long-term effects as sexual functioning problems as adults, vulnerability to later victimization, depression, suicide attempts, and substance abuse. Although they argue that most victims are not seriously harmed ("less than one-fifth evidence serious psychopathology") (1988:274), any activity in which one-fifth of the participants will many years later evidence serious psychopathology must rate as an extraordinarily dangerous activity.

Dealing With Abusers

A Candidate for Treatment?

Traditional victimology leans heavily toward victim precipitation and family dysfunction for the cause of incest and generally works to remove complete blame from the father (Moyer, 1989). Thus, many have argued that treatment of the offender is the primary concern. Daugherty, for example, has argued that after providing a means to intervene to stop the abuse, the most important requirement for new state laws on incest must be "to provide the flexibility to allow the offender to be treated and rehabilitated — not simply incarcerated for a period of time and then released" (1978:101).

Some of the findings from sociological and psychological studies of incest have fueled this argument. For example, researchers have argued that incest is the result of already socially disordered families (Cleveland, 1986; Henderson, 1983; Brooks, 1983; Nakashima and Zakas, 1977; Sgroi, 1982). A common type of offender identified in the literature is a man who is dictatorial in the family, who believes that his role is as a wage-earner, and feels that his family primarily exists to serve his needs. In a situation where he is a failure at wage-earning, where he has serious sexual and social problems with his wife, and where he confuses love with sex, he might turn to a daughter to provide him with the sex he confuses with family love (Star, 1983:35-37). Family therapists have often argued that men who fit this pattern are particularly amenable to therapy.

Another argument attacking punishment as a goal of the criminal justice system in incest cases has been that after conviction, offenders typically have an extremely low recidivism or repeat rate. Since there will be no repeat of the crime anyway, a term of imprisonment or punishment serves no purpose in preventing further offenses (Bailey and McCabe, 1979; Brecher, 1978; Forward and Buck, 1978; Gibbens et al., 1978; Gibbens et al., 1981; Maisch, 1972; Soothill and Gibbens, 1978).

Thus, the therapeutic community in general has argued that punishment only prevents effective treatment from taking place and needlessly breaks up families (Anderson and Schafer, 1967; Brecher, 1978; Butler, 1978; Forward and Buck, 1978; Giaretto, 1976; Justice and Justice, 1979; Kroth, 1979; Pittman, 1976). Katz (1983), for example, suggests that the court should be given the power to put *any* family member in an incest case into therapy, backed up by criminal penalties for noncompliance. Others see this as part of a general trend to medicalize problems of the family, reducing them to the intervention of medical "experts" as a newer form of social control (Armstrong, 1983; Donzolot, 1979; Foucault, 1980).

It is difficult to determine what is best for the child victim (Allen, 1983). A common goal is intervention to stop the abuse as soon as possible. Treatment advocates argue that punishment laws defeat this purpose because families do not report incest from a fear of family shame, disaster or excessive punishment (Kroth, 1979; Manchester, 1978). Adding to this argument is that children who were not traumatized by the incest event would be later traumatized by the criminal justice system (Schulz, 1973, 1980). Thus, the decriminalization of incest or child sexual abuse in favor of treatment goals would be of primary benefit to the victim.

Obviously, there has been great concern for keeping the incestuous family together (Gentry, 1978; Pittman, 1976). Some of the most publicized treatment efforts have been based on family therapy and an overt goal of maintaining the family after an incest experience (Giaretto, 1976; Kroth, 1979), while law reformers have traditionally argued for family unification as a goal (Bailey and McCabe, 1979, Kirkwood and Mihaila, 1979). However, it is sometimes difficult to understand the logic of a system built on a base of forced reconstitution of the family unit. As Armstrong asks (1978:205):

> With a close to fifty percent divorce rate—with people divorcing over a difference in preferred style of eggs—why, when a man

gets caught sexually abusing his daughter, is it suddenly vital
that the family be kept intact?

The assumption has been that if the father can be rehabilitated
and the family unified, the needs of the victim would automatically
be addressed. Some therapists, however, question whether a victim
of years of continual abuse can feel comfortable a few months later
living with her abuser. In addition, because victims commonly
blame themselves for their abuse and often feel extreme shame and
humiliation, a treatment system which also makes the victim feel
responsible may be extremely detrimental. Moyer (1989:15) argues
that this can be addressed by prosecuting and punishing the
offender, which "vindicates the victim and assures the victim that
she/he was not responsible for the incestuous act."

A Candidate for Punishment?

The American criminal justice system has typically justified
punishment for any, all, or a combination of reasons: retaliation or
just deserts; specific deterrence to stop an offender from repeating
the offense; general deterrence to send out a message to potential
law violators; or incapacitation to keep the offender from
committing the act while locked up. Perhaps the most problematic
is the one most widely used — general deterrence: although we use
it to justify many of our laws, we really know very little about how
it operates (Zimring and Hawkins, 1973; Blumstein et al., 1978).
Why *didn't* you commit incest? Was it due to your moral
upbringing? Religious principles? Fear of public shame if caught?
Some internalized guilt or conscience you cannot really identify?
Or fear of going to prison? How many of us can really separate these
things out and say that we only hold back from having sexual
intercourse with our children because we fear a prison term?

A major change in the literature on child sexual abuse has been
a growing presence of literature arguing for punishment of child
sexual abusers. Much of this change is due to the influence of
feminist theorists, who quite correctly point out that crimes against
females are less likely to be punished (see, e.g., MacMurray, 1989).
Feminists also ask the system to send offenders to prison as a moral
statement that announces that child sexual abuse is unacceptable
behavior. This argument has found a ready audience in a criminal
justice system which has become significantly more punitive
toward all crimes and which more than doubled the number of
persons in prison and jail during a decade (the 1980s) while the
crime rate generally remained constant.

This has been difficult for feminist theorists. On one hand, many take the position that a solution to the problem of violence against women is not going to be found without attention to the position and power accorded men in a patriarchal system and that a restructuring of the sexual division of labor is necessary for any serious change (Messerschmidt, 1986; Nelson, 1984). However, the calls that some are now making for extensive punishment under the current system for males who victimize females (e.g., Box-Grainger, 1986; Gregory, 1986) sound rather similar to the calls of conservative power structures which are quite unsympathetic to feminist aims.

It is difficult to determine what the goal of additional punishment is, since theorists who call for punishment often remain vague on goals. Some abstract idea of protection for women is often the stated goal. However, it is difficult to see how increased punishments would lessen the endemic violence against women (Daly and Chesney-Lind, 1988). Edwards (1989:11), denounces those who cannot tell the difference between male and female demands for more punishment of sex offenders. She states that the demands of feminists

> . . . cannot simply be reduced and equated with right-wing Conservative regulation, since feminists' demands for protection through law and policing and right-wing homogenized efforts toward control derive from very different theoretical conceptualization of the relation of law to the state, and very divergent political standpoints. In the apparent demand for more law and policing in the area of violence against women, feminists are simply urging the same consideration for women victims in the home as has already been given to nonspousal and nonpartner victims in the street.

What does all this mean? Certainly that there are no simple solutions to these problems. Many of us have great faith in punishment, but the dilemma is that there is no evidence that punishment does anything except provide a very expensive brutalization experience. Certainly some would argue that this is a fair trade for the brutalization the offender visited upon his victim, but unless one is satisfied by the multiplication of victims to now include one more, this has not solved very much either. As Crewdson (1988:205), certainly an opponent of treatment, argues, "there aren't enough prisons to hold all the pedophiles," and even if there were, they'd all eventually get out.

This is one of the areas of criminology where perhaps first efforts could be made to implement ideas such as those professed by the penal abolitionist movement, where mutual aid, community support and an aim of reconciliation and restoration are paramount (DeKeseredy and Schwartz, 1991).

The Child Victim and the Criminal Justice System

Do Children Lie About Child Sexual Abuse?

In some ways, the extent to which one sees problems in the courtroom with the testimony of incest victims depends on one's attitudes toward women and girls. In a courtroom where the primary emphasis supposedly is with ascertaining the accuracy of testimony, much of the concern in child sexual abuse cases has come from male doubts about the ability of females to recognize and to tell the truth.

This concern with female veracity is not new. In fact, the most difficult problems in dealing with child sexual abuse are a direct legacy of Sigmund Freud. Surprised by the large numbers of unresolved incest traumas among his patients, Freud argued that sexual trauma was a major cause of adult problems. However, he later became troubled by the growing number of patients who reported childhood sexual victimizations. Since he "knew" that this high rate could not be true, he developed one of psychology's most important child development theories in order to explain away his evidence: the need for children to resolve and displace their desire for opposite-sexed parents. Although it was developed without the benefit of ever examining a child (Wahl, 1960), and although Freud never uncovered a single instance of a false accusation of incest (Goodwin et al, 1978), his theory explains how unresolved incest desire can lead to hysteria and a confusion between fantasy and reality. Freud's idea that most child sexual assault reports were fantasy led to generations of therapists who, when seeing a sexual assault victim, were most concerned with determining why she was lying and with finding the source of her fantasies (Masson, 1984).

Other theorists have taken Freud's theories even further, arguing that in acting out Oedipal desires the highly seductive and sexually charged child leads the unwary adult into the actual sex act. Thus, some theorists have suggested that these children are in fact the cause of the problem (Swan, 1985), and have therefore exonerated the father (Woodbury and Schwartz, 1971). These dangerous theories of psychiatric researchers have been responsible for some of the problems which exist today for child victims in the courtroom.

Defense lawyers and some legal scholars have argued that the natural lying ability of females prejudices legal cases against accused child sexual assault offenders. The most important legal reference work on evidence in the courtroom, *Wigmore's Evidence*, cites approvingly a psychiatrist's argument that little girls all think like whores and that the most dangerous ones are the ones who seem to be the most innocent (Wigmore, 1940, sec. 924a):

> The most dangerous witnesses in prosecutions for morality offenses are the youthful ones (often mere children) in whom the sex instinct holds the foremost place in their thoughts and feelings. This intensely erotic propensity often can be detected in the wanton facial expression, the sensuous motions, and the manner of speech. But on the other hand one must not be deceived by a madonna-like countenance that such a girl can readily assume; nor by the convincing upturn of the eyes, with which she seeks to strengthen her credibility. To be sure, the coarse sensuousness of her demeanor, coupled with a pert and forward manner, usually leaves no doubt about her type of thought. Even in her early years can be seen in countenance and demeanor the symptoms of the hussy-type, which in later years enable one at first glance to recognize the hardened prostitute. With profuse falsities they shamelessly speak of the coarsest sex matters. Having come early into bad practices, they can weave these into their testimony and decorate their narratives with the most plausible details . . . It is just such witnesses that often bring into their picture individuals who have never been near them and that throw suspicion recklessly on the most worthy persons.

Of course, it is not necessary to delve into the history of psychology to find such assertions. Leahy, for example, argues that an important priority for courtroom proceedings is to take into account the "facts" and common knowledge that children lie, and are in fact the ones who "woo their fathers" rather than the other way around (1979:759,763). He proposes that incest law be changed to forbid the testimony of child victims unless the testimony is corroborated by other evidence. This refrain has continued to sound through the 1980s, usually in conservative and right-wing publications, as part of arguments stating that campaigns against incest and child sexual abuse are antifamily and undercut the position of the male as head of the family. There are references to Salem witchhunts by antifamily social workers (e.g., Carlson, 1985), and an insistence that not only do children commonly lie without help (Kirp, 1985), but that the stories of sexual abuse they tell are planted in their heads by psychiatrists and social workers (e.g., Eberle and

Eberle, 1986:285). Others do not want to suggest that the problem isn't real, but argue that some children lie and that many common signs of child sexual abuse can be misleading (e.g., Dillon, 1987).

On the other hand, feminist theorists began arguing early in their campaigns that children in fact rarely or never lie about such events (Forward and Buck, 1978), and research over the past 20 years has not given any reason to change this argument (Jaffe et al, 1987). Not only is the rate of false reports from children very low, but most of the false reports come from emotionally disturbed girls in their middle to late teens who are fairly easily found out (Crewdson, 1988). As Jay and Doganis (1987:123) point out: "The real problem is not whether children tell the truth, but whether adults are prepared to believe them." Worse yet, Crewdson (1988) argues that most false report charges come from adults, who *do* lie and coach their children in backing up their stories. Of course, such cases are usually found out easily, as few coached children are able to tell a compelling falsehood over a long period of time.

The Child Victim as Witness

The major problem in the prosecution of these cases is that little children do not easily fit into the structure of the court system. Most cases, of course, do not end up in court. Either charges are dropped or often offenders plead guilty to reduced charges offered in exchange for the guilty plea. However, when cases go to trial, the concern is mainly for the truth of the testimony. A common require-ment, if one disbelieves the ability of the witness to tell a story truthfully and competently, is to demand corroborating physical evidence (Leahy, 1979). Unfortunately, the very nature of child sexual abuse — that it may go on for a long time and not be uncov-ered while physical evidence can still be obtained — means that such evidence is rarely available. Requiring corroborating evidence would virtually end prosecution for child sexual abuse and incest (Ordway, 1981).

Although it has become a staple of the popular press to report that overzealous state workers are destroying the lives of innocent families by charging adults with child sexual assault (e.g., Zegart, 1989; Eberle and Eberle, 1986), perhaps more important is that few cases are brought to trial. Much has been made of the fact that many cases are "unfounded" after the initial report (e.g., Kirp, 1985), but this does not necessarily mean the reports are false. It often means that an overwhelmed justice and child protection system was unable to substantiate the charges sufficiently. In Massachusetts, all cases which pass this first hurdle (are "founded") must be referred to the District Attorney. MacMurray (1989) discovered that almost half of these referrals were still screened out for nonprosecution at the first stage of review in that office. Eventually what happens is that prosecutors only go to court on the easy cases such as stranger sexual abuse by a known pedophile (Crewdson, 1988) or incest which can be documented as having taken place over an extended period (MacMurray, 1989).

Even if the child victim is not faced with the presumption that she/he is lying, there is still the problem that children sometimes make less than perfect court witnesses (Clemens, 1983). As Ordway (1981:137) notes: "They have a subjective sense of time, an inaccurate memory—especially in regard to experiences such as incest which are repeated over time—and a limited ability to communicate what they do understand and recall."

Court Reform

The criminal justice system is not designed to meet the special needs of child victims. Often children must tell their stories dozens of times to people from agency after agency with overlapping needs and responsibilities. Meanwhile, the common practice of granting continuances causes delays that can confuse child victims, erode their memories, and undermine therapeutic efforts to help them. Then, as Whitcomb (1985:148) notes:

> When these cases do go to court, an entirely different set of problems arises for children who are called to testify. Judges may seem to loom large and powerful over small children who may feel isolated in the witness stand. Attorneys often use language children do not understand and seem to argue over everything the children say. Defense attorneys ask questions intended to confuse them for reasons children cannot comprehend. Many people are watching every move the child witness makes—especially the defendant.

Adults, particularly adults connected to the criminal justice system, tend to equate consistency with truthfulness. Obviously, children have real problems when being examined by a defense attorney. Crewdson (1988:166) explains:

> If such a contest seems like a gross mismatch, it usually is—an intelligent, well-educated trial lawyer with years of experience in questioning hostile witnesses pitted against a child who is easily confused about time, place, and the sequence of events,

who tells different parts of the same story at different times, and who links things in his mind that may not be connected.

Victim advocates have been trying to develop alternatives to allow the introduction of the child's evidence without the traditional testimony and cross-examination of the child victim. These include the "child courtroom" where juries are hidden behind one-way glass (Libai, 1980), or where juries see only a videotape of the examination of the child by an expert (Ordway, 1981). Interestingly, while more than a quarter of the states authorize some substitution of videotaped for live testimony (Crewdson, 1988), it has rarely been used (Whitcomb, 1985). The least used so far is the only one explicitly approved by the U.S. Supreme Court. It allows the use of closed circuit television to broadcast the child's testimony from another room.

A major reason none of these innovations is widely used is the defense argument that anything other than face to face contact with the victim denies the defendant his constitutional right to face and cross-examine his accusers. Courts have been generally sympathetic, as the first case law on innovations has been to rule that they cannot be used automatically, but only when the prosecutors can demonstrate that a particular child witness in a particular case will suffer emotionally. "In other words, the decision to use innovative courtroom techniques must be made on a case-by-case basis" (OJJDP, 1989a).

Meanwhile, innovations which do not involve technology are slowly being implemented or used experimentally to avoid revictimizing these children. These include using anatomically correct dolls, artwork, props, and simplified vocabulary to help the victim communicate; modifying the physical environment of the courtroom or preparing the victims by giving them a tour of the courtroom before the proceedings; introducing the victims to the judge before the trial; holding a formal "court school" to teach what happens in a trial; eliminating some of the required arrest complaints to lower the number of required testimony occasions; and others. Additionally, there has been some attempt to coordinate investigative interviews and criminal and civil proceedings as well as to accelerate the adjudication process of sexual abuse cases (OJJDP, 1989a; Whitcomb, 1985).

Conclusions

The most important issue outlined in this paper is that the solutions proposed by most theorists are problematic. Both the traditional victimology demand to medicalize the problem and the more current punishment approach follow the American ideology of individualism: social problems are individually caused and can most effectively be solved by changing/fixing the individual (Hearn, 1988). Both theories impede the policymakers' understanding of the structural causes of the problem, while at the same time expanding the network of state intervention (Nelson, 1984). One cannot deal with intrafamily relations outside the cultural context in which they occur (Gordon, 1986; Twitchell, 1987). Although some of the reforms outlined in this paper can make life a bit easier for victims, the reformer must know that these changes are doing nothing to solve the problem.

Feminist and power-control theories, on the other hand, point to the nature of a patriarchal society in which men are in charge of families, socialized to see women only as sexual objects, and taught to equate love and sex. Men often argue that they have sex with children because they love them so much. It is hard to imagine a conception of love which allows a man to harm his daughter because he loves her, to ruin her life to meet his own momentary needs (Gordon and O'Keefe, 1984). Crewdson (1988) has an intriguing theory that child sexual abusers are narcissists who constantly need reassurance that they are desired and who turn to children because children are so much more capable of idolatry than adults. What he and many others fail to point out is that all such theories are grounded in a presumptive legitimacy of male dominance in the family. If the male can coerce, dominate or terrorize his family so that its members will be more submissive to him, he may get away with battering, rape, child sexual abuse or psychological terrorism.

Perhaps the most important problem, however, is the ideology that what takes place in the family is private and beyond the view of the state. As Crewdson (1988) has pointed out, the most frustrated workers in this field are the ones who have tried to implement prevention programs, only to find strong parental opposition to teaching children that they have a right not to be forced into sex with their parents.

Bibliography

Allen, Margaret J.
   1983   "Comment, Tort Remedies for Incestuous Abuse." *Golden Gate University Law Review* 13:609-38.
Anderson, Lorna M. and Gretchen Schafer
   1967   "Children of Incest." *Pediatrics* 40:55-62.

Armstrong, Louise
   1978   *Kiss Daddy Goodnight: A Speakout on Incest.* New York: Pocket
           Books.
   1983   *The Home Front: Notes From the Family War Zone.* New York:
           McGraw-Hill.
Bailey, Victor and Sarah McCabe
   1979   "Reforming the Law of Incest." *Criminal Law Review*
           1979:749-64.
Bender, Lauretta and Abraham Blau
   1937   "The Reaction of Children to Sexual Relations With Adults."
           American Journal of Orthopsychiatry 7:500-518.
Bethea-Jackson, Gail, and Sheryl Brissett-Chapman
   1989   "The Juvenile Sexual Offender: Challenges to Assessment for
           Outpatient Intervention." *Child and Adolescent Social Work*
           6:127-37.
Blumstein, Alfred, Jacqueline Cohen and Daniel Nagin, eds.
   1978   *Deterrence and Incapacitation: Estimating the Effects of
           Criminal Sanctions on Crime Rates.* Washington, D.C.: National
           Academy of Sciences.
Box-Grainger, Jill
   1986   "Sentencing Rapists." Pp. 31-52 in Roger Matthews and Jock
           Young, eds., *Confronting Crime.* Beverly Hills: Sage.
Brecher, Edward M.
   1978   *Treatment Programs for Sex Offenders.* Washington, D.C.:
           National Institute for Law Enforcement and Criminal Justice, U.S.
           Department of Justice.
Brooks, Barbara
   1983   "Preoedipal Issues in a Postincest Daughter." *American Journal
           of Psychotherapy* 37:129-36.
Butler, Sandra
   1978   *Conspiracy of Silence.* San Francisco: Glide.
Caringella-MacDonald, Susan
   1988   "Marxist and Feminist Interpretations on the Aftermath of Rape
           Reforms." *Contemporary Crises* 12:373-92.
Carlson, Allan
   1985   "The Child Savers Ride Again." *Persuasion at Work* 8:1-10.
Clemens, M.A.
   1983   "Note, Elimination of the Resistance Requirement and Other Rape
           Law Reforms: The New York Experience." *Albany Law Review*
           47:871-907.
Cleveland, Dianne
   1986   *Incest: The Story of Three Women.* Lexington, MA: Lexington
           Books.
Crewdson, John
   1988   *By Silence Betrayed: Sexual Abuse of Children in America.* New
           York: Harper & Row.

Daly, Kathleen and Meda Chesney-Lind
    1988   "Feminism and Criminology." *Justice Quarterly* 4:497-538.

Daugherty, Mary Katherine
    1978   "The Crime of Incest Against the Minor Child and the States' Statutory Responses." *Journal of Family Law* 17:93-115.

Davis, Glen E. and Harold Leitenberg
    1987   "Adolescent Sex Offenders." *Psychological Bulletin* 101:417-27.

DeKeseredy, Walter and Martin D. Schwartz
    1991   "Left Realism and Woman Abuse: A Critical Analysis." Pp. 154-171 in Richard Quinney and Harold E. Pepinsky, (eds.), *Criminology as Peacemaking*. Bloomington: Indiana University Press.

Dillon, Kathleen M.
    1987   "False Sexual Abuse Allegations: Causes and Concerns." *Social Work* 32:540-41.

Donzolot, Jacques
    1979   *The Policing of Families*. New York: Pantheon.

Eberle, Paul and Shirley Eberle
    1986   *The Politics of Child Abuse*. Secaucus, NJ: Lyle Stuart.

Edwards, Susan
    1989   *Policing Domestic Violence*. London: Sage.

Finkelhor, David
    1987   "The Sexual Abuse of Children: Current Research Reviewed." *Psychiatric Annals* 17:233-41.

Finkelhor, David and Larry Baron
    1986   "Risk Factors for Child Sexual Abuse." *Journal of Interpersonal Violence* 1:43-71.

Finkelhor, David and Angela Browne
    1988   "Assessing the Long-Term Impact of Child Sexual Abuse: A Review and Conceptualization." Pp. 270-84 in Gerald T. Hotaling, David Finkelhor, John T. Kirkpatrick and Murray A. Straus (eds.). *Family Abuse and Its Consequences*. Newbury Park, CA: Sage.

Finkelhor, David and I.A. Lewis
    1988   "An Epidemiological Approach to the Study of Child Molestation." *Annals of the New York Academy of Sciences* 528:64-77.

Finkelhor, David, Linda Meyer Williams and Nanci Burns
    1988   *Nursery Crimes: Sexual Abuse in Day Care*. Newbury Park, CA: Sage.

Finkelhor, David and Kirsti Yllo
    1985   *License to Rape: Sexual Abuse of Wives*. New York: Holt, Rinehart and Winston.

Forward, Susan and Craig Buck
    1978   *Betrayal of Innocence: Incest and Its Devastation*. New York: Penguin.

Foucault, Michel
    1980   *The History of Sexuality*. New York: Vintage.

Gagnon, John H.
    1965   "Female Child Victims of Sex Offenses." *Social Problems* 13:176-92.

Gentry, Charles E.
  1978   "Incestuous Abuse of Children: The Need for an Objective View."
          Child Welfare 57:355-64.
Giaretto, Henry
  1976   "The Treatment of Father-Daughter Incest: A Psycho-Social
          Approach." *Children Today* 5:2-5, 34.
Gibbens, T.C.N., K.L. Soothill and C.K. Way
  1978   "Sibling and Parent-Child Incest Offenders: A Long-Term
          Followup." *British Journal of Criminology* 18:40-52.
  1981   "Sex Offenses Against Young Girls: A Long-Term Record Study."
          Psychological Medicine 11:351-57.
Gordon, Linda
  1986   "Incest and Resistance: Patterns of Father-Daughter Incest,
          1880-1930." *Social Problems* 33:253-67.
Gordon, Linda and Paul O'Keefe
  1984   "Incest as a Form of Family Violence: Evidence From Historical
          Case Records." *Journal of Marriage and the Family* 46:27-34.
Goodwin, Jean, Doris Sahd and Richard T. Rada
  1978   "Incest Hoax: False Accusations, False Denials." *Bulletin of the
          American Academy of Psychiatry and the Law* 6:269-76.
Gregory, Jeanne
  1986   "Sex, Class and Crime: Toward a Non-sexist Criminology." Pp.
          53-71 in Roger Matthews and Jock Young (eds.), *Confronting
          Crime*. (London: Sage).
Hampton, Robert L. and Eli H. Newberger
  1988   "Child Abuse Incidence and Reporting by Hospitals: Significance
          of Severity, Class and Race." Pp. 212-21 in Gerald T. Hotaling,
          David Finkelhor, John T. Kirkpatrick and Murray A. Straus (eds.),
          Coping With Family Violence. Newbury Park, CA: Sage.
Hearn, Jeff
  1988   "Commentary, Child Abuse: Violences and Sexualities Towards
          Young Peoples." *Sociology* 22:531-44.
Henderson, James
  1983   "Is Incest Harmful?" *Canadian Journal of Psychiatry* 28:34-40.
Jaffe, Peter, Susan Kaye Wilson and Louise Sas
  1987   "Court Testimony of Child Sexual Abuse Victims: Emerging
          Issues in Clinical Assessments." *Canadian Psychology*
          28:291-95.
Jay, Margaret and Sally Doganis
  1987   *Battered: The Abuse of Children*. New York: St. Martin's.
Johnson, Toni Cavanagh
  1988   "Child Perpetrators—Children Who Molest Other Children:
          Preliminary Findings." *Child Abuse and Neglect* 12:219-29.
Justice, Blair and Rita Justice
  1979   *The Broken Taboo: Sex in the Family*. New York: Human
          Sciences.

Katz, Ellen Edge
  1983   "Incestuous Families." *Detroit College of Law Review* (Spring): 79-102.
Katz, Sedelle and Mary Ann Mazur
  1979   *Understanding the Rape Victim: A Synthesis of Research Findings.* New York: Wiley.
Kaufman, Irving, Alice L. Peck and Consuelo K. Tagiuri
  1954   "The Family Constellation and Overt Incestuous Relations Between Father and Daughter." *American Journal of Orthopsychiatry* 24:269-79.
Kilpatrick, Allie C.
  1986   "Some Correlates of Women's Childhood Sexual Experiences: A Retrospective Study." *The Journal of Sex Research* 22:221-42.
Kirkwood, Laurie J. and Marcelle E. Mihaila
  1979   "Incest and the Legal System: Inadequacies and Alternatives." University of California, *Davis Law Review* 12:673-99.
Kirp, David L.
  1985   "Hug Your Kid, Go to Jail." *The American Spectator.* 18 (June): 33-35.
Kroth, Jerome A.
  1979   *Child Sexual Abuse: Analysis of a Family Therapy Approach.* Springfield, IL: Charles C. Thomas.
Landis, Judson T.
  1956   "Experiences of 500 Children with Adult Sexual Deviation." *Psychiatric Quarterly Supplement* 30:91-109.
Leahy, M.
  1979   "United States v. Bear Runner: The Need for Corroboration in Incest Cases." *Saint Louis University Law Journal* 23:731-67.
Libai, David
  1980   "The Protection of the Child Victim of a Sexual Offense in the Criminal Justice System." Pp. 187-245 in Leroy G. Schultz (ed.) *The Sexual Victimization of Youth.* Springfield, IL: Charles C. Thomas.
Lukianowicz, Narcyz
  1972   "Incest: Part I, Paternal Incest; Part II, Other Types of Incest." *British Journal of Psychiatry* 120:301-13.
Lustig, Noel, John Dresser, Seth Spellman and Thomas Murray
  1966   "Incest: A Family Group Survival Pattern." *Archives of General Psychiatry* 14:31-40.
MacMurray, Bruce K.
  1989   "Criminal Determination for Child Sexual Abuse." *Journal of Interpersonal Violence* 4:233-44.
Maisch, Herbert
  1972   *Incest.* New York: Stein and Day.
Manchester, Anthony H.
  1978   "Incest and the Law." Pp. 487-517 in John M. Eekelaar and Sanford N. Katz (eds.), *Family Violence: An International and Interdisciplinary Study.* Toronto: Butterworths.

Masson, Jeffrey Moussaieff
1984   *The Assault on Truth: Freud's Suppression of the Seduction Theory.* New York: Farrar, Straus and Giroux.
Messerschmidt, James W.
1986   *Capitalism, Patriarchy and Crime.* Totawa, NJ: Rowman and Littlefield.
Morrow, K. Brent and Gwendolyn T. Sorell
1989   "Factors Affecting Self-Esteem, Depression, and Negative Behaviors in Sexually Abused Female Adolescents." *Journal of Marriage and the Family* 57:677-736.
Moyer, Imogene L.
1989   "Changing Conceptualization of Child Sexual Abuse: Impact on the Prosecution of Cases." Paper presented at the annual meetings of the American Society of Criminology, Reno, Nevada.
Nakashima, Eda I. and Gloria E. Zakas
1977   "Incest: Review and Clinical Experience." *Pediatrics* 60:696-701.
Nelson, Barbara J.
1984   *Making an Issue of Child Abuse: Political Agenda Setting for Social Problems.* Chicago: University of Chicago Press.
Nelson, Jean
1986   "Incest: Self-Report Findings From a Nonclinical Sample." *Journal of Sex Research* 22:463-77.
Office of Juvenile Justice and Delinquency Prevention
1988   *The Police and Missing Children: Findings From a National Survey.* Washington, D.C.: U.S. Department of Justice.
1989a   *The Child Victim as Witness.* Washington, D.C.: U.S. Department of Justice.
1989b   *Preliminary Estimates Developed on Stranger Abduction Homicides of Children.* Washington, D.C.: U.S. Department of Justice.
Ordway, Dustin P.
1981   "Parent-Child Incest: Proof at Trial Without Testimony in Court by the Victim." *Journal of Law Reform* 15:131-52.
Paveza, Gregory J.
1988   "Risk Factors in Father-Daughter Sexual Abuse: A Case-Control Study." *Journal of Interpersonal Violence* 3:290-306.
Peters, S.D., G.E. Wyatt and D. Finkelhor
1986   "Prevalence." Pp. 15-59 in David Finkelhor (ed.) *A Sourcebook on Child Sexual Abuse.* Beverly Hills: Sage, as cited in Finkelhor and Lewis (1988).
Pierce, Lois H. and Robert L. Pierce
1987   "Incestuous Victimization by Juvenile Sex Offenders." *Journal of Family Violence* 2:351-64.
Pittman, Frank S. III
1976   "Counseling Incestuous Families." *Medical Aspects of Human Sexuality* (April):57-58.

Risin, Leslie I. and Mary P. Koss
    1987   "The Sexual Abuse of Boys." Pp. 91-104 in Ann Wolbert Burgess
           (ed.) *Rape and Sexual Assault*, Vol. 2. New York: Garland.
Russell, Diana E. H.
    1983   *Intrafamilial Child Sexual Abuse: A San Francisco Survey.* Final
           Report to the National Center on Child Abuse and Neglect.
    1986   *The Secret Trauma.* New York: Basic Books.
Schultz, Leroy G.
    1980   *The Sexual Victimization of Youth.* Springfield, IL: Charles C.
           Thomas.
    1973   "The Child Sex Victim: Social, Psychological and Legal
           Perspectives." *Child Welfare* 52:147-57.
Schwartz, Martin D.
    1982   "The Spousal Exemption for Criminal Rape Prosecution."
           Vermont Law Review 7:33-57.
Schwartz, Martin D. and Todd R. Clear
    1980   "Toward A New Law on Rape." *Crime and Delinquency*
           26:129-51.
Schwartz, Martin D. and Gerald T. Slatin
    1984   "The Law on Marital Rape." *American Legal Studies Association
           Forum* 8:244-64.
Sgroi, Suzanne M.
    1982   "Family Treatment of Child Sexual Abuse." *Journal of Social
           Work and Human Sexuality* 1:109-28.
Siegel, Judith M., Susan B. Sorenson, Jacqueline M. Golding, M. Audrey
    Burnam and Judith A. Stein
    1987   "The Prevalence of Childhood Sexual Assault: The Los Angeles
           Epidemiologic Catchment Area Project." *American Journal of
           Epidemiology* 126:1141-53.
Sloane, Paul and Eva Karpinski
    1942   "Effects of Incest on the Participants." *American Journal of
           Orthopsychiatry* 12:666-73.
Soothill, K. L. and T. C. N. Gibbens
    1978   "Recidivism of Sexual Offenders." *British Journal of Criminology*
           18:267-76.
Star, Barbara
    1983   *Helping the Abuser.* New York: Family Services Association of
           America.
Swan, Raymond W.
    1985   "The Child As Active Participant in Sexual Abuse." *Clinical
           Social Work Journal* 13:62-77.
Truesdell, Donna L., John S. McNeil and Jeanne P. Deschner
    1986   "Incidence of Wife Abuse in Incestuous Families." *Social Work*
           (March-April):138-40.
Twitchell, James B.
    1987   *Forbidden Partners: The Incest Taboo in Modern Culture.* New
           York: Columbia University Press.

Wahl, Charles
1960   "The Psychodynamics of Consummated Maternal Incest."
       Archives of General Psychiatry 3:2.
Wattenberg, Esther
1985   "In a Different Light: A Feminist Perspective on the Role of
       Mothers in Father-Daughter Incest." *Child Welfare* 64:203-11.
Weinberg, S. Kirson
1955   *Incest Behavior.* New York: Citadel.
Weiner, Irving B.
1964   "On Incest: A Survey." *Excerpta Criminologica* 4:137-55.
Whitcomb, Debra
1985   "Prosecution of Child Sexual Abuse: Innovations in Practice."
       U.S. Department of Justice Research in Brief (November):1-7.
Wigmore, John Henry
1940   *A Treatise on the Anglo-American System of Evidence in Trials
       at Common Law, Including the Statutes and Judicial Decisions
       of all Jurisdictions of the United States and Canada.* Vol. 7, 3rd
       ed. Boston: Little, Brown.
Woodbury, John and Elroy Schwartz
1971   *The Silent Sin: A Case History of Incest.* New York: New
       American Library.
Yorukoglu, A. and J.P. Kemph
1966   "Children Not Severely Damaged by Incest With a Parent."
       Journal of the American Academy of Child Psychiatry 5:111-24.
Zegart, Dan
1989   "Solomon's Choice." *Ms.* 17(12):78-83.
Zimring, Franklin E. and Gordon J. Hawkins
1973   *Deterrence: The Legal Threat in Crime Control.* Chicago:
       University of Chicago Press.

chapter 12

Sexual Harassment in the Criminal Justice System

Edna Erez
Pamela Tontodonato
Kent State University

Introduction

As women increase their numbers in nontraditional occupations, particularly in the criminal justice area, interest in studying their experiences has grown (see, e.g., Bowersox, 1981; Jurik, 1985; Jurik and Halemba, 1984; Kissel and Katsampes, 1980; Koenig, 1978; Martin, 1982; Parisi, 1984; Remmington, 1983). One phenomenon that surfaces in much of this research is the negative reaction of male employees to the presence of these women. Sexual harassment is one component of this reaction.

The present chapter reviews the concept of sexual harassment, the evidence concerning the types and extent of sexual harassment in the U.S., the myths surrounding its prevalence and severity, and the legal issues and remedies involved. The role of sexual harassment in perpetuating the subordination of women in society is discussed. Explanatory theories focus on the factors that shape this phenomenon: economic inequality between the sexes, gender roles and attitudes, and the role structure of the workplace.

Women and Work

Sexual harassment must be understood in the context of the role of women in the labor market. Women account for approximately 45 percent of the labor force in the U.S. (U.S. Bureau of the Census, 1988). Despite the media image of the liberated career woman, most female workers are still concentrated in traditionally female occupations such as nursing, elementary school teaching, secretarial work, and waitressing (see Taub, 1980:346, fn4,5; U.S. Bureau of Census, 1988). This phenomenon is referred to as "horizontal segregation" (MacKinnon, 1979:10). Vertical stratification by sex is also common: women tend to be concentrated in low-ranking positions (:12). Even in those fields which are dominated numerically by women, men are still in the positions of authority.

While slowly making inroads, women are still underrepresented in traditionally male professions, including the criminal justice field, which has been commonly viewed as the embodiment of masculinity (Wilson, 1982). Only about seven percent of sworn police officers (U.S. Department of Justice, 1986:248), 18 percent of lawyers and judges (U.S. Bureau of Census, 1988) and 10 percent of Federal correctional officers (Flanagan and Jamieson, 1988:76) are women.

Femaleness is a "master status" in the workplace (Schur, 1984) and working women are often treated as women first and employees second (Gutek and Morasch, 1982). Women's marital and family roles of nurturer, housekeeper, and sex object are reflected in many traditionally female jobs (MacKinnon, 1979:18). Women who work find that an emphasis is placed upon their sexuality in the workplace, often with damaging consequences. Those who advance into male-dominated fields or who move into supervisory roles encounter resistance and hostility from co- workers and supervisors, frequently with sexual overtones. In this article, we address a particular manifestation of this phenomenon, namely sexual harassment. Special attention is given to harassment faced by women in nontraditional occupations in general, and criminal justice in particular.[1]

The Concept and Definition of Sexual Harassment

Sexual harassment has a very long past and a very short history. It has existed since women first started going out to work, at least since the industrial era. However, the phenomenon did not have a name and was not recognized as a social problem until recently. One reason for this is that sexual exploitation of women has been viewed as part of the "natural order of things" and women have been seen as somehow responsible for their own victimization. Sexual harassment has also been considered a personal issue and a private problem which occurs relatively rarely.

The term "sexual harassment" was coined in 1977 at a conference at Cornell University. Once a label was created for it, it was easier to discuss and analyze the issue, but there has been and still is an enormous lack of agreement about what constitutes sexual harassment. As the following discussion will demonstrate, sexual harassment involves a continuum of behaviors and includes many ambiguous situations which are not commonly defined as sexual harassment.

The first book published on the topic, Harragen's *Games Mother Never Taught You* (1977), addressed women who were going to enter the corporate world. Harragen offered the terms "sexual molestation" or "sexual exploitation," but she does not explicitly define the kinds of behaviors that would constitute these terms. She does note, however, that most typically the offending behavior is verbal, including comments on the woman's physical characteristics and invitations for sexual contact. Harragen suggests that the typical victim is a woman who is financially vulnerable, and that the perpetrator is necessarily a male supervisor or employer who wields economic power over her. If the woman refuses the sexual relationship she may be fired, or her work performance can be unfavorably reviewed.

This definition suffers from several drawbacks: first, it ignores the notion that people can be harassed by their peers, and much harassment is of this nature; second, the definition assumes the harassee is a female while the harasser is a male. It is possible for a man to be harassed by a woman; however, it is an extremely rare occurrence simply because very few women are ever in a position to do so. In addition, sex-role socialization mitigates against women being the sexual aggressors. If men are harassed, they are most often harassed by other men (U.S. Merit Systems Protection Board, 1981).

The most famous book written on this subject is Lin Farley's *Sexual Shakedown* (1978). Farley describes sexual harassment as "unsolicited, nonreciprocal male behavior that asserts a woman's sex role over her function as a worker" (:14-15). She gives some examples of harassing behaviors, such as staring at, commenting upon, or touching the woman's body, repeated unreciprocated solicitations for dates or social interaction, requests for acquiescence in sexual behavior, demands for sexual intercourse, and, of course, rape. Farley takes the position that there is no need for a formal power differential between the parties involved for sexual harassment to occur because males in our society have inherently higher social positions and more influence in the workplace simply because they are male. They usually outnumber women in the organizational setting, and they can use sanctions such as withholding cooperation in job tasks or verbal denigration to exercise control over women workers. Further, they have structural power and resources that women do not have as yet.

A comprehensive study of sexual harassment is Catharine MacKinnon's *Sexual Harassment of Working Women* (1979). MacKinnon makes the case for viewing sexual harassment as a form of sex discrimination related to employment. Sexual harassment is defined as "the unwanted imposition of sexual requirements in the context of a relationship of unequal power" (:1). MacKinnon classifies sexual harassment into two categories: "quid pro quo" and "condition of work." The first type exists when "sexual compliance is exchanged, or proposed to be exchanged, for an employment opportunity" (:32). The second form involves a workplace pervaded by sexual harassment which is so severe, persistent, and offensive as to cause psychological and emotional damage to the employee or affect his or her work performance. Thus, a legal finding of harassment can occur even if no concrete economic loss ensued. Those involved in sexual harassment, both victims and offenders, can be either male or female.

By 1980 the Equal Employment Opportunity Commission (EEOC) formulated guidelines defining sexual harassment. These guidelines and recent case law present sexual harassment as sex discrimination, a violation of Title VII of the Civil Rights Act of 1964 (Ledgerwood and Johnson-Dietz, 1980).[2] According to the EEOC,

> Harassment on the basis of sex is a violation of Sec. 703 of Title VII. Unwelcome sexual advances, requests for sexual favors, and other verbal or physical conduct of a sexual nature constitute sexual harassment when (1) submission to such conduct is made either explicitly or implicitly a term or condition of an individual's employment; (2) submission to or rejection of such conduct by an individual is used as the basis for employment decisions affecting such individual; or (3) such conduct has the

purpose or effect of unreasonably interfering with an individual's work performance or creating an intimidating, hostile, or offensive working environment (29 C.F.R. Section 1604.11 (a), 45 Fed. Reg. 74677, 1981).

This definition reflects the MacKinnon classification of sexual harassment into "quid pro quo" and "condition of work."

Levels of Sexual Harassment

Sexual harassment involves a spectrum of behaviors. The National Advisory Council on Women's Education Programs (Till, 1980) has categorized sexual harassment into five levels.

The first level includes generalized sexual remarks and behavior. These are not necessarily designed to elicit sexual activity; rather, they are directed at a person because of his or her gender. They are closer in appearance to racial harassment, where the sentiments or actions involved are antifemale (or antimale) and are analogous to antiblack statements and behavior.[3] Such types of remarks and behavior may affect large numbers of people (for example entire offices or classrooms), and not just isolated individuals. Comments about women's supposedly lesser cognitive abilities and their mythical propensity to be jealous, vindictive, and seductive are examples of gender harassment. Analogous examples of racial harassment would include remarks concerning the alleged sexual prowess, athletic ability, or inferior intellect of African-Americans. This category of harassment also includes such items as the off-color joke, the suggestive story, the crudely suggestive remark, or ogling and staring. These behaviors are considered harassment because they are dehumanizing and indicate an implied or veiled threat. They also serve to highlight and exaggerate the differences between the members of the dominant and the subordinate groups. This kind of harassment is most common in fields that have been traditionally male-dominated, such as law enforcement or in some departments in the university setting. It must be noted, however, that sexual harassment is commmonplace even in female-dominated occupations because it is the males who are usually in the position of status and power (e.g., school principals or hospital administrators).

Examples of this type of sexual harassment in the criminal justice field are abundant. The misogynistic attitude held by some male police officers is revealed in these statements reported by a female police officer:

> "It's bad enough," this one guy said, "having one of you girls
> here; we don't have to have two in the same car."
>
> One night he ended roll call with "Let us pray that _____ [a
> woman's name] gets shot tonight" (Wexler and Logan, 1983:49)

Antiwomen sentiment is revealed in this quote from a female guard:

> I expected a negative reaction and thought I was prepared for
> it. But on my very first day, before I had even been assigned
> to a post, this male guard came up to me and asked what I was
> doing there. He said that women don't belong in men's prisons
> and told me that he would do anything he could to make my
> life miserable and force me to leave (Zimmer, 1986:94)

One female officer reported that a training officer in the academy
said,

> "This is my personal opinion; I don't think you should be in this
> job. You should go home and have babies" (Wexler and Logan,
> 1983:50)

Many female correctional officers feel that the major problem they
face at work is the male staff, not the inmates (Jurik, 1985; Peterson,
1982; Zimmer, 1986). The negative attitudes of the male guards
are so obvious that even the inmates notice it (Peterson, 1982).
Some female police officers interviewed by Wexler and Logan (1983)
reported that they have been in a squad car for eight hours with
men who refused to talk to them (49). The silent treatment is also
administered by the male guards in the correctional field (Zimmer,
1986:95).

Most of the studies of female police officers and correctional
guards reveal the emphasis placed by the men on the physical
appearance of the women. Rumor-mongering and gossiping about
the sexual preferences and behavior of the women are prevalent
(Martin, 1980; Peterson, 1982; Wexler and Logan, 1983; Zimmer,
1986). One study of female guards in New York and Rhode Island
found that most of the harassment emphasized the "femaleness"
of the women, although it was not necessarily sexual in nature
(Zimmer, 1986:94). The following comment to a female police officer
from a male peer illustrates the belief that the female officers are
viewed as sex objects:

> Officer, I don't mean any harm but I just want you to know that
> you have the biggest breasts I've ever seen on a policewoman
> (Martin, 1980:145).

The second level of harassment includes situations in which
actual sexual advances are made. This level can be distinguished

from the first by the introduction of the request for sexual encounters, often accompanied by some sort of touching. These situations do not have to be blatantly offensive, just inappropriate. The woman is the subordinate and the man is the superior; for example, a female college student with a male professor. The situation is such that a request of this kind is never free of the possibility of a threat or sanction because the person making the proposition has power over the victim. Although women are socialized into thinking that they ought to be pleased about receiving attention from powerful males, the women feel uncomfortable and disconcerted. No direct threat is made to the recipient, yet the victim feels something is wrong.

The third level includes a solicitation for sex with the promise of reward. The harasser attempts to use some sort of institutional or organizational authority to coerce or "make payment" for a sexual favor. Explicit threats are absent. Although it is very rare that the harasser uses direct and explicit language to this end, there are many ambiguous situations when such a "trade" is implied. For instance, a young woman may be invited to dinner with a supervisor, with the promise that "it would be good for your career if we got to know each other." All the levels of behavior reviewed thus far illustrate the inherent problems of interpretation and the lack of hard and unambiguous evidence in most sexual harassment cases.

The fourth level of sexual harassment introduces the notion of punishment for failure to comply with a request for sexual favors. Negative consequences ensue for noncooperation. This type of situation is generally thought of as the quintessential sexual harassment. A failing grade in a class, a negative performance evaluation at work, and dismissal from work are examples of such negative sanctions. Policewomen who refuse sexual advances may face complete enforcement of regulations or assignment to an unhelpful or nonsupportive partner (Martin, 1980). The exploitation of the position of power and authority by the harasser, which compels the victim to choose between two extremely unwelcome alternatives (the sexual encounter or the penalty), is viewed universally and unequivocally as sexual harassment.

The fifth level is the most extreme category of harassment and includes indecent exposure, gross sexual imposition, and outright sexual assaults. One female correctional officer reported that a male investigator tried to kiss her at work (Jurik, 1985:386). A male officer in Washington, D.C. gave a "playful" kiss on the back of the neck to a policewoman who was typing an arrest form (Martin, 1980:150), and a police sergeant was convicted by the police trial board of "amorous verbal and physical advances" toward a policewoman while on duty (:133, 135n). Forced intercourse may or may not be involved. This type of behavior may be the least common type of sexual harassment, although it is certainly the most devastating to the victim.

Myths Concerning Sexual Harassment

Misperceptions of the nature, seriousness, and effects of sexual harassment abound. The prevailing myths concerning sexual harassment are analogous in many ways to the myths surrounding other forms of female victimization, in particular rape and wife abuse. The first of these myths states that "this is the real world." Sexual harassment on the job seems to be so common, so much a part of popular humor and folklore that it has been accepted as somewhat of an inevitable condition, that this is what women must tolerate if they want to enter the workplace. This approach subtly implies that, "if you can't stand the heat, get out of the kitchen." It has the effect of placing the responsibility for dealing with the problem on the woman, who is somehow supposed to be able to deal with it effectively on her own, rather than placing the responsibility on the harasser. The victim should expect resistance and hostility and accept it. This attitude has also characterized the treatment of minority groups who have been subjected to the most difficult kinds of employment conditions. Economic dependence has forced these groups to tolerate the situation. African-Americans are told to expect and even accept hostile and resistant work environments because racial attitudes and stereotypes "can't change overnight."

A second myth is what Fitzgerald and Shulman (1985) have termed the "Phyllis Schlafly Myth": namely, if a woman was harassed she got what she was asking for and what she deserved. Schlafly, a proponent of maintaining women in their traditional roles and an opponent of the Equal Rights Amendment, testified in Congress several years ago that "no virtuous woman was ever harassed." This attitude has been expressed by both male and female police officers (Martin, 1980). This myth, that women who are harassed somehow bring it upon themselves and are to be blamed, is based on many centuries of Judeo-Christian thought which places the primary responsibility for controlling male sexuality at the door of female morality. The notion that women, by their dress, their behavior, or their mere presence, especially in nontraditional surroundings, somehow deserve to be sexually exploited or physically humiliated also echoes the history and experience of rape. The very same dynamics that occur in rape are played out in more subtle ways in organizations in the context of sexual harassment.

Another popular misconception is that sexual harassment is trivial or benign for the victim. Studies of sexual harassment invariably find that recipients of harassment undergo stress and psychological harm. The feelings produced by the harassment include anger, irritability, fear, anxiety, depression and powerlessness (Evans, 1978; Jensen and Gutek, 1982; Loy and Stewart, 1984; McIntyre and Renick, 1983; Tangri et al., 1982). The harassment also has physical effects on the victim (such as sleeplessness and stomach ailments) and creates negative attitudes toward work. Many victims of sexual harassment report difficulty with coworkers and supervisors, loss of motivation, and reduction in quantity or quality of work (Gruber and Bjorn, 1982; Jensen and Gutek, 1982; Tangri et al., 1982).

The economic consequences of sexual harassment on the victim are also often serious. Some victims feel compelled to quit. Others face reprisals for failure to comply with a sexual request or for being a troublemaker if they report the problem. These sanctions include being passed over for promotion, receiving a negative performance evaluation, or being fired. In the criminal justice field, the negative attitudes of the male officers are one of the major job stressors faced by female police officers (Wexler and Logan, 1983). There are additional costs incurred by the recipients of sexual harassment in the criminal justice field. Harassment (and attempts to avoid it) impedes the entry of women into the occupational subculture, which in turn robs them of important on-the-job training, psychological peer support and sponsorship, and access to inside information (Zimmer, 1986; see also Martin, 1980).

Sexual harassment is also costly to the employer. Employers, if for no other more altruistic reason, are concerned about sexual harassment because of the possible costs incurred by them in terms of litigation, bad publicity, absenteeism, employee turnover, and inferior job performance (Hoyman and Robinson, 1980; Leap and Gray, 1980).

This evidence also contradicts a fourth myth, which is the idea that women secretly enjoy the harassment. The belief that the sexual attention is pleasurable or complimentary to the recipient is widespread and resistant to change. If a woman tries to challenge this belief she will be thought of as "being coy." These kinds of protestations are taken as indicative of "feminine wiles," and that women say "no" when they mean "yes." This attitude is expressed by a criminal justice administrator queried by Zimmer (1986) about a female guard who reportedly quit after months of sexual harassment:

> I can't believe anyone propositioned her. Have you ever seen her? She just wishes someone would make an advance at her and is angry because no one did (:97)

The fifth myth states that a recipient of harassment should "just ignore it and it will go away." Women are encouraged to ignore the harassment and not get upset about it; in short, to be "good sports." This advice, usually given to the recipients of the less coercive kinds of sexual behavior, implies that if the harasser(s) does not receive a response from the victim he will get bored and stop. This is contrary to empirical evidence, however. The U. S. Merit Systems Protection Board study (1981) reported that for 75 percent of victims who ignored the harassment, its expression increased. Twenty-five percent received unwarranted reprimands from their bosses or an increase in their work load. Almost all studies that examined the issue concluded that sexual harassment usually gets worse by ignoring it, because the silence implies consent and reinforces its acceptability.

Another myth which draws on sex-role stereotypes of women is the "sour grapes" myth. The full text of this myth suggests that most charges of sexual harassment are false and/or vindictive. According to this line of thinking, such charges provide a way of getting back at a man when an office affair goes sour. This belief reveals a misunderstanding of the power dynamics that exist in institutions and organizations and fails to recognize that women have very little to gain by making false charges. In most cases they will not be believed. When they are believed, it may result in even more negative consequences for the victim, such as reprimands, demotion, transfer, or even being fired (Russell, 1986). The recipients of sexual harassment are often told they are imagining things (being too sensitive) or that they should seek some sort of counseling or help. They are also asked for definitive proof which is almost impossible to obtain.

The seventh myth states that the harassment "is an isolated incident." This myth contradicts the "this is the real world" myth, which states that "sexual harassment happens all the time, you just have to put up with it." The "isolated case" myth states that "it never happens or it's rare; you just happened to get stuck with it." As the next section shows, sexual harassment occurs at all organizational levels, particularly in traditionally male-dominated occupations. Lawsuits alleging sexual harassment have been filed against all types of organizations in the United States: universities, corporations, and even the Department of Justice.

The Extent of Sexual Harassment: Perceptions and Reality

A number of studies have attempted to estimate the prevalence of sexual harassment. However, no study has systematically documented the prevalence of sexual harassment in the criminal justice system, where most evidence of harassment is anecdotal in nature.

With several exceptions, most studies of sexual harassment are based on relatively small nonrepresentative samples from various regions of the United States. One of the earliest studies, by the Working Women United Institute (1975), found that 70 percent of the New York women surveyed reported sexual harassment on the job (Evans, 1978:204). Data from surveys of working women in New England (Powell, 1983), Connecticut (Loy and Stewart, 1984), and Florida (McIntyre and Renick, 1983), and studies of college graduates in Louisiana (Dolecheck, 1984), workers in the auto industry in Michigan (Gruber and Bjorn, 1982), and blue-collar union members in Iowa (Maypole and Skaine, 1982) obtain estimates of the prevalence of sexual harassment that range from 36 to 50 percent of the women surveyed. A study by the U.S. Merit Systems Protection Board utilizing a representative sample of federal employees found that 42 percent of female and 15 percent of male employees were sexually harassed (Tangri et al., 1982).[4] In general, less serious forms of harassment, those of a verbal nature, are more common; for example, sexual remarks, teasing, and sexual propositioning (Gruber and Bjorn, 1982; Loy and Stewart, 1984; Maypole and Skaine, 1982; Tangri et al., 1982; Zimmer, 1986). Most harassers are male (MacKinnon, 1979; Tangri et al., 1982). Some studies find coworker harassment to be more common than harassment by supervisors (Dolecheck, 1984; Maypole and Skaine, 1982; Tangri et al., 1982), although other studies argue that supervisors are more frequently the harassers (see MacKinnon, 1979). All the female correctional guards in the New York and Rhode Island survey by Zimmer (1986) reported experiencing sexual harassment.

There appear to be differences in attitudes and behavior concerning sexual harassment among men and women in traditional versus nontraditional occupations. Sexual harassment is "especially prevalent in traditionally male occupations" (Zimmer, 1986:92), although some argue that "only" a minority of these women are resented or harassed by male coworkers (O'Farrell and Harlan, 1980). Women who work in male-dominated jobs (compared to those in traditionally female jobs) are more likely to state that sexual harassment is a problem and more likely to define a given behavior as sexual harassment (Gutek and Morasch, 1982). Further, greater proportions of women in male-dominated work report "social-sexual" behaviors (e.g., sexual touching, insulting comments and gestures) compared with women in traditionally female and gender-integrated jobs (Gutek and Morasch, 1982). The women in nontraditional jobs were also more likely to report that they had experienced negative consequences due to the harassment. The men in male-dominated jobs were less likely than the men in gender-integrated jobs to label sexual behavior as sexual harassment (Konrad and Gutek, 1986).

There are differences between the sexes in perceptions of sexual harassment. Generally, males are more likely than females to view the world in sexual terms and impute sexuality in ambiguous situations between men and women (Abbey, 1982). Women identify more situations and behaviors as constituting sexual harassment than men (Collins and Blodgett, 1981; Gutek et al., 1983; Konrad and Gutek, 1986; Powell, 1986). On the other hand, a greater proportion of males than females feel that the problem of sexual harassment is not as serious as it is made out to be (Collins and Blodgett, 1981; Lott et al., 1982; Loy and Stewart, 1984; Maypole and Skaine, 1982; Tangri et al., 1982). Men are also more likely than women to attribute responsibility to the recipient of the harassment and to state that women should be able to handle such situations (Collins and Blodgett, 1981; Jensen and Gutek, 1982; Lott et al., 1982; Tangri et al., 1982).

Theories Explaining Sexual Harassment

Most explanations of sexual harassment refer to the historical and continued difference in power between the sexes. According to the conflict perspective, sexual inequality is based on a conflict of interest between men and women (Collins, 1971). Sexual harassment is viewed as a function of the inequality between men and women in the labor force and the general cultural atmosphere of sexism which supports traditional sex roles (see, e.g., Gutek and Morasch, 1982; Hemming, 1985; Hoffman, 1986; Loy and Stewart, 1984; MacKinnon, 1979). Sexual harassment exists because it is possible to exploit those with little economic power. At the same time, sexual harassment functions to perpetuate the inferior position of women in society. It is a form of social control designed to maintain the status quo (Ellis, 1981; Evans, 1978; Farley, 1978; Hemming, 1985; MacKinnon, 1979; Taub, 1980).

The case of a supervisor using his position of power to harass a subordinate (vertical harassment) is a good illustration of the so-called power differential hypothesis (Gutek and Morasch, 1982). Sexist attitudes which perpetuate sexual harassment include the belief that women are inferior to men (as is the work they do) and that a "normal" female is one who is in a dependent, supportive, and subordinate role. Women are thought to trap men with their sexuality and are thus to blame when negative consequences befall them.

Several researchers have called the adequacy of this theoretical model into question. The power differential approach cannot sufficiently explain harassment between peers (Gutek and Morasch, 1982). Other factors in the work environment contribute to its occurrence. In addition to traditional gender roles and economic inequality, occupational norms and the role structure of the work force must be examined as causes of peer harassment (Gutek and Morasch, 1982; Maypole and Skaine, 1982, 1983).

The dominant group (males) uses the informal power structure of the male peer work group to support negative and stereotyped attitudes toward working women and to harass female employees (Maypole and Skaine, 1982; see also Tangri et al., 1982). Gutek and Morasch (1982) introduce the concept of "sex-role spillover" in this regard. Sex-role spillover occurs when the workplace is permeated by "gender-based expectations for behavior that are irrelevant or inappropriate to work" (:55). For example, a male coworker may treat a female coworker as a sex object because he is responding to her in terms of his preconceived and traditional notions of what a female is instead of dealing with her as an occupant of a work role. Females are seen as "women in jobs," not fellow employees (:64). At the same time, males may act in accordance with the male sex role by being sexually aggressive. This is an especially common occurrence, according to Gutek and Morasch, for women in nontraditional occupations because males are especially unaccustomed to women as workers in male-dominated jobs.

Women who work in traditionally male occupations are often "tokens" (Hemming, 1985; Kanter, 1977; Taub, 1980). They are perceived as a threat to the dominant group, and men are forced to interact with them in ways other than traditional personal (familial) roles (Gutek and Morasch, 1982). The majority (males) may use sexual harassment as one way to emphasize the fact that these employees are different from them because they are female

(Gruber and Bjorn, 1982; Hemming, 1985; Taub, 1980). Thus, through their emphasis on the sexuality of the women workers and other sex-role stereotypes, the males emphasize the unsuitability of women for "men's work" and discourage all women from entering male-dominated fields (Farley, 1978; Gruber and Bjorn, 1982; Hemming, 1985; Taub, 1980). These conditions help explain the prevalence of peer (lateral) sexual harassment.

The problem of sexual harassment may be compounded for African-American women, who are members of a minority group in terms of both race and gender. This group is most vulnerable to harassment because of its more precarious position in the economic system and because of the stereotypes that black women are sexually accessible (Ellis, 1981; MacKinnon, 1979) and promiscuous (Young, 1986). These stereotypes further support the beliefs that black women contribute to their sexual victimization and are less damaged by sexual assaults (Young, 1986). Racism and sexism thus intertwine to accentuate such discrimination against black women. Black women may recognize sexual harassment more quickly because of their experience with racial discrimination (MacKinnon, 1979). Sexual harassment "can be both a sexist way to express racism and a racist way to express sexism" (MacKinnon, 1979:30).

White males may think that their race (and superior social status) may operate to overcome objections to their overtures for sexual encounters from females of an "inferior" social group. In addition, it has been argued that white women may be more likely to report harassment by black males because of the more positive response they expect from the system when they are "sexually degraded" by a person of another race (MacKinnon, 1979:30). However, some women may fail to report harassment by a member of another race because of fear of being labeled a racist or out of fear that the authorities will be supportive only for racist reasons (:31). Sometimes the victims and the courts have trouble disentangling the motivation for the harassment (Ellis, 1981).

Sexual and racial harassment reflect racial and sex-role stereotyping found in society at large and are a manifestation of the discrimination experienced by minority groups in society (see Hacker, 1951). Both share some common causes. Men and women, whites and blacks, are unequal in power and compete in society for limited resources. Harassment is a way to reinforce the power structure of society and maintain status and control over a particular group (Ellis, 1981). From a conflict perspective, economic inequalities underlie racial and sexual inequality (Collins, 1974).

However, society does not perceive or respond to these problems in the same manner. The court system is much more suspicious of classifications based on race than sex (Ellis, 1981) and "racial inequality is treated as a more serious problem than sex inequality" (MacKinnon, 1979:131). Ellis suggests that society's perception of sex and race discrimination is influenced by "proximity," the degree of distance within the groups:

> Race and power can sometimes be dealt with in an abstract manner: one can be insulated from racial tensions by geography, social position, or wealth. Sex and power, however, are daily issues that are always perceived in an intimate and personal way. As a result, it is in the best interest of the dominant class in society that the magnitude of the sex-power problem remain obscure in order to maintain the status quo (1981:34).

Several explanations have been suggested for the relatively common occurrence of sexual harassment of female employees of the criminal justice system. Like male employees in other fields, those in criminal justice may be uncomfortable with or threatened by working women who are peers (not subordinates). In law enforcement, the women may be seen as competitors for a limited number of higher-level jobs (Price and Gavin, 1982). In addition, the hiring of women may be felt as a blow to the status of the profession. There is a general feeling that, when a job is "easy" enough for a woman to do, it loses some of its prestige (Wexler and Logan, 1983).

The nature of the criminal justice occupational subculture may lead to a work environment particularly inhospitable to women. According to Flynn, "the law enforcement subculture has consistently stressed traditionalism, conservatism, and authoritarianism" (1982:316). Police work is the quintessential male occupation (Price and Gavin, 1982; Wexler and Logan, 1983). It is the embodiment of traditional male traits such as toughness, strength, and bravery. These qualities are considered essential to the job.[5] Thus, by definition, women are not capable of doing the job, since traditionally they are viewed as weak, indecisive, emotionally unstable, and timid. These beliefs are extremely resistant to change, even though research has found female and male officers to be similar on a psychological scale measuring personality attributes (Maglino, 1974, cited in Bell, 1982). A study of two police academies revealed that recruits come into the academy with negative attitudes toward women in police work and that some instructors explicitly articulate and reinforce sex-role stereotypes in their comments to the recruits (Pike, 1985).

When women do become police officers (and correctional guards)

and do so successfully, it calls into question what it is that makes
a man "a man" (Wexler and Logan, 1983). The self-image of the
male officer may be shaken (Price and Gavin, 1982). That is,

> (i)t may lead [the men] to question, on some level, what the real
> differences between men and women are and how masculine
> they themselves are" (Wexler and Logan, 1983:52).

The criminal justice subculture may also promote hostility toward
women because in many ways it is an "all-male clubhouse" (Wilson,
1982:372). Since police work is men's work, women are automatically an "out-group." They are thought to be different from (and
less competent than) men, and are shut out of the "old boy
network." The informal peer network is often used to harass the
females, rather than to provide the normative and psychological
support crucial for all police officers. The women are subject to
traditional sex-role stereotyping, and their "femaleness" is
emphasized to reinforce their nonbelonging and unsuitability for
the job.

Legal Issues and Remedies

Litigants in early court cases had difficulty finding an ear
receptive to the claim that sexual harassment is a form of sex
discrimination under Title VII of the federal Civil Rights Act of 1964.
Federal appellate courts came to recognize, however, that sexual
harassment was "a barrier to women's full employment
opportunity" (Livingston, 1982:7). The courts first recognized the
actionability of "quid pro quo" sexual harassment cases. That is,
harassment was only considered to be sex discrimination if the
recipient suffered some loss of a tangible job benefit (for a review
of early cases, see Dolkart and Malchow, 1987; Livingston, 1982;
MacKinnon, 1979; Rosen, 1984). Eventually, harassment which
was so severe as to cause psychological harm to the recipient
through a hostile or offensive work environment also came to be
recognized as sex discrimination (Dolkart and Malchow, 1987;
Livingston, 1982; Rosen, 1984).

In *Brown v. City of Guthrie* (1982), a female civilian police
dispatcher in Oklahoma argued that she was discriminated against
on the basis of sex, in violation of Title VII of the Civil Rights Act
of 1964.[6] Phyllis Brown was subject to sexual harassment by her
shift commander. He made sexual innuendos and gestures
repeatedly and on several occasions asked Brown to remove her
clothes. The Lieutenant asked Brown to compare herself with the
nude models in pornographic magazines which were kept in the

dispatcher's desk for the enjoyment of the police officers. The shift commander also repeatedly played back a videotape of a search performed by Brown of a female prisoner, critiqued her performance, and commented upon the physical characteristics of the prisoner. She informed the chief of police about the problem but he told her she was overreacting and so ignored the complaint. The conditions of employment became so hostile and intimidating that she felt compelled to resign her position. The Court found that Brown had established a prima facie case of sexual harassment. The police department was found liable for the discrimination perpetrated by its supervisor. (The plaintiff was awarded 60 percent of back pay and attorney's fees and costs.)

Sandra Bundy, a Vocational Rehabilitation Specialist for the D.C. Department of Corrections, argued that she was sexually harassed by several of her supervisors and that her rejection of their advances caused her advancement in the agency to be blocked and delayed (*Bundy v. Jackson*, 1981). Two of her supervisors made sexual advances toward her. When she complained to their superior, she was told that "any man in his right mind would want to rape you" (:940). This supervisor himself then propositioned her. She also pursued her complaint informally with the EEO officer and filed a formal complaint with the agency. Bundy's supervisors then began to criticize her work performance and impede her requests for promotion. The U.S. Court of Appeals, District of Columbia Circuit, held that Bundy suffered discrimination on the basis of sex (:943). Further, it held that regardless of whether the complaining employee loses any tangible job benefit as a result of the discrimination, sexual harassment amounts to sex discrimination with respect to the terms, conditions, or privileges of employment (:934, 943) when the "employer creates or condones a substantially discriminatory work environment" (:935). It thus agreed with Bundy's claim that " 'conditions of employment' include the psychological and emotional work environment" (:944). The Court also ruled that the D.C. Department of Corrections was liable for the discriminatory acts committed by its supervisory personnel since agency officials had full knowledge of the harassment and "did virtually nothing to stop or even investigate the practice" (:943).

Another sexual harassment case involving criminal justice personnel is *Henson v. City of Dundee* (1982). Barbara Henson, a police dispatcher for the Dundee, Florida police department, asserted that she and a female coworker were sexually harassed by the chief of police to the point of being compelled to resign. The chief queried the women almost daily about their sexual habits and frequently made vulgar and demeaning comments. Henson also argued that he frequently asked her to have sexual relations with him. The Eleventh Circuit Court of Appeals agreed that Henson "made prima facie showing of all elements necessary to establish violation by city of Title VII arising from supervisor's alleged sexual harassment" (:897). However, in order for sexual harassment to be a violation of Title VII, the harassment

> must be sufficiently pervasive so as to alter the conditions of employment and create an abusive working environment. Whether sexual harassment at the workplace is sufficiently severe and persistent to affect seriously the psychological well-being of employees is a question to be determined with regard to the totality of the circumstances (:904).

The court established a five-part test for proving such a Title VII claim: the employee belongs to a protected group; the employee was subject to unwelcome sexual harassment; the harassment complained of was based upon sex; the harassment complained of affected a "term, condition, or privilege" of employment, and *respondeat superior* (:903-5). That is, in order for the employer to be held responsible for the hostile environment (condition of work harassment) created by the plaintiff's supervisor or coworker, the complainant must demonstrate that the employer "knew or should have known of the harassment in question and failed to take prompt remedial action" (:905). However, the employer is strictly liable for the actions of its supervisors in the other type of sexual harassment, the quid pro quo case, where the harassment results in tangible job detriment to the employee (:909-10). Thus, according to Dolkart and Malchow (1987), the distinction between "quid pro quo" and "condition of work" harassment gave the courts some basis for decisions concerning employer liability.

The United States Supreme Court heard its first sexual harassment case in *Meritor Savings Bank, FSB v. Vinson* (1986). Mechelle Vinson, an assistant branch manager at a bank, alleged that Sidney Taylor, her supervisor, pressured her to have sex with him since (according to Taylor) he had gotten her the job. She gave in to his demands because of her fear of being fired and stated that he sexually harassed her by fondling her in the presence of coworkers, following her into the ladies' restroom, exposing himself to her, having sex with her repeatedly, and forcibly raping her. After working at the bank for four years, Vinson took indefinite sick leave and was fired two months later for excessive use of sick leave. She filed a suit under Title VII against Meritor and Taylor alleging sexual harassment.[7]

The Supreme Court affirmed that sexual harassment is sex

discrimination under Title VII and that both quid pro quo (tangible job benefit) and condition of work (hostile environment) harassment are violations of Title VII (:2404-5). In order to be actionable, the sexual harassment must be "sufficiently severe or pervasive to alter the conditions of the plaintiff's employment and create an abusive working environment" (:2406). Before a case is considered sexual harassment, it must be determined that the sexual advances are unwelcome, and the court may consider the sexually provocative speech or dress of the complainant in this determination (:2406-7). The Supreme Court also stated that having an established sexual harassment policy and grievance procedure in conjunction with a complainant who fails to use it does *not* necessarily protect an employer from liability (:2408). The Court did not provide a clear-cut ruling on employer liability for sexual harassment by supervisory employees, although it stated that employers are not always strictly liable for sexual harassment by their supervisors (:2408). It held that courts are to look to traditional agency principles for guidance in the area of employer liability.

In terms of legal remedies, a plaintiff in a sexual harassment case can be awarded back pay, reinstatement, and attorney's fees. Mental and emotional distress is not recoverable under Title VII (Dolkart and Malchow, 1987; Martucci and Terry, 1987). Many sexual harassment cases draw on tort law, including assault, battery, intentional or negligent infliction of mental distress, invasion of privacy, and failure to provide a reasonably safe workplace. Cases are pursued in this way in order to gain greater relief for the individual in terms of psychological and punitive damages (Dolkart and Malchow, 1987; Martucci and Terry, 1987).

Combatting Sexual Harassment

Sexual harassment can be prevented and reduced in several ways. Gender-integrated work places may equalize power between the sexes, increase the acceptance of women (especially in male-dominated fields), and dissipate the strength of sexist norms in the work environment (Hemming, 1985; Maypole and Skaine, 1983).

Attitudinal changes are an important part of many recommendations. Jensen and Gutek (1982) point out that merely informing people about the true extent and costs of sexual harassment will not eliminate the problem. Beliefs and attitudes must be changed on a broader level; in particular, general sex-role beliefs must be addressed (:134). Male organizational and peer group attitudes toward women must be changed so that male workers stop responding to women on the basis of sex-role stereotypes and start treating female employees as workers first and women second (Hemming, 1985). Women can also increase their power in the workplace and combat the "old-boy" network by their own networking and development of a support system (Hemming, 1985). Police departments must take seriously the hostility and harassment faced by female officers, provide channels for complaint, enforce harassment regulations, and actively change the attitudes of male officers (Martin, 1980:136).

Organizations must develop written policies governing sexual harassment which include information on the types of behavior involved, the procedures to follow in filing a grievance, and the sanctions for these violations (see, e.g., Hemming, 1985; Hoyman and Robinson, 1980; Leap and Gray, 1980; McIntyre and Renick, 1983; Powell, 1983). Training and orientation programs should incorporate information on sexual harassment, with a focus on sensitivity training for personnel managers and supervisors (Hoyman and Robinson, 1980). Top management must send a strong message that sexual harassment will not be tolerated, and organizations must respond immediately to complaints of harassment (Hoyman and Robinson, 1980; McIntyre and Renick, 1983). These recommendations are consistent with those suggested by EEOC guidelines.

The educational system can also play a role in combatting sexual harassment. Information on the extent, causes of, and legal issues surrounding sexual harassment can be incorporated into college curricula (Maypole and Skaine, 1983).

Sexual harassment should not be considered or responded to solely as an individual-level problem. It is difficult to prevent sexual harassment unless its root causes on the social-structural level— "the inequitable distribution of power that encourages harassment to occur"—are the focus of attention (Livingston, 1982:21).

Conclusions

Sexual harassment, like rape or domestic violence, is a phenomenon in which cultural stereotypes and beliefs about gender roles have resulted in the widespread acceptability of the victimization of women. Sexual harassment is detrimental because of the social and psychological costs to the victims and the devaluation of women which results. However, the major consequences of harassment for women occur in the economic sphere. Sexual harassment is both an inevitable result of women's historically inferior economic position and, at the same time, a major cause of the reinforcement and perpetuation of this position. As long as there is cultural support and legitimation of this type of victimization, this form of social control via economic means may constitute the most consequential and insurmountable barrier to the social and economic advancement of women, to their uninterrupted entry into the workplace in general, and into male-dominated occupations like criminal justice in particular.

Endnotes

[1] Certainly, women (and men) have the potential to experience sexual harassment in every field.

[2] In *Meritor Savings Bank, FSB v. Vinson* (106 S.Ct. 2399 (1986)), the Supreme Court noted that, strictly speaking, the EEOC guidelines are not legally binding, but that courts and litigants may turn to them for guidance (Bennett-Alexander, 1987).

[3] See Hacker's (1951) article on women as a minority group for a further expansion of this and related issues.

[4] It is interesting to note that this survey excludes the FBI, CIA, and NSA.

[5] This belief continues despite the fact that there is little empirical evidence to show the importance of traits such as physical strength for successful police work (see Charles, 1982; Flynn, 1982).

[6] The case also involved a claim of sex discrimination because of salary and promotion problems. This aspect of the case will not be reviewed here.

[7] The initial court (the district court) ruled against Vinson (*Vinson v. Taylor*, 23 F.E.P. Cases [BNA] 37 (D.D.C. 1980)), and the case was appealed to the D.C. Circuit Court of Appeals (*Vinson v. Taylor*, 753 F.2d 141 (D.C. Cir. 1985)). Meritor filed a writ of *certiorari* and the Supreme Court agreed to hear the case.

Bibliography

Abbey, Antonia
    1982   "Sex Differences in Attributions for Friendly Behavior: Do Males Misperceive Females' Friendliness?" *Journal of Personality and Social Psychology* 42:830-38.

Bell, Daniel J.
    1982   "Policewomen: Myths and Reality." *Journal of Police Science and Administration* 10:112-20.

Bennett-Alexander, Dawn D.
    1987   "The Supreme Court Finally Speaks on the Issue of Sexual Harassment — What did it Say?" *Women's Rights Law Reporter* 10:65-78.

Bowersox, Michael S.
  1981   "Women in Corrections: Competence, Competition and the Social Responsibility Norm." *Criminal Justice and Behavior* 8:491-99.
Brown v. City of Guthrie
  1982   22 F.E.P. Cases 1627, (W.D. Okla-DC, 1980), 30 E.P.D. 33,031.
Bundy v. Jackson
  1981   25 E.P.D. 31,710, 641 F.2d 934, (CA-DC).
Charles, Michael T.
  1982   "Women in Policing: The Physical Aspect." *Journal of Police Science and Administration* 10:194-205.
Collins, Eliza G.C. and Timothy Blodgett
  1981   "Sexual Harassment—Some See It—Some Won't." *Harvard Business Review* 59:76-95.
Collins, Randall
  1971   "A Conflict Theory of Sexual Stratification." *Social Problems* 19:3-12.
  1974   *Conflict Sociology: Toward an Explanatory Science*. New York: Academic Press.
Dolecheck, Maynard M.
  1984   "Sexual Harassment of Southern Women in the Workplace: A Problem That Must Be Faced." *Mississippi Business Review* 46:3-7.
Dolkart, Jane L. and E. Lynn Malchow
  1987   "Sexual Harassment in the Workplace: Expanding Remedies." *Tort & Insurance Law Journal* 23:181-94.
Ellis, Judy Trent
  1981   "Sexual Harassment and Race: A Legal Analysis of Discrimination." *Journal of Legislation* 8:30-45.
Evans, Laura J.
  1978   "Sexual Harassment: Women's Hidden Occupational Hazard." Pp. 203-23 in Jane Roberts Chapman and Margaret Gates (eds.), *The Victimization of Women*. Beverly Hills, CA: Sage.
Farley, Lin
  1978   *Sexual Shakedown*. New York: McGraw-Hill.
Fitzgerald, Louise and Sandra Shulman
  1985   "Tarnishing the Ivory Tower: Sexual Harassment in Education." Address to the Kent State University Administrative Staff, Kent, Ohio.
Flanagan, Timothy J. and Katherine M. Jamieson
  1988   *Sourcebook of Criminal Justice Statistics—1987*. Washington, DC: U. S. Government Printing Office; U.S. Department of Justice, Bureau of Justice Statistics.
Flynn, Edith E.
  1982   "Women as Criminal Justice Professionals: A Challenge to Change Tradition." Pp. 305-340 in Nicole H. Rafter

and Elizabeth A. Stanko (eds.) *Judge, Lawyer, Victim, Thief: Women, Gender Roles and Criminal Justice*. Boston: Northeastern University Press.

Gruber, James and Lars Bjorn
 1982   "Blue-Collar Blues: The Sexual Harassment of Women Auto-Workers." *Work and Occupations* 9:271-98.

Gutek, Barbara A. and Bruce Morasch
 1982   "Sex-Ratios, Sex-Role Spillover, and Sexual Harassment of Women at Work." *Journal of Social Issues* 38:55-74.

Gutek, Barbara A., Bruce Morasch and Aaron G. Cohen
 1983   "Interpreting Social-Sexual Behavior in a Work Setting." *Journal of Vocational Behavior* 22:30-48.

Hacker, Helen M.
 1951   "Women as a Minority Group." *Social Forces* 30:60-69.

Harragen, Betty Lehan
 1977   *Games Mother Never Taught You*. New York: Rawson.

Hemming, Heather
 1985   "Women in a Man's World: Sexual Harassment." *Human Relations* 38:67-79.

Henson v. City of Dundee
 1982   682 F.2d 897 (11th Cir.).

Hoffman, Frances L.
 1986   "Sexual Harassment in Academia: Feminist Theory and Institutional Practice." *Harvard Educational Review* 56:105-21.

Hoyman, Michele and Ronda Robinson
 1980   "Interpreting the New Sexual Harassment Guidelines." *Personnel Journal* 59:996-1000.

Jensen, Inger W. and Barbara A. Gutek
 1982   "Attributions and Assignment of Responsibility in Sexual Harassment." *Journal of Social Issues* 38:121-36.

Jurik, Nancy C.
 1985   "An Officer and a Lady: Organizational Barriers to Women Working as Correctional Officers in Men's Prisons." *Social Problems* 32:375-88.

Jurik, Nancy C. and Gregory Halemba
 1984   "Gender, Working Conditions and The Job Satisfaction of Women in a Non-Traditional Occupation: Female Correctional Officers in Men's Prisons." *Sociological Quarterly* 25:551-66.

Kanter, Rosabeth Moss
 1977   *Men and Women of the Corporation*. New York: Basic Books.

Kissel, Peter J. and Paul L. Katsampes
 1980   "The Impact of Women Corrections Officers on the Functioning of Institutions Housing Male Inmates." *Journal of Offender Counseling, Services and Rehabilitation* 4:213-31.

Koenig, Esther J.
 1978   "An Overview of Attitudes Toward Women in Law Enforcement." *Public Administration Review* 38:267-75.

Konrad, Alison M. and Barbara Gutek
  1986   "Impact of Work Experiences on Attitudes Toward Sexual Harassment." *Administrative Science Quarterly* 31:422-38.
Leap, Terry L. and Edmund Gray
  1980   "Corporate Responsibility in Cases of Sexual Harassment." *Business Horizons* 23:58-65.
Ledgerwood, Donna E. and Sue Johnson-Dietz
  1980   "The EEOC's Foray Into Sexual Harassment: Interpreting the New Guidelines for Employer Liability." *Labor Law Journal* 31:741-44.
Livingston, Joy A.
  1982   "Responses to Sexual Harassment on the Job: Legal, Organizational, and Individual Actions." *Journal of Social Issues* 38:5-22.
Lott, Bernice, Mary Ellen Reilly and Dale Howard
  1982   "Sexual Assault and Harassment: A Campus Community Case Study." *Signs* 8:296-318.
Loy, Pamela Hewitt and Lea P. Stewart
  1984   "The Extent and Effects of the Sexual Harassment of Working Women." *Sociological Focus* 17:31-43.
MacKinnon, Catherine
  1979   *Sexual Harassment of Working Women.* New Haven: Yale University Press.
Maglino, Myrna B.
  1974   A Study of Policewomen's MMPI Profiles. M.A. thesis. John Jay College of Criminal Justice.
Martin, Elaine
  1982   "Women on the Federal Bench: A Comparative Profile." *Judicature* 65:306-13.
Martin, Susan E.
  1980   *Breaking and Entering: Policewomen on Patrol.* Berkeley, CA: University of California Press.
  1989   "Sexual Harassment: The Link Joining Gender Stratification, Sexuality, and Women's Economic Status." Pp. 57-75 in Jo Freeman (ed.), *Women: A Feminist Perspective.* Mountain View, CA: Mayfield Publishing Co.
Martucci, W.C. and R. B. Terry
  1987   "Sexual Harassment in the Workplace: A Legal Overview." *The Labor Lawyer* 3:125-35.
Maypole, Donald E. and Rosemarie Skaine
  1982   "Sexual Harassment of Blue Collar Workers." *Journal of Sociology and Social Welfare* 9:682-95.
  1983   "Sexual Harassment in the Workplace." *Social Work* 28:385-90.
McIntyre, Douglas and James Renick
  1983   "Sexual Harassment and the States as Policy-Makers and Employers." *State Government* 56:128-33.

Meritor Savings Bank, FSB v. Vinson
  1986   106 S.Ct. 2399.
O'Farrell, Brigid and Sharon L. Harlan
  1982   "Craftworkers and Clerks: The Effect of Male Co-Worker Hostility on Women's Satisfaction with Non-Traditional Jobs." *Social Problems* 29:252-63.
Parisi, Nicolette
  1984   "The Female Correctional Officer: Her Progress Toward and Prospects for Equality." *Prison Journal* 64:92-109.
Peterson, Cheryl Bowser
  1982   "Doing Time With the Boys: An Analysis of Women Correctional Officers in All-Male Facilities." Pp. 437-460 in Barbara Raffel Price and Natalie J. Sokoloff (eds.), *The Criminal Justice System and Women*. New York: Clark Boardman Co.
Pike, Diane Lovewell
  1985   "Women in Police Academy Training: Some Aspects of Organizational Response." Pp. 250-270 in Imogene L. Moyer (ed.), *The Changing Roles of Women in the Criminal Justice System*. Prospect Heights, IL: Waveland Press.
Powell, Gary N.
  1983   "Sexual Harassment: Confronting the Issue of Definition." *Business Horizons* 26:24-28.
  1986   "Effects of Sex Role Identity and Sex on Definitions of Sexual Harassment." *Sex Roles* 14:9-19.
Price, Barbara Raffel and Susan Gavin
  1982   "A Century of Women in Policing." Pp. 399-412 in Barbara Raffel Price and Natalie J. Sokoloff (eds.), *The Criminal Justice System and Women*. New York: Clark Boardman Co.
Remmington, Patricia Weiser
  1983   "Women in The Police: Integration or Separation?" *Qualitative Sociology* 6:118-35.
Rosen, Helen D.
  1984   "Employer Liability for Sexual Harassment in the Workplace Under Title VII of the Civil Rights Act of 1964." *New York Law School Human Rights Annual* 2:151-76.
Russell, Diana
  1986   *Sexual Exploitation*. Beverly Hills, CA: Sage.
Schur, Edwin M.
  1984   *Labeling Women Deviant*. New York: Harper & Row.
Tangri, Sandra S., Martha R. Burt, and Leanor B. Johnson
  1982   "Sexual Harassment at Work: Three Explanatory Models." *Journal of Social Issues* 38:33-54.
Taub, Nadine
  1980   "Keeping Women in Their Place: Stereotyping Per Se as a Form of Employment Discrimination." *Boston College Law Review* 21:345-418.

Till, Frank J.
  1980   "Sexual Harassment: A Report on the Sexual Harassment of
         Students." *Report of the National Advisory Council on Women's
         Educational Programs.* Washington, DC.
U.S. Bureau of the Census
  1988   *Statistical Abstract of the United States.* Washington, DC: U. S.
         Government Printing Office.
U.S. Department of Justice
  1986   *Uniform Crime Reports.* Washington, DC: U.S. Government
         Printing Office.
U.S. Merit Systems Protection Board
  1981   "Sexual Harassment in the Federal Workplace: Is It a Problem?"
         Office of Merit Systems Review and Studies, Washington, DC: U.S.
         Government Printing Office.
Vinson v. Taylor
  1980   23 F.E.P. Cases (BNA) 37 (D.D.C.)
  1985   753 F. 2d 141 (D.C. Cir).
Wexler, Judie Gaffin and Deana Dorman Logan
  1983   "Sources of Stress Among Women Police Officers." *Journal of
         Police Science and Administration* 11:46-53.
Wilson, Nanci Koser
  1982   "Women in the Criminal Justice Professions: An Analysis of
         Status Conflict." Pp. 359-374 in Nicole H. Rafter and Elizabeth
         A. Stanko (eds.) *Judge, Lawyer, Victim, Thief: Women, Gender
         Roles and Criminal Justice.* Boston: Northeastern University
         Press.
Working Women United Institute
  1975   "Sexual Harassment on the Job: Results of a Preliminary
         Survey." Attica, NY.
Young, Vernetta D.
  1986   "Gender Expectations and their Impact on Black Female
         Offenders and Victims." *Justice Quarterly* 3:305-27.
Zimmer, Lynn E.
  1986   *Women Guarding Men.* Chicago: University of Chicago Press.

Part III

Women Professionals and the Criminal Justice System

Introduction to Part III

Women have had a great deal of difficulty entering official positions in most of the criminal justice agencies for a variety of reasons. Conflict theory is especially useful in explaining this difficulty as well as the total neglect of research on women criminal justice professionals by traditional criminologists. Not only were men in positions of authority to determine research projects but historically too few women have been employed by the criminal justice agencies to make research feasible. The small number of women could be accounted for by sex role stereotyping. Men have maintained control and authority within the system by outnumbering women and by establishing positions of authority as the domain of men.

Originally, women entered police work and corrections to supervise women during the arrest process and during their confinement in local jails and prisons. This was in accord with their stereotypical roles as nurturing caretakers of society. Except for positions as clerical workers and as administrators in women's prisons, women were excluded from administrative roles throughout the criminal justice system.

Recent Research on Women Professionals in the Criminal Justice System

Recent literature shows a slow, but progressive, movement away from the traditional concept of women's roles in criminal justice employment. The recent resurgence of the feminist movement stressed the importance of equal opportunity for women in the labor force. A number of legal decisions have resulted in policy changes with reference to the employment of women in criminal justice agencies. Since the 1972 amendment to Title VII of the Civil Rights Act of 1964, which prohibited employment discrimination based on sex, women have increasingly been hired in various criminal justice agencies. They also have been placed in line positions previously considered "for men only" (Breece and Garrett, 1975; Kennedy and Homant, 1981; Koenig and Juni, 1981; Price and Gavin, 1982; Townsey, 1980 and 1982).

Townsey (1980) has pointed out that a number of court cases have challenged the employment policies that give advantages to men. These policies involve height and weight standards, physical agility requirements, veterans' preferences, and limited pregnancy leaves. Also, several cases have charged sexual harassment on the job. Many agencies have now established guidelines to handle such cases. Legal decisions have been useful in obtaining positions for women in criminal justice agencies.

These legal decisions were especially helpful in women gaining entrance to police patrol work. Research studies, however, report that traditional police attitudes about the inherently masculine nature of police work in combination with general sex role stereotyping have hindered the movement of women into the area. Male police recruits and officers alike have resisted the acceptance of women as equal employees (Breece and Garrett, 1975; Charles, 1981; Price and Gavin, 1982; Townsey, 1980). The main objection to women police officers centers on the views of male officers that women lack sufficient strength to do the job on patrol. Yet, these views have not been supported by research.

Several research studies have examined governmental pilot programs that integrate women into patrol duties. These experimental programs have been reported in numerous cities, including Washington, D.C., New York City, Philadelphia, Denver, Miami, and Dallas (Bloch and Anderson, 1973; Breece and Garrett, 1975; Price and Gavin, 1982; Townsey, 1980). The negative attitudes of male police officers about female effectiveness on patrol were not supported by these studies. Townsey (1980) reports that women were as effective as men in all observed facets of police work.

In a study of the Michigan State Police Training Academy, Charles (1981) examined performances of men and women recruits in a variety of areas. Performance scores for men and women differed significantly only in the area of defensive tactics ability (Charles, 1981:215). Women and men performed equally well in most training areas in the academy (Charles, 1981). Male recruits, however, consistently stated in questionnaire responses that male troopers performed better than female troopers in tasks that required or could require physical strength (Charles, 1981:216). This negative attitude taints the male recruit's perception of the female officers' ability to perform police functions associated with physical aspects of the job.

The roles of women are changing and legal decisions are providing opportunities for more women to enter law schools. However, the law profession and especially the court systems are still predominantly male domains. Patterson and Engelberg (1982) state that men have maintained control of the legal profession by devising and promoting models of the legal professional. The major attribute of the legal practitioner in this model is that he is male (Patterson and Engelberg, 1982:387). As in other agencies of the criminal justice system, the higher level positions of authority (and the research projects) are controlled by men.

Scholarly work on women lawyers and judges is very limited. As more women enter the profession as criminal lawyers and judges in criminal courts, perhaps more research will be conducted on the work of these women.

Women have been employed as prison administrators and guards in women's prisons for many decades (Freedman, 1974; Rafter, 1985) but women have not been allowed to work in these capacities in men's prisons until recent years. The study of prison guards and administrators has been a neglected area of research in both men's and women's prisons. During the last decade, however, several research studies of male correctional officers in local jails and men's prisons have been published. Two research studies have been published on women guards in male prisons in the last five years (Pollock, 1986; Zimmer, 1986).

Petersen (1982:437) notes that women guards in male prisons experience some of the same conflict situations and resistance to their entrance into a previously all male environment as do women police officers. Just as the 1972 amendment to Title VII of the 1964 Civil Rights Act changed policies so that women could be employed as police officers, it also made possible the entrance of women guards in men's prisons.

Although the studies on women as professionals in the various agencies of the criminal justice system are somewhat scarce, the studies that are reported indicate strong support for the conflict perspective. That is, while some women are managing to acquire positions in the male dominated professions, most of them are being maintained at the lower levels of authority and are meeting a great deal of resistance from the men with whom they work.

New Research on Women Professionals and the Criminal Justice System

While conflict theory is applicable to the studies presented in the first two sections of this book, it is especially appropriate and even explicitly evident in the following chapters. With the current changes in sex roles for some women in our society, women have been gaining entrance into what was once an exclusively male system. However, the chapters in this section indicate that men have not always been anxious to accommodate or to accept women as coworkers. Various authors in this section explore issues regarding exploitation of women and conflict between men and women officials in criminal justice.

Although women police officers have been the subject of research more often than other professional women in criminal justice, Pike's study, "Women in Police Academy Training: Some Aspects of Organizational Response," presents an original approach to exploring new roles for women. For the first time, a woman has conducted observational research on the training of men and women police officers. The entrance of women into police work represents one indication of the changing roles of women but Pike provides evidence that adaptation to women in academies is minimal. The models of womanhood created in police training academies maintain the traditional sex role stereotypes of women and contribute to conflict between officers by strengthening the male macho image.

Martin has written a very thorough chapter, "The Changing Status of Women Officers: Gender and Power in Police Work." She documents both the early history of women's entrance into police work and the Affirmative Action Policies which changed the representation of both women and minorities on police forces. In her research study, she compares the discriminatory treatment of women who joined police work before 1980 with those who joined in 1985 or 1986. The studies by Pike and Martin both indicate that conflict theory is very applicable to the situation of women police officers as they continue to struggle for acceptance and full integration into the male dominated work structures.

Bernat's chapter, "Women in the Legal Profession," traces the historical entrance of women into the law schools and the struggle of women to gain acceptance in the legal profession. Conflict theory explains the patriarchal gatekeeping practices designed to provide men with power and the benefits of the legal profession which flow from this power. Bernat further suggests that changes in women's roles in the criminal courts are progressing slowly in this patriarchal system that values men over women.

Due to changing sex roles in society and several legal decisions women have been allowed to work as correctional officers in men's prisons. Zupan's chapter, "The Progress of Women Correctional Officers in All-Male Prisons," documents the history of women's entrance into male prisons as prison guards and carefully examines the court cases that facilitated this progress. She also documents the discriminatory actions and opposition experienced by women guards as reported by various research studies. Finally, Zupan provides a comparative analysis of the differences between male and female correctional officers.

Although women have made some progress in gaining entrance into predominantly male occupations in criminal justice agencies, women still experience opposition and discrimination from some male colleagues. These five chapters also point to several important areas for future research on women professionals in criminal justice agencies.

Bibliography

Bloch, Peter and Deborah Anderson
  1973   *Police Women on Patrol.* Washington, DC: Police Foundation.
Breece, Constance and Gerald Garrett
  1975   "The Emerging Role of Women in Law Enforcement." Pp. 96-122
          in Jack Kinton (ed.), *Police Roles in the Seventies.* Ann Arbor:
          Edwards Brothers.
Charles, Michael
  1981   "The Performance and Socialization of Female Recruits in the
          Michigan State Police Training Academy." *Journal of Police
          Science and Administration* 9:209-23.
Freedman, Estelle
  1981   *Their Sisters Keepers: Women's Prison Reform in America,
          1830-1930.* Ann Arbor: University of Michigan Press.
Kennedy, Daniel and Robert Homant
  1981   "Nontraditional Role Assumption and the Personality of the
          Policewoman." *Journal of Police Science and Administration*
          9:346-55.
Koenig, Esther and Samuel Juni
  1981   "Attitudes Toward Policewomen: A Study of Interrelationships
          and Determinants." *Journal of Police Science and
          Administration* 9:463-74.
Patterson, Michelle and Laurie Engelberg
  1982   "Women in a Male-Dominated Profession: The Women Lawyers."
          Pp. 385-97 in Barbara Raffel Price and Natalie Sokoloff (eds.), *The
          Criminal Justice System and Women.* New York: Clark
          Boardman.
Petersen, Cheryl
  1982   "Doing Time with the Boys: An Analysis of Women Correctional
          Officers in All-Male Facilities." Pp. 437-60 in Barbara Raffel Price
          and Natalie Sokoloff (eds.), *The Criminal Justice System and
          Women.* New York: Clark Boardman.
Pollock, Joycelyn M.
  1986   *Sex and Supervision: Guarding Male and Female Inmates.* New
          York: Greenwood Press.

Price, Barbara Raffel and Susan Gavin

1982 "A Century of Women in Policing." Pp. 399-412 in Barbara Raffel Price and Natalie Sokoloff (eds.), *The Criminal Justice System and Women*. New York: Clark Boardman.

Rafter, Nicole

1985 *Partial Justice: Women in State Prisons, 1800-1935*. Boston: Northeastern University Press.

Townsey, Roi

1980 "Women in Municipal Policing." A paper presented at the annual meeting of the American Society of Criminology.

1982 "Female Patrol Officers: A Review of the Physical Capability Issue." Pp. 413-25 in Barbara Raffel Price and Natalie Sokoloff (eds.), *The Criminal Justice System and Women*. New York: Clark Boardman.

Zimmer, Lynne E.

1986 *Women Guarding Men*. Chicago: University of Chicago Press.

chapter 13

Women in Police Academy Training
Some Aspects of Organizational Response*

Diane Lovewell Pike
Augsburg College

> "You can't treat a woman like you can a man."
> — Academy Instructor

Introduction

Policing is very much an organized male-oriented occupation (Drummond, 1976; Harris, 1973; Martin, 1980; Niederhoffer, 1967). Over the last decade, however, policing has undergone a change about which we know relatively little — women are becoming patrol officers. While a few studies have looked at women's performance on patrol (e.g., Martin, 1980), there is little research on the consequences of their introduction to police training. My purpose

*Although the research discussed in this article was conducted in 1978 and 1979, the observations are still relevant. Some progress has been made in the acceptance of policewomen. But as Martin suggests in the next chapter there are still barriers to full integration of women police officers.

in this chapter is to describe and explain the organizational response to women in the police academy.[1] In addition to much needed data on what actually goes on in this type of organization, the analysis explores the dilemmas created for persons in one sex role when occupational roles (and their organizational implementation) are sex linked to another. How are women characterized within the academy? What are the consequences? If "you can't treat a woman like you can a man," is it also the case that you cannot treat a woman like you can a cop?

We will examine how the models of womanhood created in training contribute to the strengthening of the male macho image. No simple "police officer" model is offered. Since female police officer remains an inappropriate status to many, in and out of the police world, it is necessary for women to adapt to a unique set of pressures, expectations, and responses. The academy's formal adaptation to women is minimal, while the response highlights their presence and their differences, in part, because female recruits are few in number. In addition, we will deal with the question of being female versus being black in policing. The findings suggest that, despite some similarities in the entrance of each minority group to policing, being black as opposed to being female generates a very different organizational adaptation and response. The situation is further complicated when one is both.

Methodology

The research for this study was conducted during 1978 and 1979 in two regional police academies. Nine weeks were spent as a participant-observer in the Eastern Police Academy (EPA), a residential facility. Four months were spent as a participant-observer in the Midwestern Police Academy (MPA), a commuter facility.[2] In addition to the observation data, interviews were conducted with staff members ($N = 19$), and questionnaires were administered to four recruit classes, the two in which I participated and two in which I did not ($N = 144$). The staff members at both academies are male, except for one female MPA instructor. The composition of the EPA recruit class is: thirty-one white males, one black male, and four white females. The composition of the MPA recruit class is: twenty-eight white males, four black males, one Hispanic male, three white females, and five black females. The analysis begins with the social organization of recruit training with respect to the characterizations of women, in and out of police work, and then turns to the specific treatment of female recruits in the classroom.

Women's Roles: Defining the Appropriate

In police academy training, characterizations of women are maintained within a particular perspective and accompanying set of expectations. Although men are characterized too, the ways women are thought of and treated create a ground against which the image of a woman on patrol becomes inappropriate. The central themes are women in general (as wives and sex objects), women and policework (victims and suspects), and women in police work.

Wives

The relationship of husbands and wives, particularly officers and police wives, is a source of both humor and concern in the academy.[3] While more common among some instructors than others, wife jokes are part of a broad style of humor in teaching.

One instructor explained to the class that there was a five-year prison penalty for carrying a gun in a motor vehicle—to which he added, "I keep sneaking one into my wife's car." Yet, the presence of female recruits creates the opportunity for husband jokes, and thus for "interruptions" in routine (Kanter, 1977:224). Most staff members are still not accustomed to the presence of female recruits:

> Is the food like what mother cooks? No, it's more like what wives cook at home—(class laughter)—or you wives, husbands. (Then noticing one of the female recruits, the instructor smiled and quipped), She hates me already (class laughter).

Women, however, are taken seriously in the role of being supportive wives of their officer-husbands. Police work has long been recognized as a source of strain on family life. One academy sponsors an evening seminar for recruits, their spouses, and friends on the academy program and police work. Slides of academy life and films on police work accompanied brief remarks by two area police chiefs. Directing most of their comments to the wives and girlfriends present, the chiefs' message stressed: police work is important, difficult, and a strain on an officer and his family; police wives have an important job to do in supporting their husbands. Support ranges from being understanding of the job pressures to making sure the uniform is sharply pressed. Wives are portrayed in a traditional role and one which maintains an image of the appropriate place for women.

Sex Objects

The characterization of women as sex objects also emerges in training.[4] In films, for example, sexy women are used to teach recruits that beautiful blondes can be fatal. One very recent film even includes an attractive female police officer, whose presence prompted the usual appreciation. Attractive women always elicit applause, whistles, and comments from the class. Jokes and comments about unattractive women in other scenes complete the popularity of beautiful women.

Instructor and recruit behavior reflect similar stereotypes. Both instructors and recruits react to the presence of women as a source of humor and entertainment while sustaining the quintessential male officer role. One instructor brought out a round of laughter by joking that (male) officers are able to hold traffic court in the back seat of the patrol car—women pay their fines there. At the residential academy, new recruits were warned that although women were now present in the dorms, there was no need for the men "to prove their masculinity." That instructor advised the women to put paper on the windows of their dorm room door—"I'd love to see you, but I haven't seen my wife all week!" And a guest instructor showing slides on ballistic laboratory facilities included one slide of two naked women. Its inclusion was an error, he explained to the class; he had been told before class to take out all "those slides" but apparently missed one. As Harris (1973:88) has written " . . . a gimmick was needed for each class if the recruits were to pay attention to them . . . sexual jokes during the lecture was one technique. A method used by instructors who accompanied their lecture with slides was to intersperse the slide collection with pictures of nudes . . . ." Male recruits, too, fall into and/or bring with them to training this style of reference to women. For example, when a group of male recruits began discussing a class on rape crisis, one commented, "There's so much (sex) around, there's no need to rape." "Yeah," another replied, "buy a broad a drink in a bar and she'll do it."

Of course, men in the academy are not unique in viewing women as sex objects, although the style in this case may reflect the working class orientation of policing as an occupation. Women use sexiness to try to distract police officers and men do buy women drinks in bars ("let him buy you a drink and he'll do it," a female recruit replied). Rather, much of the problem lies in the general separation of work and sex in our society; if women are traditionally viewed as sex objects, then the difficulty arises of how to relate to them at work. My point is that in this setting there are particular consequences of such characterizations of women because a sex-linked occupational role is challenged by nontraditional members of the opposite sex. The macho, aggressive male officer image is dependent upon the complementary image of women as sexy — not macho.[5] Casting women in this sexy role creates a sense of the "normal" and appropriate behavior of women and at the same time draws boundaries for what is deviant.

Women Ecountered in Police Work

While perceiving women as wives and sex objects reflects a general stereotype, characterizations of women as they affect police work are equally revealing and central in the organization of daily academy life.

Victims

Female victims are a special category in the police world. Viewed as helpless and/or unpredictable, women are usually more trouble for a police officer. Domestic disputes, for example, are considered dangerous and bothersome calls. One familiar scenario is that once an officer "does something" (arrests the husband, for example), the wife gets upset and turns against the cop. Although such a scenario represents only a small percentage of actual incidents, it nonetheless reflects a widespread characterization of "how women are" in these situations.

Women are also unique because social changes and demands of interest groups have created pressures for the specialized handling of the victims of sex offenses. With these pressures came the notion that female police officers should be placed in special sex offense units because they offer special skills for dealing with such cases. This policy singles out sex offense victims and female police officer skills. It also challenges the male officer's capabilities of handling such cases. At the same time, however, these female police officer roles solve dilemmas for men. Male officers are less susceptible to charges of abuse or mishandling a case if they are excluded from such situations.

Training in handling sexual assault cases specifically addresses the issue of the male officer's skills in dealing with female victims. The special attention implicitly supports the stereotype that women "of course" do a good job handling women and that men "of course" need to learn to be more sensitive. One female detective made a special effort to break down these stereotypes—"You, as a male officer, can do things for the victim that women can't do," such as help victims feel that not all men are going to hurt her. A male recruit asked how men should handle rape cases and was told, "Act like a fellow human being rather than a tough cop!"

Suspects

Female suspects required special handling too. Officer safety always comes first and searching females is particularly risky because women "unjustifiably" sue, claiming that the male officer molested them during the search. Recruits are warned to get female police officers to do such searches whenever possible.

One recruit commented after a law class on searches that regardless of the risk of being sued, he would "pat down" a female suspect for his own safety. An instructor discusses female searches at length while demonstrating on a male recruit:

> You guys can't do this with the gals . . . if dealing with female prisoners. If it's a street search, try and find a weapon—there's lots of problems and complaints, so be very careful dealing with female suspects. You gals don't have as much problem, but we do get some complaints. I guess the guys don't mind being searched by girls.

Then addressing himself particularly to the men in the class, he added:

> Be careful transporting females—they call "rape." Protect yourself against rape [charges] by noting in your mileage. Use common sense searching females . . . get a matron or female officer to do it. They [female suspects] have every hiding place you can think of.

The problem of female searches reflects real dangers and complex legal issues. Yet at the same time, the presence of female police officers can solve some of the male officer concerns about being hurt by women either physically or legally.

In addition to the potential legal risk and the extra work involved if a female officer must be found to perform the search, female suspects are dangerous. One training film lists special topics officers must deal with: drug addicts, the mentally ill, females, suicides. Another film depicting typical patrol situations featured a scantily clad woman who acted seductively during a motor vehicle stop and then pulled a gun on the white male officer. In a later scene, an extremely buxom blond wearing little in the way of clothing was engaged in conversation with an average looking middle-aged man. After a few moments, the film narrator advised that "any healthy male would have fixed on her." The message was that police officers must be observant of the total situation.

Women are also seen as devious because they behave differently in different situations. Commenting on the differences in the appearance of females (under the age of sexual consent) in the courtroom versus the barroom, one instructor explained, "She's got a training bra on in court—she was stuffed in the bar." (The humorous scenario implied that the fellow seducing her in the bar could not be expected to know she was underage.) Women often are not what they seem as another instructor explained:

> There are times when you'll have to interview women involved in crimes. My experience has been that women break down easier than men. I'm not saying you're [women] weaker, but lots of times you can tell how evil they are [referring to child abusers] by how warm they are. . . . You should keep differences between men and women in mind—don't think that they don't exist.

And when one female recruit asked a guest speaker narcotics officer if female drug dealers were "worse than males," he replied:

> It depends on how you approach it. As a cop, I reacted to how they acted to me. A man's gonna have more trouble with women because if he touches her, she can scream rape or accuse him of enjoying it—or it's hard for a man to hit a woman. But you can say "What's a good lookin' woman like you doing this for?" and she'll respond. [He added quickly] never trust 'em though.

It is important to understand that as both victims and suspects the comparison, or referent, is not "women-more-or-less-than-men." Rather, it is women vis-a-vis other categories of people encountered in police work and their appropriate behavior. While sex is a factor in this particular category, it is the category that is crucial in determining what behavior to expect and how to respond to it.

Nonetheless, out of these characterizations—wives, victims, suspects, and sex objects—sexiness, trouble, and danger emerge as factors which cut across the various police world views of what women are like. For the police, dealing with women often means more work, more trouble, although sometimes more fun. As dimensions of police culture, this is part of the recruit socialization process—how to define and handle the women all officers will encounter.

Women in Policing

"Women have no common sense."
— Recruit Comment

Special Skills

Skills in handling female victims and usefulness in female searches are probably the most commonly acknowledged (by both men and women) assets of women in patrol work. In interviews, instructors report that women offer expertise in handling children and women, have more empathy for people, and are at an advantage in their lack of motivation "to prove their manliness." As one put it, "they've got nothing to prove over a drunk." Yet while instructors feel that women have some place in policing, they differ in what that place is:

> There's a place for women. I don't think overall for street work they can do it. Women are best fitted for the job when it comes down to using resources — men are more likely to fight. Women are not suited for patrol when it comes down to a fight, but they can talk their way out of situations.

> Policewomen have a proper role in police work. It is a matter of society wanting to accept it. There's nothing wrong with policewomen in police work — [pause]. Some assignments, I don't think they should have — it's OK for them to patrol by themselves in less tough areas.

Some police officers agree that individuals vary — "a good administrator has to be able to assign people according to skills;" others say that both women and men have many skills, just different ones. The general view is that women are good with people but men have the advantage in strength.

Special Problems

The conditions under which female officers are a problem, are at a disadvantage, or have to work harder than men are more frequently noted in training than are their special skills. Recruits learn that female police officers "have to hustle more than men," "have been known to blot their lipstick on reports," and like to be "treated special." One instructor felt that women in his department received special treatment because they were assigned female recruits for field training. This was a problem because women were newer on the force and did not have the years of street experience needed to be a good field-training officer.

Women also lack physical strength, although "one of the safeguards of women in policing is men being taught not to hit women . . . . A girl relies on her ability to interact with people." Women lack aggressiveness ("they have to learn to be a leader not a follower"), and according to one instructor, women lack maturity — they are either an "over-protected daughter" or a "die-hard feminist." Only one instructor felt women did not lack any skills; in his view, "any dummy can shake a door."

The importance of physical strength in police work is a complicated issue involving biological differences, socialization factors, job requirements, and work practices. One of the arguments against women on patrol is that they are not strong enough for "the one that counts" (Martin, 1980:97). Fifty-three percent of recruits surveyed reported that they would not feel as safe with a female back-up. MPA recruits were asked whether women lack any skills, and 56 percent responded affirmatively; 36 percent of those specifically mentioned lack of physical skills (N = 78). Forty-one percent said women did not lack any skills, while 59 percent said men did not lack any skills. Of all recruits, however, 98 percent agree or strongly agree that physical skills are important in police work.

Yet, even if physical skills are perceived as important, neither academy deals with the issue of differences in strength. In the EPA, there is no physical education program. In the MPA, physical training is included but there are different standards for men and women. For example, women are allowed to do "girl's push-ups." Thus, such a style of adaptation to women in training singles out recruits on the basis of sex, not strength. Weak and overweight men did not have the option of modified push-ups.

Men and Women as Equal in Police Work

Finally, in the social organization of training, men and women are sometimes characterized as equal. There is no reason, for instance, why women cannot fire a shotgun. One instructor explained that his wife had gone through the academy and could "shoot a shotgun all day long." Another relating war stories on home gun safety said, "We've even had a number of policewomen who've been shot by boyfriends." Ironically, the unintended consequence of attempts to try to respond to men and women as equals (far less common than efforts underlining differences), is that the effort itself singles out women.

Recruits' responses are even less favorable to women than instructors' responses. One of the most revealing episodes was the guest lecture on women in policing, one of the few formal program changes focused on women. Recruits criticized the speaker's reliance on statistics, the fact that he had "only" been on patrol for a year and a half, and that he had never actually worked with a female officer. Those who objected to the placement of women on patrol were the loudest and most verbal and even my further informal inquiries elicited indifferent responses at best. One recruit rejected the attempt to formally address the issue with the comment, "Aw, that's just statistics—anybody can do that!" Staff indicated that there were plans to cancel the lecture on women in policing.

Thus, the organization's one formal attempt to deal with the presence and problems of women in policing met with negative response, highlighting women's uniqueness and the opposition to their placement on patrol. Because it was only a single session, it provided a forum for voicing set opinions rather than changing any opinions about women on patrol. The most overt confrontation of the issue of women on patrol generated the most overt criticism. In part, this may suggest that women as recruits are treated well because they are not yet officers. A fellow student is not the same as a back-up or patrol partner. When the issue is forced, the unintended consequence of a minimal formal attempt to deal with the question is to reinforce the idea that women on patrol are inappropriate. Given this inappropriateness created by such characterizations of women, we turn now to the specific treatment of female recruits in the classroom.

Women in the Classroom: Affirmation of Status

Language

Academy staff are not used to women in the classroom. The habit of most instructors is to refer to the class as if it were all male, addressing the group as "gentlemen," "guys," or "men." At the beginning of a training session, some instructors occasionally note the inaccuracy in address and correct themselves, adding boyfriend or husband to a comment, or saying "ladies and gentlemen," while others merely state once "when I say 'guys' I mean to include everyone."

It is only in the context of this issue that I ever observed a female recruit publicly object to this type of treatment in the classroom. One day an EPA instructor referred to a woman in the class as a man. When she noted it, he defended himself by saying that he only meant the reference to distinguish men from boys. To this she replied, "We're not boys either." Later in the same class, the instructor called on another female recruit, with great deliberation addressing her as Officer Smith. Some of the class snickered implying that the first recruit's protests were silly; her initial request was simply that she not be referred to as male.

Similar incidents also occurred in the MPA, but were more often cloaked in humor. Once, a managerial staff member entered the room and addressed the female instructor as "sir." She looked up and behind herself to feign (humorously) not understanding to whom the male "sir" was addressed. Despite several years of having women in the program language still reflects the maintenance of the status quo—male organization.

Language is also an issue with respect to swearing and dirty jokes. Instructors often warn female recruits of forthcoming offensive language, offering to let them excuse themselves from the room or apologizing beforehand for the language. One MPA instructor, about to tell a joke with the slang word for fornicate, told "the ladies" that they should not feel timid about leaving the room if the word bothered them. (No one left the room and he told the joke.) Not telling the joke at all did not appear to be an option. An EPA instructor remarked to a group of female recruits, "Hey! Have I said very many bad four letter words yet?" "No," one replied, "but if you don't, we will!"

Teasing

Two dominant styles in classroom interactions with women, both staff-recruit and recruit-recruit, are teasing and flirting. Teasing is directed to both men and women and is probably the major style of informal classroom interaction. Flirting with women (a type of teasing) is part of the quintessential police officer role and often—though not always—is a two-way street in the academy. Very often the basis for both flirting and teasing is sex humor.

Teasing among recruits, for example, usually focuses on women as sex objects. One female MPA recruit walking into class late was met with whistles and joking comments. During a break between classes, a male EPA recruit chided a friend for swearing in front of one of the female recruits, "watch your mouth! She has virgin ears." The friend replied, "That's the only thing virgin about her."

In another instance, a female recruit returned after break to find a parking meter where her desk had been. Jokes were made about getting her to sit on it. One fellow went over and pretended to put a nickel in the meter. Another quipped, "But George got twelve minutes!" to which a third replied, "Yeah, but he couldn't last that long." And one day the female instructor wore a skirt with her uniform instead of the usual pants. When she walked to the front of the class, there were cheers, howls and whistles. Then the assistant class coordinator followed her up to the front with his pant legs rolled up to show off his legs. The class became hysterical with laughter.

Teasing also challenges women's capacity for patrol. During an EPA break, two recruits tied a female recruit to her chair with her boot laces and slid her around the room, laughing; one yelled, "You're gonna be a cop!"

While each incident is minor and appeared to be taken in good spirit by all, such behavior nonetheless suggests that the specific classroom treatment of women parallels characterizations of women in general. The male officer model is maintained and the status of women as women is affirmed.

Flirting, on the other hand, usually occurs in the direction of male staff to female recruits or male recruit to female recruit. Some instructors flirt more than others—ranging from not at all to constantly. While flirting is generally an interaction, female recruits usually do not actively initiate this behavior in the classroom. For example, one EPA instructor remarked in class to a female recruit, "Judy, we've got to stop making eye contact in class—people will think something is going on." Another instructor asked a recruit to open a window, adding, "If you get cold, I'll put my arms around the girls."

The intent of flirting—whether to be friendly, to give women a hard time, to bolster a masculine self-image, or even if done unconsciously—is largely irrelevant for our analysis here; most likely all four are involved. But the consequences of flirting are a relevant matter. Flirting reinforces the response to women as sex objects. It means that the female recruit's status as a woman rather than as police officer is the salient status (see Epstein, 1970). Responding to females as women rather than police officers reinforces the occupational working definition of police officers as macho and male, within a style of response that reflects the working class orientation of policing.

In interpreting these selected examples it is crucial to understand that they: 1) are a way of teasing people the staff and class generally like, and 2) do not stand out as any worse than the teasing of men.

While they do indicate something about the affirmation of the status of women, it is important to remember that on the whole, daily life is pleasant. Most people like each other. Thus, we may ask, how well are women accepted in training?

Acceptance of Women in Training

Most MPA instructors state that the acceptance of women in the academy is "an individual type thing," based on individual instructors and their personalities. Extremes are represented by one who felt women are "totally accepted as equals," and another who said he did not think women were accepted at all in the academy.

Interestingly, instructors are far more negative about the acceptance of women in their police departments. While some suggest that it appears to be getting better, most report that the initial resistance was strong and is waning very slowly:

> The brass opinion is that they are a necessary evil for federal money—a third don't mind, a third will never accept women, and a third, the new police officers, want to protect women.

> I don't think they were accepted real well—it depends on the individual . . . . Many wanted to be specialized and that caused bad vibes.

Or:

> At first, not very much—now it's increased. Some individuals say they're (women) performing, some say they're not—'You can't make a man out of a woman.' There's some resentment of women in specialized units.

> They are accepted on paper very well and on a man-to-man basis. . . . But one officer once said to me 'There's only one way to get rid of bitches—have one or two get killed and we can get rid of them.'

The more positive view of acceptance in the academy may reflect some sense of "we see how it ought to be and try to present ourselves as close to that model." At the same time, given what is known about women on patrol, it may also reflect a real difference in acceptance. The academy is not the street, a distinction with important consequences as noted earlier. Furthermore, the occupational career stage can affect the degree to which the occupational role is perceived.

Second, some instructors realized that there are problems for women because they are few in number. Instructors at both

academies were asked if they felt women had any different
experience or special problems as female recruits:

> Very much so. Few have been in all male groups and the men
> don't know how to react to them other than to be flirty. . . . They
> have the problem of reacting to men and adjusting to a male slot.

> No . . . on the whole, women are more intelligent and mature
> than men.

> Yes . . . relating to such a large number of men. In the new class
> with only two gals, they get lots of remarks and have to contend
> with it—and they'll get the same on the street.

> The guys think they're a joke. . . .

> It's based on the person's personality. . . . They make their own
> problems.

> Women have trouble with upper body strength.

Most of the responses by the EPA staff centered on problems for
women in the dorms:

> It's harder for women to live in the dorms. . . . They get more
> mental abuse—lots of jokes with sex connotations.

> It's easier with four [women] but often there's only one or two.
> [Women] are at a disadvantage—males talk dirty just to
> antagonize them. They're under a lot of pressures. If I had my
> way, I'd put them upstairs. No reason [for them] to be subjected
> to this not-normal behavior—males acting abnormal because
> females are there.

> No—it's a good experience to be with other police officers.

Thus, instructors do have a certain insight into the problems
confronting women. Some recognize that women are at a disadvantage being few in number (the problem of tokenism), while
others note the exaggerated response of males (which highlights
the contrast between men and women).

Third, staff were asked whether or not the presence of female
recruits had any effect in the classroom. In interviews, about half
of the instructors report that women do not make much difference
in the classroom. Others feel the presence of women changes the
men's behavior (interestingly, not the women's):

> Men are more ill at ease . . . you get different classroom partici-
> pation if [there are] no women. Police officers are macho and
> don't like to have a girl think they are stupid if they ask
> questions, (so) are less likely to ask certain ones—they act super
> cool.

> Guys make remarks they wouldn't make to a bunch of
> guys . . . and vice versa.

> Yeah . . . it should make the majority of officers more aware of vulgarity but it doesn't seem to have that effect.

Ironically, most instructors claim that female recruits have no effect on their teaching:

> I don't teach differently; I don't think classes act any differently after the first week.

> I'm open anyway . . . some have a language barrier. Yes, I tend to be less technical; I don't think women have been exposed to things, like a breaking system.

> It makes a difference . . . I can't talk as candidly because of my values and upbringing . . . I can't feel comfortable swearing in front of women, but it's no great problem.

Thus, in the classroom the organizational response to women as female recruits complements the picture painted in characterizations of women in general. The final topic of interest in understanding the treatment of women is to examine the issue of being black versus being female.

Being Black Versus Female

Parallels exist in the legal battles undertaken by blacks and women to enter the police departments. Both groups were initially brought in to serve "people like themselves." To the extent they have remained small in numbers, both groups continue to be in a minority or token situation. Women's entrance was somewhat different insofar as their specialized placement was often to higher status units; there was no fighting over working in the ghetto.

Yet, given our understanding of how women complement the police officer role, it is important to note that blacks do not challenge the quintessential police officer role in the same way women do. In fact, some stereotypes of blacks fit quite well in the model. One can be black, yet be strong, streetwise, and masculine. The symmetry or dependency of what "women are like" in contrast to macho officers means that it is far less likely that women successfully meet the ideal-type. When they try, women risk being labeled "the butch type" or "dykes."

Blacks and women are also different with respect to organizational adaptation. Since separate but equal was declared unconstitutional, no organizational (facility, uniform, or program) changes are necessary to incorporate blacks. Sex norms (co-ed showers?) present a very different type of barrier, which at least directs organizations to different strategies of adaptation.

Other differences emerge with respect to organizational response in the classroom. The key difference is that it is all right or appropriate to make fun of women, single them out, or to tease them publicly for being female, but one does not make fun of a person for being black. In public settings, formal or informal, blacks are not responded to as blacks as a basis for interaction. With women, sex status as the basis of public interaction is routine. Interestingly, being black is the key variable. Public jokes were made about Jewish recruits and occasionally about the Hispanic (one was nicknamed "Taco").

Thus, race is a visible characteristic, like sex, and prejudice is a dimension of organizational life. However, prejudice against blacks has different consequences than prejudice against women. Prejudice may mean that while a white male officer may be willing to have a black partner (though some are not), or may rely on a black officer as a back-up, a black person is not someone to socialize with after work (Alex, 1969:205). Women, on the other hand, are generally liked by men. An officer (white male) may not want her as a partner or feel she is reliable as a back-up, but he may want to socialize with her. We do not yet understand the interactional effects of being black and female. It is hoped that our further understanding of female recruits will provide guidance in understanding the consequences of both race and sex. Both groups face the problem of being marginal to or deviant from the police officer role. Compare the following description of female officers with the one of black officers:

> Policewomen face interactional dilemmas because they are both police officers, expected to behave according to the norms governing relations among peers, and women who are expected to adhere to the norms governing male-female relations (Martin, 1980:139).

> The Negro policeman occupies a double marginal position between the marginal police role and his own marginality as a Negro. His existence is divided into two major social positions, and he cannot take either for granted. Each social situation he confronts potentially tells him something different than he expects. He is a man interchangeable with his surroundings, and performs both roles under inconsistent expectations (Alex, 1969:20-21).

Discussion

Within the formal and informal context of learning to be a rookie officer, a relatively constant outlining occurs about what is desirable in women (at least as far as men are concerned) and what men ought to desire. An important consequence of the social organization of training is a subtle delineation of the incongruity of the roles of women and police officers—officers are macho, women are sex symbols.

At one level, these findings offer support for Kanter's (1977) theory of tokens. Because women are few in number, women get more attention, are treated differently and come to be viewed in terms of stereotypes by those around them. The perceptual tendencies of visibility, contrast, and assimilation operate to make the situation for women, or for any token, unique (1977:212).[6] In terms of visibility, women in policing are under unique performance pressures. In terms of contrast, women more strongly "challenge the dominant premise" (Kanter, 1977:22) in the way in which they differ from the quintessential police officer role. Women have dealt with greater pressures toward more types of role encapsulation. The hypothesis offered here, then, is that the degree of visibility contrast, and assimilation will vary with the type of token and characteristics of the occupation and organization. Data across occupations and types of tokens are now needed to specify models of how the various dependent variables operate in different settings. As noted, sociologists have not attempted to sort out in a serious way the interactional effects of being black and female. It is not clear whether being black and female is a type of double deviance (Laws, 1975). We understand the consequences of being black, female, and a police officer even less well. People hold multiple statuses, whose relative importance and consequences need to be worked out. In the academy, black women were singled out and responded to as women, not blacks.

Finally, organizational type must be examined. To date, our understanding is biased in the direction of higher status occupations (and high status roles within those) and those involved in the main or core career stage. Wheeler (1969:54) writes:

> Just as individuals may become differently socialized because
> of differences in past experiences, motivations, and capacities
> so may they become differently socialized because of differences
> in the structure of the social settings in which they interact.

The police academy is a separate organization from the police department, despite the close organizational ties. It is a people processing organization designed solely to induct persons into police organizations by a socialization process called training (Hasenfeld, 1972). Precisely because the academy is a socializing agency, its members have a different status. One could argue that in terms of entering nontraditional occupations, recruits are less threatening than rookies or veteran officers, medical students less so than doctors, law students less so than lawyers. These statuses can make an important difference and should be explored.

Conclusions

Women will most likely continue to survive, organizationally and occupationally, as recruits and as patrol officers. Yet Kanter (1977) is right in maintaining that as long as they are few in number, change may be minimal. Given the entrenchment of the occupational roles and its effect on the social organization of daily life, it is in many ways remarkable that women have survived as well as they have. There will always be deviants, as Durkheim (1949) first noted, and by changing numbers, power, and opportunity structures we may be able to alter the content of the deviance. But change in the role of women in police training and police work, if desired, will require specific changes in the occupation and, ultimately broader changes in society.

Endnotes

[1] Organizational response refers to behaviors, structures, and processes that can be made sense of in light of other organizational behaviors and processes.

[2] In both academy programs I participated as fully as possible, including the taking of exams, role-playing exercises and field trips. I was allowed to observe, but not participate, in firearms training.

[3] All but one of the interviewed staff are married and 39 percent of the recruits in the questionnaire sample (N = 144) are married.

[4] "Sex object" is not a completely satisfactory term to me, but is intended to refer to the portrayal of women as sexy and the object of attention based on that perception.

[5] See Martin (1980:88) for how this works in the department.

[6] The study of women in management, like other sociological studies of women in medicine and law, focuses on a high status occupation. A next step is to test whether these processes operate in working class or lower status occupations. We know relatively little about women in working class jobs.

Bibliography

Alex, Nicholas
  1969   *Black in Blue: A Study of the Negro Policeman.* New York:
          Appleton, Century, Crofts.
Bloch, Peter B. and Deborah Anderson
  1974   *Policewomen on Patrol: Final Report.* Washington, DC: Urban
          Institute.
Cain, Maureen
  1973   *Society and Policeman's Role.* London: Routledge, Kegan Paul.
Connolly, Harriet
  1975   "Policewomen as Patrol Officers: A Study in Role Adaptation."
          Ph.D. dissertation. City University of New York.
Drummond, Douglas S.
  1976   *Police Culture.* Beverly Hills, CA.: Sage Publications.
Durkheim, Emile
  1949   *The Division of Labor.* Translated by George Simpson. Glencoe,
          IL: Free Press.
Epstein, Cynthia F.
  1970   *Woman's Place: Options and Limits on Professional Careers.*
          Berkeley: University of California Press.
Erikson, Kai T.
  1962   "Notes on the Sociology of Deviance." *Social Problems* 9:307-14.
Gates, Margaret
  1974   "Women in Policing: A Legal Analysis." Washington, DC: Police
          Foundation.
Harris, Richard N.
  1973   *The Police Academy: An Inside View.* New York: Wiley.
Hasenfeld, Yeheskel
  1972   "People Processing Organizations: An Exchange Approach."
          American Sociological Review 37:256-63.
Horne, Peter
  1974   *Women in Law Enforcement.* Springfield, IL: Charles Thomas.
Hughes, Everett C.
  1944   "Dilemmas and Contradictions of Status." *American Journal of
          Sociology* 50:353-59.
Kanter, Rosabeth Moss
  1977   *Men and Women of the Corporation.* New York: Basic Books.
Laws, Judith Long
  1975   "The Psychology of Tokenism: An Analysis." *Sex Roles* 1:51-67.
Lemert, Edwin
  1951   *Social Pathology.* New York: McGraw-Hill.
Manning, Peter K.
  1977   *Police Work: The Social Organization of Policing.* Cambridge,
          MA: Massachusetts Institute of Technology Press.

Martin, Susan E.
  1980   *Breaking and Entering: Policewomen on Patrol*. Berkeley, CA:
          University of California Press.
Niederhoffer, Arthur
  1967   *Behind the Shield: The Police in Urban Society*. Garden City, NY:
          Anchor-Doubleday.
Sichel, Joyce, Lucy Friedman, Janet Quint and Michael Smith
  1978   *Women on Patrol: A Pilot Study of Police Performance in New
          York City*. Washington, DC: National Institute of Law
          Enforcement and Criminal Justice.
Sullivan, Joseph F.
  1980   "All-female Class in New Jersey to Test if Women's Place is in
          State Troopers." *New York Times* (June 17):Al.
Teasley, C.E. and Leonard Wright
  1973   "The Effects of Training on Police Recruits." *Journal of Police
          Science and Administration* 1:241-48.
Thompson, James D.
  1967   *Organizations in Action*. New York: McGraw-Hill.
Wheeler, Stanton
  1969   "The Structure of Formally Organized Socialization Settings."
          Pp. 53-116 in Orville Brim and Stanton Wheeler (eds.),
          Socialization After Childhood: Two Essays. New York: Wiley.

chapter **14**

The Changing Status of Women Officers
Gender and Power in Police Work

Susan E. Martin
Department of Health & Human Services

Until the 1970s, police jobs were reserved almost exclusively for white males. Since that time, however, minorities and women have entered policing in growing numbers. By the end of 1986, minorities comprised 23 percent of sworn personnel and women nearly 10 percent (with minority females comprising 3.5 percent of the total and nearly 40 percent of all women officers). Female officers' assignments also have expanded. Once limited to working with "women, children and typewriters" (Milton, 1972), women now can be found in virtually all police units, although they continue to be greatly underrepresented in supervisory positions.

These changes in the role of women in policing have not come about easily. They required legislation, executive action, and judicial decisions to alter eligibility criteria, selection standards, and assignment and promotion practices that were discriminatory. The

first group of women assigned to patrol met with open and
organized opposition that included ostracism and harassment.
Although organized resistance has virtually disappeared, many
male officers still express skepticism about women's capabilities
as officers and oppose women's full integration into police work.

This paper explores the reasons why women were excluded from
patrol work for most of this century, the changes that have resulted
in women's broadened policing role, and the barriers that women
officers continue to face in policing. The analysis will be based on
a conflict model which emphasizes the interplay of structural
features of the workplace and the interactional patterns of behavior.

The Traditional Role of Women in Policing: 1910-1970

From the creation of the first police force in the U.S. in the
mid-19th century until 1910, women were excluded from policing;
between 1910, when the first woman became a sworn officer, until
the mid 1970s, "policewomen" were limited in number, selected
according to separate criteria from male officers, paid less than male
officers, and assigned to social work and matron (i.e., guarding
women prisoners) roles. Only in the past two decades has the
number of women officers increased and their role in policing
changed from "policewoman" to police officer.

The first women officers entered policing as specialists dedicated
to preventive and protective work with women and children. The
early "policewomen's" literature makes clear their sense of being
part of a social movement dedicated to saving "wayward" youth
and "helpless" women and their advocacy of a distinct role for
women officers. In the large departments they often were assigned
to separate Women's Bureaus, were required to have a college
education, and did not have to meet the same physical standards
as the men. Although the women were "kept at arm's length from
the main organization and, perhaps, a little despised by the
remainder of the force" (Hutzel, 1933:3), they were able to stake
a claim in policing for several reasons. They avoided direct
competition with male officers, instead accepting a limited and
special role within the department that was an extension of
women's traditional sex role. They met society's demand for better
protection of women and children. Finally, women officers provided
progressive police reformers with a response to public pressure for
changes in police practices that de-emphasized use of force and
increased the service elements of the occupational role.

Between 1930 and 1970 the duties of a few women officers

broadened to include investigative, crime lab, and vice assignments. Nevertheless, the vast majority continued to work as specialists employed in juvenile work or assigned to secretarial duties. The limitations and constraints on their recruitment, training, salary, and promotion also remained.

In 1972, the Metropolitan Police Department of Washington, D.C. became the first major municipal agency to deploy a significant number of women to patrol. Since that time there has been a gradual but continuous increase in the number of women officers and supervisors who now serve on patrol and in virtually all other assignments in police departments across the country. (For a history of the early years of women in policing, see Horne, 1980; Martin, 1980; and Price, 1985).

From Policewoman to Police Officer: The 1970s

How can the shift in women's occupational role from specialist "policewoman" to generalist officer be explained? First, police departments nationwide faced a variety of pressures to change in the late 1960s. These included rising crime rates, "manpower" shortages, urban riots, and civil disorders demonstrating mounting tensions between the police and the community they were sworn to serve. To address these problems the blue-ribbon President's Commission on Law Enforcement and the Administration of Justice (1967) called for sweeping changes of the police. Their recommendations included the subordination of strength and aggressiveness to emotional stability, intelligence, and sensitivity to minority problems in recruitment; elimination of discriminatory selection criteria; the hiring of more minority, college-educated, and female officers; and the use of women officers in patrol, vice, investigative, and administrative functions.

Second, the resurgence of the women's movement precipitated a variety of social, economic, and legal changes in the position of women in society. This movement which was both a result of and stimulus to further alteration in the labor force patterns of women, expanded the recruitment pool of female officers. It also contributed to changes in sex role attitudes that, in turn, affected women in policing by altering traditional concepts of masculinity and femininity. While the women's movement did not assure equal opportunities for female officers, it stimulated change in the social climate that affected police departments both by challenging the legal status quo and influencing social norms.

Third, legal changes made it illegal to deny a woman equal

opportunity in a law enforcement career. Prior to 1972, the employment of women in police work was limited by laws and ordinances that excluded them from patrol and thereby made them ineligible for promotion.

Since passage of The Equal Opportunity Act of 1972, which extended the provisions of Title VII of the 1964 Civil Rights Act to state and local governments, the law has been a tool to remedy earlier occupational discrimination. The law specifically prohibited agencies, including police departments, from discriminating on the basis of race, creed, color, sex, or national origin with regard to compensation, terms, conditions, or privileges of employment. It also created the Equal Employment Opportunities Commission (EEOC) to oversee enforcement of the Act.

Executive branch actions and litigation also benefitted women officers. Executive Order 11246 called for "affirmative action" in addressing patterns of discrimination; the EEOC's guidelines for implementing Title VII interpreted the term "affirmative action" to mean specific plans that include numerical goals and timetables to overcome the effects of past discrimination (Block and Walker, 1982).

Federal courts also helped establish the principles of equal employment opportunity and "affirmative action" through judicial decisions. In *Grigg v. Duke Power Co.* 401 US 424 (1971), the court stated that the purpose of Title VII is "the removal of artificial, arbitrary and unnecessary barriers to employment (i.e., sex) when the barriers operate invidiously to discriminate on the basis of race or other impermissible classifications" and placed the burden of showing the job relatedness of an employment selection procedure on employers once the procedure was shown to have a disparate impact. In many large municipal and state police departments, litigation focused primarily on racial discrimination. This resulted in court orders and consent decrees establishing racial and sexual quotas to ensure greater participation of minorities and women in policing. Other court decisions supported plaintiffs' challenges to height and weight standards and agility tests (*Blake v. City of Los Angeles*, 15 FEP 76 [D.Cal. 1977]; *Harless v. Duck* 619 F.2d 611 [1980]). As a result, when there is a charge that a person was not hired or promoted due to discrimination, the agency must be able to show that the requirements for hiring or promotion are job-related, validated, free from 'inherent bias,' properly administered, and properly graded (Barrineau, 1987:67-68).

In the 1980s, the Justice Department and the Supreme Court reinterpreted Title VII of the Civil Rights Act so as to limit the use of "affirmative action" programs and narrow the grounds on which plaintiffs can prevail in employment discrimination cases. These decisions have not eliminated court ordered or voluntary affirmative action plans that now are in place in more than half of police agencies serving populations larger than 50,000. Nevertheless, they are likely to have a chilling effect on potential plaintiffs, making it more costly and difficult to win subsequent employment discrimination cases in the 1990s.

A fourth factor in the change in women's role in policing during the 1970s were the findings from a number of evaluations of women's performance on patrol that indicated that women can perform on patrol as ably as male patrol officers (Bartell Associates, 1978; Bartlett and Rosenblum, 1977; Bloch and Anderson, 1974; Kizziah and Morris, 1977; Pennsylvania State Police, 1974; Sherman, 1975; Sichel et al., 1977). For a summary of the findings of these studies see Sulton and Townsey, 1981; for a critique see Morash and Greene, 1986. These studies made clear that sex could not be considered a bona fide occupational qualification for the job of patrol officer; women had to be given an opportunity to serve on patrol. As a result of this combination of factors, by the end of the 1970s women were assigned to patrol duties in most large police agencies.

Male Opposition to Women on Patrol

The entry of women into traditionally "male" occupations has often been resisted, but in few occupations have males fought their integration as vigorously as policing. The reasons rest on the nature of police work and the anticipated impact of women on it. The essential elements of police work involve the exercise of authority and the ability to use force on behalf of the state. Initially women, as part of the protected "weaker" class, could hardly be entrusted with the moral authority of the state or be expected to physically handle the job. Although the social position of women and the nature of policing have undergone major changes in the past century, the authoritative and physical elements of policing continue and serve to justify men's resistance to women's integration. In addition, as Martin noted (1980:79):

> The integration of women into police patrol work as coworkers threatens to compromise the work, the way of life, the social status, and the self image of the men in one of the most stereotypically masculine occupations in our society.

Police work involves a variety of tasks and responsibilities. Officers are expected to prevent crime, protect life and property, enforce the laws, maintain peace and public order, and provide a wide range of services to citizens 24 hours a day. A common thread unifying these diverse activities, however, is the potential for violence and the need and right to use coercive means to establish social control (Bittner, 1970).

Understanding that the police act as the representatives of the coercive potential of the state and the legitimate users of force helps explain a number of their attitudes and characteristics. Although most police calls involve requests for service or order maintenance functions, the crime fighting aspect of the job is visible, publicly valued, and regarded as the most satisfying part of their work by most officers. Detectives get more pay, prestige, and personal autonomy. The informal group esteems the "good pinch" (arrest) and officers who make them. Catching criminals also is associated with danger and bravery, marking police work a "man's job" although the daily reality of police work is far less glamorous.

The combination of danger and authority plus organizational pressure for efficiency has resulted in a unique set of behavioral and cognitive characteristics termed the officers' "working personality" (Skolnick, 1967). Faced with danger, officers become suspicious; feared by ordinary citizens, they often become isolated from them. Set apart from the larger world, they turn to their occupational community for support, solidarity, and social identity. Viewing the public as hostile and facing uncertain danger, officers depend greatly on each other for mutual support and physical protection. The job becomes a way of life and the occupational group and its norms provide a morality and self-conception. Those officers that do not adhere to the principal norms of policing—the rule of silence, the requirement than an officer physically back up another officer, and the rule of maintaining respect for the police—face ostracism, the silent treatment, and outright rejection as a partner (Westley, 1970).

For many years the police maintained solidarity by recruitment and selection mechanisms that assured a homogeneous group of working class white males. Outsiders were eliminated by physical requirements (women) and written tests and/or educational requirements (blacks). Background investigations and personal interviews further screened out candidates that failed to express the "correct" attitudes toward the meaning of masculinity (Grey, 1975), including an aura of toughness and aggressiveness (David and Brannon, 1976).

One of the most frequently voiced objections to women was and still is that they are less able to perform the job because they are physically smaller and weaker. In one of the few remaining occupations in which strength and physical ability still are required for the work (if only occasionally), the assignment of women to patrol implies either that the men's unique asset—physical superiority—is irrelevant, or that the man working with a woman will be at a disadvantage he would not face in a confrontation if he had a male partner.

Women provide less "muscle" to a partner, and many men feel they cannot rely on a woman to act appropriately in a physical confrontation. The view that women are unreliable and unable to defend themselves and their partners, men assert, affects their own patrol behavior, making them more cautious. For a man to rely on a male partner is part of "male camaraderie"; reliance on a woman, in contrast, is felt to be unmanly. Thus the presence of women poses a bind for a male officer who wants to depend on his partner but does not want to depend on a woman. The way out of the bind is to exclude women from patrol work.

Female officers also threaten the rule that the police should maintain respect of the citizens. In some instances the uniform and office are insufficient; the officer's personal authority and manner of conveying it are involved in gaining citizen compliance. In a society where women are viewed as objects to be dominated rather than authority figures to be feared and obeyed and where they are not used to exercising power over men, male officers fear that male citizens' denial of female officers' authority will "rub off" on the police in general. Yet the alternative, a woman exercising authority over men, is also threatening to male officers' identities.

Women officers also undermine group solidarity by altering the rules by which officers relate to and compete with each other. They inhibit the use of expressive, "raunchy" language and frequent "locker room" talk based on sports, women, and sex. Women who "talk like truck drivers" also upset the men by blurring the distinctions between the sexes that enable men to be men. The presence of women raises the specter of bonds of sexual intimacy between officers that competes with the demands of loyalty to the group. The presence of women disturbs the informal distribution of rewards because no longer does everyone compete equally; women are able to gain exemptions and favorable assignments by taking "unfair advantage" of their sex. But when this occurs, the men direct their anger at the women rather than male supervisors who permit such "inequality."

Thus the nature of police work that combines danger and the power over our highest social values—life, liberty, and justice—

has resulted in an occupation closely associated with masculinity and officers who are very reluctant to integrate women into their ranks.

Affirmative Action Policies and Changes in the Representation of Women and Minorities: 1978-1986

Despite widespread opposition to their presence, between 1978 and 1986 the proportion of women in policing increased from 4.2 to 8.8 percent of municipal officers (Martin, 1990).[1] During the same period the representation of minority officers in large and moderate sized urban departments rose from 13.8 to 22.5 percent of the sworn personnel, as shown in Table 1. Thus the representation of minorities in policing now approaches their representation in the urban population (Sullivan, 1988), but women continue to be greatly underrepresented in policing.[2] The table also suggests that although minority women make up only 3.5 percent of all officers, they comprise 40 percent of all female officers. In contrast, minority males, who comprise 14 percent of the urban police personnel, make up only 21 percent of the male officers. Most minority women officers (and, to a lesser extent, minority males) are black.

Women have made even more modest gains in obtaining promotions to supervisory ranks. In 1978 they comprised only 1 percent of all supervisors; by the end of 1986 their representation had increased to 3.3 percent of those persons with the rank of sergeant or higher. Minority women supervisors went from comprising 20 percent of women supervisors to constituting nearly one third. Nevertheless, at the end of 1986 only one out of every 100 police supervisors was a minority female.

What effect have affirmative action policies had on these increases? As indicated in Table 2, in agencies under court order to increase the representation of women and minorities, at the end of 1986 women made up 10.1 percent of the sworn personnel; in those with voluntary affirmative action plans, women made up 8.3 percent of the personnel, and in those with no such plans women constituted only 6.1 percent of the personnel. The relationship of affirmative action to the representation of minority women is even clearer.

Affirmative action also was associated with the proportion of women in supervisory positions. In departments with court-ordered affirmative action, women made up 3.5 percent of all supervisors, in those with voluntary affirmative action programs and without affirmative action plans they comprised 2.4 percent and 2.2 percent of all supervisors respectively.

Table 1

Mean Percentage of Police in Municipal Departments in 1978 and 1986 By Ethnicity and Sex

	1978			1986		
Ethnicity	**Male**	**Female**	**Total**	**Male**	**Female**	**Total**
White	83.6	2.6	86.2	72.2	5.3	77.5
Nonwhite	12.2	1.6	13.8	19.0	3.5	22.5
Total	95.8	4.2	100%	91.2	8.8	100%

Table 2

Weighted Proportion of Women Officers and Supervisors By Affirmative Action Policy Type

Type of Policy	**White Officers**	**Minority Officers**	**Total Officers**	**Total Supervisors**
Court ordered (N = 45)	5.7	4.4	10.1	3.5
Voluntary (N = 126)	5.5	2.8	8.3	2.4
None (N = 126)	4.1	2.0	6.1	2.2
Total	5.3	3.5	8.8	3.3

Because other factors such as region, city size, and minority representation also were found to be associated with the representation of women, statistical controls were used to see if affirmative action had an effect independent of these other factors. It did; both voluntary and court ordered affirmative action still were significantly associated with the proportion of women in a department after controlling the presence of other variables.

Discrimination and Harassment:
The Experience of Women Officers

Most women officers have experienced both sex discrimination and sexual harassment (which legally is a form of sex discrimination). On the basis of interviews with more than 70 female officers in five large urban departments (Martin, 1990), two-thirds of the women identified at least one instance of sex discrimination and 75 percent reported instances of sexual harassment on the job. There was no difference in the proportion of women who are sexually harassed based on the length of their police service. It appears, however, that other types of discriminatory treatment have decreased: 79 percent of the women who entered policing before 1980 but only 27 percent of those who joined in 1985 or 1986 asserted that they faced sex discrimination on the job.

Descriptions of the harassment faced by the first group of women on patrol indicated that frequently it was blatant, malicious, widespread, organized, and involved supervisors; occasionally it was life-threatening. Reports of recent incidents indicated the remaining sex discrimination is more subtle and less frequent, open, or tolerated by officials. The interviews also suggest that the women are far more sensitive to what constitutes sexual harassment and discrimination and more willing to complain about it.

The forms and sources of discrimination were varied; the anger and pain it caused, however, was strikingly vivid in the memories of many of the first generation of women on patrol. Male coworkers organized to avoid working with a woman and, when assigned a female partner, gave her the silent treatment so that "eight hours could seem like an eternity." As one woman noted:

> I was at the precinct ten days before I knew I had a partner . . . because the first ten partners called in sick and I was put to work inside the precinct. On the 11th day the other white guys called the man who was assigned to work with me and told

> him to call in sick. . . . but he came in anyway. I was in the scout
> car with him and he said to me, 'officer, wake up. Everyone's
> called in sick and they told me to do so. I just wanted to know
> why from you . . .'

Other men refused to share job knowledge or teach women skills
they routinely imparted to new men. Some women's lives were
endangered by partners and squad members who failed to instruct
on proper procedures, assist in a physical confrontation, or were
slow to provide back up. More often, however, the women were
overprotected and thus denied opportunities to take initiative which
is necessary to become an effective patrol officer.

Another way men heighten group solidarity and make clear to
women that they are "outsiders" is to sexualize the workplace
(Enarson, 1984; Swerdlow, 1989). Male officers frequently played
pranks, told jokes, and made comments that called attention to
women's sexuality or that were based on sexual stereotypes of
women. Resistance to this sexualization occasionally had life-
threatening consequences. As one woman stated:

> I had a partner who tried to pry into my private life. He called
> me stuck up when I wouldn't answer his questions. . . . When
> he put his hand on my arm, I slapped him. After that he wouldn't
> get out of the car on runs.

Some supervisors abused their authority directly by harassing
the women or indirectly by ignoring, and thereby encouraging,
mistreatment by peers. Informants recounted instances of denial
of job perks such as lockers in the station, regular scout car
assignments, and opportunities for training; overzealous and
discriminatory enforcement of rules; depression of performance
evaluations that affected transfers and promotions; sexual
harassment; denial of desired assignments; and overprotection and
"favoritism" that singled them out, isolated them from male peers,
and caused the latter's resentment.

What made their situation so frustrating was the fact that there
was little the women could do. Complaining often resulted in further
ostracism and retaliation from peers with little assurance of support
from superiors. For example, one woman who won a complaint
about her evaluation, stated that her lieutenant was so humiliated
that:

> he'd split me and my partner up, put me on inside details, and
> not give me the days off (I'd had requested).

Most women did not complain. Some remained silent because
they were trying to fit in and "didn't want to make waves"; others

looked at the "larger picture" regarding their race and sex; a third group noted that they only subsequently recognized their treatment had been illegal:

> Before EEO and sexual harassment laws, I didn't think of (what we faced) as discrimination. It was just the cost of doing the job.

The harassment, isolation, and pressure to remain silent were particularly acute for black women who often faced the "double whammy" of racism and sexism. One black woman noted, "Sometimes I couldn't tell if what I faced was racial or sexual or both." Another added, "the worst discrimination I got came from a black lieutenant." She considered suing the department but did not "'cause he's black." She added:

> I guess that makes me a racist but I looked at the overall problem it would have caused and how it would be played up in the press and didn't do it. If he'd have been anything else I'd have sued his butt.

Women's Coping Strategies

Faced with openly discriminatory treatment and the burdens of being highly visible tokens faced with performance pressures, group boundary heightening, and encapsulation in stereotyped roles (Kanter, 1977), the pioneer women adopted a variety of coping strategies. Some, overwhelmed with feelings of helplessness or the desire to remain a "lady," accepted the stereotypic seductress, mother, pet, and helpless maiden sex roles, (Kanter, 1977) welcoming or tolerating the "protection" of males and adopting a deprofessionalized policewomen role (Martin, 1980). Unable or unwilling to prove themselves "exceptions," they tended to embrace a service-oriented approach to police work, display little initiative or aggressiveness on street patrol, seek nonpatrol assignments and personal acceptance (which occasionally involved sponsorship based on a sexual arrangement with a supervisor).

Others, characterized as *police*women (Martin, 1980), identified with the policemen's culture and sought to gain acceptance by being more professional, aggressive, loyal, street-oriented, and macho than the men. In resisting traditional sex role stereotypes, however, they faced contrary stereotypic labels of "dyke" or "bitch." When they outproduced the men they were punished for overachievement. They craved acceptance, but never could quite become "one of the boys"; those that were "too friendly" paid a price by being labeled "easy."

Although most women adopted one of these two broad patterns, many actively sought to resist traditional gender arrangements and stereotypes. One resistance strategy was "striking a balance" between accepting the traditionally feminine stereotypes into which men press them and the "opposite but equally negative gender stereotype" (Jurik, 1988:292). The balancing strategies used by female prison guards included projecting a "professional image," demonstrating unique skills, emphasizing a team approach, using humor to develop camaraderie and thwart unwelcome advances, and using sponsorship to enhance positive visibility (Jurik, 1988). Many of the same strategies were used by women in policing. The women officers showed professionalism by physically proving themselves and talking their way out of situations as well as by "sticking it out, making (policing) a career." Others used humor to show their ability both to "take it" and "give it back" while avoiding a predictably "feminine" reaction or ignoring harassment. For example, one woman noted:

> When we first went on the street we didn't have locker room facilities; women had to use the public rest room to change. I went in one day and everyone got quiet. I began to wonder. . . . I turned the light on, glanced down, and saw a snake coiled on the floor. I reached for my gun but it was dead. I went out and said, "I heard of using a snake for plumbing but this is ridiculous" . . . and it was o.k. for me. I guess 'cause I reacted to situation without anger or fear, they accepted me.

Another "gave it back" by exacting petty revenge when her sergeant continued to assign her to the station to type his reports, despite her requests to work on the street, because she had made him look good by editing them. To escape the station, one day she typed a report exactly as the sergeant gave it to her, he signed it without looking at it, and was called on the carpet by the lieutenant.

Sponsorship by a supervisor or peer often led to acceptance for women officers. For a *police*woman this generally meant having a male partner vouch that she was a good (i.e., reliable) partner after a street confrontation or shooting incident. Police*women*, in contrast, tended to gain personal acceptance by acquiescing to stereotypic feminine roles and seeking sex-typed assignments. Some women gained sponsorship through romantic or sexual relationships, but sponsorship based on a "sexual bargain" tended to have long-term negative consequences.

Women's Current Status Discrimination
and Acceptance

Women officers today still face discrimination but organized resistance to their presence has ended in large departments. Recent instances of discrimination identified by informants involved pressure on women not to excel, denial of job perks, sexual harassment and sexualization of work relationships, exaggeration of women's errors, and humiliation by a partner. But women's safety is no longer jeopardized by assignment to a "killer" footbeat. Overprotection and underinstruction have diminished but not disappeared. There is a broad consensus that women are more widely accepted as officers now than they were a decade ago. "Acceptance," however, has several meanings.

As previously noted, most men initially opposed the entry of women to patrol. Recent interviews with more than 70 males of all ranks in five large urban departments suggest that vocal opponents are fewer in number and influence than in the past and supporters are more numerous and vocal. Nevertheless, the belief in male superiority remains strong.

Currently, opponents acknowledge women's presence as a "fact of life" that they deal with largely by avoidance. They cling to traditional sex role stereotypes, the belief in male status superiority based on physical domination, and the view that women cannot be "feminine" and adequate officers. As one male traditionalist asserted:

> This is a man's job. The majority of women are not capable of handling physical encounters on the street. . . . Women rely too heavily on their service revolver. . . . A woman can't be refined and be a police officer too. Women give up some of their femininity to work this job. How many women do you know that go to work prepared to kill? Women officials have met a negative response. . . . It goes back to home training; how many mothers give orders to fathers?

Many men now have more positive views of women as officers. For some these are related to successful and satisfying experiences with women partners; for others, they arise from the perception of changes in the newer generation of women and from empathy gained through marriage to a female officer. One stated, for example:

> I was one of those men who was very vocal saying this is no place for women. I admit I was wrong. I thought we'd have women killed right and left and it didn't happen. Fewer women (than

> men) are injured 'cause macho men do not want to hit a
> woman. . . . Women joining the patrol force has not hurt us and
> in fact has at least doubled our possible pool of resources. I've
> seen women work over the years and I've had to change my
> mind, much as it hurt.

Other men accept individual women as partners but are critical or
skeptical of women's performance as a group.

Although most men now take the presence of women coworkers
for granted, they continue to maintain a belief in male superiority
and behave in ways to assert it. By sexualizing the workplace, they
superimpose their sexual identities and male status superiority on
coworker equality. They also maintain stereotypes by exaggerating
women's errors, frequently referring to physical differences and
their impact on effectiveness, depicting women's routine
competence as exceptional, and insisting that women receive
"favored treatment."

Most women perceive an increase in their acceptance by male
officers. For some it is merely cosmetic; the men have not altered
their attitudes but are "not as confrontational now as they were ten
years ago." A few perceive increased resentment. Most agree with
the men's assertion that blanket stereotyping and rejection has been
replaced by greater willingness to accept an individual woman on
the basis of her performance. As one female supervisor explained,
acceptance "depends on a woman's approach and demeanor."
Women that do the job that is expected and avoid "getting cute"
are accepted; those that use their femininity to get ahead are
resented. Nevertheless, men often tolerate or encourage
stereotypically feminine behavior.

In addition, there still are double standards of behavior for men
and women and different criteria of evaluation. This is particularly
troublesome regarding failures to aid a partner and behavior in
dangerous situations that results in the label "coward." As one
woman noted:

> A new female officer lost her gun in an incident and it was all
> over the department. Males lose guns too, but are not the object
> of so many rumors.

Double standards also persist regarding language, sexual
behavior, appearance, and demeanor. Women still face the
"language dilemmas" of whether to curse or not and whether to
tolerate gross language on the part of the men. Female officers are
still frequently referred to as "girls" or are called "hon" or
"sweetheart" by male colleagues. The appearance or overweight
condition of male supervisors never came up in interviews; the

appearance of several women supervisors received comment. In sum, as a woman sergeant observed:

> There's a certain finesse a woman has to have, a certain feminine grace. If you tell it like it is and don't watch your figure or fix yourself up or have what the men expect, you won't be given quite the preference. . . . For example, they let a capable woman go from (a detective assignment) 'cause she's fat; they don't do that to a man. They'll give breaks to the biggest male toad with a foul mouth. . . . That's where I see discrimination.

Explaining the Change: Organizational, Occupational, and Cultural Factors

Despite the persistence of discrimination, sexual harassment, negative male attitudes, and double standards, women have increased in numbers, gained acceptance, and expanded their opportunities for advancement in policing in the past two decades. Contributing to these changes have been changes in departmental personnel policies and practices; the informal occupational culture; and the law, public attitudes, and sex role norms in the society at large.

Department Policies and Practices

Internal changes begun during the 1970s have continued to alter the occupational role and work environment of the police. These include (1) changes in recruitment, selection, assignment, and promotion procedures plus development of policies that prohibit sexual harassment; (2) efforts to "professionalize" and unionize the police; (3) an emphasis on community relations in police work; and (4) legal limitations on use of violence and physical force by officers. These changes have opened police work to women and minorities and have undercut the solidarity of the formerly all-white male work group.

In the long run, the proportion of female officers can be no greater than their proportion among applicants and persons accepted by police departments. Application and selection rates, in turn, are shaped by the eligibility criteria and recruitment and selection mechanisms. Since passage of the Equal Employment Opportunities Act in 1972, eligibility criteria for police applicants have been dramatically altered. Higher educational standards for female than male officers, minimum height and weight standards, and maximum age limits have been virtually eliminated (Fyfe, 1987; Milton, 1972; Sulton and Townsey, 1981). Consequently, the pool of eligible candidates for policing includes virtually all healthy high school graduates.

Selection procedures, too, have changed. Although 76 percent of municipal agencies today use a pretraining physical agility or fitness test (Fyfe, 1987), the previous emphasis on upper body strength that eliminated women applicants has been replaced by tests that include fitness, flexibility, and endurance exercises, and usually are scored on age and sex-based standards. In addition, oral interviews have been standardized, and questions about marriage and family plans are illegal.

Women still are underrepresented among all applicants for police jobs but appear to be accepted in proportion to their application rate. They made up 20 percent of the applicants for police positions in 1986, 21 percent of those persons accepted for training, and 19 percent of those completing the academy (Martin, 1989).

Analyses of the limitations on women's occupational attainment have tended to focus either on the characteristics of individual workers and the impact of sex-role socialization (Blau and Duncan, 1967; Deaux 1984; Treiman and Terrell 1975) or the structural features of the occupation or organization and the ways they shape occupational rewards (Baron, 1984; England, 1984) and work-related attitudes and behaviors (Kanter, 1977). Three recent studies that have incorporated both individual and structural perspectives while focusing on relations of power in the work place (Reskin and Roos, 1990; Robinson and McIlwee, 1989; Zimmer, 1986) help guide the analysis of the changing status of women in policing.

Policing traditionally was dominated by a strong informal power structure based on personal ties and political maneuvering that has worked against women. Although informal influence and sponsorship remain important aspects of "getting ahead" in police work, structural changes in the past decade have opened many new opportunities for women. The adoption of formal procedures for obtaining desirable nonpatrol assignments and changes in promotion procedures have been particularly important. Equal employment opportunity requirements have led to more frequent posting of position announcements, written specification of selection criteria (including written examinations), and procedures for challenging arbitrary decisions. Many chiefs, if only to avoid litigation, have called for the assignment of women to every unit, creating new opportunities.

Promotion procedures also have been altered to reduce or eliminate the effect of supervisor evaluation and seniority which greatly handicapped the first cohort of women. These procedures also give greater weight to the written examination and an oral interview or assessment center analysis that increasingly is standardized. Greater supervisor accountability, a more hetero- geneous group of supervisors, and the presence of equal employment opportunity procedures also have reduced "rational bias" discrimination (Larwood et al., 1988). Such discrimination occurs when a subordinate acts on beliefs about whether a show of bias seems likely to be rewarded or punished by others. Larwood et al. (1988) found that subjects were less likely to discriminate in personnel decisions when they got cues indicating that persons with power over them disapproved of it; in the absence of such information, they made discriminatory decisions based on their beliefs concerning the preferences of their bosses. As support for such behavior decreases, so does discrimination itself.

Greater bureaucratic rationality and governmental regulation constraining the influence of the informal social structure gives women who are self confident more opportunities to use their personal and interactional resources to advance (Robinson and McIlwee, 1989). Many of the women officers that gain desirable assignments and promotions, in turn, enter a cycle of empowerment that further increases opportunities to move up. As one woman observed, "I wasn't as assertive as a sergeant as I was as a lieutenant and I've grown more assertive as a captain." Others have taken advantage of new mechanisms through which to assert legal rights. As a result, as one woman explained:

> Now, if a man walks on me, I'll look him in the eye and stomp him back. Ten years ago I wouldn't. . . . It's the times that have changed . . . maybe me also. . . . Before, I didn't want to make waves on job. I had to ask an assistant D.A. who wanted to commend me in letter to the chief not to do it because if my lieutenant saw it, pressure would have come down on me all the harder. . . . We have more rights today . . . because we now have a union and officers now speak up.

Women rarely formally file complaints because doing so is likely to hurt their careers. But many have learned how to use the system to handle grievances informally. Some have threatened to file discrimination complaints in order to obtain informal redress of such situations as arbitrary assignments, depressed supervisory evaluations, and sexual harassment. Others have turned to women supervisors informally for assistance with problems.

Most agencies now have EEO and sexual harassment policies and officers responsible for their enforcement. They vary, however, in how vigorously they carry out these policies. Where the chief has made clear through his actions that sexual jokes, touching, or other forms of sexual harassment are unacceptable, officers appear to be more circumspect in their behavior.

The movement to professionalize policing that was initiated in the late 1960s also has facilitated the integration of women. It led to structural changes such as closer supervision of officers, increased accountability of supervisors, universalistic rules, and a "management cop culture" that challenges the previously-prevalent "street cop culture" (Reuss-Ianni, 1983). This has weakened the solidarity of the informal culture based on officer homogeneity.

Two additional changes that have facilitated the integration of women officers are the rise of community-oriented policing and increased police liability for use of excessive force. Data from five case study departments suggest that women are assigned to community services units, are focused on crime prevention and addressing community problems more frequently than male officers, and find the work more satisfying than men do.

Changes in liability have led to a diminution of the aggressive "take names and kick ass" style of policing and an increase in the value of interpersonal skills in dealing with citizens.

Change in the Informal Culture of Policing

When the first generation of women officers were met with organized opposition from a cohesive informal work group, the men that were sympathetic toward women officers were silenced by the threat of ostracism and retaliation. Now supporters of women in policing are able to speak more freely while opponents cannot count on other men to support their negative opinions of women and minorities.

The lack of seniority, an important factor in the informal culture, magnified the powerlessness of the first generation of patrol women. Those women now exercise the prerogatives of seniority. For example, one woman with 16 years of patrol experience referred to the men on her shift as "my babies" and noted "the younger men respect me, ask my opinion."

Age and maturity also have reduced the need for acceptance felt so keenly by the first generation of women; familiarity has diminished the constant pressures to prove themselves. As one woman noted:

> You reach a certain point of acceptance and don't have to go
> through these routines. . . . At first, everywhere I went I had to
> prove myself; now I don't.

Initially, women were excluded from the informal social activities
of the work group. Consequently they missed out on an important
source of information, feedback, and the opportunity to make
contacts, cultivate sponsors, and build alliances that contribute to
occupational success (Martin, 1980).

In the past decade, women's participation in police officers'
informal social activities has increased, signaling changes in the
police culture and broader societal values and reducing women
officers' isolation. In all case study departments, the "stag-party"
atmosphere of off-duty drinking parties has diminished, and the
range of social activities in which women participate has broadened.
One man asserted:

> Attitudes have completely changed over the last eight
> years. . . . (E)ven the good girls in the precinct may come by (to
> shift change parties); . . . now you get labeled as outcast if you
> don't.

Another man summed up the changes:

> The guys treat the women a lot more normal now. The girls
> shoot, run, and play tennis with the guys and socialize in a
> platonic way.

Despite these changes, women are only partially integrated into
the informal activities and influence structure. Some women choose
not to socialize outside of work due to family responsibilities or
concern with gossip. Others avoid participating in certain types of
activities, such as hunting and fishing trips.

Societal and Cultural Changes

Men's prior socialization gives them an advantage over women
when they enter police work (Martin, 1980). Males are more likely
than females in their youth to have played "cops and robbers,"
fantasized about police work, used firearms, and participated in
contact sports which introduced them to key elements in the police
subculture such as the controlled use of violence, teamwork, and
group loyalty. Females, conversely, are likely to have been taught
to be "little ladies," skilled in verbal manipulation but not physical
assertiveness (Martin, 1980).

In the past decade definitions of acceptable "masculine" and
"feminine" behavior have expanded and patterns of sex role

socialization have been modified. Girls now have more opportunities to participate in athletics, play on teams, and become physically
fit, diminishing the physical differences between men and women.
They also are more likely to have planned a career and have a
female officer as a role model. Boys now are taught that sensitivity
and expressiveness are desirable traits; many see their fathers participating in domestic work and their mothers holding full-time jobs.

Rookie male and female officers' educational and prior work
experiences also are converging. Both are likely to have taken shop
and home economics courses in secondary school. Few officers of
either sex have been in the military. The decrease in the proportion
of police who are veterans (almost all of whom were male) has closed
the experience gap faced by the first group of women on patrol who
worked with men accustomed to military discipline. Officers of both
sexes who are part of the new generation of officers are far more
likely than their predecessors to challenge authority and the rank
structure.

Increased public acceptance of women officers also has diffused
some of the men's fear that citizen resistance to females would
undermine the authority of their office. Instead, male officers
discovered that citizens often feel less threatened by a female officer
and that their presence defuses situations.

These cultural changes have eased some of the burdens that their
prior socialization and differentness put on the women officers.
Nevertheless, men and women still bring different experiences to
a job whose definition rests on the officer's ability to take control,
using physical means if necessary, giving male rookies an
advantage.

Summary and Conclusion

Initially excluded from policing, then assigned a limited role that
was an extension of the traditional female sex role, women only
entered the mainstream of police work in the 1970s. The first
cohorts of women officers faced strong opposition by a cohesive
informal work group that sought to drive them out. While some
coped with the pressures by resigning or obtaining nonpatrol
assignments, others made clear that women can perform well as
patrol officers and supervisors. Through that decade and the 1980s
the number, opportunities, and power of women in policing have
slowly expanded.

This progress appears to have been facilitated by both structural
and cultural changes that affected society's laws, norms, and

values; by the police informal subculture; and by departmental policies and practices. Equal Employment Opportunity laws and policies have opened up many occupations previously reserved for men, including policing, and have resulted in changes in selection, promotion, and assignment criteria. Changing sex role norms also have eased slightly the conflict between sex role expectations of women as women and occupational role demands of them as police officers. The influx of women and minority officers, in turn, has contributed to weakening the solidarity of the informal influence structure.

Despite these changes, the barriers to full integration of women officers that are built into the formal and informal structures of the work organization and the culturally prescribed habits of male-female interaction remain strong. Only major alterations in the nature of the work and in culturally defined patterns of gender-related behavior will eliminate them. Such changes appear to be underway at a slow and uneven pace.

Endnotes

[1] The data in the remainder of this paper, unless another source is cited, are drawn from a two-phase study recently completed by the author. That study included a mail survey of all state police and all 446 municipal departments serving populations of 50,000 or greater. The survey sought information on (1) departmental policies and practices regarding recruitment, selection, and promotion; (2) the number and percentage of male and female officers by ethnic group, rank, and assignments; (3) male and female officer turnover rates; and (4) the existence and nature of other personnel policies related to women.

The second phase involved case studies in five large urban agencies: Birmingham, Detroit, and Washington, D.C., where the representation of women officers and supervisors is above the mean for large agencies and Chicago and Phoenix, where women's representation is at or below the mean. The case studies involved (1) interviews with high-ranking officials regarding policies related to the integration of women; (2) analysis of data on performance provided by four of the departments for a sample of male and female officers matched by race, rank, and length of service; and (3) interviews with 112 male and female officers and mid-level supervisors in the five case study agencies.

[2] In 1985 blacks made up 12.1 percent of the American population; Hispanics 6.4 percent. Because both minority groups tend to live in cities rather than suburban or rural areas, however, they probably remain somewhat underrepresented in urban police agencies. In contrast, women represent 52 percent of the population and 44 percent of the labor force.

Bibliography

Baron, James N.
  1984   "Organizational Perspectives on Stratification." *Annual Review of Sociology* 10:37-69.
Barrineau, H.E. III
  1987   *Liability in Criminal Justice.* Cincinnati, OH: Pilgrimage.
Bartell Associates
  1978   *The Study of Police Women Competency in the Performance of Sector Police Work in the City of Philadelphia.* State College, PA: Bartell Associates.
Bartlett, H.W. and A. Rosenblum
  1977   *Policewoman Effectiveness.* Denver, CO: Civil Service Commission and Denver Police Department.
Bittner, Egon
  1970   *The Functions of Police in Modern Society.* Chevy Chase, MD: National Institute of Mental Health.
Blau, Peter and Otis Dudley Duncan
  1976   *Women and the Workplace: The Implications of Occupational Segregation.* Chicago: University of Chicago Press.
Bloch, Peter and Deborah Anderson
  1974   *Policewomen on Patrol: Final Report.* Washington: Urban Institute.
Block, W.E and M.A. Walker (eds.)
  1982   *Discrimination, Affirmative Action, and Equal Opportunity.* Vancouver: The Frazier Institute.
California Highway Patrol
  1976   *Women Traffic Officer Project.* Sacramento, CA: Author.
David, Deborah and Robert Brannon (eds.)
  1976   *The Forty Nine Percent Majority: The Male Sex Role.* Reading, MA: Addison-Wesley.
Deaux, Kay
  1984   "From Individual Differences to Social Categories: Analysis of a Decade's Research on Gender." *American Psychologist* 39:105-16.
Enarson, Elaine
  1984   *Woodsworking Women: Sexual Integration in the U.S. Forest Service.* Birmingham: University of Alabama.
England, Paula
  1984   "Socioeconomic Explanations of Job Segregation." Pp. 28-46 in H. Remick (ed.) *Comparable Worth and Wage Discrimination.* Philadelphia: Temple University Press.
Fyfe, James
  1987   *Police Personnel Practices, 1986.* (Baseline Data Report Volume 18, Number 6). Washington, D.C.: International City Management Association.

Gray, Thomas C.
  1975   "Selecting for the Police Subculture." Pp.46-56 in Jerome H.
          Skolnick and Thomas C. Gray (eds.) *Police in America*. Boston:
          Little Brown.
Horne, Peter
  1980   *Women in Law Enforcement*. Springfield, IL: Charles Thomas.
Hutzel, Eleanor
  1933   *The Policewoman's Handbook*. New York: Columbia University
          Press.
Jurik, Nancy C.
  1985   "An Officer and a Lady: Organizational Barriers to Women
          Working As Correctional Officers in Men's Prisons." *Social
          Problems* 32:375-88.
Jurik, Nancy C.
  1988   "Striking a Balance: Female Correctional Officers, Gender Role
          Stereotypes, and Male Prisons." *Sociological Inquiry* 58:291-305.
Kanter, Rosabeth M.
  1977   *Men and Women of the Corporation*. New York: Basic.
Kizziah, C. and M. Morris
  1977   *Evaluation of Women in a Policing Program: Newton,
          Massachusetts*. Oakland, CA: Approach Associates.
Larwood, L., E. Szwajkowski, and S. Rose
  1988   "Sex and Race Discrimination Resulting from Manager-Client
          Relationships: Applying the Rational Bias Theory of Management
          Discrimination." *Sex Roles* 18:9-29.
Martin, Susan E.
  1980   *Breaking and Entering: Policewomen on Patrol*. Berkeley:
          University of California Press.
Martin, Susan E.
  1989   "Women on the Move? A Report on the Status of Women in
          Policing." *Police Foundation Report*. Washington, D.C.: Police
          Foundation.
Martin, Susan E.
  1990   *On The Move: The Status of Women in Policing*. Washington,
          D.C.: Police Foundation.
Milton, Catherine
  1972   *Women in Policing*. Washington, D.C.: Police Foundation.
Morash, Merry and Jack Greene
  1986   "Evaluating Women on Patrol: A Critique of Contemporary
          Wisdom." *Evaluation Review* 10:230-55.
Pennsylvania State Police
  1973   *Pennsylvania State Police Female Trooper Study*. Harrisburg,
          PA: Pennsylvania State Police Headquarters.
Price, Barbara
  1985   "Sexual Integration in American Law Enforcement." Pp. 205-13
          in W.C. Heffernan and T. Stroup (eds.) *Police Ethics: Hard Choices
          in Law Enforcement*. New York: John Jay University Press.

President's Commission on Law Enforcement and the Administration of
    Justice
    1967   *Task Force Report: The Police.* Washington, D.C.: U.S.
            Government Printing Office.
Reskin, Barbara F. and Patricia A. Roos
    1990   *Job Queues, Gender Queues: Explaining Women's Inroads into
            Male Occupations.* Philadelphia, PA: Temple University Press.
Reuss-Ianni, Elizabeth
    1983   *Street Cops and Management Cops.* New Brunswick, NJ:
            Transaction.
Robinson, J. Gregg and Judith S. McIlwee
    1989   "Women in Engineering: A Promise Unfulfilled?" *Social
            Problems* 36:455-72.
Sherman, Lawrence J.
    1975   "Evaluation of Policewomen on Patrol in a Suburban Police
            Department." *Journal of Police Science and Administration*
            3:434-38.
Sichel, Joyce L., Lucy N. Friedman, Janice C. Quint, and Mary E. Smith
    1978   *Women on Patrol: A Pilot Study of Police Performance in New
            York City.* Washington, D.C.: National Institute of Law
            Enforcement and Criminal Justice.
Skolnick, Jerome H.
    1966   *Justice Without Trial.* New York: Wiley.
Sullivan, Peggy S.
    1989   "Minority Officers: Current Issues." Pp. 331-46 in R. Dunham and
            G. Alpert, *Critical Issues in Policing.* Prospect Heights, IL:
            Waveland Press.
Sulton, Cynthia and Roi Townsey
    1981   *A Progress Report on Women in Policing.* Washington, D.C.:
            Police Foundation.
Swerdlow, Marian
    1989   "Men's Accommodations to Women Entering a Nontraditional
            Occupation: A Case of Rapid Transit Operatives." *Gender and
            Society* 3:373-87.
Treiman, Donald and K. Terrell
    1975   "Sex and the Process of Status Attainment: A Comparison of
            Working Women and Men." *American Sociological Review*
            40:174-200.
Westley, William
    1970   *Violence and the Police.* Cambridge, MA: MIT Press.
Zimmer, Lynn E.
    1986   *Women Guarding Men.* Chicago: University of Chicago Press.

chapter 15

Women in the Legal Profession

Frances P. Bernat
Pennsylvania State University

Women's entrance into the legal profession has come neither quickly nor easily. Throughout most of United States' history, women have been barred from the practice of law. Much of the growth in the number of women lawyers has occurred in the past twenty years. According to Kym Liebler (1990:25), "(b)etween 1970 and 1985, the number of women lawyers in the nation grew rapidly from 13,000 to 122,000." Slightly lower numbers were provided by the Bureau of Justice Statistics in a 1986 report. Their report indicated that between 1970 and 1986 the number and percent of women lawyers increased from 11,000 (4 percent) to 106,000 (17 percent) (Schafran, 1987:192). According to Cynthia Fuchs Epstein (1983), the number of women lawyers in 1980 was 62,000 (12.4 percent). Thus, the "real" growth has occurred in the past ten years.

Minority representation in the legal profession is also not reflective of their rates in the general population. Currently, it has been estimated that there are about 25,000 black attorneys (3.4 percent) and about 15,000 Hispanic attorneys (2 percent) in the United States (Yuda, 1990). Black women attorneys accounted for 0.8 percent of the lawyers in the United States in 1987 — less than 6,000 (Burleigh, 1988).

These numbers are troubling. The view of law as a profession for men, indeed white males, has meant that both overt and covert forms of discrimination have disadvantaged women practitioners. Although women today comprise between one third and one half of any given law school class, and are expected to account for about one third of all lawyers in the United States by the year 2000 (Liebler, 1990), women lawyers have yet to be fully integrated into the inner circles of the legal profession and to be accepted to the same degree as male lawyers. Discrimination against women has historically kept women out of the legal profession and has continued to define the practice of law in male terms.

The First Women Lawyers

Karen Berger Morello (1986), in her historical analysis of women lawyers, stated that the first woman to practice law in colonial America was Margaret Brent in 1638. Brent was asked by the governor of the Maryland colony, Leonard Calvert, to be the executor of his estate. Within days of his death, Brent presented herself as Calvert's executor and lawyer, and received letters of administration from the Maryland Assembly which empowered her in that capacity (Morello, 1986).

For eight years after Calvert's death, Brent litigated 124 court cases on behalf of his estate. Among Calvert's outstanding debts were monies owed to soldiers who had helped Calvert reclaim his governorship. These soldiers threatened full-scale rioting in Maryland if they did not receive payment out of Calvert's estate. In the end, Brent was credited by the Maryland Assembly for the adept manner in which she settled the claims against the estate and appeased the soldiers. Nonetheless, Brent moved out of Maryland in disgust after the Assembly refused to give her the right to vote (Morello, 1986).

From colonial times until the mid-1800s, not much is known about the practice of law by women. We do know that women were prohibited from attending law schools and were denied admission to the state bars during this time period. It is most likely that the few women who appeared in court to litigate claims were there on their own behalf. The first woman to address the United States Supreme Court (1975), for example, was Lucy Terry Prince, a black woman who successfully defended a land claim (Morello, 1986). It is also possible that women who moved out west in the 1800s were able to practice law in local courts. Admission to the state bar was not mandatory on the part of lawyers who wished to appear before these courts, and many women were needed to fulfill traditionally male jobs. The Chicago Legal News in February, 1869, chronicled Mary E. Magoon as having practiced law in North English, in Iowa County (Morello, 1986).

The underlying rationale which barred women from the legal profession was simply that they were women. It was felt that law was synonymous with male characteristics and traits. Differences between the sexes were highlighted and exploited to keep women from a world of business, law and books. As Catharine MacKinnon (1987:8) has commented, "Difference is the velvet glove on the iron fist of domination." The power differential which existed between men and women was insulated from any challenge on the part of women when they did not have access to the political and legal system.

The first woman to be officially recognized as a lawyer in the United States was Arabella (Belle) Babb Mansfield. She was admitted to the Iowa State bar in June, 1869 (Epstein, 1983; Morello, 1986; Wortman, 1985). Marlene Stein Wortman (1985) contends that women did not actively pursue entrance into the legal profession earlier than 1869 because they generally did not see themselves as being separate from men. She stated:

> Why did women first seek admission to the bar in 1869 and not earlier? The answer must begin with the observation that a professional, more particularly a lawyer, was a person vested with the right to command, direct, and advise others. Before a woman could realistically entertain the idea of a legal career, women had to have the right to own and use property and had to see themselves as separate persons with interests different from those of men. The struggle for married woman's property rights had advanced this perspective. Women then had to move to the next stage, of thinking of themselves as persons exercising authority. The suffrage movement speeded this process. The right to become lawyers, officers of the court, some suffragists believed would enhance women's status and claims to the franchise (Wortman, 1985:217).

During the 1830s and 1840s, women began to struggle for the right to own their own property and the right to vote. Women's involvement in the abolitionist movement had the effect of making women realize their own self-worth. In 1848, a women's conference was held in Seneca Falls, New York, and women argued for their independence and individual rights (Cincinnati Law Review, 1983). It wasn't until a number of years after this convention that women suffragists seeking to strengthen women's legal posture were able to force some states to admit them into the legal profession. These victories came easier in some of the more liberal western states than in the provincial northeast (Morello, 1986; Wortman, 1985).

To be eligible for admission to a state bar, persons had to either clerk for a requisite period of time with a licensed practitioner or attend law school. The most usual method was a clerkship. Practicing male lawyers could choose who would work with them and were virtual gatekeepers of the profession. For women desirous of a legal career, clerking was not generally a viable option. First, male lawyers refused to allow women to clerk with them. Women who did clerk usually did so with supportive male family members (husbands or brothers). Second, women realized that a legal education would provide them with greater credibility. Because male lawyers sought to keep women out of the profession by perpetuating the view that being a lawyer was synonymous with being a man, women had to prove that they were capable of practicing law by showing that they were intellectually astute and that they could successfully complete legal studies. Nonetheless, entrance into law schools also proved to be a difficult road for women. Men were also gatekeepers at the law school doors.

The first law school to admit women was Washington University in St. Louis, Missouri. In 1869, it admitted Lemma Barkloo and Phoebe Cousins. Barkloo left the school after her first year and successfully passed the Missouri bar exam; Cousins became the school's first female law student to graduate after two years of coursework (Morello, 1986). The first female to graduate from a law school in the United States, however, was Ada Kepley who graduated from the University of Chicago law school in 1870 (Morello, 1986). The first black woman to graduate from law school was Charlotte Ray who graduated from Howard University and passed the D.C. bar in 1872 (Burleigh, 1988).

Entrance into law schools also proved to be a challenge for many women. In eastern, urban schools and at the Ivy League colleges, women were denied admission to law schools well into the twentieth century. One of the last law schools to change its discriminatory admission practices and accept women was Harvard — which finally admitted 12 women in 1950 (Morello, 1986).

The reasons given for excluding women from the legal profession, and from law school, were essentially moralistic in tone. Males who oversaw the entrance of persons into law (judges, lawyers, law school professors and bar admission boards), argued that law was a hard-nosed, "male" profession which could impune the "delicacy" of a female's biological character. For example, when the Illinois Supreme Court in 1870 denied Myra Bradwell's admission to the state bar it stated:

> That God designed the sexes to occupy different spheres of action, and that it belonged to men to make, apply and execute the laws, was regarded as an almost axiomatic truth. . . . (cited in Morello, 1986:18).

After the state court's decision to deny Bradwell admission to the state bar on basis of gender, she decided to appeal her case to the United States Supreme Court. In *Bradwell v. Illinois* (1873), the court held that the Fourteenth Amendment's privileges and immunities clause did not apply to causes of action involving occupational freedom. Thus, the majority court's opinion hinged on a strict interpretation of law. It is in Justice Bradley's infamous concurring opinion that the moralistic nature of the court's holding is to be found. Justice Bradley argued:

> Man is, or should be, women's protector and defender. The natural and proper timidity and delicacy which belongs to the female sex evidently unfits it for many of the occupations of civil life. The constitution of the family organization, which is founded in the divine ordinance, as well as in the nature of things, indicates the domestic sphere as that which properly belongs to the domain and functions of womanhood (cited in Wortman, 1985:257).

A few years later, a similar statement was expressed by the Wisconsin Supreme Court when it denied the application of a female attorney to practice before that appellate bench. In Goodell (1875), the court remarked:

> The law of nature destines and qualifies the female sex for the bearing and nurture of the children of our race and for all life-long calling of women, inconsistent with these radical and sacred duties of their sex, as is the profession of the law, are departures from the order of nature; and when voluntary, treason against it. . . . The peculiar qualities of womanhood, its gentle graces, its quick sensibility, its tender susceptibility, its purity, its delicacy, its emotional impulses, its subordination of hard reason to sympathetic feeling, are surely not qualifications for forensic strife. Nature has tempered woman as little for the juridical conflicts of the court room, as for the physical conflicts of the battle field (cited in Wortman, 1985:250).

State statutes and law school admissions standards had to be changed before women could have unobstructed access into the legal profession. Due to the pioneering efforts of the first women lawyers, states (and law schools) began to remove gender language from their admission criteria. In 1918, the American Bar Association, which had previously refused to admit women, began to accept women into its membership. By 1920, women were admitted to practice law in almost every state; Alaska admitted its first woman attorney in 1950 (Feinman, 1985; Morello, 1986). Nonetheless, the number of women lawyers in the early part of the twentieth century remained low. Women comprised 1.1 percent (558) of all lawyers in 1910 and 1.4 percent (1,738) in 1920. Between 1950 and 1970, women accounted for about 4 percent of all lawyers (Epstein, 1983).

Patriarchal Gatekeeping

Many nineteenth century women suffragists believed that if they worked hard and showed that they had the mental agility to practice law, then they would be fully accepted into the bar. It was their hope that they could effectuate legal change which would ultimately provide them with the right to vote and other important freedoms. While women received the right to vote in 1920, full acceptance into the profession has yet to be achieved (see Copleman, 1986; Hall, 1990; Prinz, 1986; Schafran, 1986; Women Lawyers Journal, 1989). Women are struggling to be fully integrated into senior partnerships in law firms (Blodgett, 1986; Epstein, 1983; Liebler, 1990; Repa, 1988; Women's Rights Law Reporter, 1986), tenured professorships in law schools (Allen and Wall, 1987; Fossum, 1980; Moss, 1988) and judgeships at the local, appellate and federal levels (Allen and Wall, 1987; Cook 1980, Cook, 1985; Hall, 1990; Klein, 1980; Knowles, 1982; Women's Rights Law Reporter, 1986). Additionally, women are fighting for social changes at the workplace which will end covert forms of discrimination, and respond to the particular needs of women attorneys (Burleigh and Goldberg, 1989; DeBenedictis, 1989; Graham, 1986; Hall, 1990; Peterson, 1981; Stark, 1986).

The Practice of Law

Patriarchy is a social system designed to provide men with power and the benefits which flow from it. Under patriarchy, male roles are equated with positions of power and prestige while female roles are equated with subordinate social positions. The exclusion of women from roles reserved for males is based on a belief that women are inferior and in need of protection. However, total exclusion of women from all spheres is difficult for a patriarchal society to maintain. Once total exclusion from a previously defined male social role becomes an impossible gate to keep closed to women, other gates are created to prevent full entry. For the legal profession, once women could no longer be prohibited from entry into it, other obstacles were raised to prevent women from gaining full access into the field. These new gates consist of *occupational specialization*, labeling some areas of legal practice as being appropriate for women, and occupational immobility, labeling women as being unable to perform leadership responsibilities in a law firm. These gatekeeping tactics are presented in the discussion which follows.

Upon graduation from law school, female graduates may have difficulty in finding employment in private firms (Charne et al, 1986; Epstein, 1983; Sheridan, 1981). One problem which women face is having job interviewers ask inappropriate questions about the applicant's marital status and whether she has any children. Sheridan (1981) reports that one job applicant, who had graduated third in her class, was "dismayed" when asked if her husband would allow her to work. Such questions are not uncommon. The New Jersey Supreme Court's Task Force on Women in the Court's first year report (in June, 1984), found that:

> Despite the existence of state and federal statutes prohibiting employment discrimination, female job applicants are often asked inappropriate questions at both law firm and judicial clerkship interviews. Women survey respondents reported recurring instances in which they were asked questions concerning their intentions to have children, use of birth control, the availability of child care and whether they had their spouse's consent to work (Women's Rights Law Reporter, 1986:144).

According to Charne, Becker and Kerns (1986), while women accounted for more than 30 percent of all law school graduates in 1984, they accounted for only 13 percent of practicing attorneys. They believe that gender bias may be at the root of the discrepancy.

Women who do practice law tend to be employed in government service positions (including public defender, public prosecutor and legal aid offices), specialize in areas such as probate, family law and real estate, or be asked to perform specialized functions within a law firm such as legal research (Epstein, 1983; Patterson and

Engelberg, 1982). One federal publication on career opportunities
for women in law provided this advice for female job applicants:

> Women's opportunities seem best in those law specialties where
> their contributions to the field have already been recognized.
> Some of these are real estate and domestic relations work,
> women's and juvenile legal problems, probate work (about a
> third of all women judges are probate judges), and patent law
> for those who have the required training in science (cited in
> Patterson and Engelberg, 1982:391).

Cynthia Fuchs Epstein (1983) found that many women hired by
private law firms were routinely delegated work which would not
require them to go into a courtroom. One male associate in a large
firm reported that women "are sent to the library and they write
briefs, which is what everybody does for a couple of years, but then
people get kind of pulled out of that and told to go at least argue
motions and stuff—but the women don't get as precisely a fair shot"
(Epstein, 1983:104).

Consequently, women lawyers practicing in private firms are not
going to develop courtroom experience which may be crucial when
it comes time for promotions and pay increases. Deborah Graham
(1986:54) reported that a 1985 American Bar Foundation survey
found that "6 percent of the women in private law firms were
partners as compared to 20 percent of the men." Abrahamson and
Franklin (1986) found in their study of the Harvard Law School class
of 1974 that by 1985 only 23 percent of the women had made
partner compared to 51 percent of their male classmates. Both male
(80 percent) and female (88 percent) attorneys agree that men are
paid more than women (Patterson and Engelberg, 1982). It has been
estimated that upon their graduation from law school, women earn
$1,500 less than their male counterparts; within ten years, the
salary discrepancy ranges from $9,000 to $18,000 a year (Patterson
and Engelberg, 1982).

Sexual bias also affects the employment choices of women
lawyers. They are not as likely as men to work in the private sector
(71 percent of all women lawyers work in the private sector
compared to 82 percent of all male lawyers). And, when they are
in private practice, they are more likely to work alone or in small
firms than are their male counterparts (Patterson and Engelberg,
1982). Many women lawyers realize that they do not want to work
for a firm in which they are not treated with respect. Sexual
harassment of women associates is a silent poison which may force
women to quit their jobs or suffer in silence (Burleigh and Goldberg,
1989). Problematically, it is not always easy to determine when

sexual harassment has occurred. The United States Supreme Court's 1986 decision in *Meritor Savings Bank FSB v. Vinson* found two forms of sexual harassment: making sexual favors as a condition of employment and creating a hostile environment (Burleigh and Goldberg, 1989). However, many women are reluctant to report inappropriate remarks and off-color jokes about women which make them feel uncomfortable. These women may think that they are either too sensitive or worry that they may lose their jobs (Burleigh and Goldberg, 1989).

Working for a private law firm can be very difficult. Senior partners expect their junior associates to work long hours and to bring in business for the firm. Rainmaking, a term which refers to the ability of an associate to make "rain" or money for the firm, is a major factor in whether a person is made partner (Epstein, 1983; Liebler, 1990; Repa, 1988). As Barbara Kate Repa (1988:70) noted, rainmaking is difficult for women who have been excluded "from all-male clubs and social activities where the seeds for new business are thought to be planted and cultivated." Women lawyers are more likely to have clients referred to them because of their professionalism rather than to attract clients from their personal contacts (Epstein, 1983; Graham, 1986; Repa, 1989).

In recent years, women have attempted to enhance their ability to be rainmakers by forming women law associations and support groups while attempting, at the same time, to pierce "old-boy" networks (Alden, 1986; Repa, 1988; Sheridan, 1981). Deborah Graham (1986:58) reported that the California State Bar Association was the first bar "to urge its members to work for reform within the exclusive clubs to which they belong" in an effort to help end the exclusion of women attorneys from these business and social circles. In recent years, the American Bar Association's House of Delegates adopted recommendations which seek to prevent continued practices which prevent the full integration of women into the profession (*Women Lawyers Journal*, 1989).

When women are in court they may experience gender bias from the trial judge. Women attorneys have been called "honey," "little lady," and "little girl," or referred to by their first names when their male colleagues are referred to by "Mr. _____" (Blodgett, 1986; Copleman, 1986; Eich, 1986). The New Jersey Task Force survey, mentioned above, reported that women attorneys (78 percent) experienced incidents in which they felt that they had been disadvantaged by a judge because they were women (Eich, 1986; Schafran, 1987; *Women's Rights Law Reporter*, 1986). Judge Eich (1986:23) stated:

It is almost inconceivable that a judge would comment in open
court on a male attorney's handsome vested suit, his haircut
or age, much less his aftershave lotion or his anatomical good
looks. And one can only imagine the consequences were the
judge to make similar remarks to a black male attorney — calling
him 'young man' or even 'boy' (really no more than equivalent
terms to 'young lady' or 'girl') or to refer to his color.

Sexual bias in the courtroom affects not only the interpersonal
relationship between the judge and the female attorney, it can affect
the outcome of the case (Eich, 1986; Schafran, 1987). Women
lawyers are fighting a presumption of incompetence (Blodgett,
1986; Copleman, 1986; *Women's Rights Law Reporter*, 1986). The
practice of law is defined in male terms. Thus, to be a competent
lawyer means that one is aggressive, tough, nonemotional,
ambitious, and upwardly mobile (Blodgett, 1986; Hall, 1990;
Liebler, 1990; Schafran, 1987). One sexual stereotype of women
is that they are emotional: If the female attorney takes an aggressive
posture in litigation, a judge may perceive her behavior to be
unnecessary histrionics or hysteria. Like wise, if a woman appears
to be too cool in court, she may be perceived as being unsupportive
of her client's cause (Blodgett, 1986). Minority women lawyers have
the additional burden of being mistaken for clients when they
appear in court (Burleigh, 1988). Such sexual bias works to
undermine female counsel's credibility and professional stature.

However, it is clear that women attorneys are competent
practitioners. Both male and female attorneys surveyed by the New
Jersey Task Force on Women in the Courts agreed that gender did
not affect the competence of legal representation. Women attorneys
worked hard to champion their client's causes (*Women's Rights
Law Reporter*, 1986).

Criminal Law Practice

Many of the observations discussed above pertain to women who
practice in the criminal justice system. Many women lawyers seek
employment as prosecutors and public defenders because the
public sector provides them with a better avenue for equal
employment opportunities. According to Clarice Feinman (1985;
1986), government employment provides women with an
opportunity for tenure, benefits, regular hours, and a chance for
promotions. However, women in the criminal justice system appear
to be delegated responsibilities associated with women's legal
practice. As Edith E. Flynn (1982:320) noted, "women working as

prosecutors at federal, state, and county levels . . . are relegated mostly to domestic and juvenile matters, while highly visible criminal and civil cases are often reserved for men." Thus, the areas of litigation which may serve as areas of political or economic advancement are withheld from them.

Social Change in the Profession

Many of the first women lawyers felt compelled to be tough competitors with their male colleagues (Finelli, 1986); after all, they had to blaze a trail under conditions of overt discrimination and hostility. But as the number of women in the profession grew, a "second generation" of women lawyers no longer felt the need to be "super-women." They began to adapt law office management to their own characteristics and lifestyles (Finelli, 1986).

Among the particular challenges women face is how to balance family-life with their career. Many women today are no longer waiting to make partner before beginning a family. Instead, they have begun to make changes in the practice of law which will accommodate their family needs. Many women have sought maternity leave changes which provide women with necessary leave of absence without jeopardizing their employment status— the so-called "Mommy Track." Nonetheless, women have felt pressured to return to work as soon as possible after their baby is born (Graham, 1986). Since the primary responsibility of child care in a family is placed upon women, recent research has shown that women professionals who try to balance career and family responsibilities are disadvantaged in the "progress and rewards" of their careers. (Figueira-McDonough and Sarri, 1987:21). Nonetheless, many women want to have both a family and a career.

One course of action some women have taken is to place primary importance on child-rearing and secondary importance on career development. In this regard, women have begun part-time work in law firms (Abrahamson and Franklin, 1986; Graham, 1986; Peterson, 1981). Convincing law firms that part-time work is a viable option has been difficult. Some law firms believe that part-time lawyering is impractical because part-timers might require greater supervision or be unavailable to meet with clients and other attorneys to discuss progress in a case (Peterson, 1981). Other firms hire part-timers but assign the attorney "full-time" work schedules (Graham, 1986). Other courses of action undertaken by women attorneys include starting their own legal practices with built-in flexible hours or opting out of the practice of law for a period of time

(Stark, 1986). Regardless of the career path ultimately chosen, women lawyers are showing that they can be effective without being so-called "superwomen."

Women lawyers face many of the challenges that women in other professions and occupations face. Sex role stereotypes which define women's primary role as wife and mother must be challenged if women are to be accepted for their competence and ability in the profession. However, when women are working and raising a family, the profession must bend to accommodate the increased pressures and demands that these working professionals face. It is not a question of "having it all;" it is a question of being accepted as women who work.

Conclusion

Like women in many other areas of employment, women attorneys have to deal with gender issues which affect the nature and quality of their employment. As women entered the gates which kept them out of the profession, they found that new gates existed. These gates have obstructed their passage to the more prestigious and powerful career paths which are unobstructed for male lawyers. *Occupational standards* are defined in male terms; to be successful means that a lawyer is aggressive, adversarial and rational. *Occupational choices* are presented in gender specific terms; women lawyers are expected to work in areas of law that do not conflict with sex role expectations, such as domestic relations law and governmental service. *Occupational advancement* is primarily designed for men; women lawyers are not considered to be capable of performing leadership functions in law firms.

Years of overt and covert discrimination have made it difficult for women to be accepted in this male dominated and defined profession because the walls which protect the inner sanctums of it are strengthened by a system of patriarchy which protects and values men over women. Progress has been made because of the steps taken by women to overcome the barriers and the "glass-ceilings" which have confronted them. Women are forging ahead in the hopes that they can be accepted for who they are and for the professionalism which they bring to their career.

Bibliography

Abrahamson, Jill and Barbara Franklin.
1986   *Where They Are Now: The Story of the Women of Harvard Law 1974*. Garden City, NY: Doubleday.

Alden, Sharyn
1986   "Networking: Women's Bars Offer Support." *Wisconsin Bar Bulletin* 59 (June): 32-36.

Allen, David W. and Diane E. Wall
1987   "The Behavior of Women State Supreme Court Justices: Are They Tokens or Outsiders?" *The Justice System Journal* 12:232-44.

Blodgett, Nancy
1986   "I Don't Think That Ladies Should Be Lawyers." *American Bar Association Journal* 72 (December):48-53.

Burleigh, Nina
1988   "Black Women Lawyers: Coping With Dual Discrimination." *American Bar Association Journal* 74 (June):64-68.

Burleigh, Nina and Stephanie B. Goldberg
1989   "Breaking the Silence: Sexual Harassment in Law Firms," *American Bar Association Journal* 75 (August): 46-52.

Charne, Irvin B., Barbara J. Becker and E. Ann Kerns
1986   "Women Lawyers in Firms: Assets not Liabilities." *Wisconsin Bar Bulletin* 59 (June).

Cincinnati Law Review
1983   "Women and the Law: From Abigail to Sandra." *Cincinnati Law Review* 52:967-76.

Cook, Beverly Blair
1985   "Women Judges in the Opportunity Structure." In Laura Crites and Winifred L. Hepperle (eds.), *Women, The Courts, and Equality*, pp. 143-74. Newbury Park, CA: Sage.
1980   "Political Culture and Selection of Women Judges in Trial Courts." In Debra W. Stewart (ed.), *Women in Local Politics*, pp. 42-60. Metuchen, NJ: Scarecrow Press.

Copleman, Martha
1986   "Sexism in the Courtroom: Report from a Little Girl Lawyer." *Women's Rights Law Reporter* 9:107-8.

DeBenedictis, Don J.
1989   "California Women Lawyers Surveyed." *American Bar Association Journal* 75:26-27.

Eich, Judge William
1986   "Gender Bias in the Courtroom: Some Participants Are More Equal Than Others." *Wisconsin Bar Bulletin* 59 (June):22-24 + .

Epstein, Cynthia Fuchs
1983   *Women in Law*. Garden City, NY: Anchor Books.

Feinman, Clarice
1986   *Women in the Criminal Justice System*, 2nd ed. New York: Praeger.

1985   "Women Lawyers and Judges in the Criminal Court." In Imogene
        L. Moyer (ed.), *The Changing Roles of Women in the Criminal
        Justice System: Offenders, Victims, and Professionals*,
        pp. 271-75. Prospect Heights, IL: Waveland Press.
Figueira-McDonough, Josefina and Rosemary C. Sarri
1987   "Catch-22 Strategies of Control and the Deprivation of Women's
        Rights." Pp. 11-33 in Josefina Figueira-McDonough and
        Rosemary Sarri (eds.), *The Trapped Woman: Catch-22 in
        Deviance and Control*. Newbury Park, CA: Sage.
Finelli, Susan C.
1986   "The 'Second Generation' Professional Woman in the Law Firm."
        Legal Administrator (Fall):65-66.
Flynn, Edith E.
1982   "Women as Criminal Justice Professionals: A Challenge to
        Change Tradition." Pp. 305-340 in Nicole Hahn Rafter and
        Elizabeth Anne Stanko (eds.), *Judge, Lawyer, Victim, Thief:
        Women, Gender Roles, and Criminal Justice*. Boston:
        Northeastern University Press.
Fossum, Donna
1980   "Women Law Professors." *American Bar Foundation*
        1980:903-14.
Graham, Deborah
1986   "It's Getting Better, Slowly." *American Bar Association Journal*
        72 (December):54-58.
Hall, Sophia H.
1990   "Women in Law: Have We Come a Long Way?" *Women Lawyers
        Journal* 77:4-7.
Klein, Joan Dempsey
1980   "Women Judges Join Together." *Judges Journal* 19:4 + .
Knowles, Marjorie Fine
1982   "The Legal Status of Women in Alabama, II: A Crazy Quilt
        Restitched." *Alabama Law Review* 33:375-406.
Liebler, Kym
1990   "Women in the Law." *Pennsylvania Lawyer* 12 (March):25-28.
MacKinnon, Catharine A.
1987   *Feminism Unmodified: Discourses on Life and Law*. Cambridge,
        MA: Harvard University Press.
Morello, Karen Berger
1986   *The Invisible Bar: The Woman Lawyer in America 1638 to the
        Present*. New York: Random House.
Moss, Debra Cassens
1988   "Would This Happen to a Man?" *American Bar Association
        Journal* 74 (June):50-55.
Patterson, Michelle and Laurie Engelberg
1982   "Women in a Male-Dominated Profession: The Women Lawyers."
        Pp. 385-97 in Barbara Raffel Price and Natalie J. Sokoloff (eds.),
        *The Criminal Justice System and Women: Offenders, Victims,
        Workers*. New York: Clark Boardman.

Peterson, Karen I.
   1981   "Women Lawyers Meet Challenge of Dual Roles." *Michigan Bar Journal,* May:249-50.
Prinz, Laurie
   1986   "In Retrospect: Resistance to Women Lawyers Slow to Die." *Wisconsin Bar Bulletin* 59 (June):11-14.
Repa, Barbara Kate
   1988   "Is There Life After Partnership?" *American Bar Association Journal* 74 (June):70-75.
Schafran, Lynn Hecht
   1987   "Practicing Law in a Sexist Society." In Laura L. Crites and Winifred L. Hepperle (eds.), *Women, The Courts, and Equality,* pp. 191-207. Newbury Park, CA: Sage.
   1986   "Educating the Judiciary About Gender Bias: The National Judicial Education Program to Promote Equality for Women and Men in the Courts and the New Jersey Supreme Court Task Force on Women in the Courts." *Women's Rights Law Reporter* 9:109-28.
Sheridan, Kathleen
   1981   "Women in Law: With a Woman on the Supreme Court, Has Anything Changed?" *Barrister* 8 (Summer):44-48.
Stark, Sharon
   1986   "Juggling Children and Career." *Wisconsin Bar Bulletin* 59 (June):17-21.
Women Lawyer's Journal
   1989   "ABA Commission On Women in the Profession Report." *Women Lawyer's Journal* 76:8.
Women's Rights Law Reporter
   1986   "The First Year Report of the New Jersey Supreme Court Task Force on Women in the Courts — June 1984." *Women's Rights Law Reporter* 9:129-77.
Wortman, Marlene Stein (ed.)
   1985   *Women in American Law: From Colonial Times to the New Deal,* Vol. 1. New York: Holmes and Meier Publishing.
Yuda, Geoffrey
   1990   "Minorities in the Law." *The Pennsylvania Lawyer,* March:8-15.

chapter 16

The Progress of Women Correctional Officers in All-Male Prisons

Linda L. Zupan
Illinois State University

History of the Integration of Women Correctional Officers

The employment of women as prison guards was virtually unheard of prior to the mid-1800s. In the earliest penal institutions male and female prisoners lived communally and were watched over by male guards. In the late 18th century, female offenders were moved to separate wings of male prisons, but were still guarded by men. The women prisoners were often subjected to physical abuse and sexual exploitation. It was not uncommon for female prisoners to be beaten and raped by their male keepers or forced into prostitution by male wardens (Freedman, 1981:16). In response to the lobbying efforts of female prison reformers, male guards were eventually replaced by female matrons. In 1822, the first female jail matron was appointed in Maryland. In Auburn prison, the first female guards were hired in 1832, seven years after a separate wing for women offenders was opened (Young, 1932:4).

The creation of separate reformatories for women offenders in the late 19th and early 20th centuries, provided additional employment opportunities to women in corrections. In some states the legislation that established reformatories for females also mandated that the new institutions be administered and staffed entirely by women (Parisi, 1984:93). For women with college educations in teaching, social work, and education, the newly created reformatories offered the opportunity to apply their skills and knowledge, and to develop independent careers (Pollock-Byrne, 1990:109-12). However, the work was far from ideal. Low pay, long work hours and weeks, and unpleasant work conditions frustrated even the most dedicated of the women (Rafter, 1985:75).

In later years, many state legislatures repealed the laws prohibiting the employment of males in female reformatories, thus opening the door for males to assume administrative positions in institutions for women. By 1966, all but ten female institutions were administrated by male wardens or superintendents (Allen and Simonsen, 1981:295). The primary reasons for repeal of the laws were a shortage of qualified women to manage the reformatories and a lack of faith on the part of male legislators in the administrative abilities of women (Pollock-Byrne, 1990:109).

It was not until the 1970s that any substantial change occurred in the role of women in institutional corrections. During this decade women fought for, and eventually won the right to be employed as correctional officers in prisons for men. Two factors are credited for the significant changes that occurred in the 1970s. The first was a growing dissatisfaction among women with the limited opportunities available to them in institutional corrections. A report by the Joint Commission on Correctional Manpower and Training in 1969 confirmed that women occupied only a periphery role in corrections. Although women comprised 40 percent of the nation's labor force in 1969, they accounted for only 12 percent of the correctional work force (National Advisory Commission on Criminal Justice Statistics and Goals, 1973:476). In institutional corrections, women were either limited to working in direct service positions in female facilities where job and advancement opportunities were severely restricted by the small size of the facilities or were employed in clerical and support staff positions in all-male institutions where pay and job status were low (Chapman, et al., 1983:27).

The second major force behind the change was the passage of

amendments to the 1964 Civil Rights Act in 1972. The Civil Rights Act of 1964, more specifically Title VII of the Act, prohibits employment discrimination on the basis of sex. When originally passed, the Act applied only to private sector employment, but in 1972, the U.S. Congress passed amendments to the Act that extended the prohibition against employment discrimination to public employers at the state, county and local levels. Armed with the weight of Title VII behind them, women brought suits against correctional officials who refused to hire them as correctional officers in all-male prisons. Prior to 1977, women were generally successful in using Title VII to gain employment in male prisons, but in 1977 a critical ruling by the U.S. Supreme Court threatened to subvert the progress made by women (Zimmer, 1983:202). In the case of *Dothard v. Rawlinson*, the Court ruled that under certain circumstances, women could be prohibited from correctional officer jobs in male prisons.

Although the decision of the Court has been widely debated and discussed, the facts of the case are simple. Diane Rawlinson, a recent college graduate with a degree in correctional psychology, applied for a correctional counselor (guard) position with the Alabama Board of Corrections. Rawlinson was denied the position because she failed to meet the minimum height requirement established by the Board. Rawlinson filed suit against the Alabama Board of Corrections charging that the height requirement discriminated against women and violated Title VII. She also challenged a policy implemented by the Board while her case was pending that barred women from holding positions that required contact with male prisoners.

The federal district court which originally heard the case ruled that the minimum height and weight requirements violated Title VII. The court also struck down the policy barring women from contact positions with inmates on the basis that the state had failed to prove that women could not perform the job. On appeal, the U.S. Supreme Court upheld the lower court's decision on the minimum height and weight requirements but reversed the ruling on the no contact policy. Without supporting proof, the Court held to the assumption that the presence of women would threaten the security of the all-male, maximum security prison. In the opinion for the majority, Justice Potter Stewart disclosed the presumptive reasoning of the Court:

> The essence of a correctional counselor's job is to maintain prison security. A woman's relative ability to maintain order in a male, maximum-security, unclassified penitentiary of the type

Alabama now runs could be directly reduced by her womanhood. There is a basis in fact for expecting that sex offenders who have criminally assaulted women in the past would be moved to do so again if access to women were established within the prison. There would also be a real risk that other inmates, deprived of a normal heterosexual environment, would assault women guards because they were women. In a prison system where violence is the order of the day, where inmate access to guards is facilitated by dormitory living arrangements, where every institution is understaffed, and where a substantial portion of the inmate population is composed of sex offenders mixed at random with other prisons, there are few visible deterrents to inmate assaults on women custodians (433 US 321:335-36).

While great concern was expressed that the ruling of the Court in *Dothard* would be used to exclude women from employment in all-male prisons, a number of analysts have noted that no other department of corrections has successfully used the case for that purpose (Jacobs, 1981; Potts, 1983; Zimmer, 1983). In cases following *Dothard*, courts continually attempted to balance the employment rights of women with the institution's need for security.

Inmates also contested the employment of opposite sex guards on the grounds that their presence infringed on inmate privacy. A number of suits challenged the deployment of opposite sex officers in shower, toilet, and dressing areas (see for example, *Forts v. Ward*, 1979; *Bowling v. Enomoto*, 1981; *Avery v. Perrin*, 1979; and *Gunther v. Iowa*, 1980). Others challenged the practice of opposite sex "pat search" frisks (see for example, *Smith v. Fairman*, 1983; *Sam'i v. Mintzes*, 1983; *Madyun v. Franzen*, 1983; and *Bagley v. Watson*, 1983).

In these cases, the courts generally attempted to balance the employment rights of women with inmate privacy needs by ordering changes in institutional policies and/or in the physical structure of the prison. In the case of *Fort v. Ward* (1979), for example, the court ordered that inmates be allowed to cover the windows on their cell doors for 15 minutes each day. The court also ordered that translucent shower screens be erected on all showers.

Despite the decision in *Dothard*, many state correctional departments complied with Title VII mandates and changed policies prohibiting the employment of women correctional officers in all-male prisons. By 1981, all but four state correctional systems (Alaska, Pennsylvania, Texas and Utah) employed women as correctional officers in all-male prisons (Morton, 1981:10).

According to Chapman, et al., (1983:27) the number of female correctional officers increased from 9.2 percent of all correctional officers in 1973 to 12.7 percent in 1979. By 1981, women comprised approximately six percent of the officer force in all-male prisons, and in nine states more than ten percent of the correctional officer force in all-male prisons was female.[1] Not surprisingly, the primary reason cited by correctional officials for the increased employment and utilization of female officers was Title VII of the Civil Rights Act (Morton, 1981:10).[2]

The Federal Bureau of Prisons acted as early as 1975 to integrate women correctional officers in all of its prisons except the maximum-security penitentiaries (Feinman, 1986). By 1980, 8 percent of the correctional officer force in all-male federal institutions was female (Ingram, 1980:276). Women comprised anywhere from one to nineteen percent of the correctional officer staff in federal institutions.

Changes were also occurring in the role of women correctional officers in the nation's jails. The nature of this change is evident in the experience of the New York City Department of Corrections. Prior to 1980, women correction officers were prohibited from working in the city's various male-only facilities. In consequence, the only positions available to them were in the Women's House of Detention and the jail ward of Elmhurst Hospital. In 1981, following a court decision that required the state corrections department to deploy females to their male prisons, city correctional officials instituted a policy that allowed women officers to assume positions within any of the city's jails, including the all-male facilities. The only areas restricted from the women were the inmate showers or areas where male inmates were strip-searched (Steier, 1989:n.p.).

Following the change in deployment policy, the percentage of women holding uniform positions in the New York City Department of Corrections increased from ten percent of the total guard force to almost 25 percent. Women currently comprise a larger percentage of the uniformed employees of the corrections department than in any other uniformed New York City department. Only 11.8 percent of New York Police Department uniformed officers, 9 percent of the Transit Police Department, and less than 1 percent of the Fire Department are female (Steier, 1989:n.p.).

The change in deployment policy also affected the number of women hired by the department. Between October 1987 and October 1988, 417 women and 869 men were hired, about one woman for every two males (Steier, 1989:n.p.).

A recent study of the employment of women in local jails reveals that 21.5 percent of the total correctional officer force in the 107 largest jail systems in the nation are female (Zupan, 1990:6). In some counties such as Fulton County, Georgia, women comprise over 40 percent of the jail's guard force. Certainly, one explanation for the relatively high percent of women officers is that jails are coeducational institutions detaining both male and female inmates, and that women employees are needed to supervise female inmates. However, among the 107 jail systems in the study, more than 75 percent deploy women officers to supervise the housing units of male inmates (Zupan, 1990:8).

Current Status of Women Correctional Officers

Currently, about 15 percent of the total correctional officer force in both male and female state facilities is female (Contact Center, Inc., 1988:9). States vary as to the percentage of women correctional officers. The lowest percentages of women officers are employed in Idaho where only 5.1 percent of the total correctional officers force is female and in North Carolina where only 5.8 percent of the force is female. Mississippi employs the largest percentage of women; 36 percent of the state's guard force is female.

The percentage of women correctional officers assigned to all-male prisons also varies between states. In Alabama, for example, a full 85 percent, or about 272 of the state's 324 female correctional officers work in male prisons. In contrast, in North Carolina, less than 1 percent of the state's 221 female correctional officers work in male prisons.

Although this type of census data is important in discerning patterns and progress in the employment of women correctional officers, it reveals little about the type of women who work in all-male prisons. Unfortunately, there is a surprising lack of comprehensive information on the demographic characteristics of the women themselves. One of the few studies to examine the background and personal characteristics of women correctional officers was conducted by Jurik and Halemba (1984). In their study of 40 female and 139 male correctional officers in a medium-minimum security prison in the southwest, the authors found that the women officers were more highly educated, were more likely to come from a professional and urban family background and were more likely to be divorced, separated, or single than were their male co-workers (Jurik and Halemba, 1984:555-57). In her study of correctional officers in New York and Rhode Island, Zimmer

(1986:45) also found that female officers were more highly educated than their male counterparts, but the differences in educational achievement were small. Fifty-four percent of the male officers in her study had some college education while 55 percent of women officers had some higher education. The majority of women in Zimmer's (1986:45) sample came from fairly traditional work backgrounds. Prior to their application to the prison, many of the women had worked in low paying, traditionally female jobs or had been unemployed. In contrast, male officers were more likely to have prior military or criminal justice experience. Jurik (1985:382) also found that women had less "anticipatory socialization" than their male counterparts. In her study, 38 percent of female officers reported previous employment experience in either corrections or a related field; 68 percent of the males had previous experience in these areas. While 46 percent of the males had prior military experience, none of the women had served in the military.

Jurik and Halemba (1984:557-58) also detected differences between male and female officers as to their reasons for pursuing a career in corrections. When asked about factors influencing their career decisions, women officers were more likely than men to give intrinsic reasons, such as an interest in human service work or in inmate rehabilitation. Male officers also cited an interest in human service work or in inmate rehabilitation but were more likely than women to mention extrinsic factors such as job security, salary, fringe benefits, or the unavailability of alternative work as their reasons for accepting employment at the prison. In contrast, most of the women in Zimmer's (1986:40-43) study indicated financial benefits or the lack of alternative job opportunities that require minimal education and experience as their primary reasons for entering corrections. Interestingly, none of the women in her study entered the job with aspirations for a career in corrections.

Zimmer (1986:43-45) further found that the women in her study were considerably conservative in their sex-role attitudes. This is in direct contrast to the popular image of women in nontraditional occupations as groundbreaking, pioneering, women's rights advocates. Fifty-six percent of the women officers believed that women should not work during their children's formative years. Only 17 percent "strongly favored" passage of the Equal Rights Amendment and only 38 percent believed that husbands and wives should have equal power within the family (Zimmer, 1986:43-44). The women did, however, overwhelmingly support the concept of equal pay for equal work.

The Additional Burdens of Being a Women Correctional Officer in an All-Male Prison

Few would argue against the assertion that the job performed by correctional officers is a demanding one. Among the factors which make the job difficult are a hostile and involuntary clientele, a rigid and hierarchical authority structure, conflicting goals and expectations, an overabundance of rules and regulations, an unpleasant physical work environment, and a chronic lack of resources. Like their male counterparts, female correctional officers routinely deal with these unfavorable aspects of the job, yet unlike male officers, females also endure a number of additional hardships placed on them simply because of their sex. The most apparent burdens with which they must cope include tokenism, differential treatment by male supervisors and administrators, and opposition by male co-workers.

Tokenism

Despite the progress of the last two decades to integrate women correctional officers into all-male prisons, they still constitute a numeric minority in most institutions. Considerable pressure is placed on women officers because they are minorities or "tokens" within the prison organization. First, tokens tend to be highly visible within the organization and as such, their performance, as well as their mistakes, are closely scrutinized and discussed by those around them (Kanter, 1977:206-42). Zimmer (1986:105) noted that the women officers in her study received a disproportionate amount of attention due to their high visibility. Male inmates and officers regularly dissected the appearance, behavior and actions of the women. The mistakes of women were quickly communicated throughout the prison and were discussed for weeks. Consequently, many of the women became self-conscious and avoided taking risks that would make them stand out even further.

Second, differences between tokens and the dominant group tend to be exaggerated while similarities between the two groups are often overlooked (Kanter, 1977:206-42). Other than sex, the most glaring difference between male and female correctional officers is their physical size and strength. It is to these differences that male officers most frequently point in arguing against the employment of women correctional officers in all-male prisons. As a consequence of being "different" from their male co-workers, women are never fully accepted or assimilated into the predominately male work group (Zimmer, 1986:105).

Finally, the actions or behavior of one token are often attributed to all members of the token group (Kanter, 1977:206-42). Such overgeneralizations are common in prisons where male officers and supervisors tend to judge all women officers by the actions and behavior of only a few. When one woman officer performs unsatisfactorily it is readily assumed that all women officers will perform unsatisfactorily. The reverse opinion is seldom held. Rarely is it assumed that all women officers will perform effectively simply because one woman does. Typically, an outstanding woman officer is viewed as an exception. The tendency to judge all women by the actions or behavior of one places tremendous pressure on women officers. Not only must they prove themselves but they must also prove that other members of their sex can do the job.

Differential Treatment by Supervisors and Administrators

Although in many prisons formal personnel policies prohibit overt discrimination on the basis of sex, the actions of prison officials, particularly first-line supervisors, often result in the disparate treatment of women officers. Such differential treatment of women officers is common in the deployment practices of first-line supervisors. In the institutions Zimmer (1986:86-88) studied, supervisors were given discretionary power in the assignment of guards. Male supervisors who feared for the safety of female officers, or who believed that women were unfit for the job, assigned them to low-risk positions requiring little direct contact with inmates. This type of discriminatory assignment was particularly prevalent during the officers' field training. Although the function of field training was to provide officers with experience in a variety of positions within the prison, women officers received experience in only a narrow range of low-risk positions (Zimmer, 1986:80-82).

Discrimination by male supervisors in the assignment of female officers was also found in the prison studied by Jurik (1985:384-85). Male supervisors who doubted the abilities of female officers or who believed that their presence infringed on inmate privacy refrained from assigning women to cellblocks, housing units or yards where they would have close contact with inmates. Instead, women were assigned to control rooms, visitation and clerical areas where they had little inmate contact.

Both Zimmer and Jurik noted that the discriminatory treatment by male supervisors severely handicapped women officers. Zimmer (1986:83-84) found that differential assignments, particularly during the field-training period, prevented the women from learning important tasks and from gaining valuable experience in a variety of positions. Women were also denied opportunities to build confidence in their skills and abilities, particularly in the supervision and control of inmates. Jurik (1985:384) observed that differential assignments limited women's promotion opportunities as they lacked prerequisite experience in certain posts and positions. Finally, the differential treatment women received served to further antagonize male co-workers who viewed them as being given safer, plusher jobs while they were forced to work the more dangerous ones.

Jurik (1985:385-86) observed that discrimination by male supervisors also occurred in their formal evaluations of female officers' performance. Supervisors in the studied prison were not provided clearly defined and objective criteria on which to evaluate the performance of correctional officers. As a result, evaluations of women officers were subject to the biases of the male supervisors. Since the evaluations were later used in the promotion process, women who were evaluated by male supervisors antagonistic to their employment were clearly disadvantaged.

The failure on the part of prison officials to provide clear guidelines, or to clarify existing guidelines, also had adverse effects on women officers. Petersen (1982:455) found that ambiguities in policies regarding inmate privacy caused confusion for women officers and inhibited their performance. For example, prison policy prohibited women from strip searching inmates except in "emergency situations." Prison administrators failed to adequately clarify what constituted an emergency situation. Male officers interpreted the women's confusion over their strip searching duties as a sign that they were shirking from unpleasant tasks.

Opposition By Male Co-workers

A final burden with which female correctional officers must cope is the opposition of male co-workers. In study after study, researchers have consistently found that male officers generally oppose the employment of women correctional officers and resent their presence in all-male prisons (Fry, et al., 1985; Holeman and Krepps-Hess, 1983; Petersen, 1982; Simpson and White, 1985).[3] The only exception concerns the relationship between black and Hispanic male and female co-workers. Zimmer (1987:133-34) found that friendly relationships often developed between minority male and female officers. The basis of this friendship was a shared perception that white male officers opposed and harassed both women and minorities.[4]

The reasons male officers commonly give for their opposition to female officers are based primarily on the male officers' distorted perceptions of women. Women are perceived as lacking the physical size and strength necessary to handle aggressive inmates, or to back-up male officers in violent situations. Male officers fear that the lack of strength not only places the women in peril but also endangers inmates and co-workers (Jurik, 1985; Parisi, 1984; Simpson and White, 1985). Related to this is the perception that women lack the psychological strength to withstand the stresses and strains of the job as well as inmate attempts at manipulation and intimidation (Jurik, 1985; Zimmer, 1987). Male officers also believe that female officers will endanger prison security by engaging in sexual relations with inmates or will get promoted by engaging in sexual relations with supervisors and administrators (Jurik, 1985; Owen, 1985; Petersen, 1982; Zimmer, 1985). Finally, male officers believe that women will be unable to perform unpleasant tasks such as frisking and strip searching inmates or supervising shower and toilet areas because of infringements on inmate privacy and that they will be forced to assume more than their fair share of the dirty work.

Outside observers point to a more compelling reason for the opposition of female officers. They suggest that the presence of women challenges the "macho" image of the job and calls into question the commonly shared belief that extreme masculinity is a prerequisite for effective performance as a correctional officer (Crouch, 1985; Horne, 1985; Owen, 1985; Zimmer, 1987).

Regardless of the reasons for the opposition, the fact that it exists has adverse consequences for female officers who must deal with both the overt and covert expression of their co-workers' resentment. One way male officers demonstrate their resentment is by harassing female officers. In one study, women officers reported being the victims of rumors, innuendoes, and allegations of sexual misconduct spread by their male colleagues (Petersen, 1982:453). In another study, the harassment women officers received ranged from outright statements of opposition by male officers to more subtle and sexual forms of harassment such as joking, teasing, and name calling (Zimmer, 1986:90-100).

Perhaps a more serious consequence of male co-worker opposition and resentment is that women are denied access to the prison guard subculture and to the benefits the subculture provides. As has been noted by a number of correctional scholars, the prison guard subculture plays a critical role in socializing officers to the demands of the job and in protecting them from the hardships of the work. Because women officers are denied entry into the established subculture, they must either do without or seek out alternative sources of support that may or may not be readily available.

Differences Between Female and Male Correctional Officers

Because of the unique circumstances women encounter as correctional officers in all-male prisons, it is commonly assumed that their response to the job is different and distinct from that of male officers. The data, however, fail to support this assumption. Although relatively few studies have compared male and female correctional officers, the research that does exist suggests that sex has little influence in the work-related attitudes, evaluations and performance of officers.

Evaluations of the Work Conditions

Jurik and Halemba (1984:559-60) assessed correctional officer perceptions of a variety of work-related conditions including opportunities for advancement, chances to increase knowledge and skills, and the amount of task variety, authority, discretion, and influence in policy decisions. The only difference they found between female and male officers concerns the perceived amount of discretion. Male officers indicated that they did not have enough discretion to properly perform the job; women exhibited a desire for more structure in the job.

Jurik and Halemba (1984:558-59), however, detected differences between female and male officers in their attitudes toward co-workers and superiors. Women officers were more likely to express negative attitudes toward male co-workers and to indicate that many of their problems at work were caused by male co-workers. There were no substantial differences in the attitudes of female and male officers toward their superiors. Both tended to have negative feelings toward their superiors and to believe that the majority of their work-related problems were caused by superiors.

Work Adjustment

Fry and Glaser (1987) investigated differences between female and male officers on various social psychological aspects of work adjustment and staff integration. More specifically, the researchers compared officer evaluations of stress, organizational commitment, co-workers, inmate services, and impact of the job on the individual officer. Overall, few differences were detected between the work adjustment and integration of female and male officers. The only significant difference found was in regard to inmate services; females were much more negative in their evaluations of inmate services. The researchers concluded that "women are at least as well adjusted and integrated as men in prison work" (Fry and Glaser, 1987:51).

Job Satisfaction

A common expectation is that women officers will be more negative in their affective evaluations of the job because they must continually deal with the consequences of tokenism, differential treatment, and co-worker opposition. The research, however, fails to support this assumption. Cullen, et al. (1985:524) found no significant difference between the level of job dissatisfaction experienced by male and female officers. Jurik and Halemba (1984:560-63) also noted little difference in the levels of job satisfaction reported by female and male officers. In addition, these researchers found that the women officers' negative attitudes toward male co-workers had little impact on their levels of job satisfaction.

Stress

Another common assumption concerning the affective response of women correctional officers, is that the job is more stressful for women because they must deal with the burden of being female in a male-dominated organization. The data tend to support this assumption. Although Cullen, et al., (1985:524) reported that gender was unrelated to levels of life stress experienced by officers, they found that women officers experienced a significantly higher level of work-related stress than did male officers. This finding is further supported by the results of studies conducted by Stinchcomb (1986) and Zupan (1986).

Attitudes Toward Inmates

If traditional sex-role stereotypes are to be believed, women correctional officers would be more positively oriented toward inmates, less punitive toward them and more sensitive to their needs than their male counterparts. The findings from research conducted by Crouch and Alpert (1982) are often used as evidence that women are indeed less punitive and aggressive toward inmates. In this study, the authors measured officer attitudes toward punishment and aggressiveness in inmate encounters during academy training and six months into the job. They found that the sex of the officers influenced changes in attitudes. Although males and females entered the training academy with similar scores on measures of punitiveness and aggressiveness, after six months on the job, males became increasingly more punitive and aggressive while females became more tolerant and nonpunitive. Although widely cited, the findings of this study are often misconstrued. In describing their methodology, the authors clearly note that after academy training the officers were assigned to totally different institutions. Male officers were assigned to male-only institutions while women officers assumed positions in female-only institutions. Instead of gender influencing changes in attitudes toward inmates, it is more likely that differences in the environments, inmates and role expectations between male and female institutions produced the changes.

More appropriate assessments of the influence of gender on attitudes toward inmates have compared female and male officers within the same institution. These studies suggest that gender plays only a small, if not insignificant role, in the officer attitudes toward inmates. Jurik and Halemba (1984:558-59), for example, measured the degree to which officers held negative (punitive) attitudes toward inmates and found no significant difference between female and male officers. According to the authors (1984:558), the fact that female officers were no more positive or negative toward inmates "refutes the stereotype that women [are] more sensitive to the needs of inmates than men." This finding was also supported in research conducted by Zupan (1986). In this study, the author found that although male and female officers evaluated the needs of inmates very similarly, neither were sensitive enough to accurately identify inmate needs. As with the research of Jurik and Halemba the findings in this study contradict the conventional view that women correctional officers possess greater interpersonal skills and are more sensitive to the needs of people around them (Zupan, 1986:352-53).

Work Styles

Zimmer (1986:108-47) investigated the manner in which women officers coped with the demands of the job and found that they adopted one of three roles. In the "institutional role," women adhered closely to institutional rules and tried to maintain a highly professional stance. Although these women tried to enforce rules in a fair and consistent manner, their preoccupation with obedience to the rules often caused them to become rigid and inflexible. Women who assumed the "modified role" believed that they could not perform the job as well as men and therefore sympathized with male officers who opposed the presence of women officers. These women tended to fear inmates and to avoid direct contact with them. To perform the job, they relied heavily on their male co-workers for back-up. Women who adopted the "inventive role" relied on inmates for support. They expressed little fear of inmates and, in fact, preferred working in direct contact with them. Although Zimmer (1986:109) argued that these roles are unique to women, she failed to provide conclusive evidence that they are different from the work styles of male officers.

Previous research indicates that these roles are not necessarily unique to women officers. Male officers also cope with the demands of the job by adopting very similar work styles (Jacobs and Retsky, 1975:23). Some officers assume a repressive style. These officers tend to adhere closely to and rigidly enforce the rules of the facility. Other officers adapt to the job by establishing friendships with inmates. Still others deal with inmates by avoiding contact with them. The roles adopted by male officers are clearly similar to the roles assumed by female officers.

Performance

When women are asked to evaluate their performance vis a vis their male co-workers, they generally give themselves positive ratings. Kissel and Katsampes (1980:226), for example, reported that 8 percent of the women in their sample felt completely satisfied with their performance while the remaining 92 percent were "for the most part" satisfied with their performance. All of the women in the study described their performance as equal to that of their male counterparts.

Other studies have utilized behavioral and organizational measures of performance but have found few differences between female and male officers. Holeman and Krepps-Hess (1983) compared the performance of 168 matched pairs of female and male correctional officers on a variety of performance measures. No significant differences were observed between female and male officers on their performance appraisal ratings, number of accommodations or reprimands, or amount of sick leave used.

Assault Rates

As discussed previously, most male co-workers oppose the presence of women correctional officers in all-male prisons on the grounds that their lack of physical strength and size endangers officer safety and facility security. Bowersox (1981:496-98) observed that safety fears often led male officers to be more protective of female than of male officers. In contrast, women officers believed that they could defend themselves. They felt that the fears of their male co-workers were unwarranted and they resented male offers of protection. In one of the few studies to address differences in frequency and outcome of assaults against female and male officers, Shawver and Dickover (1986:32-33) found little to confirm the safety fears of male officers. According to this study, women officers were assaulted significantly less than their male counterparts. Furthermore, when women were assaulted they were about as likely as male officers to be injured or to suffer a major injury.

Shawver and Dickover (1986:32-33) also investigated the claim that increases in the number of women officers within the prison results in increases in the number of assaults against male officers. From their analysis, the researchers found no relationship between the percentage of women officers employed in the prison and the number of assaults on male staff.

Attrition Rates

The issue of staff turnover in prisons has received only scant attention in the correctional literature. Turnover among female officers has received even less notice. The few studies that do exist present contradictory findings as to differences between the attrition rates of females and males.

One study, conducted by the Federal Bureau of Prisons reported that the termination/resignation rate among women officers in federal institutions was higher than that of males (Ingram, 1980:276). Anywhere from 11 to 32 percent of the staff who left were female. Ingram (1980:276) noted, however, that very few of these women resigned because of job demands or the work environment. In contrast, data released by the New York City Department of Corrections revealed that between October 1987 and October 1988, 356 male jail officers resigned compared to only 110 women, a ratio of 3.5 male resignations to every 1 female resignation (Steier, 1989:n.p.).

Concluding Comments

Over the last two decades, researchers have closely followed the progress of women correctional officers in all-male prisons. Not only have they meticulously documented the integration process but have also focused much needed attention on the treatment women receive in the prison organization. The research, however, is far from complete.

Presently, there is a critical need for more research to compare the objective behaviors of female and male officers rather than simply their attitudes and perceptions. There is also a need for researchers to take a different approach in order to unravel the effects of the structural features of the prison organization on the behavior and attitudes of both female and male officers.

All too often, researchers approach the study of women correctional officers with the assumption that their job orientations and work-related attitudes and behaviors are different from those of male officers. The unique orientations, attitudes and behaviors of women are either credited to their sex or to the burdens they encounter in the male-dominated prison organization. What has yet to be adequately addressed is the role that the structural features of the prison organization play in affecting the job orientations of female *and* male officers.

The literature on correctional institutions documents a variety of structural factors that play a considerable role in molding correctional officer behavior and attitudes, irrespective of the officers' individual characteristics (see for example, Jacobs and Kraft, 1978:316-17). These same structural features may, in fact, obliterate job related differences between female and male officers. Therefore, we would expect to find less variation in attitudes and behavior *between* the sexes and greater variation within the sexes. Although relatively few comparative studies of female and male officers exist, these studies indicate that gender has only a minor and inconsequential influence on officer evaluations of working conditions, adjustment to the job, work group integration, job satisfaction, work styles, performance and assault rates. Only through additional, more rigorous comparative studies of this type can the hypothesized effect of the structural features on officer behaviors and attitudes be assessed. Once the effects of the prison's structural features on both male and female officers have been analyzed, attention can then be focused on a more pressing issue — determining the extent to which these features are inherent to organizations created and dominated by males.

Endnotes

[1] These states included Louisiana, Wyoming, Kentucky, Oklahoma, South Carolina, Kansas, Nevada, Michigan and Virginia.

[2] Other reasons cited included: the need for female officers to conduct certain tasks such as searching female visitors; application by qualified females; shortages of male applicants; and, expansion of the work force (Morton, 1981:10).

[3] A study of women jail correctional officers in Colorado conducted by Kissel and Katsampes (1980) is the only exception to these findings. In this study male officers were found to be generally positive toward women officers. Almost 88 percent of the men felt that "male and female complement each other on performance of duties" (1980:225). There are a number of flaws in this study. The most serious is the small number of sampled males (25). A second problem concerns the large percentage of women officers in the studied jail. According to the authors over 34 percent of the correctional officer staff is female. The high proportion of females prohibits generalization of the findings to most prison settings where the percentage of women is much smaller and where women are in the "token" minority.

[4] With the exception of Zimmer's (1986) peripheral discussion of the relationship between male and female minority officers, very little attention has been given to the influence of race or ethnicity on women correctional officers. Obviously, this is a fruitful area for future research.

Bibliography

Allen, Harry and Clifford Simonsen
    1980   *Corrections in America.* New York: MacMillan Publishing Company.
Avery v. Perrin
    1979   473 F. Supp. 90.
Bagley v. Watson
    1983   579 F. Supp. 1099 (D.C. Ore.).
Bowersox, Michael S.
    1981   "Women in Corrections: Competence, Competition, and the Social Responsibility Norm." *Criminal Justice and Behavior* 8:491-99.
Bowling v. Enomoto
    1981   514 F. Supp. 201.
Chapman, Jane R., Elizabeth K. Minor, Patricia Rieker, Trudy L. Mills and Mary Bottum
    1983   *Women Employed in Corrections.* Washington, DC: U.S. Government Printing Office.
Contact Center, Inc.
    1988   *Corrections Compendium* 13:9-20.

Crouch, Ben M.
  1985   "Pandora's Box: Women Guards in Men's Prisons." *Journal of Criminal Justice.* 13:535-48.
Crouch, Ben M. and Geoffrey P. Alpert
  1982   "Sex and Occupational Socialization Among Prison Guards: A Longitudinal Study." *Criminal Justice and Behavior* 9:159-76.
Cullen, Francis T., Bruce G. Link, Nancy T. Wolfe, and James Frank
  1985   "The Social Dimensions of Correctional Officer Stress." *Justice Quarterly* 2:505-33.
Dothard v. Rawlinson
  1977   433 U.S. 321.
Feinman, Clarice
  1986   *Women in the Criminal Justice System* (2nd Edition). New York: Praeger Publishers.
Forts v. Ward
  1980   621 F.2d. 1210 (2nd Cir.).
Freedman, Estelle B.
  1981   *Their Sisters' Keepers: Women's Prison Reform in America, 1830-1930.* Ann Arbor, MI: University of Michigan Press.
Fry, Lincoln J. and Daniel Glaser
  1987   "Gender Differences in Work Adjustment of Prison Employees." *Journal of Offender Counseling, Services and Rehabilitation* 12:39-52.
Fry, Lincoln J., Daniel Glaser, Barbara Mathieu, and James Mathieu
  1985   "The Integration of Female Correctional Officers in the California Prison System." Paper presented at the annual meeting of the Southern Sociological Association, in Charlotte, North Carolina.
Gunther v. Iowa State Men's Reformatory
  1980   612 F.2d. 1079, cert. denied 446 U.S. 996 (8th Cir.).
Holeman, H. and B. Krepps-Hess
  1983   *Women Correctional Officers in the California Department of Corrections.* Sacramento, CA: Final Report of Research Contractors to the Department.
Horne, Peter
  1985   "Female Corrections Officers: A Status Report." *Federal Probation* 49:46-54.
Ingram, Gilbert L.
  1980   "The Role of Women in Male Federal Correctional Institutions." Pp. 275-81 *American Correctional Association (ed.) Proceedings of the One Hundred and Tenth Annual Congress of Correction.* College Park, MD: American Correctional Association.
Jaccbs, James B. and Harold G. Retsky
  1975   "Prison Guard." *Urban Life* 4:5-29.
Jacobs, James B. and Lawrence J. Kraft
  1978   "Integrating the Keepers: A Comparison of Black and White Prison Guards in Illinois." *Social Problems* 25:304-18.

Jacobs, James B.
  1981   "The Sexual Integration of the Prison's Guard Force: A Few
          Comments on *Dothard v. Rawlinson*." Pp. 57-85 in B. H. Olsson
          (ed), *Women in Corrections*. College Park, MD: American
          Correctional Association.
Jurik, Nancy C.
  1985   "An Officer and a Lady: Organizational Barriers to Women
          Working As Correctional Officers in Men's Prisons." *Social
          Problems* 32:375-88.
Jurik, Nancy C. and Gregory J. Halemba
  1984   "Gender, Working Conditions and the Job Satisfaction of Women
          in a Non-Traditional Occupation: Female Correctional Officers in
          Men's Prisons." *The Sociological Quarterly* 25:551-66.
Kanter, Rosabeth Moss
  1977   *Men and Women of the Corporation*. New York: Basic Books.
Kissel, Peter J. and Paul L. Katsampes
  1980   "The Impact of Women Corrections Officers on the Functioning
          of Institutions Housing Male Inmates." *Journal of Offender
          Counseling, Services and Rehabilitation* 4:213-31.
Madyun v. Franzen
  1983   704 F. 2d. 954.
Morton, Joann B.
  1981   "Women in Correctional Employment: Where Are They Now and
          Where Are They Headed?" Pp. 7-16 in B. H. Olsson (ed.), *Women
          in Corrections*. College Park, MD: American Correctional
          Association.
National Advisory Commission on Criminal Justice Standards and Goals
  1973   *Corrections*. Washington, DC: U.S. Government Printing Office.
Owen, Barbara A.
  1985   "Race and Gender Relations Among Prison Workers." *Crime and
          Delinquency* 31:147-59.
Parisi, Nicolette
  1984   "The Female Correctional Officer: Her Progress Toward and
          Prospects for Equality." *The Prison Journal* 64:92-109.
Petersen, Cheryl Bowser
  1982   "Doing Time With the Boys: An Analysis of Women Correctional
          Officers in All-Male Facilities." Pp. 437-60 in B. Raffel Price and
          N. Sokoloff (ed.), *The Criminal Justice System and Women*. New
          York: Clark Boardman.
Pollock-Byrne, Joycelyn M.
  1990   *Women, Prison, and Crime*. Pacific Grove, CA: Brooks/Cole
          Publishing Company.
Potts, Lee W.
  1983   "Employment Opportunity Issues." *Federal Probation* 47:37-44.
Rafter, Nicole
  1985   *Partial Justice: State Prisons and Their Inmates, 1800-1935*.
          Boston: Northeastern University Press.

Sam'i v. Mintzes
1983   544 F. Supp. 416.
Shawver, Lois and Robert Dickover
1986   "Research Perspectives: Exploding a Myth." *Corrections Today.* August:30-34.
Simpson, Sally and Mervin White
1985   "The Female Guard in the All-Male Prison." Pp. 276-300 in I. Moyer (ed.), *The Changing Role of Women in the Criminal Justice System.* Prospect Heights, IL: Waveland Press.
Smith v. Fairman
1982   678 F.2d. 52, cert. denied 461 U.S. 907 (7th Cir.).
Steier, Richard
1989   "Women Flourishing in Correction Dept." *A.J.A. Newsletter* Winter:n.p.
Stinchcomb, Jeanne B.
1986   "Correctional Officer Stress: Looking at the Causes, You May Be the Cure." A paper presented at the annual meeting of the Academy of Criminal Justice Sciences, in Orlando, Florida.
Young, Clifford
1932   *Women's Prisons Past and Present and Other New York State Prison History.* Elmira, NY: Summary Press.
Zimmer, Lynn
1983   "The Legal Problems of Implementing Title VII in the Prisons." *ALSA Forum* 7:199-221.
Zimmer, Lynn E.
1986   *Women Guarding Men.* Chicago: The University of Chicago Press.
Zupan, Linda L.
1986   "Gender-Related Differences in Correctional Officers' Perceptions and Attitudes." *Journal of Criminal Justice* 14:349-61.
Zupan, Linda L.
1990   "The Employment of Women in Local Jails." A paper presented at the annual meeting of the Academy of Criminal Justice Sciences, in Denver, Colorado.

Postscript

The major thesis of this book, as expressed in Chapter 1, is that conflict theory is an appropriate perspective to explain the traditional research and theory of male criminologists. The theory also is useful to examine the differential attitudes and behavior of criminal justice officials toward women and men offenders, victims, and professionals. The feminist perspective, which has received some recognition by mainstream criminology in the last few years, also helps explain the process whereby men have established themselves in positions of dominance in the field of criminology. Traditional sex role stereotyping has allowed for the socialization of men into occupational roles as breadwinners and women into domestic roles as housewives and mothers. This has created and maintained the patriarchal system that provides men with the power to control the criminal justice system.

However, women's roles have been slowly changing and there has been an increased interest in research on women offenders, victims, and professionals, as well as a moderate increase in women employed as professionals in criminal justice agencies. The chapters in this book demonstrate the increased acceptance of feminist theory by some criminologists. The papers also indicate that these changes have made a difference in research on women and in opportunities for women in most aspects of the criminal justice system. Legal decisions have been made that have changed the criminal statutes that discriminated against women offenders. There also are new laws and policies that require protection for women who are victims of domestic crimes by men and provide equal employment opportunities for women and protection against sexual harassment for women in criminal justice agencies. Other chapters point to new programs for women offenders that recognize the need for these women to become economically and socially independent in order to function effectively in modern society.

In reporting research that indicates these changes, many of the authors in this volume note that the full implementation of these new laws, policies, and roles for women has been hindered by a system that continues to be dominated by men. Thus, conflict theory is relevant to all the chapters in this book. Several of the authors have also included feminist theory in writing their chapters.

The new and revised chapters in this volume have integrated material on race, ethnicity and international groups wherever that information was available. The international studies that have been conducted are predominantly in the areas of prostitution, pornography and violence against women. Most of these studies also are limited to Australia and Western European countries, such as Britain and the Netherlands. More research needs to be conducted on these groups, especially concerning Hispanics, Native Americans, and Asians as well as other third world cultures. The ethnic diversity in Hawaii and its impact on women's crime and how the criminal justice system in that state handles women victims and offenders is another area that needs to be researched.

While one chapter in this edition has included research on lesbians, this has been a highly neglected area by criminologists and is limited to battering relationships. This is an important area, since one study suggests that many shelters and heterosexual victims are reluctant to include lesbian victims in their programs. This research, however, has the potential of presenting false stereotypes of lesbian relationships, even though research shows that most battering occurs in heterosexual relationships. More research and service programs for lesbian victims are needed in the area of battering, but it also is essential that criminologists begin to explore other issues in criminology related to lesbians and gays.

Although the numbers of older women involved in criminal situations are small, feminist criminologists have an obligation to conduct research to explore this highly neglected area. Some research has been done on fear of crime among older women (e.g, Hanrahan's recently completed dissertation). Much more is needed so that criminologists can understand the needs of these women. Furthermore, the limited available evidence suggests that the few older women in prison are mostly "warehoused" and are without programs to meet their special needs.

Feminist criminologists also have noted the bias in most criminological theories. These theories are predominantly written by white, middle class males and are based on research studies of male offenders, victims, and professionals. Thus, these theories have a gender, race, and class bias. Not only do they ignore women, but they assume that the official data are accurate in identifying young, black males as the greatest offenders. (A more diversified research methodology, including qualitative and historical studies, may be necessary to develop an objective/adequate data base for more meaningful theory construction). Conflict theorists have challenged the basic premises of these positivist theories regarding black crime and have called attention to the crimes of the elite that are ignored by the traditional legal and justice systems. Feminists also stress the importance of research and theories concerning the participation of women in elite crime.

Even though this volume has included some material in the areas noted above, there is still much work to be done. If criminology is to be a discipline free of bias, both feminist and mainstream criminologists must begin to include groups with differential power, e.g., women, racial/ethnic minorities, older adults and children, all social classes, the physically challenged, and lesbians and gays in their research. A research agenda that is diversified and international (i.e., inclusive instead of exclusive) in scope is necessary to build a framework for creating a general theory of crime and criminal behavior.

Author Index

Subject Index

Sex Discrimination (see sexual
   harassment)
Sex Role(s), (stereotypes) 114,147,
   156-157, 159, 187, 207,
   228-229, 255, 256, 268,
   277,282, 296, 300,301, 302,
   316, 329, 345 (also see sexual
   stereotypes)
Sex Role Spillover, 239
Sexism, 70, 231, 234, 238, 292
Sexual
   Assaults, 164, 165 (see also
      sexual violence)
   Behavior, 238
   History, 165
   Promiscuity, 77
   Scripts, 156
   Stereotypes, 160
Violence, 147, 148, 153-157,
   163-175 (see also rape, sex
   abuse)
Sexual Harassment, 15, 147-149,
   345
   Conflict Perspective, 238, 240
   Causes of
      Economic Inequality, 239, 246
      Male Domination, 236, 240
      Power Control, 230, 238-240
      Stereotyping, 236, 238, 240,
         241-242
   Correction Officers, 333
   Criminal Justice System,
      231-232, 237-238, 241,
      242-244
   Definitions, 229-231, 315
   Effects on Victims, 234-235, 246
   Female Guards, 232-233,
      236-237, 246
   Female Police Officers, 232-233,
      235, 240, 290-292, 294,
      298
   Gender Harassment, 231
   Legal Profession, 314-315
   Male Occupations in, 237-38
   Levels of, 231-234
   Males of, 228-230, 237
   Minorities of, 240, 333

Myths, 234-237
Peers, 229, 237, 239, 241-242
Race, 240
Sex Discrimination, 230,
   242-243
Theoretical Explanations,
   238-242
   Gender Roles, 239
   Power Differential Hypothesis,
      239-240
Types of,
   Hostile Work Environment,
      230, 242, 244
   Quid Pro Quo, 230-231, 242,
Workforce, in, 256
Sexual Stereotyping
   Workplace, 228-229
   Cause of Sexual Harassment,
      236, 238, 240, 241-242
Shooting, 87
Sigmund Freud, 213
Snitches, 41
Social Conflict Theory/Approach
   (see Conflict Theory)
Social-Sexual Behavior, 238
Sociobiologists, 155
Spouse abuse (see domestic
   violence)
Spousal homicide (see homicide)
State Bar Associations (see
   individual states)
State v Chambers, 61
State v Costello, 60
Status Offenses, definition, 61
Stealing (see theft)
Stitch Rule, 182
Street walker (see prostitution)
Suffragettes, 309-310, 312

Temperance, 36
Theft (see offenses, female)
Theories (see individual theories
   by name)
   Child Development 213,
      Conflict, Labeling, Lerner's
      Theory, Narcissists Theory,
      Patriarchy, Power Control,
      Social Conflict, Tokenism,